7
DEADLY
SCENARIOS

Also by Andrew F. Krepinevich

The Army and Vietnam

7 DEADLY SCENARIOS

A MILITARY FUTURIST EXPLORES WAR IN THE 21ST CENTURY

ANDREW F. KREPINEVICH

BANTAM BOOKS

7 DEADLY SCENARIOS
A Bantam Book / February 2009

Published by
Bantam Dell
A Division of Random House, Inc.
New York, New York

Book design by Susan Turner
Maps by Robert Bull

Bantam Books and the Rooster colophon are registered trademarks
of Random House, Inc.

Library of Congress Cataloging-in-Publication Data
Krepinevich, Andrew F.
7 deadly scenarios : a military futurist explores war
in the 21st century / Andrew F. Krepinevich.
p.   cm.
ISBN 978-0-553-80539-0 (hbk.)
1. War—Forecasting.   2. Military planning—United States.   3. National security—
United States.   4. Twenty-first century—Forecasts.   I. Title.   II. Title: Seven deadly
scenarios.   III. Title: Military futurist explores war in the 21st century.
U21.2.K78 2008
355'.033073—dc22
2008039164

Printed in the United States of America
Published simultaneously in Canada

www.bantamdell.com

10 9 8 7 6 5 4 3
BVG

To My Family

CONTENTS

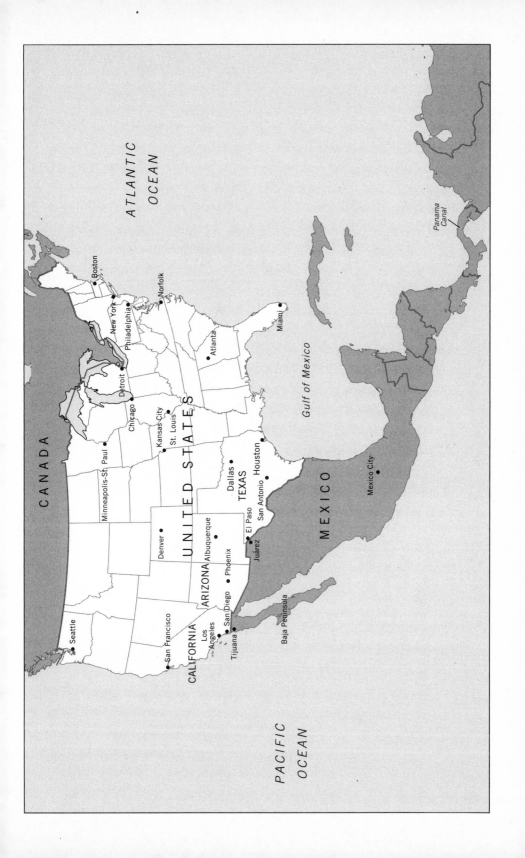

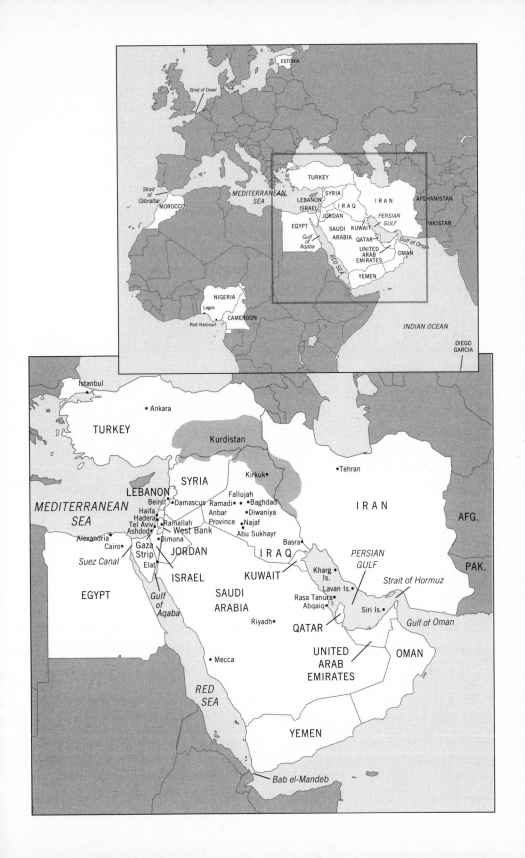

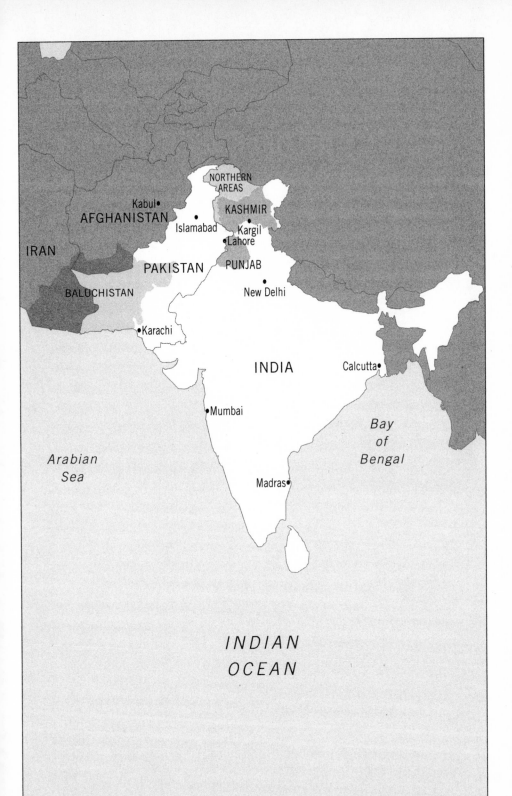

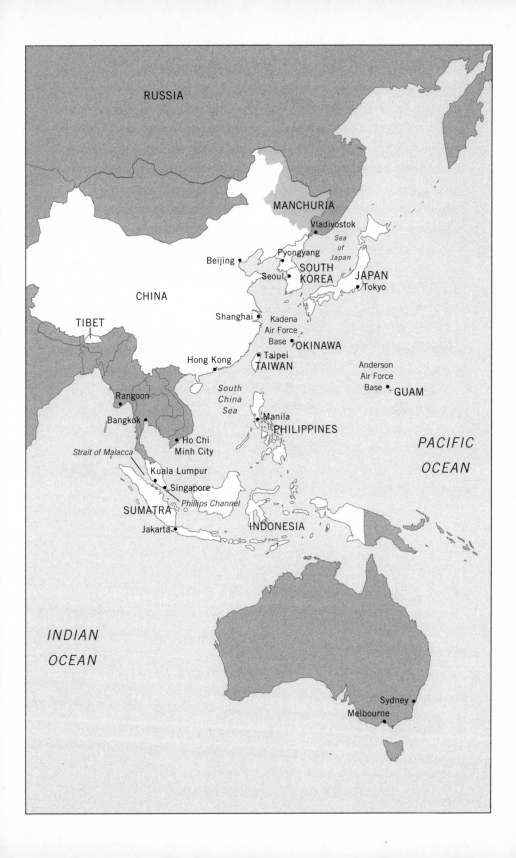

DEADLY
7
SCENARIOS

Introduction

A GLIMPSE OF THE FUTURE

People only see what they are prepared to see.
—Ralph Waldo Emerson

PEARL HARBOR

DAWN WAS BREAKING ON SUNDAY MORNING, THE SEVENTH DAY OF the month, on the island of Oahu. Aside from its status as a tourist mecca, the island was home to several major American military facilities, including the huge naval base at Pearl Harbor and the Army's Hickam airfield. For the soldiers and sailors, the day began like any other Sunday, with a skeleton crew on duty while many others slept off their Saturday night's revelries.

But this was no ordinary Sunday.

For over a week, unknown to the island's commanders, a large fleet had been steaming toward the Hawaiian Islands, operating under strict radio silence and without running lights to avoid detection. The fleet sailed to the north of the islands, far beyond the normal shipping lanes, to reduce the chances of being detected by U.S. naval patrols or commercial ships. This time of year found the northern Pacific storm-tossed, and as the fleet pressed on toward its target, it adjusted its course to sail inside rain squalls.

Early that Sunday, following a high-speed run, the fleet's aircraft carriers came within one hundred miles of Pearl Harbor, their principal target. An hour before daybreak pilots scrambled into their planes. Shortly thereafter the carriers launched their strike aircraft, more than 150 in all, a mix of fighters, dive-bombers, and torpedo planes, which quickly moved into formation and headed through the night sky for Oahu. Their mission: execute Raid Plan No. 1. As the aircraft approached Pearl Harbor, the weather cleared, as if on cue. This enabled the strike formations to use the battery of searchlights at Kahuku Point as a navigation aid to guide them toward their targets.

Dawn was now breaking. As sunlight streamed over the horizon, the airborne strike force pressed home its attack over Pearl Harbor, achieving complete surprise. Dive-bombers and torpedo planes went to work on the ships lying at anchor along Battleship Row, where the U.S. Navy's capital ships were berthed. Fighter aircraft peeled off and strafed the airfield, hitting parked planes, fuel storage tanks, and hangars. Army Air Corps pilots rushed to take off after the attacking force, but by the time they were aloft, the attackers had completed their strikes and vanished. Failing to locate the attackers, the Army aircraft returned to base, whereupon a second wave of carrier strike aircraft hit them. A *New York Times* reporter on the scene reported that the attacks were "unopposed by the defense, which was caught virtually napping."[1]

Surveying the results, the American defenders were filled with anger—and relief. The attack, executed on the morning of Sunday, *February 7, 1932,* occurred at the outset of a U.S. Army–Navy war game called Grand Joint Exercise 4. Rear Admiral Harry Yarnell, commander of the newly commissioned American aircraft carriers *Saratoga* and *Lexington,* had launched the attacking planes. The "bombs" dropped were flour bags, which could be found splattered on the Navy's ships still sitting at anchor.

Red-faced, the Army Air Corps commanders sought to minimize the

1. This account is taken from Thomas Wildenberg, *Destined for Glory* (Annapolis, Md.: Naval Institute Press, 1998), pp. 95–96; David C. Evans and Mark R. Peattie, *Kaigun* (Annapolis, Md.: Naval Institute Press, 1997), p. 473; Ryan David Wadle, "United States Navy Fleet Problems and the Development of Carrier Aviation, 1929–1933," unpublished paper, August 2005, at https://txspace.tamu.edu/bitstream/1969.1/2658/1/etd-tamu-2005B-HIST-Wadle.pdf, accessed on December 21, 2006; and Jack Young, "The Real Architect of Pearl Harbor," Association of Naval Aviation, Spring 2005, at www.findarticles.com/p/articles/mi_qa3834/is_200504/ai_n15743392/print, accessed on December 20, 2006.

attack's results. They argued that the damage incurred to Hickam Field was minimal, and asserted that they had found and attacked Yarnell's carriers. Finally, they protested the attack on legal grounds—it was improper to begin a war on Sunday!

The war game's umpires sided with the Army. Their report made no mention of Yarnell's attack but concluded that "it is doubtful if air attacks can be launched against Oahu in the face of strong defensive aviation without subjecting the attacking carriers to the danger of material damage and consequent great loss in the attack[ing] air force."[2]

Nearly ten years later carriers of the Imperial Japanese Navy, attacking Pearl Harbor on Sunday, December 7, 1941, proved that Admiral Yarnell, not the umpires or the Army, had gauged the future correctly. The admiral had been willing to confront uncomfortable possibilities, whereas others had not. Although America was shocked by the Japanese attack, many in the Navy were not. As Admiral Chester W. Nimitz, the architect of the Navy's victorious campaign against Japan, ruefully admitted, "Nothing that happened in the Pacific was strange or unexpected."[3]

THE DAWN OF BLITZKRIEG

NEARLY SIX YEARS AFTER ADMIRAL YARNELL'S "SURPRISE ATTACK" on Pearl Harbor, in the fall of 1937 the world witnessed by far the largest field exercises held in Germany since the Great War that had led to its humiliation at Versailles. These maneuvers were conducted on the North German Plain. Some eight infantry divisions took part. (The entire U.S. Army today comprises only ten divisions.) But the size of the enterprise was not its only notable aspect: appearing for the first time in these exercises was the Wehrmacht's Third Panzer Division and the First Panzer Division's First Panzer Brigade. These formations had not existed during the Great War. Indeed, they had only just been formed. The two novel units were unusual in several respects. Most conspicuous was their emphasis on mechanization. They boasted a massive number of tanks, some eight

2. Jack Young, "Real Architect."
3. Chester W. Nimitz to President of Naval War College, September 24, 1965, Naval Historical collection, Naval War College, Newport, R.I.; cited in Thomas B. Buell, "Admiral Raymond A. Spruance and the Naval War College," *Naval War College Review*, March 1971, p. 33.

hundred in all. Their appearance in the exercise produced a heightened sense of expectation, which extended all the way up the army's chain of command to the German General Staff. Rather than the two-day length typical of most annual exercises, these maneuvers were to span a full week.[4]

The Third Panzer's attack plan involved using its infantry forces to engage enemy troops defending a bridgehead, while its armored forces attacked the defenders' left flank. The objective was for the Panzers—the German word for armor, or tanks—to break through the enemy lines. The attack was everything the Wehrmacht's most ardent Panzer advocates could have hoped for. After a hundred-kilometer approach march, the division went into the attack, quickly forcing the enemy to commit its reserves. Even these proved insufficient to arrest the Panzers. The following day the Third Panzer not only broke through the enemy front but penetrated deep into its rear area. Confronted with armored forces prowling behind its shattered lines, the enemy's position quickly unraveled. What had been planned as a week-long exercise was decided in only four days.

The chief of the German General Staff, General Ludwig Beck, on hand to observe the field maneuvers, was less than enthusiastic about the results. He believed that the umpires' rulings were too generous to the mechanized forces. The Panzer Division was ordered removed from further play. Still, General Beck admitted that the "friendly" force had "solved the problem allotted to it, through a well-planned, swift, and energetic use of its means." General Franz Halder, who would succeed Beck as chief of the General Staff a year later, was stunned by the "fluid mobility" in the Third Panzer's operations.[5] Indeed, the world had witnessed the first major demonstration of *blitzkrieg,* or "lightning war."

Despite General Beck's skepticism and the reservations of some officers about what had transpired, many other officers, men like General Heinz Guderian, were more enthusiastic about the potential of mechanized

4. Robert M. Citino, *The Path to Blitzkrieg: Doctrine and Training in the German Army, 1920–1939* (Boulder, Co: Lynne Rienner, 1999), p. 239–40. Note that the 1935 maneuvers took place before the Panzer divisions had been created, while the 1936 maneuvers focused on testing the quality of noncommissioned officers and men in the much-expanded Army.
5. Ibid., p. 241.

air-land warfare. Consequently, the German military continued to explore its possibilities, and did so more aggressively than any other military. Like the U.S. Navy's "attack" on Pearl Harbor, Germany's field exercise gave the world a glimpse into the future. But other militaries generally discounted or even ignored what had happened on the North German Plain. Less than four years later Germany's armies would conquer nearly the entire continent. They accomplished this striking feat by employing a more elaborate version of the new way of fighting first demonstrated during those four days in the autumn of 1937. Indeed, blitzkrieg—massed armor moving rapidly, supported by air power— would dominate land warfare for the next half-century.

MILLENNIUM CHALLENGE

IN THE LATE SUMMER OF 2002 THE U.S. MILITARY PREPARED TO CONduct what some were calling "the largest, most expensive, and most technically elaborate war game in U.S. history."[6] The Pentagon spent roughly a quarter-billion dollars to stage Millennium Challenge 02, which was planned to last three weeks and include all the military services. By the time the exercise concluded on August 15, more than 13,000 troops had participated in waging the mock war in seventeen simulation locations and nine live-force training sites.[7]

The scenario for Millennium Challenge was set five years into the future, in 2007. It involved military action against a breakaway part of Iran. A retired Marine Corps officer, Lieutenant General Paul van Riper, was selected to command the "Red," or enemy, Iranian side. Van Riper saw from the outset that his forces were totally outgunned by the American military forces ("Blue") arrayed against him. To survive the coming battle, let alone win it, he would have to outthink the numerically and technologically superior U.S. forces.

Van Riper decided to use motorcycle messengers to transmit orders,

6. Michael Schrage, "Military Overkill Defeats Virtual War and Real-World Soldiers Are the Losers," *Washington Post*, September 22, 2002, p. B05, at www.washingtonpost.com/ac2/wp-dyn/A47121-2002Sep21?language=printer, accessed on December 22, 2006.
7. Sean Naylor, "War Games Rigged?" *Army Times*, August 16, 2002, at http://www.armytimes.com/print.php?f=1-292925-1060102.php, accessed on December 22, 2006.

negating the Americans' high-tech eavesdropping capabilities. As the Blue fleet sailed into the Persian Gulf in preparation for war, Van Riper instructed his flotilla of small boats to mingle with the flow of commercial traffic and shadow the warships.

By the time the Blue commander issued an ultimatum to Red to surrender or face destruction, Van Riper was ready to attack the American fleet. To ensure communications security, he sent the attack order via the morning call to prayer, broadcast from the minarets of Iran's major mosques. At this signal the Red force of small boats, along with a handful of aircraft, attacked.

The attack centered on weaknesses in some very sophisticated U.S. capabilities, such as the Navy's Aegis air defense system. Knowing the technical limitations of the Aegis radar system, Van Riper and his team simply "overloaded" its capacity with salvo launches of cruise missiles from small ships, aircraft, and land-based sites. Red also made wide use of "stealth" technology, such as the camouflage nets and screens that had long been commercially available from companies in Sweden and Russia. Van Riper employed many other simple means to great effect: to avoid having the Americans detect his strike aircraft's locations through signals intelligence, or SIGINT, he used light signals rather than tower-to-pilot radio conversations to launch their attack.[8]

Operating in constricted waters, the U.S. fleet was vulnerable to a surprise attack. Like its naval ancestors at Pearl Harbor over sixty years earlier, the American fleet suffered terrible damage. Some sixteen warships ended up either damaged or sunk in what would have been the worst naval disaster in over half a century. Senior officers at Joint Forces Command (the headquarters overseeing the exercise) were stunned. As the German Panzers had done in that long-ago autumn, Van Riper and his motley band were making a mockery out of the exercise.

Joint Forces Command officials stopped the exercise, then proceeded to "refloat" the Blue fleet. But Van Riper continued to pose unpleasant problems for the American forces. To "overcome" these problems, the exercise umpires artificially constrained Van Riper's forces. They told him not to use certain Red forces, or to use them in nonsensical ways.

---

8. Lieutenant General (Ret.) Paul Van Riper to the author, June 17, 2008.

For example, they ordered Van Riper to move his antiaircraft weapons to locations where they could not engage Blue aircraft supporting Army and Marine Corps landings. The Red air defense forces that could not be moved were told to turn off their target-acquisition radars.

Confronting such an accommodating enemy, the American forces, with their "new" fleet, quickly defeated the Red forces and "validated" their preconceived notions of how to fight, along with the billions of dollars in new equipment being ordered to support them.[9] One of the Joint Forces Command's admirals sarcastically observed, "We don't conduct field exercises, we do demonstrations."[10] Agreeing, Van Riper sadly concluded that "MC 02 was a demonstration . . . not an experiment in line with JFCOM's charter."[11]

As news of Van Riper's action spread through the press, JFCOM attempted to control the damage. The public was informed that "Blue play and Red play was merely to facilitate the experiment and enable it to look at the different pieces. It was not to see who would win." But prior to the exercise, General William "Buck" Kernan, commander of Joint Forces Command, had told Pentagon reporters that the success of Millennium Challenge was based on the assumption that the U.S. force would be fighting a determined and relatively unconstrained Opposing Force (OPFOR). "This is free play," Kernan declared. "The OPFOR has the ability to win here."[12]

9. This account of Millennium Challenge 2002 is taken from Schrage, "Military Overkill," p. B05; Naylor, "War Games Rigged?"; Julian Borger, "Wake Up Call," *Guardian* (London), September 6, 2002, at www.globalsecurity.org/org/news/2002/020906-iraq1.htm, accessed on December 22, 2006; U.S. Department of Defense, Briefing, Air Force Brigadier General Smith, JFCOM Joint Warfighting Center, at www.defenselink.mil/Utility/PrintItem.aspx?print=http://www.defenselink.mil/transcripts/ 2002/t05222002 _t0522jfcom.html, accessed on December 24, 2006; and General Van Riper, conversation with the author.
10. Confidential interview with the author.
11. General Van Riper to the author, June 17, 2008. Effects-based operations are defined by JFCOM as "a process for obtaining a desired strategic outcome or effect on the enemy through the synergistic and cumulative application of the full range of military and non-military capabilities at all levels of conflict."
12. General Van Riper believed that JFCOM's refusal to release his full report on the exercise, which detailed its problems, stemmed at least in part from the fact that it contained copies of internal e-mails showing that the exercise was scripted after the "sinking" of sixteen U.S. Navy warships, and not the "free play" reported to congressional staffers and the media. Van Riper to the author, June 17, 2008.

But it did not have such ability, and as a consequence the American military may have missed a chance to prepare itself better for the future. Fortunately, the U.S. military is large, and responsibility for preparing for tomorrow's threats does not reside with one organization or individual. Still, many defense experts agree that a single Pentagon office, directed for over three decades by one man, has proved better at providing early warning to the country's senior national security leaders than any other.

YODA

ANDREW MARSHALL IS A QUIET, KINDLY-LOOKING MAN, NOW IN HIS ninth decade. Although intimately familiar with the workings of the Pentagon, he somehow looks out of place there, like someone who has strayed from one of the tour groups that visit the building.[13] Yet he has achieved legendary status among those in the strategic studies world whose business it is to think about the future, and to identify the dangers that may threaten the security of the American people and their way of life. Marshall is the only senior policy official to have survived the 2001 transition from the Clinton administration to the Bush administration. This feat, while remarkable, had become routine for Marshall, who has served in his position in *every administration,* Republican or Democrat, for thirty-five consecutive years, dating back to the Nixon administration.[14]

Marshall is brilliant, almost certainly a genius. Along with other legendary strategic thinkers like Herman Kahn and Albert Wohlstetter, he was one of the "wizards of Armageddon" who developed the foundations of nuclear strategy during the golden age at RAND, the Defense Department's first and foremost think tank.[15] Among these "wizards," Marshall's status is similar to that of J. K. Rowling's Professor Albus Dumbledore, the benevolent and great wizard who heads a school whose

---

13. Peter J. Boyer, "Downfall," *New Yorker,* November 20, 2006, p. 58.
14. The author served in Andrew Marshall's office from 1989 to 1993 and in the years since has served as a consultant to Marshall's office.
15. The term comes from the title of Fred Kaplan's book, *The Wizards of Armageddon.*

faculty is composed of other wizards.[16] Marshall has also been described as the Pentagon's Yoda, the Jedi Master who stands as the wisest member of the Jedi Council. Like Dumbledore and Yoda, Marshall has taught his methods of analysis to a number of America's foremost strategists.[17]

Marshall has endured because he has tried to help senior Defense Department officials, and the secretary of defense in particular, understand *how* to see the future rather than *what* to think or do. To use a medical analogy, Marshall is perhaps the nation's foremost strategic diagnostician. His role has been to diagnose the emerging security environment: What are the principal forces at work that will shape that environment? How might these forces change the world in ways unfavorable to U.S. security—or how might they be exploited to strengthen national security?

Diagnosing a disease correctly is indispensable to determining the appropriate treatment. Marshall has left "writing the prescription" to the Pentagon's senior leaders. Or as Marshall puts it, "I'd rather have decent analysis in response to the right set of questions than brilliant analysis focusing on the wrong set of questions." His ability to help senior government officials focus on the right set of questions makes him valuable and enables him to remain in the background—and in his position.

In Washington, a town of self-promoters, Marshall is a throwback who practices and preaches the old adage that "there is no end to the good a person can do if he doesn't care who gets the credit." While nearly everyone else in town obsessively "keeps score," Marshall is

16. Daniel Ellsberg, conversation with the author. Ellsberg achieved notoriety as one of RAND's "whiz kids" and as the person who leaked the Pentagon Papers. For an overview of Professor Dumbledore, see www.answers.com/topic/albus-dumbledore, accessed on December 27, 2006.
17. Among those who have learned from Marshall are professors Eliot Cohen (Johns Hopkins School of Advanced International Studies), Aaron Friedberg (Princeton University), and Stephen Peter Rosen (Harvard University). Marshall also counts former senior government officials such as Barry Watts, James Roche, and Dennis Ross among his pupils. Collectively, this group is sometimes referred to as the "Jedi Warriors." Moreover, as mentioned in the acknowledgments of their most notable works, scholars ranging from Graham Allison *(Essence of Decision)* to Roberta Wohlstetter *(Pearl Harbor: Warning and Decision)* have been powerfully influenced by Marshall.

distinguishable by his studied disinterest in this game. He is content to have others take his ideas and run with them—and take credit for them—as long as they are acted upon.

SCENARIOS: PREPARING FOR AN UNCERTAIN FUTURE

TODAY THE UNITED STATES IS CONFRONTING PERHAPS THE GREAT-est set of challenges to its security since the end of the Cold War. One of Marshall's principal tools for preparing for future threats while they are still dark clouds on the distant horizon rather than storms that are already upon it is the use of scenarios—stories about how future events might come to pass. Such scenarios can be used to help the Pentagon make better decisions in an uncertain world.[18] Admiral Yarnell's "attack" on Pearl Harbor, the Third Panzer Division's remarkable breakthrough maneuvers, and General Van Riper's use of a third-rate Middle Eastern military to confound the world's most powerful armed forces all showed how the future might unfold. If such scenarios are sufficiently plausible and sufficiently worrisome—posing a credible and serious potential threat to American security—then senior national security decision-makers should devote time and resources to address them.

Scenarios can help Pentagon planners confront difficult questions that the secretary of defense poses to them: What are the most pressing challenges that the military will face in the coming years? Is it possible to deflect them? How can we shape them in ways that make them less dangerous? What kind of military will the United States need to confront them? Is it similar to the one that exists today, or very different? Is it similar to the military that the Pentagon currently plans to field in the coming years?

There are simply too many uncertainties regarding the course of future events to provide precise answers to these questions. Military-related technologies are progressing and diffusing too rapidly to assume that the future conflict environment will merely be a linear extrapolation of

18. Peter Schwartz, *The Art of the Long View* (New York: Doubleday, 1991), pp. 3–4.

the recent past. Existing and potential enemies have the incentive and increasingly the means to present the U.S. military with challenges very different from and more formidable than those to which it is accustomed. The attacks of 9/11, the ongoing insurgencies in Afghanistan and Iraq, the progressive nuclearization of Asia, China's fielding of anti-satellite weapons, the cyberwar waged against Estonia, and the Second Lebanon War between Israel and Hezbollah provide ample evidence of a major shift in the character of conflict.

Some argue that the best course of action is simply to await events and adjust to threats as they confront us. But this approach essentially avoids thinking about the future. It represents a strong vote for "business as usual" and a mindless stay-the-course mentality that assumes that tomorrow will be only slightly different from today. This approach fails just when it is most needed, when a new type of threat emerges. The U.S. Army, for example, was optimized in its organization, structure, and equipment to fight the Second Gulf War as a latter-day version of the First Gulf War. It was quite unprepared for the modern insurgency that emerged after the fall of Baghdad.

The Pentagon cannot afford to await events. It must make decisions today on what military capabilities will equip America's fighting forces decades from now. Congress has already approved expenditures of hundreds of billions of dollars to create tomorrow's military. It takes years to introduce a new operational concept, or a new method of conducting military operations, and perfect it into a finely honed doctrine, and it takes additional years to reorganize and reequip the military to operate according to that doctrine.

So are we building the right military today? If we are not, the nation will have wasted enormous sums of money. As Senator Sam Nunn once noted, no matter how hard Congress tries, it can only spend the same dollar once. Failure here represents an enormous problem for a nation already swimming in a fiscal ocean of red ink. Worse, building the wrong military potentially jeopardizes the security and well-being of America's citizens and of its allies and partners around the world. For those who fail to prepare properly, the penalty can be catastrophic. After the Japanese attack on Pearl Harbor, it took nearly a year—and the good fortune that enabled the "Miracle at Midway"[19]—before the United States could retake the initiative in the war. France was far less fortunate. When Germany turned its blitzkrieg war machine on her in the spring of 1940, her armies had far too little time to take corrective action. Paris fell in less than six weeks, and the French lived under Nazi occupation until liberated by the Allies four years later.

The key to minimizing the risk of being surprised and of suffering catastrophic failure is not to ignore risks in the hopes of muddling through but rather to take uncertainty into account to identify areas of potential risk, and to employ planning tools, like scenarios, to narrow the range of uncertainty where possible. Once we identify critical risks, we can create "hedges" or "strategic options" that will facilitate rapid course adjustments, should the U.S. military find itself in a substantially different competitive environment. The U.S. Navy was caught napping at Pearl Harbor, but even during the lean budget years of the 1930s Depression, it had built in hedges against an uncertain future. These hedges existed in the form of a handful of aircraft carriers that fortunately were at sea the day the Japanese attacked. In the months that followed the attack, the Navy exercised the "strategic option" it had created by shifting its shipbuilding program to emphasize carriers. The silver lining in the Fleet Problem that witnessed Yarnell's attack is that it encouraged the Navy to continue experimenting with this new kind of ship.

LEAVING THE COMFORT ZONE

WE ALL HAVE A VISION OF THE FUTURE, WHETHER WE REALIZE IT OR not. Typically our default vision is that tomorrow will look pretty much like today. This vision works reasonably well for individuals, and it can work for Pentagon planners too, during periods of gradual change, such as during the Cold War, when the Soviet Union provided the United States with a relatively predictable enemy. In those years the key centers

---

19. The "miracle" was that a strikingly inferior U.S. fleet inflicted a decisive defeat on the Imperial Japanese Navy, in which the Americans lost but one carrier while the Japanese lost four. The term comes from Gordon W. Prange, Donald M. Goldstein, and Katherine V. Dillon, *Miracle at Midway* (New York: McGraw-Hill, 1982).

of prospective conflict—Central Europe, the Atlantic Ocean, the Korean Peninsula—were well known. The types of war the Soviets could wage—an advanced version of blitzkrieg warfare, combining air power and mechanized ground forces, and submarine warfare—were well understood, as were the instruments of war. During the Cold War the United States and Soviet Union were engaged in a relatively well-defined competition to see who could make the best tank, the best piece of artillery, the best fighter aircraft, and so on.

Today the United States confronts a very different set of enemies—radical Islamists and hostile nuclear rogue states like North Korea (and prospectively Iran)—than it did during the Cold War. And China's rise to great power status, which some view as a positive sign, raises eyebrows in the Pentagon, where Beijing's ongoing military buildup is a source of growing concern. How do these new rivals, who culturally are quite distinct from the Cold War–era Soviets, see themselves advancing their agenda? What means will they use to achieve their goals? And when will they make their move?

The principal potential battlegrounds of military competition are no longer in Europe and the Atlantic; once the focal point of Cold War concerns, they are now strategic backwaters. The new area of instability and conflict runs from the eastern shores of the Mediterranean Sea to the Sea of Japan—what Pentagon planners refer to as the "Arc of Instability." American forces now find themselves fighting protracted wars in Afghanistan and Iraq, events that would have seemed fantastic less than a decade ago. In what improbable places will the U.S. military find itself operating over the next decade?

The forms and instruments of war are changing as well. In traditional areas of warfare, no one has replaced the Soviet Union. Today the United States has no serious competition when it comes to building a better tank or nuclear submarine. America's enemies—both existing and potential—realize that if the Soviet Union could not successfully challenge the United States by competing symmetrically, by building similar kinds of military capabilities, then they will have to pursue very different paths. But what new paths will they travel? And how will they challenge U.S. security? If conflict emerges, what might it look like?

DON'T TRY TO PREDICT THE FUTURE—YOU CAN'T

WHILE THE PENTAGON WOULD DEARLY LIKE TO KNOW THE ANSWERS to these questions, it is simply not possible. Too many factors have a hand in shaping the future. Of course, Pentagon planners may blithely assume away all uncertainty and essentially bet that the future they forecast is the one that will emerge. In this case the U.S. military will be very well prepared—for the predicted future. But history shows that militaries are often wrong when they put too many eggs in one basket. In the summer of 1914, as World War I was breaking out, Europeans felt that the war would be brief and that the troops might be home "before the leaves fall." In reality the Allied and Central Powers engaged in over four years of horrific bloodletting. In World War II the French Army entered the conflict believing it would experience an advanced version of the trench warfare it had encountered in 1914–1918. Instead, France was defeated by the Germans in a lightning campaign lasting less than two months. Finally, in 2003 the Pentagon predicted that the Second Gulf War would play out with a traditional blitzkrieg. Instead, it turned into an irregular war, a "long, hard slog."[20]

Militaries seem prone to assuming that the next war will be an "updated" version of the last war rather than something quite different. Consequently, they are often accused of preparing for the last war instead of the next. This is where rigorous, scenario-based planning comes into play. It is designed to take uncertainty explicitly into account by incorporating factors that may change the character of future conflict in significant and perhaps profound ways. By presenting a plausible set of paths into the future, scenarios can help senior Pentagon leaders avoid the "default" picture in which tomorrow looks very much like today.

If the future were *entirely* uncertain, scenario-based planning would be a waste of time. But certain things are predictable or at least highly likely. Scenario planners call these things "predetermined elements." While not quite "done deals," they are sufficiently well known that their probability of occurring is quite high. For example, we have a very good

20. Secretary of Defense Donald Rumsfeld to General Dick Myers, Paul Wolfowitz, General Peter Pace, and Doug Feith, Subject: Global War on Terrorism, October 16, 2003.

idea of how many men of military age (eighteen to thirty-one) there will be in the United States in 2020, since all of those males have already been born, and, barring a catastrophic event, the actuarial data on them is quite refined. We know that China has already tested several types of weapons that can disable or destroy satellites. We know that dramatic advances in solid-state lasers have been made in recent years and that more advances are well within the realm of possibility. These "certainties" should be reflected in all scenarios, while key uncertainties should be reflected in how they play out across the different scenarios.[21] If scenario-based planning is done well, and if its insights are acted upon promptly, the changes it stimulates in the military may help deter prospective threats, or dissuade enemies from creating threatening new capabilities in the first place.

SCENARIOS AND STRATEGY

THE INSIGHTS DERIVED FROM SCENARIO-BASED PLANNING, PROPERLY done, are indispensable to those charged with crafting U.S. national security strategy. This is because the essence of strategy is identifying asymmetric advantages, both our own and those of our rivals, both existing and prospective. General Rupert Smith observes that "the essence of the practice of war is to achieve asymmetric advantage over one's opponent; an advantage in any terms, not just technological."[22] Leading private sector experts on strategy share his view. Richard Rumelt notes:

> As a strategist you try to identify, create, or exploit some kind of an edge. So how do you find that advantage? Well, it's not always staring you in the face. And you look at asymmetries. You look *at* asymmetries and you try *to create* them. . . . [W]hen you are trying to create or exploit the advantage . . . the first thing you need is an asymmetry.[23]

21. Kees Van der Heijden, *Scenarios: The Art of Strategic Conversation* (Hoboken, N.J.: John Wiley & Sons, 2005), pp. 4–6.
22. Rupert Smith, *The Utility of Force: The Art of War in the Modern World* (New York: Alfred A. Knopf, 2007), p. 377.
23. Barry D. Watts, Memorandum for the Record, "Strategy Seminar," Center for Strategy & Budgetary Assessments, September 25, 2007, p. 7. (Emphasis in the original.)

The crafting of strategy is a race between ourselves and our rivals to identify asymmetric advantages and exploit them. When Rumelt met with the head of Apple, Steve Jobs, he asked Jobs what his long-term strategy would be. Jobs just smiled and said, "I am going to wait for the next big thing."[24]

Of course in a military competition the "next big thing" is typically derived from an insight that some new development—or some capability that has been around but was previously overlooked—has the potential to provide a major asymmetric advantage. The military that arrives at this insight first, and exploits it quickly, will realize a great advantage over its rivals. Early in the last century the development of blitzkrieg and of fast carrier task forces were "next big things" that gave those who first understood their value a great advantage. Correspondingly, those who missed these insights were typically surprised, as were the French in 1940. Awareness, according to the great strategists, is critical. Carl von Clausewitz once observed that surprise lies "at the foundation of all undertakings," and "surprise becomes the means to gain superiority." Thus "surprise lies at the root of all operations without exception."[25] Clausewitz's Eastern counterpart, Sun Tzu, concurred, declaring that "all warfare is based on deception."[26]

Scenarios can help us identify where our rivals have advantages and thus may surprise us, and where we may do the same. The effect requires considerable research and thought. As Kees Van der Heijden warns, "You must spend time hunting for surprises . . . [otherwise] it is difficult not to come up with the obvious."[27] Scenario building requires research into the key trends, or "drivers," that will likely exert the greatest influence on the future security environment. President Dwight Eisenhower understood the need to work to identify the insights that will

24. Dan P. Lovallo and Lenny T. Mendonca, "Strategy's Strategist: An Interview with Richard Rumelt," *McKinsey Quarterly,* August 2007, p. 4.
25. Carl von Clausewitz, *On War,* ed. and trans. Michael Howard and Peter Paret (Princeton, N.J.: Princeton University Press, 1976), p. 198; and B. H. Liddell Hart, *Strategy,* 2nd ed. (New York: Meridian Books, 1991), p. 343.
26. Sun Tzu, *The Art of War,* trans. Samuel B. Griffith (Oxford, U.K.: Oxford University Press, 1971), p. 66.
27. Van der Heijden, *Scenarios,* p. 59.

confer advantage and avoid surprise. "Plans are useless," he once observed, ". . . planning is indispensable."[28]

WHY DO WE HAVE A HARD TIME CHANGING OUR VISION?

DESPITE THE VALUE OF SCENARIO-BASED PLANNING AND THE Pentagon's commitment to it, the Pentagon still has a hard time taking a more comprehensive view of the future. Somehow it does not fully embrace this kind of planning. Why? Why did it not take to heart General Van Riper's ability to use the forces of a third-rate military power to present novel problems for the U.S. armed forces?

Unfortunately, there is no simple answer, and no easy remedy. Certainly for most organizations change is an unnatural act. Bureaucracies—and the Pentagon has one of the world's largest—are organized primarily to execute complex routines that enable *the existing way of operating* to be accomplished efficiently. Bureaucracies are not optimized for innovation or change. Often, the more successful an organization becomes, the more difficult it is to convince its principals of the need for change. The U.S. military's overwhelming dominance, which elicits comparisons with Rome's imperial legions, has bred an attitude of success if not hubris. Only recently, in Vietnam and Iraq, has the military stumbled, but even here the blame has fallen more on the nation's political leadership than on the military. Consequently, especially powerful forces are at work within the military to defeat those advocating change. After all, if the system isn't broken, why fix it?

Another barrier to change lies in the military's training and education systems, which are only now catching up even with the recent changes in warfare, let alone anticipating those that might be on the way. Michael Porter, an expert on the problems of corporate adaptation, notes that "training emphasizes the one correct way to do anything; the construction of specialized, dedicated facilities solidifies past practice into expensive brick and mortar; the existing strategy takes on an aura of invincibility and becomes rooted in the company

28. Richard Nixon, *Six Crises* (Garden City, N.Y.: Doubleday, 1962), p. 235.

culture."[29] Porter might well have drawn this observation from military organizations. Only recently has the Army begun to adapt its training facilities to the kind of irregular warfare now endemic to Iraq—that is, it adapted only after the threat has manifested itself. But such lateness is neither new nor unique to the Army. During the Vietnam War the U.S. Navy and Air Force proved slow to adapt their pilot training to the new challenges they confronted.[30] But what about getting ahead of the game? What about adapting in anticipation of change, rather than waiting until after the danger is upon you?

Finally, the impetus for change is muted by the realization that real change will likely alter the military's pecking order. Subcultures of a military service that are viewed as peripheral may become dominant, while the currently dominant subculture may have to cede pride of place or even be marginalized. One reason the U.S. Navy did not adopt carrier aviation more enthusiastically was the opposition of the service's "Gun Club"—the battleship admirals whose ships represented the dominant expression of naval power, albeit in an era that was passing from the scene. People naturally resist changes that make them or their group less important. The result is that organizations tend to discount information that suggests that major change is necessary. An organization in effect uses its "immune system" to isolate or expel individuals or ideas that challenge the prevailing, more institutionally comfortable vision of the future.

Overcoming unwarranted institutional resistance to change is a principal objective of scenario-based planning. Even here problems can emerge, as organizations comfortable with the status quo promote the scenarios that support their preferred vision of the future. The key is to pick plausible scenarios in which the challenges to the security environment are quite different from those of today. The scenario set should represent the full range of plausible futures. This does not mean developing an infinite number of scenarios to match the infinite number of possible futures. Experience has shown that senior leaders can best deal

---

29. Michael E. Porter, "The Competitive Advantage of Nations," *Harvard Business Review*, March–April 1990, p. 78.

30. Barry D. Watts, *A Net Assessment of Training and Education for Combat as a Source of Sustainable Military Advantage*, unpublished paper, August 2006, pp. 39–43.

with a handful of scenarios, more than a few but certainly fewer than ten. Above ten they begin to "lose the forest for the trees." The key, then, is to choose the scenarios carefully, so that they adequately represent the range of plausible futures, even if they do not account for every specific possible future. Does this mean that the United States may still find itself surprised? Yes, but properly done, a scenario-planning process will reduce the likelihood of its being caught totally unawares. Moreover, a properly crafted set of scenarios will suggest when the world might be moving toward an alternative future. In this way it can provide early warning of a shift in the security environment, thereby better enabling the military to prepare for it.

THINKING ABOUT THE NEXT WAR

ON AUGUST 1, 1991, A FEW MONTHS AFTER THE END OF THE FIRST Gulf War, Andrew Marshall and I met with a small group of advisers at the Office of Net Assessment in the Pentagon. At the time I was serving as one of Marshall's military assistants. During the meeting Marshall announced his intention to undertake an assessment of a different kind from the Soviet-oriented efforts that had dominated the office's work since its establishment in 1973.

Marshall said this assessment would explore whether a major shift in the character of military competition was under way—what Soviet writers had referred to as a "military-technical revolution." It was not clear to him, however, that such an assessment was possible. The consensus of the group was that the issue was too important not to address, despite the prospective difficulties. Marshall agreed. The task of leading and writing the assessment fell to me.

While this meeting formally initiated the assessment, Marshall and I had discussed the issue informally for nearly a year prior. Indeed, he had been thinking about the matter for perhaps a decade. He and I had several key talks prior to the August meeting. Of particular importance was a meeting on December 19, 1990, during the buildup of U.S. forces in the Persian Gulf prior to the First Gulf War. The purpose was to develop a framework for assessing the postwar security environment. During our conversation Marshall indicated his intention to move beyond

Cold War military balance assessments, even though the Soviet Union still existed.[31] Two days later we met again, and Marshall declared that the office needed to focus more on how military competitions might change. He suspected they might change dramatically. Among the issues he asked me to begin thinking about were how to define our competition if the Soviet Union's power continued to wane, how to take into account the growing lethality of conventional warfare, and how rapid advances in technology might change concepts of warfare.

We met again on January 24, 1991, during the early days of the Gulf War air campaign. Our conversation focused on whether we were witnessing a fundamental discontinuity in military operations, and how we might identify a new blitzkrieg form of warfare if it were on the horizon. Marshall also wanted to know if we might be able to identify the magnitude of the shift as well as its form.

I spent the better part of a year drafting a preliminary assessment, and another year producing a more detailed version. In writing the assessment, I benefited from numerous one-on-one meetings with Marshall. I chaired a number of meetings of experts from within the Defense Department and from the greater security studies community. Perhaps most important, Marshall included me in a number of meetings with senior civilian and military leaders to explore the issue.

Toward the end of the assessment, we agreed to include a brief scenario to explain how, despite America's enormous military advantages, others might adapt to the rapidly changing military environment and exploit it to their advantage. While developing the scenario, I outlined it to Chris Lamb, who at the time was working in the Defense Department's Office of Special Operations and Low-Intensity Conflict (SOLIC, or in Pentagon-speak "So-lick"). Chris suggested a name for the enemy depicted in the scenario. The enemy, said Lamb, was not fighting "fair" but was engaged in a kind of rough-and-tumble "street fight" with the United States. Hence the scenario's title: "The Streetfighter State." I expanded upon the scenario in 1996.

---

31. Military balance assessments, or net assessments, focus on key regional or functional areas of a military competition. Thus there were regional assessments of the military balance in Central Europe between NATO and the Warsaw Pact, and functional assessments in areas like nuclear forces and maritime forces.

What follows is the scenario in its entirety. It provides an example of how scenarios, properly crafted, work. They do not predict the future; they do, however, highlight the kinds of challenges for which a military must prepare. Thus while the United States has yet to engage Iran (the Streetfighter State presented in the scenario), the American and other militaries later did encounter the kinds of military challenges presented in the scenario. Unfortunately, the warnings we raised, like those in Millennium Challenge 02, were not sufficiently heeded.

"THE STREETFIGHTER STATE"

It is October 2016. The United States is about to confront the first major act of regional aggression in over a quarter century. This time the aggressor is Iran, but it takes a very different path than that chosen by Iraq in 1990.

For Iran the new century has meant both internal and external turbulence. Internally, the Iranian people have grown weary of over a quarter century of Islamic fundamentalist rule. The mullahs, in attempting to defuse growing discontent, have tried to apply the "Chinese" model by engineering rapid economic growth to mute political (and sectarian) opposition. Thus between 1998 and 2003 Iran adopts a much more friendly approach to the West. Tehran suspends its support of terrorism. Threats to blockade the Strait of Hormuz cease. Attempts are made to cultivate better relations with Saudi Arabia and the other Gulf States.

The reaction from the West is overwhelmingly favorable, except from the United States. Washington objects to Iran's decision to purchase commercial nuclear reactors from Russia, along with other arms purchases from China. Tehran retorts that it remains a member of the Non-Proliferation Treaty (NPT), that its nuclear program is peaceful and operating under International Atomic Energy Agency (IAEA) safeguards, and that given the relative instability of the region, it is only prudent to engage in a slow-paced modernization of its armed forces.

Washington's European allies, growing increasingly distant from America over economic issues and NATO's inability to deal successfully with the Balkan crisis, embrace the Iranian peace initiative. From

London to Paris, Berlin to Rome, the Americans are seen as catering to their long-term visceral dislike of Iran's fundamentalist regime. Soon European and Japanese energy firms are operating in Iran, focusing especially on developing that nation's huge reserves of natural gas.

Although the results are initially promising, sustaining high economic growth rates proves difficult to achieve. Indeed, developments "conspire" to work against the Iranian leadership's hope of pursuing the Chinese model. First, there is the continued transition in the developed world from "industrial" to "information" economies, which acts to flatten the growth of energy demand. This transition also is beginning to emerge in the newly industrializing countries, many of whom are skipping some phases of industrialization on their way to information-based economies. Second, alternatives to carbon-based fuels are coming "on line," especially nuclear power (in Japan and China) and renewable energy sources (i.e., solar, wind). Third, the long decline in Russia's energy production is finally reversed in 2009. Fourth, the lifting of sanctions on Iraq in 2002 brings that country fully back into the oil market—while creating a growing security threat to Iran.

The Iranian fundamentalist leadership's inability to generate rapid economic growth through "accommodation" with the West is made clear with the reverse energy "shock" of April 2014, when the factors described above produce a temporary collapse of oil and gas prices. Efforts to enforce limited production agreements among exporting producer states prove fruitless. This leads to a political backlash in Iran, with hard-line fundamentalists in the ascendant. The hard-liners argue that Iran is again being exploited by the West, which is accused of depressing oil prices while supporting Iran's prospective enemies in Baghdad (through the lifting of sanctions) and Saudi Arabia (through the sale of advanced arms, including a theater missile defense system that is manned and maintained primarily by Americans).

The hard-line faction in Tehran argues that the only way to ensure Iran's economic growth and political stability is to achieve freedom from Western exploitation. This requires confronting the West and altering dramatically the world energy equation in favor of the "exploited" oil- and gas-producing and -exporting states. The Iranian military is instructed to prepare to execute long-held plans to block the Strait of

Hormuz and to target Saudi and other Gulf oil state production facilities. The target date is November 2016.

It turns out that Washington's suspicions regarding the Iranian nuclear weapons program are not without foundation. By the fall of 2014 Iran has an inventory of eight nuclear weapons, which are mated to eight of its nearly 1,400 ballistic missiles. The Iranian military also boasts over 2,000 cruise missile systems, over 800 advanced conventional munitions (e.g., laser- and optically guided bombs), and wide access to commercial satellite communications networks. Iran also possesses limited chemical munitions stocks, nearly 7,000 antiship mines (some quite advanced), and some late-generation "traditional" systems (e.g., tanks, aircraft, surface warships), including five diesel submarines capable of conducting clandestine mine-laying operations. Finally, Iran has maintained a core terrorist network in the Middle East and Europe, with a limited network in the United States.

Iran's political and strategic culture is such that it is willing to accept what the United States would consider a disproportionate amount of punishment, including casualties, and collateral and environmental damage, and to wage a protracted struggle if necessary to accomplish its strategic objectives. Finally, Iran's leadership understands the American political and strategic culture and is prepared to exploit it.

On November 6, 2016, Iran executes its war plan. Iranian ballistic and cruise missile forces disperse. Mine seeding of the Strait of Hormuz commences. Iranian submarines begin their "underwatch" patrols of the mine fields. Antiship missile batteries (e.g., the Silkworm and Seersucker) position themselves along the approaches to the strait. Iran's small air force, equipped primarily with antiship missiles, disperses.

The Iranian leadership moves to deep underground shelters for its protection. Fiber-optic landlines and satellite "subscriber" service on systems like Iridium handle essential communications. Overhead reconnaissance is provided by Russian satellites. (Russia is only too happy to both reduce the influence of the United States and the European Union [EU] in the region and realize windfall energy profits during the crisis, and after, assuming the Iranian ploy is successful.)

Next, the Iranian leadership declares that three conditions must be met before the strait will be reopened and the flow of oil resumed. First, *all Western forces must depart the region, including U.S. support forces in Saudi Arabia. Second, Saudi Arabia must dramatically curtail its oil and gas production. Third, tankers transiting the Strait of Hormuz must pay a transit fee to Iran. The mullahs believe that, if they can achieve these objectives, the key, enduring effect will be to make the Saudi Kingdom and the Gulf Cooperation Council states wards of Iran.*

Recalling the Gulf War, Tehran issues a warning to all states in the region. Cooperation with any powers "external to the region" will lead to "dire consequences" being visited upon the cooperating state. Several options are open to Iran in making good on this threat. First, it might employ weapons of mass destruction, even though its arsenal is very limited. Second, it might conduct a precision strike on oil and gas fields in the region. Third, it could threaten environmental or "dirty" war, (e.g., destroying water supplies, detonating industrial plants that employ toxic chemicals, striking oil wells, etc). Iran's hope is that these threats will deter potential U.S. allies, especially within the region of conflict. Ideally, these concerns could be sufficient to preclude U.S. military action. As an aside, Iran plans to attack Israel, with a nuclear weapon if necessary (although Iranian leaders believe this will not be necessary), in order to weaken any U.S.-Arab coalition.

Still, there is no guarantee that attempts to exploit fault lines in a U.S.-led coalition will prove successful. In short, the Iranian leadership realizes that it may find itself opposed by a U.S.-led coalition prepared to take military action. Should this occur, Iran is prepared to make the war as sanguinary and protracted as possible. The hard-line fundamentalists are prepared to exploit the social dimension of strategy to offset Iran's clear disadvantages in the technical dimension. In short, Iran's leaders are banking that Americans do not have the will to engage in protracted conflicts, especially those that are bloody, if U.S. national survival is not perceived to be at stake.

If U.S. and other extraregional coalition members prepare to project their forces into the region, they will find themselves confronting several challenges. The Iranian armed forces are instructed to attack any port or airfield employed by the United States or its allies to introduce forces into the region. (The option also is open to strike these targets preemptively, prior to the arrival of U.S. forces.) This may include mis-

siles armed with nuclear, chemical, or even biological warheads. Conventional attacks, employing integrated packages of missile and air strikes, are another possibility.

The Iranians do not intend to challenge American and other coalition naval forces directly. Their objective is not command of the seas, but rather sea denial. Tehran uses information obtained through third-party commercial satellites to plot the movement of U.S. forces at sea, and for early warning and targeting purposes. Washington is faced with the dilemma of allowing its forces to be observed in this manner or of attempting to deny this information to the Iranians by convincing Russia to cease providing satellite information to Iran. Other alternatives involve employing electronic warfare against satellite or ground stations, or perhaps even contemplating attacks on the satellites themselves.

Iran lacks the means to conduct long-range strikes against U.S. forces on the open seas with high confidence of success. It hopes to make up for this shortcoming by combining its handful of modern diesel submarines and mine barriers to slow and canalize U.S. movement (an action that would be especially effective around the strait), and covering fires in the form of missiles or long-range aircraft that might be employed selectively against high-value U.S. targets (e.g., aircraft carriers), if they can be located.

If U.S. forces prepare for deep-strike operations on key Iranian targets, the mullahs intend to make these targets exceptionally difficult to strike, even with advanced conventional munitions and near-real-time intelligence. First, many key targets are "cloaked" with human shields of hostages (ideally American or coalition member nationals, many selected from firms operating in Iran). Second, key elements of the Iranian military are positioned in densely populated areas. In some instances, these elements are co-located alongside Iran's nuclear reactors or power plants, or industrial plants that utilize significant quantities of highly toxic chemicals as part of their manufacturing process (i.e., "Bhopals in waiting"). The Iranian people, declare the mullahs, are ready to die to defend their faith against the "Great Satan."

If need be, the Iranian leadership is prepared to intentionally destroy several "dirty" targets, while accusing the United States of causing the catastrophe. Again, Tehran's aim is to prevail by employing a superior strategy against a technologically superior force, even at a cost in human and material resources that would be unacceptable when viewed from the value system of advanced Western industrial states. Once these targets are destroyed, Iran plans to "retaliate" in kind by striking similar targets in coalition states located within the region. These strikes could be executed by mobile ballistic missile or cruise missile systems, or by special operations sabotage teams. Attempts also will be made to appeal directly to the U.S. public and international opinion to stop the war.

If, for whatever reason, the Iranian denial strategy fails and the U.S.-led coalition conducts successful forced-entry operations following the neutralization of most Iranian long-range systems and their corresponding C3I network, the Iranians have a fallback plan. It involves countering U.S. and coalition ground forces' operations to physically control the country.

The Iranian forces will not employ the armor-heavy, combined-arms Cold War–era conventional operations favored by the Iraqis and the Bottom-Up Review planners. They will not attempt to "close with and destroy" coalition forces. Nor will they sit and await a coalition attack in prepared defensive positions constituting a "front line." Rather, they will initiate unconventional warfare operations against coalition forces. Iranian forces will operate in small, independent groups, diffusing the target base and making effective U.S. deep-strike attacks difficult. Small but numerous enemy partisan units will attempt to infiltrate past the coalition screening forces and conduct hit-and-run or suicide attacks on U.S. and allied rear base areas.

The objectives of such operations would be to raise U.S. costs, especially in time and blood, and to fracture the coalition. To this end, the Iranian leadership will likely attempt to establish sanctuaries for its forces, either in remote, inhospitable areas of the country or in neighboring states that are willing to act as benevolent neutrals. From these locations the Iranians could support unconventional operations, and could also stockpile weapons like cruise missiles that are difficult to target, but which themselves can strike effectively at long ranges. As coalition forces occupy the country, they would find themselves engaged in an unconventional war that would negate much of their military effectiveness. The Iranians hope to pose the United States with a "best case" outcome that sees coalition forces winning a Pyrrhic victory, with no easy or early end to the conflict in sight.[32]

INSIGHTS FROM "THE STREETFIGHTER STATE"

AGAIN, SCENARIOS DO *NOT* ATTEMPT TO PREDICT THE FUTURE. Rather, their purpose is to identify and highlight potential changes—especially disruptive changes—in the threat environment. "The Streetfighter State," written well over a decade ago, envisions that energy issues will trigger a military confrontation.[33] If the scenario were written today, with the benefit of hindsight, the trigger might be geopolitical in nature (such as a U.S.-Iranian confrontation over Iran's support of radical Islamist forces in Iraq or Lebanon). Or it might be military-technical in nature, as Iran acquires nuclear weapons capability. Given that, what "red flags" ought this scenario to have raised in the minds of military planners in the mid-1990s?

First, it envisions an absence of direct combat between similar forces. Gone are the central elements of Cold War–era combat: tanks against tanks, fighter aircraft against fighter aircraft, artillery duels, and the like. It posits that symmetrical warfare—combat between forces that generally look similar to each other—is becoming progressively unlikely. This marks a major break from the U.S. military's twentieth-century experience. The Kaiser's army in World War I looked very much like our own, as did Germany's Wehrmacht in World War II. The Imperial Japanese Navy's carrier divisions closely paralleled the Americans' own fast carrier task forces. Germany's submarine warfare campaigns were exceeded in their effectiveness only by the U.S. Navy's relentless submarine campaign against Japanese shipping in the Second World War. During the Cold War, Soviet tank armies opposed American tank forces in central

32. Andrew F. Krepinevich, Jr., *The Conflict Environment of 2016: A Scenario-Based Approach* (Washington, D.C.: CSBA, 1996), pp. 11–16.

33. Oil prices have risen to record heights recently. Yet over the long term it seems a fair bet that oil prices will move higher than the $70 per barrel price in place at the time this book went to press. Setting the price in 2016, however, is risky business. The history of oil has been marked by price spikes in both directions. Put another way, the oil market over the last century and a half has proved to be a nonlinear phenomenon. See Daniel Yergen, *The Prize* (New York: Simon and Schuster, 1991).

Europe, while both sides sought to build ever more capable fighter air-craft, submarines, and the like. For the American military, the twentieth century was the Century of Symmetrical Warfare. But in the scenario above this warfare era, like the twentieth century itself, has come to an end, and defense planners must take this disruptive shift into account.

Second, the scenario envisions the problems posed by a more pro-liferated world, one of rogue states armed with nuclear weapons. How might a country's possession of even a small nuclear arsenal alter the way in which the United States projects military power? The prob-lem has emerged first in North Korea, but the timeline for dealing with a nuclear-armed Iran still holds up well, even a decade after the scenario was published.

Another problem raised by the scenario is the ongoing proliferation of missiles among a broader set of rivals. Irregular Iranian forces armed with significant numbers of missiles pose a difficult challenge to U.S. forces. In 2006, Hezbollah struck Israel with nearly 4,000 rockets in the Second Lebanon War. By 2016, the scenario's time frame, will nonstate enemies have access to precision-guided rockets? It is a problem that U.S. and partner militaries ignore at their peril.

The scenario highlights the growing problem that even advanced naval forces, like those of the United States, will have in narrow or re-stricted waters. Six years after this scenario was published, Millennium Challenge 02 highlighted this problem in a more direct way.

Finally, the scenario warns of the problem of irregular warfare. The Iranians respond to the American "victory" by reverting to guerrilla warfare, attempting to erode America's will through a protracted war. That will sound familiar to those with even a casual interest in Amer-ica's experience in Iraq following its "regime change" military campaign in 2003.

Did the "Streetfighter State" scenario predict the future? Hardly. But did it provide what is essential to military planners—an under-standing of how warfare might change and the key challenges that could emerge from that change? Absolutely.

Are there threats to international security and stability on the dis-tant horizon that defense planners may be overlooking? Equally impor-tant, are there potential disruptive events that could occur in the near term, even today, that are not being given proper attention? The scenarios that follow are the author's attempt to address these questions. Like the "Streetfighter State" scenario, they present credible new military challenges on which the Pentagon might usefully focus its attention.

The reader should note the use of footnotes, both to provide citations for the references used to identify key trends and to further enrich the narrative. With regard to the latter, those citations with dates later than the fall of 2008 have been created solely to enhance the narrative. They are not meant to represent citations in the traditional sense.

1

THE COLLAPSE OF PAKISTAN

A situation threatening the security of Pakistan's nuclear arsenal and collapse of its command and control could only be brought about by subversion from within the military. Were this to happen, it would signify the Islamists' penetration of the last bastion of credible power in Pakistan.

Brigadier (Ret.) Arun Sahgal
United Service Institution[1]

LESS THAN THREE MONTHS AFTER ASSUMING OFFICE, PRESIDENT Martin Simmons faces perhaps the greatest threat to America's security since the 1962 Cuban Missile Crisis. As Congress rushes to confirm the remaining members of the president's national security team, the dramatic events of the past eight weeks, which began with the assassination of Pakistan's president on February 24, are now coming to a head. Also emerging is a clear picture of the danger posed by Pakistan's Islamist

---

1. Rahul Bedi, "Who Is in Control of Pakistan's Nuclear Arsenal?" *London Daily Telegraph*, December 29, 2007.

army faction and its militant Muslim allies, who hope to exploit that country's growing civil disorder to seize power and create a radical Islamist state.

ASSASSINATION

THE CRISIS CAME SUDDENLY. PRESIDENT REHMAN DHAR WAS PLAN-ning a trip to the United States. Islamist[2] officers in Pakistan's shadowy intelligence service, the Directorate of Inter-Services Intelligence (ISI), apparently leaked the planning details to a clique of Islamist army colonels. The purpose of Dhar's trip, as we now know, was to request the deployment of American troops to Pakistan as the lead element of an international military force. The Pakistani president hoped to win U.S. backing and, ultimately, broad international support for his campaign to impose order on several provinces that are the center of a rapidly metastasizing militant Islamist insurrection. The Jihadist[3] sanctuaries located in these frontier areas have long provided support to terror campaigns in Afghanistan and India. More recently, they have extended their reach, claming responsibility for the "Stockholm Massacre" train bombings that killed more than two hundred, and the assassination of moderate Muslim leaders in Egypt and Morocco.

Armed with President Simmons' support, President Dhar planned to address the United Nations General Assembly to request the world body's backing for deploying an international peacekeeping force to his country. The purpose was to avoid a possible war with India, whose government had become increasingly anxious following last fall's increase in Jihadist guerrilla and suicide attacks in Kashmir, which Dhar proved unable to suppress.

Whether Dhar could have succeeded in his mission will never be known. Pakistan's president never made it to the airport. On February 24, 2013, his heavily armed motorcade was ambushed by renegade Pakistani Army units under the command of the Islamist faction, who were

---

2. As used here the term *Islamists* refers to those elements in the Pakistani armed forces that are associated with the radical Muslim movement.
3. The term *Jihadist* refers to nonstate entities that are part of the global radical Muslim movement, as typified by organizations like al Qaeda.

likely supported by Jihadist elements. In less than ten minutes the president and nearly all his forty-seven-man bodyguard were cut down.[4] A video of the massacre taken by the militant Islamists has been shown repeatedly by al-Jazeera and other Muslim media.[5] Reflecting their mastery on the "war of ideas" battlefield, Islamist military leaders and their cleric allies proclaimed the assassination the work of the Indians and Americans. This has produced large anti-American and anti-Indian public protests in Pakistan and parts of the Arab world. More than a million Pakistanis demonstrated both in Lahore and in Rawalpindi. At the same time public opinion polls revealed that these same people voice admiration for the Muslim radicals for ridding them of the pro-Western Dhar.[6]

"THE CENTURY'S GREATEST CRISIS"

THE SITUATION IN PAKISTAN CONTINUED DETERIORATING INTO MID-April, as the world's second-largest Muslim state slipped toward open civil war. The military was divided between army Loyalists, who had ruled the country off and on for decades amid various ineffectual civilian

---

4. Pakistan's recent history has been marked by a number of attempted assassinations. In August 1988, President Muhammad Zia al-Haq was killed in a plane crash that some believe was planned, and not an accident as reported. During his time as president, General Pervez Musharraf survived several assassination attempts, including one in December 2003 which saw a powerful bomb detonated only minutes after the general's car crossed a bridge in Rawalpindi. Less than two weeks later, a second attempt was made on Musharraf's life by suicide car bombers, who killed over a dozen bystanders but failed to kill or injure the Pakistani president. In December 2007, former Pakistani Prime Minister Benazir Bhutto was killed in a gun and bomb attack while campaigning in Rawalpindi. Edward Jay Epstein, "Who Killed Zia?" *Vanity Fair,* September 1989, at http://www.edwardjay epstein.com/archived/zia.htm, accessed on September 16, 2008; Salman Masood, "Pakistani Leader Escapes Attempt at Assassination," *New York Times,* December 26, 2003, at http://query.nytimes.com/gst/fullpage.html?sec=health&res=9807E6DD173EF935A15 751C1A9659C8B63, accessed on September 16, 2008; and Matthew Moore and Emma Henry, "Benazir Bhutto Killed in Gun and Bomb Attack," *Telegraph,* December 29, 2007, at http://www.telegraph.co.uk/news/worldnews/1573792/Benazir-Bhutto-killed-in-gun-and -bomb-attack.html, accessed on September 16, 2008.
5. Less graphic versions have been shown by the Western media. Those with strong constitutions may download the video at the al-Jazeera website, http://english.aljazeera.net.
6. The Muslim world's ability to hold mutually incompatible views simultaneously was demonstrated in the period after the 9/11 attacks, when Muslims reveled in their ability to strike a blow at the world's superpower, while also believing that the World Trade Center attacks were the work of the CIA or Israelis.

governments, and the Islamist army faction, whose sympathies are with the militant Muslim groups. The Loyalist army leaders attempted to perform their traditional role of imposing order within the country. This time, however, they had to contend with Islamist elements within the armed forces, led by a clique of young colonels and a few junior generals, who command perhaps a third or more of the country's military. The Islamist faction supports the formation of a "true" Islamic republic, to be ruled by the country's radical Islamist parties in league with the army's "young Paks," and with the support of many of the nation's Sunni religious leaders.

There has been a spate of reports, many confirmed, of minor clashes between these two army factions, even as the world remains hopeful that all-out civil warfare can be avoided.[7] Of greatest concern is the disposition of Pakistan's arsenal of nuclear weapons, estimated to number 80 to 120, each of which is capable of causing greater destruction than the atomic bombs that destroyed the Japanese cities of Hiroshima and Nagasaki at the end of World War II. These weapons are believed to be located at half a dozen or so sites around the country, most of which are currently controlled by Loyalist forces. At least one site, however, is controlled by Islamist units. Both U.S. and other national intelligence services have concluded that sympathetic elements of the ISI have provided Islamist officers leading the breakaway army units with the activation codes needed to arm the nuclear weapons under their control.[8] If so, there may be little to prevent these weapons from being used.

These events confirm the worst fears of many security experts, who

---

7. See William Dawson, "South Asia on Verge of War," *Los Angeles Times,* April 14, 2013, p. 1; Joanne Szerbenny, "India, Pakistan Brace for War," *Boston Globe,* April 13, 2013, p. 1; and Harry Oats, "Pak Radicals on Collision Path," *New York Times,* April 13, 2013, p. 1.
8. While Pakistan has improved its control over its nuclear weapons in recent years, it is not clear if it has transitioned, either partially or fully, to requiring access codes to arm nuclear warheads. It does store its weapons disassembled, and key components are kept at different locations. However, the Islamist army factions have evidently managed to secure the key components required to completely arm a nuclear weapon. What is uncertain is whether access codes are needed, and if they are, whether the breakaway elements have them. Greg Miller, "Pakistan's Nuclear Arsenal a U.S. Worry," *Los Angeles Times,* November 8, 2007; Joby Warrick, "Pakistan Nuclear Security Questioned," *Washington Post,* November 11, 2007, p. 1; and William Dawson, "Pak Nukes Armed and Ready," *Los Angeles Times,* April 17, 2013, p. 1.

have argued that once Pakistan began to slide toward anarchy, the nuclear command and control structure would soon collapse.[9] As one noted, "Pakistan tends to leak. It has leaked vital weapons information in the past, and it may now be leaking nuclear weapons themselves."[10]

Fortunately, Pakistan's ballistic missile units apparently remain under the control of Loyalist elements.[11] These missiles are the most effective means the Pakistanis have of delivering a nuclear warhead at long range. Two air bases with aircraft capable of delivering nuclear weapons are controlled by Islamist forces, but this danger pales in comparison to claims by two Jihadist groups that they have been provided with several nuclear weapons each and have begun moving them to "alternate locations" for safekeeping.[12] These claims have recently been confirmed by an Islamist colonel. Speculation is that the Islamist military elements intentionally transferred the weapons to gain leverage, not so much over their Loyalist rivals as with the international community, to preclude the intervention that Dhar had sought. The danger also exists that these weapons might be smuggled abroad for use against any states that side with the Loyalists to suppress the Islamist forces. The principal targets of such attacks would appear to be India and the United States. In an attempt to reassure an increasingly unnerved U.S. public, senior Defense Department officials have launched a mini–media blitz to point out the difficulties involved in transporting a nuclear weapon halfway around the world and positioning it in an American city. India's leaders, given their country's long border with Pakistan, are far less sanguine regarding this threat. They cite repeated statements by Pakistani opinion leaders advocating the use of nuclear weapons if need be to ensure the recovery of Kashmir, a long-disputed province lying between the two

---

9. Bedi, "Who Is in Control?"
10. Miller, "Pakistan's Nuclear Arsenal."
11. Just as fortunate, all three hundred-plus U.S. military trainers and advisers in Pakistan have managed to make their way to Pakistani Loyalist bases. Had some of them been taken hostage by the radical Islamist army faction or by militant Muslim groups, an already difficult situation would have been greatly complicated. Evidently the Americans had planned for such a contingency and, following receipt of a coded message, rendezvoused at certain "rally points," to be picked up by U.S. helicopters and transports guarded by Army Rangers. See Donald Faher, "U.S. Troops in Daring Escape," *Atlanta Constitution,* March 12, 2013, p. 1.
12. John Sherman, "Pak Nukes on Loose?" *Los Angeles Times,* March 22, 2013, p. 1.

countries. For example, in an interview on the Waqt television channel that was published by the mainstream right-wing Urdu daily *Roznama Nawa-i-Waqt*, senior Pakistani newspaper editor Majeed Kaira discussed Kashmir's importance to Pakistan, called it "the jugular vein" of Pakistan and added that Pakistan should not hesitate to use nuclear weapons to take it from India. Kaira, who is also editor in chief of the English daily *The Nation*, declared:

> It is better to die fighting than to die from famine. Kashmir is our biggest issue, and showing flexibility on this matter is tantamount to treason. Anyone who shows flexibility on the issue, I will consider a traitor.[13]

Colonel Sajjad, one of the Islamist army leaders, has declared that, in addition to the nuclear bombs provided to the militant groups, other weapons, "at least twelve," have been removed from storage and dispersed, to ensure that the Islamist army elements "retain a nuclear capability" should the storage sites be attacked by air strikes for the purpose of eliminating the weapons. The colonel has declared that "horrific consequences" would befall any foreign power that attempted to destroy the weapons by a preemptive attack.[14]

Despite their advantage in numbers—well over half of the army has remained loyal to the government in Islamabad—time is clearly not on the Loyalists' side. Islamist army elements have fanned the flames of street demonstrations by calling for the civilian government and the army's leadership to resign, citing the failure of both to provide for the country's security and prosperity in over sixty years of rule. While radical Islamist demonstrations have previously been limited to Baluchistan and the Northwest Frontier Province, they have recently expanded to

13. Kashmir is said to be Pakistan's "jugular vein" because it provides much of the country's water supply. Kaira said that U.S. think tanks are predicting that Pakistan will become "another Somalia" by the end of the decade, owing to growing problems with its water supply. Kaira went on to say that "the establishment of an Islamic welfare state in Pakistan is our objective, and to achieve this objective we will use any means at our disposal—including nuclear weapons." The interview appeared in *Roznama Nawa-i-Waqt*, March 24, 2013, p. 1.
14. W. David Wallace, "Islamist Colonel Threatens Nuclear Destruction," *New York Times*, March 28, 2013, p. A1.

other parts of the country, to include Peshawar Province, long a source of recruits for the country's military. Indeed, during the Pakistan Army's episodic efforts to bring stability to the country's ungoverned areas, increasing numbers of troops have defected to the radicals' side rather than fight against their fellow tribesmen.

Compounding the problem, after years of Pakistan's "exporting" Jihadists to conduct terrorist attacks elsewhere, foreign Jihadists—members of militant Muslim organizations with links to al Qaeda and other Muslim extremist groups—have been slipping into Pakistan in increasing numbers since last fall. They have swollen the local militants' ranks while further radicalizing Pakistan's Jihadist groups. The introduction of foreign militants comes as no surprise, as al Qaeda has long cited the regimes in Saudi Arabia (owing to its possession of Islam's holiest sites and its great oil wealth) and Pakistan (because of its large population and its nuclear arsenal) as its two principal targets for subversion. Thus the army's Loyalist elements confront two adversaries: breakaway Islamist army units and a growing numbers of Jihadists, along with a population that, with every passing day, is losing confidence in the army and the country's traditional political parties. British prime minister William Winthrop describes the situation as "the century's worst crisis."[15]

THE SLOW DISINTEGRATION OF PAKISTAN

IMMEDIATELY FOLLOWING DHAR'S ASSASSINATION, JIHADIST ELE-ments, including radical Sunni mullahs, organized street demonstrations where Pakistanis called upon the government to step down and yield to the creation of a fundamentalist Islamic state. Initially the demonstrations were concentrated in the Northwest Frontier Province and in Baluchistan to the south, both hotbeds of the Jihadist movement. However, within a week the demonstrations spread to other parts of the country, thanks to the Islamist army leaders' effective use of the media, the Internet, and the encouragement of radical mullahs who, as they preached in the mosques, reminded the faithful of their duty to rise up against the government.

15. John Czarzasty, "Brit PM Pledges Support," *New York Times,* April 4, 2013, p. A3.

The lights at the White House have been burning late into the night for weeks now. The president, we are told, is in close contact with world leaders including those of the other permanent members of the UN Security Council—Britain, China, France, and Russia—to formulate a plan for international intervention in Pakistan, should diplomacy fail to defuse the crisis. The White House press secretary has stated the president's intention to speak to the American public in a nationally televised address within the next few days. In his address the president plans to inform the nation—indeed, the world—of recent developments and present a plan for moving forward to resolve the crisis. There is growing speculation that the address may coincide with the onset of military operations by the United States, Britain, and India. American and British land and air forces have been staging in Afghanistan for several weeks now, and a combined Anglo-American fleet is now steaming within easy reach of Pakistan's southern coast.

Many Americans, shocked by these events, are asking: How did it come to this?

Sadly, the signs of impending disaster have been visible for some time. They call to mind the exchange between President Franklin Roosevelt and British prime minister Winston Churchill. Toward the end of the Second World War, the president asked Churchill what name should be given to the war that had wrought such devastation. Churchill immediately replied, "The Unnecessary War." Just as Europe failed to arrest the rise of Nazi Germany prior to World War II, if the ongoing crisis in Pakistan leads to a major conflagration, be it in South Asia or farther afield, no one will be able to say the world community did not see it coming. Pakistan's destablization has been in the works for the better part of a decade now. As Britain's foreign secretary recently observed, "The current crisis reminds one of watching as rising floodwaters gradually overwhelm a dike. You see the danger, but too late, and are powerless to stop it."[16] Whether the international community is powerless to stop Pakistan's slide toward anarchy is debatable; what is not is that it is happening.

16. Donald Kerr, "Pakistan's Long Road to Collapse," *Los Angeles Times*, March 12, 2009, pp 14–15.

While the process of disintegration has accelerated in recent years, Pakistan has arguably been in decline for decades. Since its inception the country has been ruled by a succession of civilian governments and, when they failed, the Pakistani Army, the country's only competent institution and long recognized as the backbone of the state. Still, unlike the Arab world, Pakistan has had several periods of extended rule by democratically elected governments, from 1947 to 1958, from 1971 to 1977, from 1988 to 1999, and more recently from 2008 to the present. Yet none of these governments proved able to raise Pakistan out of poverty or to compete with the country's great rival, India. If anything, they proved more corrupt, less competent, and more likely to violate individual Pakistani civil rights than the military regimes that preceded and succeeded them.

Indeed, Pakistan's most successful period, economically speaking, occurred during the military rule of General Muhammad Ayub Khan, from 1958 to 1969, while its most calamitous periods occurred during the rule of a civilian, Zulfikar Ali Bhutto, who pursued a path of socialist nationalization during the better part of the 1970s that reversed the progress made under General Khan.[17] But the generals that followed Ali Bhutto had a mixed record themselves. General Muhammad Zia al-Haq, who ruled from 1977 to 1988, managed to do little better despite substantial American assistance during the Soviet occupation of Afghanistan and a steady stream of remittances from Pakistanis working in countries along the Persian Gulf. Zia's rule coincided with American and Pakistani support for the Jihadists fighting Soviet occupation forces in Afghanistan during the 1980s. As their radical Muslim ideas began to take hold in Pakistan, Zia unwisely attempted to maintain his regime's legitimacy by instituting a separate Islamic court system, promoting Islamist army officers, and encouraging the formation of madrassa schools (many funded by Saudi Arabia's ruling family or wealthy Saudi individuals) to teach Wahhabism, a strident form of

---

17. Bhutto was overthrown by General Zia al-Haq, and ordered hanged by Pakistan's Supreme Court on charges that he had authorized the murder of a political opponent. Many observers considered the charges to be fraudulent. See British Broadcasting System, "Deposed Pakistani PM Is Executed," April 4, 1979, at http://news.bbc.co.uk/onthisday/hi/dates/stories/april/4/newsid_2459000/2459507.stm, accessed on September 16, 2008.

Islam. In so doing, Zia propelled his country along the path toward the current crisis.

Another major factor in Pakistan's slide is the country's military, which has often placed its own interests above those of the Pakistani people. The army leadership has been responsible for diverting huge amounts of the nation's wealth to itself. Its generals have successfully lobbied for, or simply taken, a substantial cut of the national economic pie to sustain the military competition with India, whose population and GDP are seven times greater than Pakistan's. In recent years, the military has absorbed roughly 30 percent of the country's budget, while much of the rest has gone to debt service. Reflecting their status in Pakistani society, military officers enjoy a range of entitlements. For example, retired officers often receive large plots of land at far below market cost. This culture of entitlement and the resentment among ordinary Pakistanis that has grown over the years have bred the kind of anger and bitterness that fuel the current crisis.

The results of this long-term fiscal mismanagement are now painfully plain for all to see and epitomize the British foreign secretary's depiction of a dike slowly reaching the bursting point. Thanks to Pakistan's long run of excessive military spending and high foreign debt, little funding is available to make improvements in the nation's infrastructure or its education system, or to invest in more efficient forms of production. Compounding these problems are the nation's growing water shortages, which have been a source of increasing concern in recent years. Within the next decade Pakistan's rapidly growing population will reach a quarter-billion people attempting to scrape out a living in a country rapidly becoming as dry as the Sahara Desert. Islamabad had hoped to delay the profound economic and social consequences of this combined demographic and ecological disaster into the 2030s or at least the 2020s. However, the failure to take preventive measures such as water conservation and recycling, which most experts agree should have begun in the 1990s, has only accelerated the day of reckoning.[18]

18. The problem is further exacerbated by global warming, which has led to the progressive melting and evaporating of the Himalayan glaciers. The decline of this source of water for river-based irrigation has caused Pakistan's agricultural crisis to arrive earlier than most expected. This has been an important factor in the current uprising.

A lack of investment in infrastructure and education finds Pakistan lagging in its efforts to enter the information age, while its neighbor India has taken a leading role. While the international community has come to view India as a rising regional power, it looks at Pakistan and sees a government whose competence does not even extend to its own borders. This is especially galling to the Pakistani people, who have long measured themselves against their Indian neighbors. Moreover, the military's continued demand for ever greater resources, in its vain attempt to match the Indian military in a competition it cannot win, has placed increasing stress on the nation's purse.

Confronted by the ongoing breakdown in civil order in many parts of the country, on March 2 Pakistan's acting president, General Muhammad Mehmood Ahmad, called upon the army to restore order. Many army units responded to the general's command; however, those units commanded by Islamist officers refused to take action. More than that, these units' officers openly supported the Jihadists' demands.

THE RISE OF RADICAL ISLAMISM: THE MADRASSAS

WHERE HAD PAKISTAN'S JIHADISTS COME FROM? PART OF THE ANswer lies in the long decline of Pakistan's education system. In an age when intellectual skills count for more and more in a nation's ability to compete economically, the poor stewardship of the country's finances by a succession of Pakistani governments progressively gutted an already weak education system. The problem has been compounded by the country's dramatic population growth, which roughly *doubled* between 1977 and 2002. Today over 40 percent of Pakistan's population is under the age of twenty. Undereducated, and un- or underemployed, the unskilled and frustrated young men and, increasingly, women comprising this "youth bulge" must compete not only with fellow Pakistanis but with young people around the world for a job in the global economy. Too numerous to be absorbed into Pakistan's economy, and hampered by a lack of education, many young people have been left behind in the quest for a place in the country's workforce and society and as such have proved fertile ground for recruitment by militant Muslim groups.

By neglecting its educational infrastructure, Islamabad paved the way for the rise of the madrassas. These privately funded religious schools educate millions of young men and women in the Muslim world, and they are particularly influential in parts of the developing world where government education systems do not reach, as in many areas of Pakistan. For orphans and the poor, especially in rural areas, the madrassas provide essential social services, including education, room, and board.

While the majority of madrassas are not "terrorist factories," as some in the U.S. Congress allege, they do tend to be narrow-minded institutions.[19] And some, especially those funded by Muslims in the Persian Gulf region, such as wealthy Saudis, do promote extreme ideologies.[20] In these madrassas, subjects like music and science are ignored. Often the students learn only the Qur'an and then only a radical interpretation (many moderate Muslims would say misinterpretation) of the sacred texts. Those children who express an interest in pursuing a profession in, say, medicine, rather than becoming mujahideen—Muslim guerrillas or terrorists (the term *mujahideen* literally means "struggler") engaged in jihad (struggle)—are subjected to severe indoctrination, or what Westerners might call brainwashing or reprogramming. As one madrassa principal observed regarding a few of his more reluctant charges, "By the time I work on them for a few months, they will want to be mujahideen too."[21] The system for recruiting Jihadists can be

19. A typical madrassa curriculum includes courses in Arabic, Tafsir (interpretation of the Qur'an, or Koran), S (Islamic law), Hadith (recorded sayings and deeds of the Prophet Muhammad), Mantiq (logic), and Islamic history. Depending on the educational demands, some madrassas also offer additional advanced courses in Arabic literature, English, and other foreign languages as well as science and world history. Mumtaz Ahmad, "Madrassa Education in Pakistan and Bangladesh," at http://www.apcss.org/Publications/Edited%20Volumes/ReligiousRadicalism/PagesfromReligiousRadicalismandSecurityinSouthAsiach5.pdf, accessed on September 16, 2008; and P. W. Singer, "Pakistan's Madrassahs: Ensuring a System of Education, Not Jihad," Brookings Institution Analysis Paper #14, November 2001, accessed at http://www.brookings.edu/views/papers/singer/20020103.pdf, accessed on September 16, 2008.
20. From 1996 to 2001 Saudi Arabia and Pakistan were two of only three countries (the other being the United Arab Emirates) to recognize the Islamist Taliban regime in Afghanistan. Many of al Qaeda's leaders, including Osama bin Laden, are Saudis, and Pakistan maintained close ties (and provided support) to the Taliban during its rule.
21. Jessica Stern, "Meeting with the Muj," *Bulletin of Atomic Scientists*, January–February 2001, p. 44.

summed up in the words of one Pakistani Muslim cleric: "The rich Saudis donate money, and the poor Pakistanis donate their sons."[22]

Between 500,000 and 2 million Pakistanis are enrolled in madrassas. According to recent estimates, radical madrassas comprise "only" 10 to 15 percent of the country's total.[23] They have made an ongoing effort, spanning the better part of two decades, to radicalize some 50,000 to 300,000 young Pakistanis at any given time. As has now become evident, the influence of Pakistan's madrassas has been growing rapidly in recent years, despite former president Pervez Musharraf's orders to shut down the radical madrassas in the wake of the 9/11 attacks and his July 2005 ruling that all foreign students must have the approval of their respective governments.[24] As is now evident, these rulings were generally ignored.

During the latter part of March 2013 both Islamist and Loyalist army elements continued tightening their control over their sections of the country, rather than engage each other in direct conflict. The restraint showed by the army factions was not practiced by the Jihadists, who engaged in sporadic acts of violence against Loyalist forces and government officials. Fortunately, to this point their actions have not triggered a full-blown clash between the country's military forces, although that certainly seems to be the Jihadists' aim. Most disturbing, of course, was the revelation by Colonel Ashraf, in a now famous al-Jazeera interview, that Islamist army units were now in control of at least one of the country's nuclear weapons storage sites.[25]

THE UNGOVERNED AREAS AND THE RADICAL ISLAMIST MOVEMENT

THE ISLAMIST ARMY FACTION'S ABILITY TO EXERT INFLUENCE IN the Northwest Frontier Province and Baluchistan was aided considerably by local Jihadist elements, which had over the years come to dominate these provinces politically and socially. In fact, not since its inception in

22. Monica Swenson, "Oil Windfall Fuels Terrorism," *Washington Post,* August 4, 2011, p. A9.
23. Stern, "Meeting with the Muj," p. 43.
24. In addition, all madrassas in Pakistan were directed to register with the government. Neither directive was carried out. The latter declaration followed the attacks on London's subway system, which were perpetrated in part by men who had been educated in Pakistan's madrassas.
25. The interview is online at www.aljazeera.net, accessed on April 11, 2013.

1947 has Pakistan's government ever exercised complete sovereignty over its territory. This became very apparent to Washington following the 9/11 attacks and the subsequent U.S. military operations in Afghanistan, which drove the Taliban regime and its al Qaeda allies across the border into Pakistan's Federally Administered Tribal Areas (FATA), where they have long enjoyed sanctuary despite the efforts of American special forces and loitering airborne strike systems to defeat them.[26] Most fleeing Taliban, al Qaeda, and foreign Jihadis fled to the FATA, but others found their way into the Northwest Frontier Province, Baluchistan, and Pakistani urban areas. Despite repeated entreaties by Washington, Islamabad has never seriously attempted to impose order on the province.

A succession of "cease-fires" between the government and the militant Muslim groups (e.g, the Taliban) and local tribal leaders has done little save to provide the latter with a sanctuary from which they can wage their campaign of subversion against Pakistan and Afghanistan. The situation has only grown worse in recent years as Baluchistan, which lies to the south of the FATA, along Pakistan's border with Iran, has also become a center of support for Jihadist elements. Within these two provinces radical elements have created a foundation upon which to build a broader base of support among ordinary Pakistanis fed up with the secular political parties and the army. This became evident following the 9/11 attacks, when a network of safe houses established throughout Pakistan supported a number of al Qaeda leaders.

While Islamism holds sway in several provinces, the movement has also found expression in Pakistan's Islamist political parties, which began to flex their muscles as President Musharraf reversed course after the 9/11 attacks and sided with the United States against Afghanistan's Taliban regime—a regime that the ISI had helped put in place and sustain. In the October 2002 elections the Islamist parties exceeded all expectations, winning 20 percent of the vote nationwide while gaining control of the assemblies in the Northwest Frontier Province and Baluchistan. Prior

26. U.S. and other Western intelligence organizations have concluded that both Osama bin Laden and Mullah Omar (the Taliban leader who ruled Afghanistan prior to the U.S. invasion in the fall of 2001) are in hiding in the Federally Administered Tribal Areas, a region bordered by Afghanistan to the east, Pakistan's Northwest Frontier Province and the Punjab to the east and northeast, and Baluchistan to the south, in which the government has traditionally had no legal authority.

to this election, the Islamists had never won so much as 5 percent of the vote. However, if the Islamists hoped for a "mullah-military alliance" to emerge out of the elections, displacing the country's traditional—and horrendously ineffectual—secular political parties, they were quickly disillusioned. Indeed, these parties have increasingly been displaced by Jihadists operating from the FATA and the radical movement within the Pakistani Army.

Still, the country's Islamist parties are not without their successes. The current crisis confirms that the country's militant Muslim parties have realized their goal of penetrating the military's officer corps. The Jamaat-e-Islami party hoped to win over senior generals so that the next coup would be an "Islamist coup." Greater success, however, was achieved by the Jamait-ul-Ulema-e-Islam (JUI) party, which, while smaller, is more radical and is centered among the Pashtun peoples of the Northwest Frontier Province and northern Baluchistan. The JUI's success in penetrating the junior officer corps can be seen in the composition of the army's Islamist military faction, which is dominated by colonels supported by many of the army's rank and file. Not to be outdone, the Jamaat-e-Islami party claims credit for infiltrating the ISI and converting several key senior officers to the Islamist cause. These officers have apparently been instrumental in providing intelligence on Loyalist military forces to the Islamists and, most important, information on how to bring together the components needed to arm a nuclear weapon and to engage and bypass the launch activation codes (assuming Pakistan has installed them) on Pakistan's nuclear weapons.[27]

Ironically, the Pakistani military's slide toward Islamism has been aided in no small way by the United States, which broke off its military training and advisory programs in 1990 (following the Soviet Union's withdrawal from Afghanistan) over concerns that Pakistan was developing a nuclear weapon. Pakistani officers, rather than forming relationships

---

27. Following the attacks of 9/11, the United States worked covertly with the regime of then-President Musharraf to formulate launch codes that would minimize the risk that Pakistan's nuclear weapons could be employed without the authority of the country's senior military leader or its head of state. Washington has yet to confirm or deny its role in this effort, or to state whether ISI officers have the ability to defeat the safeguards. Nor has the United States or Pakistan publicly confirmed that the Pakistanis ever actually installed the launch code technology on their weapons. Ruth Alley, "Have Pakistan's Nukes Been 'Rendered Safe'"? *Wall Street Journal,* April 22, 2009, p. A3.

with their American counterparts, were isolated from them and more easily swayed by militant Muslim rhetoric. While military-to-military exchanges were resumed following 9/11, they were too little, too late.

The Islamist army leaders are also receiving support from several Jihadist terrorist and insurgent groups that, ironically, were formed by the Pakistani Army to wage guerrilla warfare against India as a means of advancing Islamabad's aims to secure Kashmir. The province, located in the northern part of India, is currently divided among China, India, and Pakistan and has been at the center of the conflict between India and Pakistan since they became independent in August 1947. Both countries view the entire Kashmir region as disputed territory and have fought two of their three full-scale wars over the issue, in 1947 and in 1965. More recently, in 1999, there was a limited border conflict (also referred to by some as the Third Kashmir War) in the Kargil area of India-controlled Kashmir. Pakistan suffered defeats in all three wars.

Owing to its lack of success in conventional forms of warfare, the Pakistani military took a page from its successful efforts with the United States in defeating the Soviet occupation of Afghanistan in the 1980s: it organized and supported Jihadist terrorists and guerrillas, helping them infiltrate into India's section of Kashmir to conduct their attacks. Yet over time this new approach accomplished little of benefit to Pakistan. First, it undermined efforts to improve relations with India, perpetuating Islamabad's ruinous spending on defense. Second, it led to the formation of a sizable Jihadist guerrilla force inside Pakistan that, as we now see, has sided with the army's Islamist elements. As Sartaj Aziz, Pakistan's former foreign and finance minister, recently observed, "For every ten [Jihadists] who are trained here to fight in Kashmir, one goes and the rest stay in Pakistan to cause trouble."[28]

RUN-UP TO THE CURRENT CRISIS

WITH THE REVELATION THAT THE ISLAMIST ARMY FACTION IS IN possession of at least two dozen nuclear weapons and is actively moving to disperse a sizable portion of them, it is clear that time is no longer on

---

28. William Spracher, "Militant Muslim Backlash Hits Paks," *Wall Street Journal,* June 18, 2012, p. A1.

the side of the Loyalists or the international community. The growing dis-order in Pakistan only reinforces the situation's urgency. Jihadist efforts to erode Pakistan's civic order, in an effort to trigger an all-out war between the army factions, have been building for several years now and are cur-rently at fever pitch. Their goal, of course, is to create widespread chaos in Pakistan, which they believe offers them the best chance of seizing power.

The witches' brew of a destabilizing youth bulge, declining economic growth, a growing ecological crisis, receding education opportunities, never-ending tensions with India over Kashmir, and the seemingly ever-lasting incompetence of Pakistan's military and secular political parties has eaten away at the country's civic foundation. The Islamist cancer grew throughout the decade, even as the world's attention was focused on the war against Islamism in Afghanistan and Iraq, on Iran's push to pro-duce a "Persian Bomb," on the global economic meltdown, and on wild fluctuations in the oil markets stemming from lower economic growth rates, instability in the Persian Gulf, and the ongoing conflict in Nigeria.

While Musharraf pledged his support for U.S. efforts to defeat the Jihadists following the 9/11 attacks, by mid-decade he was silently ac-quiescing to crackdowns by Islamist groups against what they consid-ered "un-Islamic" aspects of society. Over the past year this Pakistani "culture war" became widespread. It began in the expanding Islamist strongholds of the Northwest Frontier Province and in Baluchistan. The-aters and movie houses were forcibly closed, and those that tried to re-main open were sacked by Jihadist vigilantes. In Lahore, Jihadist thugs climbed billboards to deface the images of women not depicted wearing the traditional Muslim dress. Rampaging Jihadist students at Karachi Uni-versity destroyed musical instruments, calling them "satanic." The grow-ing usurpation of women's rights was epitomized by a horrific episode in which a Baluchi council of elders, implementing their interpretation of sharia,[29] sentenced a young woman in southern Punjab to be gang-raped to satisfy a violation of honor allegedly committed by her brother.[30]

---

29. Sharia is Islamic law. As Islam makes no distinction between the religious and the sec-ular, Islamic law covers not only rituals but every aspect of an individual's life. As Islamist forces have grown in power in Pakistan, so has the writ of sharia.
30. The traditional practice of "honor" killings has made a strong comeback with the rise of the Jihadists. They involve the murder of women by family members who deem that

Even though the story was picked up by the global media, the general response among Western nations was to express deference to Islamist norms.[31] Somewhat reminiscent of the Nazis in Germany and the Communists in Russia, the Islamists, although still a minority in Pakistan, claim to speak not only for themselves but for an entire people—indeed, an entire faith.

It comes as no surprise, then, that foreigners and native Pakistani Christians have been subjected to "Islamist justice." Bomb attacks on churches and church-run schools have effectively forced Christians underground, particularly after the August 2010 firebombing of the Catholic hospital in Hyderabad that tended to the sick and needy of all faiths, and the brutal beating and execution last October of four Catholic nuns working at a Karachi relief organization.[32] It barely requires stating that Pakistan's microscopic Jewish community has effectively been extinguished, as nearly all Jews have by now fled the country.

As the world saw in Iraq, even Muslims are not safe from Jihadist violence. Muslims of the Sunni sect comprise roughly 80 percent of Pakistan, while about 20 percent is Shi'a Muslims.[33] The Jihadists view Shi'a

---

their behavior has blackened the family name. Examples of such acts are elopement and refusal to accept an arranged marriage. Such common Western practices as cohabitation out of wedlock would, of course, qualify as well.

31. Opposition to these depredations has been strongest in the United States, as witnessed by the series of women's rights marches that followed in the wake of this barbaric episode. In the eyes of Islamists, women are permanently relegated to second-class status, which they share with infidels (nonbelievers) and slaves. Women, however, are uniquely disadvantaged: a male nonbeliever may convert to Islam, and a male slave may be set free, but a woman's inferior status is perpetually locked in place. As the above example shows, this inferiority is played out in many ways. In general, Islamic laws severely discriminate against women when it comes to sexual crimes. For example, they effectively deny protection for a woman against rape, since four male witnesses must confirm its occurrence.

32. William Spracher, "Jihadist Religion 'Cleansing' Continues," *Wall Street Journal*, October 29, 2012, p. A1.

33. The majority of Muslims are Sunnis. Orthodox Sunni Islam believes the Qur'an is the final authority given by Allah, and there is no further revelation. Shi'a Muslims, on the other hand, believe that Muhammad appointed his son-in-law, Ali, to succeed him as the rightful imam, to receive divine inspiration and authority from Allah, and to expand the message of the Qur'an. Some extremist Sunni groups, such as the Taliban or al Qaeda, advocate persecuting Shi'a Muslims as heretics. For example, Abu Musab Al-Zarqawi, the notorious leader of al Qaeda in Iraq during the early insurgency period in that country, in 2005 urged his followers to kill Shi'a. Al-Jazeera, "Al-Zarqawi Declares War on Iraqi Shia," at http://english.aljazeera.net/archive/2005/09/200849143727698709.html, accessed on September 16, 2008; and Al-Ahram Weekly, "Zarqawi's Double Face," at http://weekly.ahram.org.eg/2006/799/re5.htm, accessed on September 16, 2008.

Muslims as infidels to be exterminated and have directed a steady stream of violence at them in recent years. Adopting the techniques used by Jihadists in Afghanistan and Iraq, Pakistani Jihadists have used suicide bombers and improvised explosive devices (IEDs) to strike at Shi'a gathering places, such as mosques and town markets, at times killing hundreds at a stroke. Over the past eighteen months they have pursued a campaign against key figures in the Shi'a community. The goal of this campaign is clearly to intimidate Pakistan's Shi'a leaders into leaving Pakistan. In the weeks following Dhar's assassination, the Jihadists are enjoying increasing success, as growing numbers of middle- and upper-class Shi'a are fleeing the country.

The principal individual targets of the Jihadists' assassination efforts are government officials, senior military officers, non-Islamist political party leaders, and members of the professions (e.g., physicians). The assassination of several Pakistani Loyalist generals by militant Muslims has greatly embittered Loyalists toward their erstwhile brethren. While assassinations of senior Pakistani officers have occurred throughout the country's turbulent history, the fact that the Islamist army faction likely provided information to the groups plotting the assassinations is seen as much more than a mere violation of professional courtesy.[34]

Over the past two years the country has been starved for foreign investment, which plummeted following a series of attacks on foreign business interests, culminating in the November 2010 suicide truck bombing of the Avari Hotel in Lahore, a favorite of visiting business executives. As the Shi'a elite leave, they are taking their money with them, which will only compound Pakistan's problems. The Jihadists' purpose in these attacks has been to accelerate Pakistan's economic collapse and to mobilize nationalist support against foreign "exploiters."

Judging by events, they have succeeded. Demonstrations against the government, which had been on the rise throughout 2010, grew in scale and intensity as the year came to a close. A clear sign that public

---

34. Lieutenant General Mushtaq Ahmed Baig, the country's surgeon general, was killed while being driven home from his office. That attack, as well as more recent assassinations, was primarily the work of al Qaeda and the Taliban. Farhan Bokhari, "Pakistani General Assassinated," *Jane's Defence Weekly,* March 5, 2008, p. 15; and William Spracher, "Pak Generals in Crosshairs," *Wall Street Journal,* August 29, 2012, p. A1.

order was breaking down came when the disturbances spread to Punjab Province in mid-April. This may have been the tipping point in the struggle to maintain order in the country. As one observer noted, "The army has shown again and again that it can control mass unrest in Pakistan as long as it does not spread to northern Punjab, from where most of the army's own soldiers are recruited."[35] The forces of disorder within Pakistan clearly agreed. Leaks from U.S. intelligence reports have revealed that it was then that Islamist leaders within the military saw the time as ripe for action.[36]

In the absence of strong governmental leadership following the brutal assassination of President Dhar and the consequent confusion deliberately fostered by the Islamist military and Jihadist elements, the situation in Pakistan has deteriorated rapidly. Since their standoff with Islamist army units began in early March, the Loyalist army commanders have felt they lacked sufficient force to move against the Islamists' units and their Jihadist allies, now concentrated in the Northwest Frontier Province and Baluchistan. For their part, the Jihadists show no sign of letting up on their campaign of assassinating moderate civilian and military leaders and sabotaging key parts of Pakistan's economy. When several Loyalist Pakistani army units defected to the Islamists last week, another wave of alarm spread concerning the safety of those nuclear storage sites controlled by Loyalist forces.[37]

Nor has the international community been quick to act. When President Simmons addressed the nation on March 10, he called upon America's allies and the United Nations to approve prompt military action to stabilize the situation, secure the country's nuclear weapons, and avert civil war. Realistically speaking, however, the only countries with the means for intervening in force are the United States and India—the very targets of Pakistani street rioters and the Islamists.

---

35. Anatol Lieven, "A Difficult Country: Pakistan and the Case for Developmental Realism," *National Interest,* Spring 2006, p. 47.

36. W. David Wallace, "Military Radicals Fuel Tensions," *New York Times,* December 1, 2012, p A1.

37. Concerns have now also arisen with regard to Pakistan's stockpile of fissionable materials—uranium-235 (that is to say, nuclear-weapons-grade uranium) and plutonium. James Thorton, "More to Fear Than Weapons Alone," *Washington Post,* April 3, 2013, p. A1.

WHAT IS TO BE DONE?

WHAT ABOUT THE UNITED NATIONS? THUS FAR THE WORLD BODY, as in the preceding crises in Iraq and Iran, has proved incapable of acting decisively. On March 26, after several weeks of inconclusive Security Council discussions, India's prime minister Agarwal declared that New Delhi would not tolerate indefinitely the ongoing instability in neighboring Pakistan. Agarwal has repeatedly declared that Pakistan is capable of striking every city in India using an arsenal of plutonium warheads fabricated with material from a production reactor at Khushab in Punjab.[38] The Indians also have long been concerned that Pakistani terrorists will attack their nuclear weapons sites as part of an overall surprise nuclear strike.[39] While India's leader declared his country's strong desire for a peaceful resolution to the crisis in Pakistan, and stated his hope that a conflict between the two countries could be avoided, he warned both the Loyalists and Islamists against any use of nuclear weapons, against India or any other state in the region. Indian leaders clearly fear that if any of these weapons are in the hands of the Jihadists, they may attempt to smuggle them across the border, perhaps into Kashmir, to create a spectacular terrorist event. Consequently, India has suspended all bus and train links between the two countries and placed its armed forces on high alert.

In an attempt to rouse the Security Council to action, the Indian prime minister has also taken pains to remind other potential Jihadist targets—especially Russia and the United States—that they and their interests are at risk from "loose" nuclear weapons. The Indian leader's speech, which was broadcast worldwide, called to mind President John Kennedy's speech during the Cuban Missile Crisis nearly fifty years ago, particularly the prime minister's warning that "any nuclear attack upon

38. The use of plutonium enables the making of lighter, more compact and deadlier weapons than highly enriched uranium, the other fuel for a nuclear explosion. "It means we can make smaller weapons that are easier to fire at longer range," notes former Pakistani defense minister Lieutenant General Talat Masood. Smaller warheads also enable the use of ballistic missiles as delivery systems, as their payloads are far less than that of a combat aircraft. Dean Nelson, "Pakistan Upgrades Nuclear Arsenal," *London Sunday Times*, July 30, 2006. China assisted the Pakistanis in developing the improved warheads.
39. These fears extend back at least to 2006. "Official Says Nuclear Sites May Be Attacked," *Los Angeles Times*, July 29, 2006.

India by Pakistan, no matter how it occurs, no matter what faction is responsible, will be considered an attack by all of Pakistan, leading to a devastating response against that country."[40]

The speech triggered intense diplomatic efforts among the world's leading powers. Few countries believe it is possible for the Pakistanis to sort things out among themselves. There are broader issues involved as well. If the Islamists emerge victorious and install themselves as the country's new leadership, it will represent a stunning defeat for the civilized world in the war against radical Islamist elements. Shielded by its nuclear arsenal, a radicalized Islamic Pakistani Republic would become a major sanctuary and breeding ground for Jihadists, who would go abroad as they have since 9/11, attempting to subvert other Muslim states and increasing the likelihood of attacks against non-Muslim countries. Equally disturbing, no one can be certain that such a radical regime would view the use of nuclear weapons as a measure of last resort, to be considered only under the direst circumstances.[41] The transfer of several nuclear weapons to the Jihadists announced by Islamist army leaders can only fuel these concerns. Given this act, can the world be certain that an Islamic regime would not share or sell its nuclear weapons to others? All recall that Dr. Abdul Qadeer Khan,[42] the Pakistani physicist, ran (with

40. On October 22, 1962, President Kennedy declared, "It shall be the policy of this Nation to regard any nuclear missile launched from Cuba against any nation in the Western Hemisphere as an attack by the Soviet Union on the United States, requiring a full retaliatory response upon the Soviet Union." See www.americanrhetoric.com/speeches/jfkcuban missilecrisis.html.

41. India's proclamations are interpreted by many to mean that it will use nuclear weapons against Pakistan to ensure that an Islamic regime does not possess a nuclear arsenal. William Spracher, "India Threatens Use of Nuclear Weapons," *Wall Street Journal*, March 26, 2013, p. A1.

42. In January 2004, Khan confessed to having been involved in an international network of clandestine nuclear proliferation from Pakistan to Libya, Iran, and North Korea. On February 5, 2004, General Pervez Musharraf announced that he had pardoned Khan. Musharraf later confirmed that Khan had sent gas centrifuges and centrifuge parts to North Korea, and possibly uranium hexafluoride. During the 1980s and 1990s, Western governments became increasingly convinced that covert nuclear and ballistic missile collaboration was taking place between China, Pakistan, and North Korea. Of particular concern was the apparent export of Pakistan's nuclear technology to North Korea in exchange for ballistic missile technology. Following the September 11, 2001, terrorist attacks and the subsequent U.S. invasion of Afghanistan, the Americans found that al Qaeda had made repeated efforts to obtain nuclear materials from Pakistan to build either a radiological bomb or a crude nuclear bomb. Two Pakistani scientists admitted

China's help)[43] what amounted to a nuclear arms bazaar with North Korea and Iran, among other states, before finally being "outed" by foreign intelligence efforts in 2002. Can we expect an Islamist regime to be more circumspect with regard to nuclear proliferation than those that occupied the seats of power in Islamabad in the 1980s and 1990s, who were ostensibly cooperating with the United States? It hardly seems so.

All but one Security Council member—China—appears willing to act. Beijing has joined in calling for a peaceful resolution to the crisis but maintains that the current instability is an internal matter and not within the purview of the United Nations. A more cynical—and perhaps more accurate—view is that the Chinese are positioning themselves to establish a preferred relationship with a radical Islamist regime, should one emerge. This would be consistent with the direction in which events appear to be headed, barring some form of intervention. Moreover, it hardly bears mentioning that, alone among the world's great powers, China has established close relationships with militant Islamist regimes, Iran in particular, that are oil exporters. As shown by their active support for nuclear programs in Iran, North Korea, and Pakistan, the Chinese have adopted a far more sanguine view with regard to the dangers of nuclear proliferation and appear to have few qualms about working

---

having had talks on the topic with Osama bin Laden himself. Khan's dealings extended to Iran as well. The IAEA reported that Iran had established a large uranium enrichment facility using centrifuges based on the stolen URENCO designs, which had been obtained "from a foreign intermediary in 1987." The intermediary was not named, but many diplomats and analysts pointed to Pakistan and specifically to Khan, who was said to have visited Iran in 1986. The Iranians turned over the names of their suppliers and international inspectors quickly identified the Iranian centrifuges as Pak-1s, the model developed by Khan in the early 1980s. William J. Broad and David E. Sanger, "A Tale of Nuclear Proliferation: How Pakistani Built His Network," *New York Times*, February 12, 2004, at http://query.nytimes.com/gst/fullpage.html?res=9F00E1D6133AF931A25751 C0A9629C8B63, accessed on September 16, 2008; David E. Sanger, "The Khan Network," paper presented at the Conference on South Asia and the Nuclear Future, Stanford University, June 4–5, 2004; Carnegie Endowment for International Peace, "A. Q. Khan Nuclear Chronology," *Non-Proliferation*, Vol. VIII, No. 8, September 7, 2005, accessed at http://www.carnegieendowment.org/static/npp/Khan_Chronology.pdf, accessed on September 16, 2008; and William Langeweische, "The Wrath of Khan," *Atlantic Monthly*, November 2005.

43. It must be noted that Khan also covertly acquired sensitive nuclear information and equipment from several European countries.

with some of the world's most repressive regimes to advance their economic and security goals. Beijing may see a nuclear-armed Islamist Pakistan as a major worry for both the United States and India, which China views as attempting to constrain its growing ambitions in Asia.

The global peace movement has emerged as China's most formidable ally in its efforts to block international action. The movement's leaders (if one can describe such an amorphous group as having any true leadership) are arguing that intervention may precipitate the very dangers the United States and India seek to avoid: it may lead the Islamist army colonels to use the nuclear weapons in their possession against India, the intervention forces, Loyalist army units, or even Shi'a population centers. They posit that even if an intervention succeeds in defeating the Islamist army elements, the Jihadists would almost certainly attempt to use any nuclear weapons in their possession. Consequently, peace advocates (or "appeasers," to use but one of the terms employed by their skeptics and detractors) believe the United States and India must negotiate with the Islamists. That is the message of the large-scale demonstrations in several U.S. and western European cities, which have "spontaneously" spread to many cities in China and the Arab world.

How should the United States respond? Since Pakistan detonated its first nuclear weapon some fifteen years ago, every American president has worried about what might happen if this unstable country ever descended into disorder. The Pentagon, which has primary responsibility for responding in such a contingency, is the focal point for planning. Yet the military, preoccupied with the threat posed by Saddam Hussein's Iraq, the Long War against militant Islamists, and moves by Iran and North Korea (both former signatories to the Nuclear Non-Proliferation Treaty) to develop nuclear arsenals, accorded this contingency a relatively low priority, in terms both of planning and of developing capabilities to address it. The Defense Department's last major strategic review, conducted in 2009, known as the Quadrennial Defense Review, noted the problem of proliferation and even alluded to the possibility that nuclear materials might be put on the market by new "Dr. Khans." However, even mentioning a contingency involving Pakistan (once declared by President George W. Bush to be a "major non-NATO U.S. ally"), let alone planning for one, has been viewed as too sensitive politically.[44] Thus planning languished.

Moreover, senior American military leaders, while aware of Pakistan's increasingly fragile state, shuddered at the implications of confronting such a threat, given the American people's growing unwillingness to commit their sons and daughters to military service during the conflicts in Afghanistan and Iraq, and the Bush administration's refusal to make the difficult choices to increase taxes and to reduce spending on popular government programs in order to free up funding to bolster military preparedness for the Pakistan contingency.

Despite the fervent hopes that a crisis might be avoided, it is now upon us. Two overarching security problems must be addressed. First, and most critically: How can Pakistan's nuclear weapons—both those in storage and any "loose nukes"—be identified and secured without running the risk of their being used? Second: How can Pakistan, a country with a population over six times that of Iraq, be made secure or stabilized, lest it become a "Jihadi factory"?[45]

General (Ret.) Stephen J. Czarsinki, who served as the U.S. Army's senior military commander in Iraq until his retirement last fall, observed recently that Pakistan presented a problem in "both form and scale" for the U.S. military:

> The problem of finding unsecured nuclear weapons in a country that size is very different from any in our military experience. As for stabilizing that country, Pakistan's sheer size, both in land mass and population, far exceeds in scale anything we have confronted in

44. The Pentagon's 1992 Defense Planning Guidance, which provides instruction to the military on what kinds of contingencies ought to be the subject of planning, contained several "politically incorrect" scenarios. This classified document was leaked to the press and widely publicized—and criticized. Consequently, the scenarios were modified to include only those that were "inoffensive" to American and ally political sensitivities. Future efforts to develop planning scenarios were hobbled by this experience.

45. The term, which has become popular in the Pentagon, was coined by Admiral James "Buster" Corrigan, vice chairman of the Joint Chiefs of Staff. See Admiral James "Buster" Corrigan, Testimony, Senate Armed Services Committee, April 24, 2013, at http://armedservices.senate.gov/hearings.htm, accessed on April 30, 2013.

previous stability operations in our history. Consider, Mr. Chairman, that at the height of the "Surge" of U.S. forces in Iraq we had roughly 20 brigades working to bring order to a country of around 27 million. The population of Pakistan is about seven times as large, which would mean a surge of 160 brigades, using Iraq as a model. The entire United States Army, including the Reserves, has but 76 brigade combat teams. If we deployed every Army combat unit to Pakistan, we would not have half the number we would likely need to bring order to that country.

This, of course, would make little sense. First, stabilizing Pakistan would almost certainly be a long-term proposition, requiring an extended deployment of our forces. We would therefore have to rotate forces into and out of the country over time. Our Army is organized to have one-third of its brigades deployed, one-third preparing to deploy, and one-third refitting after a deployment. Out of an Active force of 48 brigades, this means we can sustain 16 of them forward deployed over an extended period of time. As for our Reserves, owing to the fact that its soldiers are civilians who are only periodically called up for duty, the Army estimates that only 4 or 5 of its 28 brigade combat teams can be deployed forward on a sustained basis. In short, the Army has the capability to deploy some 20 brigades on a sustained basis, not 76, nor 160.

Second, the Army has brigades deployed to other parts of the world. There are currently 4 in Iraq and 3 in Afghanistan, and 1 in Europe. Take away those 8 and you have the capacity to deploy only 12 to Pakistan on a sustained basis. Of course, this would leave us with little or no effective strategic reserve if a crisis developed elsewhere in the world.

Of course, the Marines have deployed brigade-sized formations in Afghanistan and Iraq. However, their numbers are not sufficient to make a major difference in what we could deploy to Pakistan,[46]

46. General (Ret.) Stephen J. Czarsinki, Testimony, House Armed Services Committee, "The Challenge of Stability Operations," April 24, 2013, at www.house.gov/hasc/hearing_information.shtml, accessed on April 30, 2013. The Marine Corps is organized into three active and one reserve divisions, comprising a total of twelve brigade-sized ground force elements, nine active and three reserve.

When questioned about how the military might secure Pakistan's nuclear arsenal, the general went on to state what is now widely understood. Emissions from a nuclear weapon, in the form of gamma rays, X-rays, and neutrons, travel only short distances, perhaps a few hundred yards at the very most. Even modest levels of shielding (for example, using thin sheets of lead) reduce these emissions substantially. This means that any effort to develop a means of detecting these weapons at great distances, such as by a satellite in space or even by an aircraft flying at an altitude of only few thousand feet, will fail.[47] While some farsighted officials urged the Defense Department years ago to pursue a "Manhattan Project"[48] to develop the technology to solve the problem, the laws of physics pose a fundamental barrier to success.[49]

Some hope, however, can be found in the unclassified version of prepared congressional testimony offered last year by the director of national intelligence (DNI)[50] who, along with the general heading the

47. Nuclear weapons are radioactive and they are very dense. There are three basic ways of detecting them: "passively" detecting the radiation they emit, "actively" detecting very dense objects (e.g., with X-rays), or "actively" detecting by irradiating them and observing the resulting fissions. Passive detection is the only practical means of searching large areas for nuclear weapons. For reasons of cost and complexity, bathing large areas in X-rays or neutrons is not feasible.

Nuclear weapons are also very difficult to detect at any significant range (especially if shielded by even a modest layer of lead), since neither the plutonium nor the highly enriched uranium used in a nuclear weapon is highly radioactive. Moreover, highly enriched uranium (HEU, or U-235) emits far less neutron and gamma radiation than plutonium. Thus HEU is difficult to identify through passive detection. Plutonium is substantially easier for passive systems to detect, since it has dramatically higher neutron and gamma ray emissions. See http://www.nti.org/e_research/cnwm/overview/technical5.asp, accessed on October 9, 2008.
48. The Manhattan Project was the United States' effort during World War II to design and build a nuclear weapon. The project received the highest possible priority and proceeded on a crash basis.
49. There have been reports that DARPA, the Defense Advanced Research Projects Agency, is working to develop small, cheap radiological sensors. The concept behind this effort is to create a "radiological sensor net" (RSN) by seeding an area with these sensors, which can be deployed through various means, including airborne insertion. Even then, however, success would require fairly precise intelligence on the suspected location of the "loose nuke." See John Smith, "DARPA Tackles 'Loose Nuke' Problem," *Aviation Week and Space Technology*, April 29, 2013, pp. 23–25.
50. The director of national intelligence (DNI) is the most senior U.S. intelligence official and is responsible for coordinating the intelligence community's efforts. The DNI is the principal intelligence adviser to the president and the statutory intelligence adviser to the National Security Council. The position of DNI was created after the 9/11 attacks on New York and Washington.

National Security Agency (NSA),[51] argued for a different solution to the problem. The DNI testified:

> Dealing with terrorists possessing nuclear weapons will require a highly integrated intelligence effort, whose central element will be human intelligence (HUMINT). We must penetrate terrorist organizations with our covert operatives, and find ways of "turning" members of those organizations into willing informers. To be sure, we will continue our efforts, along with those of the Defense Department, to intercept terrorist communications and to exploit technical means of locating these weapons. But HUMINT must be the central element of our efforts in this area.[52]

It appears that the success or failure of any U.S. or international effort to secure Pakistan's nuclear weapons will rely, to a high degree, on how well America's "spies," and those of cooperating states, have been able to infiltrate Pakistan's Jihadist groups, and on the friendships that military officers, U.S. and British in particular, have been able to form over the years with their Loyalist Pakistani counterparts.

But even assuming that Pakistan's nuclear weapons can be located, there is still significant uncertainty as to whether they can be disabled or secured. Even if intelligence correctly pinpoints the location of the nuclear weapons storage sites controlled by Islamist Pakistani Army units, the United States still confronts several problems in seizing or destroying these weapons. First, any air strike or insertion of ground forces would likely require surprise to succeed. Forewarned, the Islamists would likely reposition the weapons or, even worse, try to use them. If surprise were achieved, however, U.S. and other military observers believe another problem must be addressed: the weapons are likely stored in deep underground chambers, impervious to destruction by even the

---

51. The NSA is part of the U.S. intelligence community. It is also an independent agency within the U.S. Department of Defense. The NSA was established in 1952. Its primary purpose is encoding and decoding communications intelligence and protecting U.S. information systems.
52. Director of National Intelligence, Testimony, House Permanent Select Committee on Intelligence, April 22, 2013, www.house.gov/int/hearing_information.shtml, accessed on April 30, 2013.

most powerful American "bunker buster" precision-guided munitions, sometimes referred to as "smart bombs." There have been reports that the U.S. government has developed very low-yield, highly accurate "precision" earth-penetrating nuclear weapons in anticipation of this problem.[53] However, it is doubtful that any U.S. president would authorize the first use of American nuclear weapons, even under these circumstances.

Finally, it might be necessary to destroy or neutralize *all* of Pakistan's nuclear weapons (or at least those not given to the Jihadists) simultaneously. The Islamist army elements would have great incentive to employ at least some of the weapons that survived any U.S. strike, lest they be lost in any follow-on attacks. The likely targets of Islamist nuclear retribution strikes would be Pakistani Loyalist forces, India, and U.S. forces in neighboring Afghanistan. If Loyalist units are hit, the temptation on their part to retaliate in kind against Islamist forces or Jihadist strongholds may be irresistible. Should India be attacked, a full-scale nuclear exchange involving dozens, and perhaps hundreds, of warheads may ensue. There are indications that New Delhi would retaliate with scores of nuclear weapons to ensure it destroyed every Pakistani nuclear weapon.[54]

While U.S. air and missile defenses now positioned in the area may be able to intercept some Pakistani nuclear weapons launched against India, there are no guarantees that they will be able to intercept every aircraft or missile. It is, of course, possible that the attacks may be mounted employing nontraditional means (e.g., by smuggling a weapon across the Indian border, employing a small commercial aircraft on a "kamikaze" strike, or trucking one into a Loyalist area). Simply put, there is no shortage of risks involved in taking action, as military planners readily concede. If the United States attempts to take out Pakistan's nuclear forces and fails to eliminate them all, Washington may be blamed for acting but not succeeding, even though doing nothing may be the worst option of all. Again we come back to the critical importance of having detailed intelligence regarding the location of Pakistan's weapons and the ability to strike quickly and effectively.

53. Tim Keppler, "The Pentagon's 'Black' Nukes," *New York Times*, September 18, 2011, p. C1.
54. Harry Oats, "A South Asian Nuclear War?" *New York Times*, April 23, 2013, p. A1.

The challenges associated with securing the nuclear weapons trans-ferred to the Jihadists are no less formidable, even assuming the U.S. military can identify where the weapons are located. If the weapons are held by a small group of Jihadists, and if their location can be precisely defined, and if the location is in a sparsely populated area, the clandes-tine insertion of elite U.S. Special Operations Forces (SOF) troops would be one possible means of securing the weapons, particularly if they are inserted immediately following an air strike that kills or disperses the Ji-hadists. But this option relies for its success on an uncomfortable num-ber of "ifs."

In any event, a combined air-SOF strike may prove difficult to pull off. Although their development has long been discussed, another prob-lem confronting the U.S. military is its lack of long-range stealthy SOF aircraft, both planes and helicopters, to move these forces over the great distances that will be required to penetrate deep into Pakistan, while also avoiding detection. Equally worrisome is how the captured nuclear weapon and the U.S. troops guarding it will be evacuated. It is unlikely that the aircraft that transport the Special Forces will be able to land in Pakistan, let alone refuel there.[55] Yet another concern is that if the weapons are found to be in a densely populated area, a much larger force will be required to seize them, reducing the chances for surprise while greatly increasing the possibility of civilian casualties.

It would take days to organize and transport such a large force. Mil-itary commanders thus confront the problem of time. Once intelligence reports the suspected location of a weapon, the clock is ticking. If the Jihadists are smart, and one must assume they are, they are likely mov-ing their weapons on a regular basis. The longer it takes to organize and deploy a "snatch" team and the associated forces, the greater the chance that they will arrive to find—nothing. This planning factor is critical for U.S. commanders. The military has only a small number of Special Forces and even less in the way of air transportation assets. It cannot

55. There are rumors that India and Afghanistan may make bases available for U.S. trans-port aircraft, but this does not solve the problem of where these aircraft can land inside Pakistan to recover U.S. troops and secure the weapon(s). Helicopters, of course, can land in exceedingly small spaces. However, they are greatly limited in their range. Thus the question: How would they be refueled?

afford a failed snatch mission. A just-published article in *Jane's Defence Weekly* states that the entire U.S. military has sufficient assets to conduct at most two or three of these snatch raids simultaneously.[56] Thus the intelligence must be of the highest grade, U.S. forces must operate with the greatest speed, and the operations must be superbly coordinated. Once the Jihadists realize that the snatch operations are under way, their incentive to use these weapons, rather than have them seized, will likely increase dramatically.[57]

For their part, advocates of a negotiated resolution to the crisis are arguing that negotiations be given more time to work, and that Pakistan's borders be sealed off for the time being and all traffic entering and departing the country be monitored in order that the loose nukes might be "quarantined." This, they assert, will prevent loose nuclear weapons from leaving the country. What they fail to explain, however, is how this can be accomplished. Admiral Harrison Hayes, the U.S. chairman of the Joint Chiefs of Staff, has publicly stated that quarantining Pakistan is a practical impossibility. First, the Iranians cannot be trusted to participate in such an operation, even if their Shi'a brethren are being persecuted. Second, the U.S., Afghan, and allied NATO militaries, despite their best efforts over the past eight years, have been unable to seal the rugged border between Pakistan and Afghanistan. Third, India has been unable to stop the infiltration of Jihadists into Kashmir, despite decades of effort directed to that end. Finally, it would take months to deploy the enormous number of troops needed to even attempt to accomplish the

---

56. John Colbin, "U.S. Lacks Forces to Seize 'Loose Nukes,'" *Jane's Defence Weekly,* March 17, 2013, p. 28.

57. Such weapons typically have special codes that must be entered before they can be activated; senior administration officials fear that the codes could plausibly have been provided by Islamist moles within the ISI. In discussing this issue on NBC's *Meet the Press,* one U.S. senator argued that if the Jihadists want to detonate a weapon on their own soil, it "would give us one fewer weapon to recover." This may be true; however, it ignores the possibility that Pakistanis—and others advocating negotiating at any cost—may blame the United States and its allies for what might amount to the first hostile use of a nuclear weapon since the August 1945 attacks on Japan. Should this use occur in a heavily populated area, the outcry among these groups would be even greater. Nor can one discount the possibility that the Jihadists and their sympathizers might assert that the explosion was that of a U.S. nuclear weapon. In short, problems abound, while solutions are few. *Meet the Press,* NBC News, April 8, 2013, transcript at www.msnbc.msn.com, accessed on April 29, 2013.

task. As a practical matter, any loose nukes could be across the border long before American and other troops could be positioned to block them.[58] In a rare show of solidarity, all of the permanent members of the Security Council have rejected this option, which America's UN ambassador succinctly described as a "non-starter."[59]

However, the United Nations has yet to agree on a course of action. Given China's refusal to endorse preventive measures, there is little hope that the world body will act in a timely and forceful manner. Consequently, the United States and other like-minded states, Britain and India in particular, have engaged in talks of their own aimed at defusing the crisis.

Assuming the Islamists and Jihadists can have their nuclear fangs removed, Pakistan will still be on the cusp of chaos, if not engulfed by it. How can this enormous failed state be stabilized? It is clearly beyond the American military's capabilities. As General Czarsinki noted, the Army or the National Guard already have a substantial number of soldiers deployed (along with the Marines) to stabilize Afghanistan and Iraq. Moreover, the cost of stabilizing Afghanistan and Iraq has, at its peak, run over $100 billion a year. A back-of-the-envelope calculation reveals that the United States would require an army three to four times the size of the current force, and some $200 to $400 billion a year to have a chance of stabilizing Pakistan, assuming the same approach is applied. The United States, still recovering from the "great recession" of 2008–2011, is neither willing nor able to undertake such an open-ended commitment on its own.

Clearly some difficult choices will have to be made. If the United States is to intervene to secure Pakistan's nuclear weapons and stabilize the country, it will need either the support of allies or a resumption of conscription to achieve the force levels that are likely to be required. It may need both. The question is: Is this possible? According to unsubstantiated press reports, India has pledged its support and is mobilizing

---

58. Merely attempting to inspect every bit of cargo leaving and entering Pakistan would be a herculean task. Moreover it would quickly create severe economic dislocations within the country by reducing the "velocity" of trade upon which Pakistan relies for its existence.

59. Donald Kerr, "UN Ambassador Rejects 'Quarantine' Option," *Los Angeles Times*, April 1, 2013, p. 3.

its military toward this end.[60] Rumors are circulating that a number of European states, primarily Britain and France, have offered to contribute their special operations forces and some ground forces, along with elements of their navies, for the purpose of securing Pakistan's coastline against attempts by Islamist army leaders and Jihadists to depart the country, or to smuggle nuclear weapons out. Both London and Paris have reportedly positioned forward in India (as has the United States in Afghanistan) so-called consequence management teams.[61] These teams are specialized in dealing with the aftermath of a nuclear attack. The United States is also working with democratic Muslim states, Turkey and Indonesia in particular, in the hope of getting them to commit peacekeeping forces from their sizable armies. As for a return of conscription, public opinion polls show the American people overwhelmingly oppose it.

This is the situation we confront as the president prepares to address the nation later this week. While the crisis in Pakistan comes as a shock to most Americans, to many observers, including senior government officials, it is hardly a surprise at all. To them, the greatest surprise is that Pakistan did not implode sooner. While it is hoped the president will report on some dramatic diplomatic breakthrough, media reports of U.S. and Indian troop movements indicate that it is more likely that military action is imminent. If so, the combined forces of the U.S.-led coalition may already be in the process of executing their initial strikes as the president speaks. The fate of millions may well hang in the balance.

60. James Thorton, "U.S.-India in Alliance Talks," *Washington Post,* April 8, 2013, p. A1.
61. There are confirmed reports that a major Japanese naval task force has transited the Strait of Malacca, entered the Indian Ocean, and is steaming toward Pakistan. The task force's purpose is not yet known, and Tokyo refuses even to confirm the fleet's existence. Several military experts, however, believe the ships have two missions: first, to support efforts to control the Pakistani coast; and second, ballistic missile and air defenses. Donald Kerr, "Preparations on for Nuke War," *Los Angeles Times,* April 5, 2009, p.1; and William Spracher, "EU, Japan Militaries on Move," *Wall Street Journal,* April 14, 2013, p. A1.

2

WAR COMES TO AMERICA

Humans are creatures of habit. Furthermore, even when confronted with reasonably documented new facts that they understand intellectually, they frequently fail to grasp the new message at the visceral level. The opportunities for mass destruction and "Armageddon on the cheap" have proliferated. Communication and new means of transportation essentially have wiped out the comforts of international isolation. Geography still matters, but it no longer provides a safe haven for any state.

— Martin Shubik, "Terrorism, Technology
and the Socioeconomics of Death"

NOT LONG AFTER THE FIRST ATOMIC BOMBS WERE USED AGAINST Japan in the final days of World War II, some began to think of how such terrible weapons might be used against the United States. Robert Oppenheimer, known as the "Father of the Atomic Bomb" for his leading role in developing the weapon, told Congress that a small number of men, less than half a dozen, "could destroy New York" by smuggling a nuclear weapon into the city. When a senator asked how such a weapon, smuggled inside a crate, could be detected, the famous scientist responded, "With a screwdriver."[1] Oppenheimer was effectively saying that detecting a nuclear weapon, especially one that is properly shielded, is difficult almost to the point where nothing short of visual identification will suffice.

Nearly thirty years later, in late 1974, the FBI received a message

1. Steve Coll, "The Unthinkable," *New Yorker,* March 12, 2007.

from an individual claiming that he had hidden a nuclear weapon some-where in Boston and would detonate it unless he received $200,000. A team of experts rushed in with scientists from the U.S. Atomic Energy Commission to locate the weapon and secure it. The operation quickly dissolved into a Keystone Kops comedy of errors. The group's radiation detection gear arrived at the wrong airport. When the gear was located, it was discovered that the tools needed to install the equipment had been left behind. As one of the researchers commented, "If they were count-ing on us to save the good folk of Boston . . . well it was bye-bye Boston."[2]

TEN DETERMINED MEN

IN THE FALL OF 2003 SECRETARY OF DEFENSE DONALD RUMSFELD penned a memo to his senior civilian and military advisers, sharing some of his innermost fears about the ongoing war with radical Islamists. No matter that the radical Islamists lacked an army, or a state—in fact, pre-cisely because they lacked the trappings of a traditional enemy—they were going to be difficult to defeat. In the end, Rumsfeld concluded, the United States faced "a long, hard slog."

The Long War, as it has become known, raised fears that the cluster of loosely aligned radical Islamist groups around the world would some-day gain access to weapons of mass destruction. The greatest concerns have focused on the enemy's obtaining nuclear or biological weapons. Al Qaeda documents captured following the U.S. invasion of Afghani-stan revealed that the group was intent on acquiring these weapons.[3]

In his office at the Pentagon, Andrew Marshall was now asking, "How much destruction can ten determined men create?" Since antiq-uity, the answer to that question had been "Not much." But with the dif-fusion of knowledge of how to fabricate biological weapons, and with nuclear weaponry proliferating to an ever-greater number of states, the answer seemed certain to change, and perhaps soon.

2. See en.wikipedia.org/wiki/Nuclear_Emergency_Support_Team, accessed on June 8, 2008.
3. According to the CIA, al Qaeda has been trying to acquire weapons of mass destruc-tion, including nuclear weapons, since the early 1990s. David Ignatius, "Al-Qaeda's Nu-clear Weapons Pursuit," *Washington Post*, October 18, 2007, at www.signonsandiego .com/uniontrib/20071018/news_lz1e18ignatiu.html, accessed on June 12, 2008.

Over the past decade a series of government commissions have warned of the dangers inherent should nonstate groups come into possession of weapons of mass destruction. Experts warned that terrorist organizations armed with biological or even nuclear weapons would have every incentive to use such weapons to cause the kind of mass destruction and panic they hope will enable them to realize their goal of a fundamental change in the international order.

Academics like Harvard's Graham Allison and defense establishment veterans like former defense secretary William Perry and former senator Sam Nunn warned that something must be done to curb proliferation and impose safeguards.[4] Fred Iklé, a close colleague of Andrew Marshall's and an expert on nuclear strategy, has become the movement's John the Baptist. However, he is the herald not of mankind's salvation but of its destruction. Iklé warns of the heightened instability that will characterize a proliferated world and the growing likelihood that nuclear weapons will be used.[5]

These warnings elicited some response. The United States instituted the Proliferation Security Initiative, a loose coalition of states that agreed to share intelligence about states attempting to transfer fissionable materials, or even weapons, to other nations or nonstate entities. The United States and Russia have also been dramatically reducing their nuclear arsenals, which achieved enormous size during the Cold War, as an act of good faith toward the goal of eventually eliminating nuclear weapons altogether. At the Cold War's end, senators Sam Nunn and Richard Lugar authored legislation to establish the Cooperative Threat Reduction Program, to provide funding to ensure that Russia's

4. Allison has written extensively on the threat of nuclear terrorism. See, for example, Graham Allison, "How to Stop Nuclear Terrorism," *Foreign Affairs,* January–February 2004; and Graham Allison, *Nuclear Terrorism: The Ultimate Preventable Catastrophe* (New York: Henry Holt, 2004). Sam Nunn and William Perry have written recently on the importance of taking steps to reduce the number of nuclear weapons and on the need to prepare for the consequences of their use. See George P. Shultz, William J. Perry, Henry A. Kissinger, and Sam Nunn, "A World Free of Nuclear Weapons," *Wall Street Journal,* January 4, 2007; William J. Perry, Ashton B. Carter, and Michael M. May, "After the Bomb," *New York Times,* June 12, 2007; and Sam Nunn, "The Race Between Cooperation and Catastrophe," Speech before the IAEA Conference, March 16, 2005, at www.nti.org/c_press/speech_nunniaea_031605.pdf, accessed on June 8, 2008.
5. Fred Charles Iklé, *Annihilation from Within* (New York: Columbia University Press, 2006).

nuclear arsenal would remain secure in the wake of the Soviet Union's collapse.

Despite these and other efforts to maintain control over weapons of mass destruction, radical groups persisted in their efforts to acquire and use them. In 1995 a radical Japanese sect, Aum Shinrikyo, set off nerve gas on a Tokyo subway, and shortly after the 9/11 attacks on New York and Washington, some as-yet-unknown group or individual used anthrax to conduct an attack through the mail in the United States.[6] The principal fear, however, remained that of an attack by atomic weapons. The Pentagon and other arms of the United States government began investing substantial funds to develop technologies to detect the presence of fissionable material at a distance, so as to enhance the ability to intercept any efforts to smuggle such materials, including in weaponized form, into the United States. At the same time, an effort began to field some "render safe" teams. These teams have the mission of disarming any nuclear weapons that are intercepted while being smuggled into the country.

While Americans continued to go about their daily business, the rough outline of a way to block the covert introduction of nuclear weapons into the country took shape. The government deployed nearly two thousand radiation detectors to ports and border-crossing points, including ports overseas where cargo bound for the United States would be taken on board. Detectors were also emplaced at airports, aboard Coast Guard ships, at rail centers, and in mail facilities. Nuclear Emergency Support Teams (NESTs), composed of scientists, engineers, and technicians trained to locate nuclear weapons, are prepared to deploy on short notice.[7]

6. In August 2008, Department of Justice and FBI officials released documents and information indicating that charges in the anthrax attacks case were about to be brought against Dr. Bruce Ivins. However, Ivins committed suicide before any charges were filed. Consequently, the case never went to trial. See http://www.fbi.gov/anthrax/ amerithraxlinks.htm, accessed on October 19, 2008.
7. NESTs were created in the wake of the 1974 fiasco in Boston described above. Formerly known as the Nuclear Emergency Search Team, these teams provide technical assistance to the FBI, the lead federal agency for terrorism response within the United States. Department of Energy, National Nuclear Security Administration, "Nuclear Emergency Support Team (NEST)," www.nv.doe.gov/library/FactSheets/NEST.pdf, accessed on June 11, 2008. Other nuclear detection programs include the SLD-Core Program, originally designed to assist Russia in safeguarding against the smuggling of nuclear and fissile materials out of that country (the program has since been expanded to the former Soviet Union

While these efforts are significant, critics have repeatedly argued that, given the enormous consequences that would ensue from a nuclear or biological attack on the United States, they are inadequate. They noted that only eight years after India and Pakistan detonated nuclear weapons and began constructing arsenals, North Korea followed suit, with one senior DPRK official informing one senior U.S. counterpart that "it's up to you whether we transfer them."[8] Iran pressed on with its nuclear program while the international community engaged in feckless attempts to threaten and cajole it to cease. Observing all this, several Arab states asserted that they too needed their own "peaceful" nuclear energy programs.

Now, within the span of a few months, the debate is over. The nuclear Cassandras, to their horror and that of the nation, have been proved right.

REMEMBER THE ALAMO?

WHILE IT STANDS IN THE SHADOWS OF TEXAS'S TWO MAJOR CITIES, Dallas and Houston, San Antonio is second to none when it comes to its status as a major U.S. military hub. The city is home to several major Air Force bases, an intelligence center, and a major medical facility.

At precisely 8:28 a.m. on the morning of March 6, 2011, just as the city's morning rush hour is at its peak, a blinding flash of light rips through the downtown area. Nearby buildings are immediately vaporized. Buildings farther off buckle and collapse. Those outside the immediate impact area have their windows blown out. A local TV station's traffic helicopter captures the blast at a distance of nearly nine

---

states, Greece, and several East European states); the Megaports Initiative, begun in 2003 to equip large international seaports with radiological detection equipment; and the Container Security Initiative, designed ultimately to evaluate all containers bound for the United States for radiological and nuclear materials. See also Gary W. Philips, David J. Nagel, and Timothy Coffey, *A Primer on the Detection of Nuclear and Radiological Weapons* (Washington, D.C.: Center for Technology and National Security Policy, May 2005); and James Goodby, Timothy Coffey, and Cheryl Loeb, *Deploying Nuclear Detection Systems: A Proposed Strategy for Combatting Nuclear Terrorism* (Washington, D.C.: Center for Technology and National Security Policy, July 2007).

8. Wesley Pruden, "Better to Escape into Dreamland," *Jewish World Review,* September 15, 2006.

miles away. As the telltale mushroom cloud begins to rise from the city, the traffic reporter remarks, "My God, it's an atomic bomb! May God help us."[9]

In this age of modern communications, the news flashes quickly throughout the United States and around the world. President Reynolds is quickly spirited to his airborne command post. Congress disperses to an "alternate location," and Washington goes into "lockdown" mode. Military forces ring the capital, and NEST teams begin an intensive search to locate any nuclear weapons that might have been placed covertly in the city.[10]

At the Pentagon, word goes out to all U.S. military commands around the globe raising their alert status to DEFCON (Defense Condition) 2, just one level short of full-scale war. Strategic Command's nuclear forces are placed on high alert, while at the North American Air Defense (NORAD) Command's headquarters, military specialists pore over incoming satellite imagery to determine if they somehow missed a missile launch indication that would identify the source of the attack—and to detect any additional missile launches that would indicate a follow-on strike.

By ten a.m. the Department of Homeland Security is raising its alert level to red. At the same time, security measures at American seaports and airports are heightened. Coast Guard ships move into place off major American ports to screen approaching vessels, questioning their captains and inspecting their manifests.

In San Antonio, first-responders—firefighting forces, police, emergency medical assistance personnel, and others—move quickly toward the devastated area but are highly limited in what they can do because of the residual radiation and lack of protective gear. Most remain outside the "hot" zone in the immediate blast area, lest they absorb lethal

---

9. Jorge Sanchez, "San Antonio Hit by Nuke Blast," *Chicago Tribune*, March 7, 2011, p. 1.
10. The military's Joint Special Operations Command (JSOC) has highly skilled units—by some accounts more skilled than NEST teams. While the NEST teams have the lead for domestic incidents and the JSOC teams are responsible for overseas contingencies, the latter are likely supporting the former in responding to the crisis. See Daniel Dawes, "Special Forces Hunt for Nukes," *Newsday*, March 20, 2011, p. 3.

doses of radiation. They are joined, but only after hours have passed, by radiological decontamination teams from the Texas National Guard, which has been mobilized to deal with the catastrophe. By early afternoon many of the city's first-responders are (unknown to most of them) working in contaminated areas. Tragically, their heroism comes at a terrible price. As few are equipped to deal with the residual radiation and fallout that accompanied the nuclear blast, dozens suffer lethal doses of radiation poisoning. Even those working along the external periphery of the hot zone have likely taken on enough radiation to incur a much higher lifetime risk of contracting cancer and other diseases. To avoid the fallout, city residents are directed to stay out of the devastated area and to remain indoors. Inevitably, this produces the near-chaos that has become increasingly familiar to the nation and the world, as images of it splash across television screens everywhere: workers suffering from radiation sickness separated from their families in suburbia; contaminated animals being shot on sight; and mothers isolated from their children.[11]

The lead shot on the evening news, not only in America but around the world that night, centers on two images: the footage from the traffic helicopter with the reporter's horrified voice-over; and on-the-scene reporters standing at locations where the severely damaged Alamo mission—the shrine to Texas's independence—can be seen in the distant background.

NO FINGERPRINTS?

THAT EVENING PRESIDENT DAVID REYNOLDS ADDRESSES THE NATION from an undisclosed location. He informs the American public that NORAD's review of its satellite observation data, combined with the live footage of the city as the bomb went off, shows no indication that the weapon was delivered by any kind of missile or aircraft. Simply

11. The searing image of Susan Davis, sobbing and on her knees in despair, as she vainly begs National Guard troops to let her enter the contaminated area to search for her two missing children, will long remain a part of the nation's consciousness. The photograph has appeared in countless print and broadcast media. See Susan Dawes, "A Picture of Fear," *Time*, November 17, 2011, p. 32.

stated, the bomb was prepositioned in the city covertly and then detonated, perhaps remotely.

The president informs the country that he has directed a series of
steps be taken in response to the crisis. They include placing the military
on high alert; mobilizing the National Guard to support recovery operations in San Antonio and to help seal the U.S. border with Mexico;
placing U.S. nuclear forces on high alert; and directing the Justice Department (including the FBI) and Department of Homeland Security to
provide support to states and municipalities as they conduct searches to
determine whether they might also be harboring a nuclear time bomb.

Finally, the president appeals to all Americans not to panic but to
go about their daily lives. He pledges that "we will find those responsible for this infamous attack. When we do, retribution will be swift and
sure."[12] It is a statement he will come to regret, as much as former President George W. Bush came to regret his declaration pronouncing the
"end of major combat operations" in Iraq eight years ago.

Over the next few weeks, as the death toll mounts, it becomes clear
that this attack dwarfs the 9/11 strike, which claimed some 3,000 lives.
On March 23 San Antonio's mayor, Juan Melendez, announces that over
29,000 people have been confirmed as dead, while over 60,000 others
have sought medical attention for serious injuries sustained in the attack.[13]

The response in America takes several forms. There is an enormous
outpouring of sympathy and support for the citizens of San Antonio,
manifested both publicly and privately. Other states and municipalities
send search and rescue teams to locate and recover those trapped in the
rubble of collapsed buildings. Charities and relief organizations provide
food, clothing, and shelter to displaced citizens. Their efforts are greatly
enhanced by the donations of the American people and, gratifyingly,
many foreign governments and citizens.

The American people are also angry and in a mood for vengeance

---

12. Martin Goldman, "President Vows 'Swift and Sure' Response," *New York Times*,
March 7, 2011, p. A1.
13. Martin Goldman, "Death Toll at 29,000," *New York Times*, March 18, 2011, p. A1.
Mayor Melendez was fortunately out of town the day of the attack, although much of his
government staff either perished in the blast or suffered debilitating injuries. The city, like
others that have suffered attacks, remains under martial law.

against those who would kill so many so wantonly. But they are also puzzled. Despite the most spectacular act of terrorism in recorded history, no group has stepped forward to claim responsibility for it.

The job of fingering the culprit is left to U.S. intelligence, and to the nuclear forensics teams that have secured samples of the radioactive materials generated by the bomb blast. While nuclear forensics is a limited science—it is better at ruling out the source of a nuclear blast than identifying it—it is better than nothing. Three types of atoms are of high interest to nuclear forensics teams. First, they look for fissile material (such as highly enriched uranium or plutonium) that did not undergo fission. This offers some clues as to the sophistication of the weapon's design. Second, they look for new atoms created by nuclear fission, which can provide clues as to how the weapon was designed. Third, they look for atoms of materials near the fission core of the weapon, which can help determine the components of the weapon used. These three methods, along with others that remain classified, can help identify the weapon's design type and, with some luck, point an accusatory finger at its originator.[14]

While nuclear forensics is capable of revealing a great deal about the fissile material at the heart of a nuclear device, it is not foolproof. As one expert notes, "If you want to identify [material] uniquely, then you need some samples to compare it with. Otherwise, you're like someone with a DNA sample and no DNA bank." Scientists have sought to create an international database of nuclear material that could help them identify, more quickly and accurately, the origins of the fissile material in the event of a terrorist nuclear attack. Unfortunately, at this point nuclear forensics is far more capable of telling us where the materials in a nuclear weapon did not come from than where they did.[15]

---

14. For an overview of nuclear and radiological detection capabilities, see William Dunlop and Harold Smith, "Who Did It? Using International Forensics to Detect and Deter Nuclear Terrorism," *Arms Control Today*, October 2006. See also Joint Working Group of the American Physical Society and the American Association for the Advancement of Science, *Nuclear Forensics Role, State of the Art, and Program Needs*, at http://cstsp.aaas.org/files/Complete.pdf. Accessed on June 12, 2008.
15. Matthew B. Stannard, "New Tools for a New World Order," *San Francisco Chronicle*, October 29, 2006.

THE RED CONNECTION

THE FORENSICS EFFORT REVEALS THAT THE WEAPON HAS A "SOVIET" nuclear fingerprint. To the president and his advisers, however, the notion that the Russians would smuggle a weapon into the United States and detonate it in San Antonio makes no sense. The Russians have several thousand nuclear weapons and the missiles to deliver them. Given the absence of effective U.S. defenses against ballistic missiles, Moscow could strike the United States on a large scale with virtual impunity. Moreover, given the long Cold War history between the two nations, Russian leaders run the risk that the United States will identify the bomb design as likely of Soviet origin. This could trigger a full-scale U.S. nuclear attack against Russia, of the kind President Kennedy threatened during the Cuban Missile Crisis.[16] Why launch an attack with a single weapon that invites an overwhelming U.S. nuclear response? Why risk being detected smuggling the weapon into the United States? What could Russia possibly gain from this attack? Adding to the surreal atmosphere in the White House situation room is the knowledge that the Russians have not placed their nuclear forces on alert.[17]

Rather than go public and announce the weapon's likely origin— and possibly stir the wrath of the American public—the president decides to inform Russia's leader, President Dmitry Medvedev, of the evidence that U.S. intelligence has accumulated and demand a response. This most secret exchange is communicated personally by the U.S. secretary of state, who flies covertly to Medvedev's retreat near St. Petersburg, where he meets alone with the Russian leader.[18]

The president's confidence in his initial judgment regarding the

16. During the 1962 crisis, which was precipitated by the Soviet introduction of nuclear weapons into Cuba, President Kennedy declared, "It shall be the policy of this nation to regard any nuclear missile launched from Cuba against any nation in the Western Hemisphere as an attack on the United States, requiring a full retaliatory response upon the Soviet Union," at http://edition.cnn.com/SPECIALS/cold.war/episodes/10/documents/kennedy.speech, accessed on June 5, 2008.
17. House Armed Services Committee; Hearings on the U.S. Nuclear Posture, March 28, 2011, at www.house.gov/hasc/hearinginformation.shtml, accessed on April 5, 2011.
18. Details of the meeting and other internal administration deliberations during the crisis are provided in James Wentworth's series of extended articles "Crisis of the Country," *Washington Post*, June 8, 9, 12, 2011. Cited hereafter as "Wentworth Reports."

Russians' culpability is sustained when, on March 28, the FBI intercepts a truck on the interstate highway outside Seattle found to be carrying a dirty bomb. This type of weapon contains radioactive material and a conventional high explosive. It cannot create a nuclear explosion, but it can spew radioactive material over a relatively limited area. The driver and his crew are fortunately subdued before they can activate the weapon. The would-be perpetrators are identified as members of a radical Islamist organization with ties to many others, including al Qaeda. The interrogation of these terrorists reveals little else.[19]

President Reynolds instructs the FBI director not to release any information regarding this seizure, so as not to alarm the public. Miraculously, in this era in which Washington has become a "city of leaks," secrecy is maintained.

So too in Russia. The Russians may have lost the Cold War to the Americans for a host of reasons but not because of an inability to keep secrets. Following his conversation with the president, Medvedev immediately directs an investigation into Russia's nuclear stockpile and orders heightened security of its nuclear storage sites. An inventory of Russia's weapons begins; U.S. security teams are invited to assist, using negotiations under the Nunn-Lugar program as a cover.

One problem the Russians confront is that no one knows exactly how many nuclear weapons were fabricated during the Soviet era.[20] In a time of central planning where every industry had a quota, and where managers would sometimes stockpile production over and above their quota to cover future shortfalls, record-keeping, even for nuclear weapons, was not precise. Both the Americans and the Russians know they may not be able to determine whether a weapon—or weapons— has gone missing.

---

19. The FBI apparently debated the merits of employing "aggressive interrogation techniques" with these men to determine if other weapons of mass destruction are being emplaced. Domestic and international criticism of such techniques in the war against radical Islamists (e.g., using them with prisoners at Guantánamo Bay) leads to this type of interrogation being rejected. The Bureau is unable to determine if there is a link between the "dirty bombers" and the attack on San Antonio.

20. Former senior official of the government of France, confidential discussion with the author, Paris, June 2004.

On April 5 President Medvedev calls President Reynolds on the Moscow-Washington "hotline," the communications system linking the two leaders. Medvedev informs the president that Russian security services have in custody a "criminal element" comprising members of the Russian mafia and the Russian military. "Intensive interrogation" (that is to say, torture) of these individuals reveals that nine Soviet-designed atomic demolition munitions (ADMs) have been sold on the black market to Islamic militants believed to be linked to al Qaeda and several groups associated with it.[21] These groups are operating in a number of locations, among them Chechnya, Afghanistan, Iran, Spain, and the United States. The ADMs are believed to have yields in the range of 1 to 15 kilotons, or between 1,000 and 15,000 tons of TNT. By comparison, the atomic bomb dropped on Hiroshima is estimated to have had a yield of roughly 13,000 tons.

Medvedev informs President Reynolds that the Russian government deeply regrets the lapse in security. He reminds the president that Russia has long feared that radical Muslim elements inside his country would get and use a radiological or nuclear device against the Russian people. Medvedev recounts several incidents, including two of which U.S. intelligence had no knowledge, of terrorist attempts to use dirty bombs in Russian cities.[22] The Russian president tells his American counterpart that he is prepared to place the full resources of his government into finding and punishing those responsible. Medvedev also pledges over $4 billion in relief aid to the people of San Antonio.

The two leaders discuss at length whether this information should be kept from the public. The news that perhaps eight nuclear weapons (nine, less the San Antonio bomb) may now be in the hands of radical Islamists might give rise to panic. They agree that, for the time being, this discovery must remain secret. They also concur that each will inform the other if he decides to "go public." President Reynolds admits to

---

21. "Wentworth Reports," *Washington Post*, June 9, 2011, p. A16.
22. In one early case, in November 1995, Chechen separatists buried a canister of radioactive cesium-137 in a Moscow park, then told a Russian television network where to locate it. Alex Rodriguez, "Radioactive, Unprotected: A 'Dirty Bomb' Nightmare," *Chicago Tribune*, February 15, 2007, p. 1.

Medvedev that even though only his most trusted advisers are privy to this information, he fears that the press will soon gain access to it.[23] Medvedev replies that he will confront the same problem as his investigation widens.

Following the conversation with Medvedev, the president holds a meeting of his National Security Council. During the meeting the CIA briefs the council on Russia's nuclear arsenal. Despite the efforts of Nunn-Lugar, the council is told, supplies of radioactive materials capable of being used in a dirty bomb are relatively abundant in Russia. In particular, Russia's many northern lighthouses, more than six hundred in all, are equipped with radioisotope thermoelectric generators using radioactive strontium-90 to create electricity. The lighthouses are largely unguarded. Many lack even a basic security fence.[24] The president and his security team are also informed that despite spending billions of dollars to help the Russians secure their nuclear arsenal, major parts of the arsenal remain outside the Nunn-Lugar program, and even the parts that are within it sometimes suffer from lax security.[25] Following the briefing, Secretary of Defense Wilton Summers raises the possibility that the Russians might intentionally provide militant Muslims with atomic weapons, but he abandons the idea as too risky "even for the Russians" to pursue.

The president quickly contacts the leaders of Afghanistan and Spain. Walking a fine line between truth and deception, the president informs them the United States has intelligence that radical Muslim groups in their countries may have been involved in the attack on San Antonio. Again, to avoid panic, he does not mention the other "loose nukes" that may be at large in their countries. Reynolds offers the assistance of U.S. intelligence, which both countries accept. Russia meanwhile undertakes an intensive search to identify and "liquidate" the terrorist cells.

Iran is a different matter. The mullahs that rule over the country

23. Nancy Czerbeck, "President Concealed 'Loose Nuke' Intelligence," *Los Angeles Times,* July 22, 2011, p. 1.

24. Rodriguez, "Radioactive, Unprotected," p. 1.

25. Carla Anne Robbins and Alan Cullison, "In Russia, Securing Its Nuclear Arsenal Is an Uphill Battle," *Wall Street Journal,* September 26, 2005, p. A1.

have been responsible for the two greatest U.S. foreign policy fiascos in the last forty years: the sacking of the American embassy in Tehran and the ensuing hostage crisis, and the erosion of the United States' position in the Middle East region following the invasion of Iraq in 2003.

The president is reminded that in closed testimony before Congress in November 2009, his director of national intelligence reported that Iran now had sufficient fissionable material to construct several nuclear weapons, and that the mullahs might already have these weapons. Would a nuclear-armed Iran, some of whose leaders seem to be awaiting the imminent appearance of the Twelfth Imam, run the risk of directing militant Muslims to undertake a nuclear attack on the United States?[26] Or would the Iranians "merely" assist a radical Islamist plot already under way? One question that remains at the forefront of the president's mind and those of his senior advisers is: Who did this to us?

The question is also on the minds of the American people, who want the perpetrators identified and destroyed. Around-the-clock news coverage, along with intense blogosphere activity, keeps the public's anger and fear at a high level. Public speculation as to who is responsible for the attack ranges from the Chinese to radical Islamists to American survivalists. No one raises the Russians as the possible source of the weapon used in San Antonio.

THE SPARTACUS EFFECT

APRIL 16, 2011, IS A SUNNY, WARM SPRING DAY IN CHICAGO. THE city is enjoying the first days marking the end of an unusually cold winter. (The local weather reports note that in the days before global warming the city's seniors would have called it a "typical" winter.) Shortly before noon—history will record it precisely at 11:44 a.m.—the heat of a man-made sun disrupts the city's daily hum. A nuclear blast rips through the city's core. More powerful than the San Antonio explosion,

26. According to Twelver Shi'as, Imam Hujjat al-Mahdí is the Twelfth Imam and the Mahdi, the ultimate savior of humankind. They believe that the Mahdi was born in 868 and has been hidden by God (referred to as the Occultation), and that he will reappear when the world has fallen into chaos.

the Chicago weapon generates its telltale mushroom cloud that boils up over the city in a matter of moments. Landmarks like the Sears Tower simply disappear, calling to mind New York City's Twin Towers on the morning of 9/11. Only this time no one in the tower escapes death.

Security cameras and cell phone cameras provide grainy footage of the calamity, which quickly spreads to the news media and, just as rapidly, to the Internet. Thanks to the experience gleaned from the San Antonio attack, disaster relief teams arrive en masse from around the country, along with radiological decontamination units. As in San Antonio, local and regional hospitals are overwhelmed by the casualties, as are the field hospitals set up by National Guard units. Other hospitals around the country and in Canada that specialize in burn casualties are alerted, even though many are filled to capacity with cases from the March attack.

Again, as with San Antonio, local utility service in many areas on the periphery of the blast is disrupted. Meanwhile, a panic ensues among citizens over whether they may have been exposed to fallout and its consequences. The topic had been a staple on the cable news channels following the San Antonio attack.

The cost in human life is staggering. Estimates are that over 32,000 prompt fatalities have been sustained, along with over 80,000 severe casualties, a substantial number of whom are not expected to live. The economic costs, both direct and indirect, are estimated to run into the hundreds of billions of dollars.[27]

Nuclear forensics confirms, within a few days, that the weapon used is of the same design type as the one used in San Antonio. But whereas the weapon used there had a yield of around six kilotons, the one used in Chicago is estimated at eleven kilotons, or slightly less than the Hiroshima bomb. The second Soviet atomic demolition munition has been "found." If Medvedev is right, there are seven more on the loose.

On the night of the Chicago attack President Reynolds addresses the nation from the Oval Office. The location, while traditional, is this

27. "America's Nightmare," *Economist*, April 21, 2011, p. 30.

time also symbolic. The president has remained in Washington, even though cities are clearly the target of these attacks. The president informs the American public that there is compelling intelligence to indicate that the attacks are the work of radical Islamist elements that have gained access to stolen Russian nuclear weapons. The president does not, however, inform the public that there may be additional nuclear weapons at large. He reassures the American people that the Russian government is cooperating fully and encourages urban dwellers to remain in their cities and to go about their daily lives. Reynolds announces a range of expanded initiatives designed to ensure that a third attack never comes. The armed forces are fully mobilized, as is the Coast Guard. Municipal police forces are put on extended duty. Cargo entering the United States is subjected to a higher level of inspection and search.[28] As in the case of San Antonio, many countries send disaster relief teams and supplies to Chicago.

The president instructs U.S. forces engaged in what the Pentagon calls "global man-hunting" operations—covert operations, primarily by special forces units—to be intensified and to strike at militant Muslim groups, especially their leadership, wherever they can be found. Nations including Pakistan, Syria, and Yemen are informed that the United States is prepared to strike any and all suspected radical Islamist group targets, including those within their borders, as an act of "self-defense" under the United Nations charter.

At home the nation's blogs, cable news channels, and talk radio shows blister from the firestorm of anger raging in the American people. In the Information Age, a nation's ability to whip itself into a frenzy makes the yellow journalism of another age seem tame by comparison.[29] Calls for retaliatory nuclear strikes on major Arab Muslim cities now attract support from a growing number of Americans, as does the idea of

28. President David Reynolds, Address to the Nation, April 16, 2011, at www.white-house.gov, accessed on April 27, 2011.
29. The term "yellow journalism" dates back to the late nineteenth century. The term originated during circulation wars between Joseph Pulitzer's *New York World* and William Randolph Hearst's *New York Journal* between 1895 and about 1898. Both papers sensationalized the news to help drive up circulation. Encyclopedia Britannica, "Yellow Journalism," at http://www.britannica.com/EBchecked/topic/652632/yellow-journalism#tab=active~checked%2Citems~checked&title=yellow%20journalism%20—%20 Britannica%20Online%20Encyclopedia, accessed on September 16, 2008.

deporting all Muslims living in the United States.[30] Amid this discussion there is coverage of an increasing number of hate crimes against the American Muslim community. Hate graffiti (e.g., "The only good Muslim is a dead Muslim," "Let's send them all to 'paradise' ") and acts of arson against mosques and Muslim places of business increase sharply.

Privately, the president is consumed with anxiety. He knows he has taken a calculated risk with the safety of the American people. Seven nuclear weapons are unaccounted for. For all anyone knows, they may already be embedded in other U.S. cities. Perhaps hundreds of thousands of American lives are at risk. Yet the president knows that if he directs the evacuation of American cities, terrorists might set off a hidden weapon in a city before the population can depart. He also risks triggering a panic. Moreover the United States is not prepared for such evacuations. Where would these people go? Who would care for them? Finally, he understands that the U.S. economy would suffer catastrophic damage in the event of mass evacuation. He decides that, like the British people confronted with the Nazi "blitz" bombings during World War II, the American people must remain in their cities and weather the storm.

The following day, April 17, a radical Islamic group with ties to al Qaeda publicly claims responsibility for the attacks on San Antonio and Chicago. It also declares that it is a nuclear power and is capable of conducting additional attacks on American cities if its demands are not met. These demands are that all U.S. and other foreign forces be withdrawn from all Islamic countries, including Iraq, Pakistan, Afghanistan, and the Persian Gulf states. They demand that the United States terminate its "alliance of death" with the "Jew-dogs that occupy Muslim lands" (i.e., the state of Israel).[31] Finally, they demand that America cease exporting its "cultural filth" to the Islamic world by submitting television programming, movies, the printed word, and Internet sites to designated imams for review and approval.[32]

---

30. Perhaps the most notable example of this view was voiced by a former Air Force chief of staff, retired General Knowling Howell, who observed that "in the nineteenth century we wiped out entire tribes of Indians for much less than what the Arabs are doing to us today." General (Ret.) Knowling Howell, *This Week*, ABC News, April 24, 2011, at abcnews.go.com/ThisWeek, accessed on July 12, 2011.
31. Hashim Nabouk, "Militants Set Terms," *Wall Street Journal*, April 18, 2011, p. A1.
32. Nancy Czerbeck, "Radical Muslims Dictate Terms," *Los Angeles Times*, April 18, 2011, p. 1.

Shortly after this declaration, other radical Islamist groups—eight in all—also claim responsibility for the attacks. The president's national security advisor, Dr. William Frenzel, tells the president it reminds him of the movie *Spartacus*. In the movie the Romans, having defeated the rebel army led by Spartacus, demand he be turned over to them. All the men in the rebel army proceed to claim that they are Spartacus. Like the first radical Islamist group, each of the others has its own set of demands. Many are similar. Included among the additional ones are the release of all Muslim prisoners held by Israel; massive Western "reparations" to the Arab world to amend for the "exploitation" of its peoples; and requirements that all Muslims in Europe and America live under sharia (Islamic religious) law. When the president asks Frenzel how the Romans dealt with the problem, he replies, "They killed them all. That way they knew they had gotten Spartacus." The president is reported to have replied, "I guess General Howell would find that solution agreeable. Well, I'm no butcher. At least not yet."[33]

That day the president's National Security Council meets at an "undisclosed location," where the country's senior civilian and military leaders debate how the United States can best respond in the wake of the most devastating attacks in the nation's history. There is enormous pressure on the president to take action. The growing public anger over the administration's inability to fight back is palpable. The president notes that during the Cold War, an attack like this would have resulted in a U.S. nuclear retaliatory strike against the aggressor state. But here there is no state against which to retaliate. There is only a collection of radical groups, most of which probably had no role in the attacks. Ironically, he notes, Russia, the "provider" of the weapons used, is attempting to help the United States.

When the president mentions the tale of Spartacus in alluding to his difficulty in identifying the true source of the attacks, Secretary of Defense Wilton Summers also notes that the Romans solved the problem by crucifying all his army's survivors, and that many Americans would

---

33. The motion picture takes a number of liberties with history, but Dr. Frenzel's description accurately reflects the account it presents.

welcome a broad attack on Arab states "like Syria and Lebanon" and the occupation of Persian Gulf oil fields as a means of providing reparations to the United States for the attacks. Reynolds curtly informs his defense secretary that this course of action is not an option. Army General Thomas Nast, the chairman of the Joint Chiefs of Staff, notes that, whatever the merits of this course of action, the U.S. military lacks the manpower to occupy the Gulf States' oil fields while providing support for the ongoing massive relief operations inside the United States; assisting federal, state, and local authorities in the border states to screen incoming cargo; and maintaining currently deployed forces in Afghanistan and Iraq. But this is not the last time the subject of waging a counterterror campaign against Muslims, especially those from the Arab world and Pakistan, is raised.

The director of national intelligence informs the president that no group has presented compelling evidence that it is the true source of the attacks. Intelligence agencies from dozens of countries are assisting in the effort to identify and destroy the source of these attacks. Russian intelligence has reported that those who sold the ADMs to the radical Islamists have no idea what group they may have represented, or whether the weapons were later transferred to other radical groups. The director of the Department of Homeland Security reports that while some Americans are moving out of the cities, most are staying put. They realize they need their jobs. But many who can are sending their children to live with relatives or friends in the outer suburbs or rural areas.

Congress, as it often does following the onset of a national security crisis, generally supports the president. But, as the radical Islamist demands are made known, a small but highly vocal minority calls for the administration to enter into talks with the attackers. Anything, they argue, is better than suffering another such attack. Another, larger group of members of Congress argue that the United States should deliver an ultimatum to those Muslim governments that have been cited as sponsors of terrorism to hand over the radical Islamists in their countries or risk nuclear attack on their cities.

"MY FELLOW AMERICANS"

IN THE PREDAWN HOURS OF APRIL 28 TWO CESSNA AIRCRAFT piloted by militant Islamist suicide bombers take off from a remote airstrip in northern Mexico and head on their one-way journey, each taking a different route. NORAD detects one plane and scrambles Air National Guard fighters to intercept the unidentified aircraft. After two warnings to leave U.S. airspace, the Cessna is shot down as it approaches San Diego. American Special Forces and NEST teams arrive shortly thereafter, along with two "render safe" teams possessing special training in deactivating nuclear weapons. Several Russian nuclear weapons specialists accompany them. The third weapon is located and disarmed.

The second, apparently more experienced, kamikaze pilot flies low to exploit ground clutter and employ terrain masking. As the United States long ago disbanded its continental air defenses,[34] he is able to evade detection and, shortly after ten a.m., successfully detonates his weapon as his plane approaches ground level in the heart of San Diego. Fortunately, this fourth weapon suffers from pre-initiation, and the blast generates only a fraction of its potential yield.[35] Nevertheless, it kills over 3,000 people immediately, while over 20,000 suffer serious wounds, many of them fatal. (The ultimate death toll exceeds 7,500.)

Within an hour of the attack on San Diego, just as news of the attack is being broadcast, in the Maryland suburbs north of Washington, D.C.,

34. During the 1950s and 1960s the United States maintained an extensive air defense system against the threat of Soviet atomic attack using long-range bombers. The Air Force maintained a sizable force of fighter interceptors, and the Army deployed scores of surface-to-air missile batteries as part of the Army Air Defense Command (ARADCOM). When the Soviet Union began deploying large numbers of nuclear-armed intercontinental ballistic missiles (ICBMs) in the 1960s—missiles against which these defenses were ineffective—the decision was made to disband ARADCOM and draw down the country's air defense fighter force.

35. Pre-initiation, or pre-ignition, occurs when two subcritical masses containing a mixture of plutonium-239 (Pu-239) and plutonium-240 (Pu-240) are brought together through a chemical explosion that produces a premature chain reaction. The result is an explosion that releases far less energy—and destructive force—than a weapon that is properly detonated. The chemical explosion is used to enable a subcritical mass of plutonium to achieve the supercritical mass needed for the virtually complete fissioning of the nuclear material. Dietrich Schroeder, *Science, Technology and the Nuclear Arms Race* (New York: John Wiley & Sons, 1984), pp. 32–33.

local police stop a panel truck traveling at a high rate of speed. The driver and his companion are of Middle East extraction. Moving quickly, the police open the cargo door in time to stop two other men from activating what turns out to be a Soviet-era ADM, which is recovered.[36] Intensive interrogation of the drivers reveals that they were running late for their rendezvous with three other accomplices who were to help them position the weapon inside Washington itself. The fifth nuclear weapon has been identified and, thankfully, recovered.

As word spreads of the foiled second air attack on San Diego and the intercepted attack on Washington, and as footage of the devastation in San Diego is broadcast, panic grips the American people. A spontaneous, albeit still limited, evacuation begins in many U.S. cities, especially those close to the border. Americans discern that the attacks, and attempted attacks, present a pattern: all the cities targeted lie within a few hundred miles of an international border or the ocean. The public also knows that the United States is being subjected to repeated nuclear attacks, and that the Reynolds administration seems unable to stop them, although it has successfully intercepted perhaps half of them. The American people do not know that the administration is dealing with (or at least is reasonably confident that the threat is limited to) nine nuclear weapons.

President Reynolds, at this point, is under tremendous strain. His staff fears he may be on the verge of a nervous breakdown. He struggles over whether to inform the American public that four weapons remain unaccounted for, or to keep that information secret. His instincts tell him he must "level" with the American people, lest the public believe the enemy has dozens of these weapons at its disposal.

That afternoon, as the president prepares to address the nation, two developments confirm his instinct to reveal, at last, the true nature of the threat confronting the nation. First, he receives word from the *Washington Post*'s senior editor that the paper has what it believes to be compelling evidence of the number of weapons.[37] Second, President

---

36. "Wentworth Reports," *Washington Post*, June 12, 2011, p. A1.
37. "Wentworth Reports," *Washington Post*, June 8, 2011, p. A1.

Medvedev calls the president to inform him that Russian state police have recovered two of the ADMs, which were about to be sold to a Chechen Muslim separatist group. This leaves but two of the nuclear weapons still unaccounted for. Buoyed by this news, and realizing that the *Post* may not prove willing to sit on its story, the president decides to share what he knows of the danger with the public.

At eight p.m. eastern daylight time President Reynolds, seated at his desk in the Oval Office, addresses the American people in a broadcast that is beamed around the world. "My fellow Americans . . ."

The president reports on the attack against San Diego and notes that over 60,000 Americans have been killed in the world's first "protracted" nuclear war. He assures the nation that every measure is being taken to prevent another attack, and cites the interception of two weapons that day and the recovery of another two inside Russia. Then comes the "headline paragraph":

> Based on information gathered by the Russian intelligence service, and provided to me by President Medvedev, it appears that two weapons remain unaccounted for. These weapons are believed to be in the hands of radical Islamists, who are attempting either to sell them or to use them against the United States or one of our partners in the war against these barbaric extremists. We, along with the intelligence and security services of over eighty of our allies and partners around the globe, are engaged in the most intensive manhunt in history to identify the location of these weapons and bring to justice those who have perpetrated these crimes against humanity.[38]

"RAG-HEADS 60,000; U.S. 0"

THE NEXT DAY'S HEADLINES FIND THE ATTACK ON SAN DIEGO CON-signed to the below-the-fold spot in the *New York Times* and *Washington Post*, while the revelation of two unaccounted-for nuclear weapons

---

38. President David Reynolds, Address to the Nation, April 29, 2011, at www.whitehouse .gov, accessed on May 3, 2011.

("President Reports Two 'Loose Nukes'") races across in banner head-lines.[39]

The public's reaction remains dominated by fear and anger. The spontaneous evacuation of U.S. cities increases its pace—many urban residents cite the need to leave until the unaccounted-for weapons are recovered. It's a temporary departure, they say. The economic and so-cial effects are becoming more profound. Economic experts report that the U.S. economy is in danger of falling into a recession as severe as the one from which the nation has just recovered.[40] Meanwhile the urban poor lack the means of the more affluent city dwellers to relocate until the crisis passes. Fearing riots, the governors of over thirty states, in-cluding Massachusetts, New York, Pennsylvania, Michigan, California, and Texas call up National Guard units to patrol their major urban areas—both to work with local authorities to detect or intercept an attack, and to deal with potential riots. But these units are clearly inadequate to the task of helping to provide food, shelter, and sanitary conditions to what is the largest mass exodus of people in the nation's history.

At the same time Army units are dispatched to the U.S.-Mexican border to beef up border security, and the Navy is directed to support Coast Guard efforts to maintain the integrity of the U.S. coastline. But with many troops deployed overseas in combat zones and others at-tempting to provide disaster relief support to the cities that have been attacked and to those citizens fleeing other urban areas, the American military simply cannot meet all the demands placed on it. Adding to the problem is the fact that an unusually high percentage of National Guard troops are, in their civilian lives, employed in public safety jobs as po-licemen and firemen. As one governor put it, "Calling up the National Guard is like robbing Peter to pay Paul. I get my guardsmen, while my mayors lose many of their police and fire people."[41]

America's fear is exceeded only by its anger. Attacks on Muslims are still not widespread, but they are increasing at an alarming rate. Reports

39. Martin Goldman, "President Reports Two 'Loose Nukes,'" *New York Times,* April 30, 2011, p. A1.
40. Robert Denois, "U.S. Economy Headed for a Crisis?" *Business Week,* May 4, 2011, p. 42.
41. Nancy Czerbeck, "Guard Callup Hurts Local Areas," *Los Angeles Times,* May 5, 2011, p. 6.

of U.S. Special Forces strikes against suspected radical Islamists are seen as pinpricks compared to the hammer blows raining down on the United States. Looking at the death toll, one U.S. tabloid headline sums up the thoughts of many: "Rag-Heads 60,000; U.S. 0."[42]

The president's public support, which had soared in the immediate aftermath of the San Antonio attack, has now plummeted. Most Americans see his efforts as weak and ineffectual. A few members of Congress have publicly called for impeachment proceedings, citing the president's willful withholding of information regarding the number of nuclear weapons at large. The president, they argue, hid the dangers confronting the nation from the American people, then proved incapable of protecting them from those dangers.

At a meeting of the National Security Council on April 30 at an "undisclosed location," a consensus is reached that some form of dramatic action is needed to restore the American people's morale and their confidence in their government. It is suggested again that the United States respond by attacking known sponsors of those radical Islamist groups that are claiming responsibility for the attacks. "Send them all to paradise and let Allah deal with them," argues one angry principal.[43] If the radical Islamists have no state, another argues, attack the states that are giving them aid and comfort and providing them with sanctuaries.[44]

Senator Jay Williams, the senate majority leader, who is present at the meeting, asks: What about presenting an ultimatum to these countries? Turn over members of these groups to the United States for trial? Nearly all present quickly dispatch this idea to the trash heap, bombarding it with objections: the governments will deny they are harboring these groups. They will play for time—"We need time to locate these people"—while relocating radical leaders to hiding spots. If they cooperate, they will raise the hostility of their own people. And even if we get hold of the people we want, some ask, what will we do with them?

42. "Rag-Heads 60,000; U.S. 0," *New York Daily News*, May 1, 2011, p. 1.
43. Martin Goldman, "President Weighs Options," *New York Times*, May 1, 2011, p. A1. The unnamed principal is believed to be Defense Secretary Summers.
44. "Wentworth Reports," *Washington Post*, June 12, 2011, p. A1.

Put hundreds or thousands of them on trial? Incarcerate them indefinitely at Guantánamo? Even if this made sense, the national security advisor to the president notes, it would take months, if not years, to bring about. The American people want action, not litigation.[45]

The discussion returns to the radical Islamist state sponsors. Should we demand something of them or simply attack them? And if we attack them, how do we go about it?

Vice President Jeremiah Jones notes that if we had been subjected to a nuclear attack by a state, we would have retaliated until it surrendered. The fact that states like Iran and Syria are harboring and aiding these groups enables them to attack the United States. Summers notes that this may be the time to destroy Iran's nuclear program, before it can enable future attacks on the United States like the attacks occurring now.

The chairman of the Joint Chiefs of Staff, General Nast, briefs the president and his advisers that the military has drawn up a range of strike options and has drafted plans for an extended campaign against state sponsors of the groups that claim responsibility for the ongoing attacks. The options include the use of nuclear weapons. Targets include military facilities, nuclear power and weapons programs, national infrastructure, and cities. The city target option is code-named "Old Testament" reflecting its view of justice as "an eye for an eye."

Secretary of State Margaret Smith argues for patience. Such attacks could dissipate much of the international sympathy that has been generated for the United States in the wake of the recent attacks. Furthermore, she argues, the kind of attacks being discussed, and the follow-on campaigns against these countries, could create even more radical Islamist enemies. Smith argues for a series of ultimatums, to be issued by the United States and the international community, to those governments sponsoring radical Islamist groups.

Defense Secretary Summers drily responds that the world's sympathy for America could reach even greater heights if the two unaccounted-for weapons were detonated in the United States. The country is now at

45. Ibid., pp. A9–A10.

war, he says, against a group of states and nonstate entities that are practicing a form of ambiguous aggression against the United States. The United States can attempt to sue for some kind of peace, although with whom he hasn't a clue; or it can accept the fact that it is at war—a war that has already caused more damage to the American homeland in a few weeks than all of World War II—and mobilize its full resources to defeat its enemies. Summers declares he has no interest in negotiation; he is interested only in the total cooperation of these rogue states, and their capitulation to American demands for unfettered access, so that they may avoid "their complete and utter destruction." It is time for the nation to mobilize its resources to fight the war that has been waged against it ever since radical Islamists seized the first American hostages at the U.S. embassy in Tehran over thirty years ago. Summers concludes by threatening to resign if decisive action is not taken soon.

The president asks whether pursuing such a course of action might remove any chance of deterring those holding the two remaining weapons from using them. The director of national intelligence, Robert Cooley, replies that the groups who claim responsibility for the attacks have typically responded to acts of strength, not weakness.

Faced with such a momentous decision, the president informs his crisis team that he will take a few days to mull over his options before coming to a decision, which he will then announce in an address to a joint session of Congress and the nation.[46]

On May 4, as the president is weighing his options, central Boston is leveled by a nuclear detonation. Forensics indicates that the weapon had apparently been positioned in the cellar of one of the city's mosques. Over 12,000 prompt fatalities are incurred, and over 43,000 casualties. The governor of Massachusetts reports that these figures would be far higher had it not been for the ongoing evacuation of the city. The nuclear forensics teams report that the weapon is of a design similar to the others detonated or intercepted. This leaves one weapon unaccounted for.

Four days later, on May 8, during a U.S. Coast Guard inspection of a cargo ship approaching U.S. territorial waters in the Gulf of Mexico

---

46. The preceding description of this momentous meeting is found ibid., pp. A1, A9–A15.

off the coast of Florida, a nuclear weapon detonates, destroying both the cargo ship and the Coast Guard cutter. On May 17 the DNI informs the president that the intelligence community, backed up by the results of nuclear forensics, believes that this is the final missing Soviet ADM.

The president addresses a joint session of Congress and the nation on May 18. He reports that U.S. and foreign intelligence services have concluded that the danger of new nuclear attacks in the foreseeable future is negligible, and he encourages Americans to return to their cities and their normal lives. The president announces that the United States will work with its allies and partners, together and through the United Nations, to pressure those states suspected of supporting radical Islamist elements to cease all such activities.[47] In the interim the United States is intensifying its worldwide military operations to locate and destroy radical Islamist groups with the cooperation of over eighty other countries.

The response to the president's address is lukewarm at best. Less than a week after the speech, Summers resigns in protest, as do two members of the Joint Chiefs of Staff. The president is lauded for avoiding a much wider conflict and for attempting to get the country's economy "moving again," and he is excoriated for failing to attack "the source of the barbarous forces" and eradicate them once and for all. Most Americans adopt the latter perspective, and the president's approval ratings sink below 20 percent. Privately, he tells those closest to him that he is willing to suffer public disapproval in order to spare the country the dangers of a full-scale war. Nevertheless, in early September the House of Representatives begins hearings to determine if the president should be impeached.

Throughout the summer the country's security forces remain on heightened alert. The nation braces for further attacks, but none come; by late autumn most cities, with the exception of the four that had suffered nuclear attacks, have regained nearly all of their prewar population. Congress establishes a special commission to examine the causes of the attacks and to determine if anything could have been done to prevent them.

47. Following the attack on Chicago, the United Nations voted to relocate "temporarily" to Geneva, Switzerland. Indications are that the move will be permanent.

In November, DNI Cooley reports to the president that while the increased intensity of military operations has produced some success, new terrorist cells are forming more quickly than existing ones are being destroyed. Many in the Muslim world see the "War of Fire," as they call it, as a decisive victory for the radicals, and an increasing number of followers are joining the movement.

Two days before Thanksgiving, the president is awakened shortly after midnight by a phone call from Cooley. A radical Islamist group has contacted the CIA and provided detailed knowledge of the series of nuclear attacks that occurred from March to May. The information is such as to represent irrefutable proof that this group perpetrated the attacks. There is a pause. Cooley then states, "Mr. President, they inform us that they have other nuclear weapons in the United States and will begin using them within a week unless we meet their demands, which are as follows . . ."

3

PANDEMIC

*While we will consider all options to limit the spread of a
pandemic virus, we recognize complete border closure
would be difficult to enforce, present foreign affairs com-
plications, and have significant negative social and economic
consequences.*

Homeland Security Council, *National Strategy
for Pandemic Influenza* (May 2006)

SOUTH OF THE BORDER, DOWN MEXICO WAY . . .

THE STREETS OF MANY AMERICAN CITIES AND TOWNS ARE NEARLY
deserted. News reports offer viewers and readers images of communities tightly shuttered, as if bracing for an oncoming hurricane. But it is
not a hurricane that finds Americans avoiding one another "like the
plague."

Meanwhile, as the United States increasingly resembles a vast collection of semi–ghost towns, to the south literally millions of people are
on the move. They are traveling in just about every form of transportation imaginable—from cars and buses to bicycles and motor scooters.
With gasoline increasingly difficult to find, many have been reduced to
moving on foot. This mass of humanity is coursing along the roads

through northern Mexico toward the southwestern United States. This human wave also moves in thousands of makeshift watercraft that the U.S. Navy has dubbed the "Plague Flotilla" and the "Avian Armada." The mass of Mexicans, now estimated at nearly eight million, has no organizing force directing it, yet all its participants are unified toward one goal: crossing the border into the United States, in the hope of gaining access to this country's medical system—which ironically in many areas has simply ceased functioning in any meaningful way. This mass migration is the product of the largest and most deadly pandemic since the Great Influenza of 1918, a pandemic that is driving Mexico's population north—a human tidal wave about to crash across America's borders.

THE PANDEMIC "PLAGUE"

MANY AMERICANS ARE STUNNED AT THE DEVELOPMENTS OF THE last six months, yet the warning signs have been clear for over a decade. Over five years ago eminent members of the public health community warned that "the current, ongoing epidemic of H5N1 avian influenza in Asia is unprecedented in its scale, in its geographic distribution, and in the economic losses it has caused." They went on to note ominously that "recent evidence suggests that H5N1 has accumulated mutations that have made it increasingly infectious and deadly in mammals." In late 2003, nearly eight years ago, H5N1 began appearing in domestic poultry. It then spread across Asia. Tens of millions of birds died of influenza, and hundreds of millions were culled to protect humans after thirty-four confirmed human cases of H5N1 influenza in Thailand and Vietnam resulted in twenty-three deaths. The news made the papers, but barely. Public awareness of the danger quickly faded, although experts warned at the time that "to stop, or even slow, a pandemic would require an internationally coordinated, 'all-out' response in the early stages of human-to-human transmission."[1] Today, the world is paying an in-

---

1. Stanley L. Knobler, Allison Mack, Adel Mahmoud, and Stanley M. Lemon, eds., *The Threat of Pandemic Influenza* (Washington, D.C.: National Academies Press, 2005), pp. 12, 13, 21.

calculable price, in terms of both human life and material wealth, for failing to heed their warnings.

Here in America the best defense against pandemic influenza appears to be isolation. People are instinctively shunning one another to avoid contracting the virus. With antiviral drugs in short supply, Americans are trying their best to avoid coming into contact with those who may be carrying the disease. Television and radio public service announcements offer guidance on "cough etiquette." Shopping centers are now typically referred to as "mallsoleums," silent memorials to the country's unofficial state religion of secular materialism. While retail stores have suffered a dramatic decline in sales, online shopping firms are faring somewhat better, although sellers are struggling with a shortage of people to pack, ship, and deliver their goods, as many workers either have succumbed to the virus or are practicing self-isolation to avoid coming into contact with infected persons. Economists are unanimous in their belief that the country and the global economy are rapidly slipping into another major recession.

Nearly all schools are closed, and playgrounds are deserted. Most schools ended their terms prematurely, sending their students home as much as a month in advance. Also shuttered are daycare centers and preschool facilities, as mothers who work outside the home now have to take leaves of absence to care for their young. In other times, this may have put them at risk of losing their jobs. But the rapid economic slowdown finds many employers happy to grant such requests. Some working mothers organized informal childcare arrangements in order to stay on the job; sadly, these childcare "pods" (as they became known), where young children were brought together in sizable numbers, proved to be great incubators for influenza. Following an NBC *Nightly News* exposé detailing the high mortality rate of "pod" children, many state and local governments cracked down on the practice, which has apparently all but ended following the well-publicized suicides of over a dozen women whose children died apparently having contracted pandemic influenza while mingling with "podmates."[2]

2. "The Influenza Pods," *Nightly News,* NBC News, June 30, 2011, transcript at www.msnbc.msn.com/id/3032619/, accessed on July 19, 2011.

For those who cannot stay home, wearing sanitary masks is the order of the day. The images of Americans everywhere wearing white masks, so common today, would have seemed fanciful only a few months ago. In some rural communities, law enforcement officials and community volunteers in their service have set up roadblocks restricting the movement of people into and out of their jurisdiction. While illegal, all but a few of these local blockades remain in force—federal, state, and local authorities have their hands full as their flu-depleted staffs work to maintain public order at key facilities like hospitals.

The masks and the growing restrictions on personal freedom of movement are but two symbols of how life has changed in the United States. The summer movie season has been washed away by the government's ban on public gatherings.[3] Meanwhile baseball, the national pastime, is experiencing a "silent season." Major league baseball tried for a few days to play televised games in empty stadiums, then canceled its schedule when several players came down with pandemic influenza, or "the plague," as many Americans are calling it. Baseball fans will no doubt long remember the image of the New York Yankees' star pitcher David Bromwell collapsing on the pitcher's mound during a game and lapsing into convulsions while his teammates frantically tried to help.[4]

Interestingly, the one public place where people do congregate—and where large gatherings are not yet banned by the government—is in the nation's houses of worship. This has led to an ongoing contentious court battle between those advocating a prohibition on religious services in the name of public safety, and those defending services, as one pastor famously stated, "in the name of God."[5]

3. There has been, however, an explosion in the movie-rental business, especially via download over the Internet. Several of this summer's blockbusters, including the final movie in the *Harry Potter* series and the first episode in the third of three *Star Wars* trilogies, have been released directly through the Internet, and are doing a booming business. See Henry Herbert, "Internet Blockbusters: Flu Fluke or New Wave?" *Wall Street Journal,* July 25, 2011, p. A1.

4. Bromwell would die two weeks later. With the baseball season all but effectively canceled, fans are increasingly focusing their attention on how well their team is faring against the plague, both in absolute terms and against rival teams. See Chic Anderson, "Pandemic Shifts Balance of Power in NL East," *New York Post,* July 22, 2011, p. 84.

5. Father Jeremiah Doyle, of St. Raymond's parish, Bronx, *Nightly News,* NBC News, June 28, 2011, transcript at www.msnbc.msn.com/id/3032619/, accessed on July 12, 2011.

While most public places are deserted, hospitals are overburdened by too many patients, too few beds, and depleted staff, as more and more doctors, nurses, and support personnel succumb to the disease. In the 1918 pandemic, some 675,000 Americans died. With the U.S. population three times as great today, over ninety years later, some are projecting that 2 million Americans will die before this pandemic runs its course. If so, the death toll would be over five times as many deaths as were suffered by the United States in all of World War II.[6]

A GLOBAL ECONOMY IN CRISIS

THE PANDEMIC THREATENS MORE THAN AMERICANS' LIFESTYLES and commuting patterns. In a world of global supply chains, it is lapping at the foundation of the country's economic system. America's residential real estate market is once again in a state of near-collapse, as fears grow that a massive death toll in the United States would greatly decrease the demand for housing. Commercial real estate is starting to feel the pinch too, as telecommuting becomes more widespread with white-collar Americans trying to avoid the workplace. This has led to strains on the country's communications network, as growing numbers of telecommuters work the nation's phone lines, cell towers, and Internet.

Meanwhile, thanks to the development of global logistics networks over the past three decades, on a typical day tens of thousands of standardized containers are loaded on and off ships at American ports, while thousands of eighteen-wheeler trucks move across the country's borders with Mexico and Canada. The challenge of maintaining the velocity of trade, so critical to the country's economic health, while also preventing infected persons and livestock from entering the country, has proved to be an impossible task, especially once it became clear there were insufficient supplies of antiviral drugs to provide to dockworkers and port officials and still meet other priorities. Not surprisingly, many dock-

6. For the American death estimate, see http://1918.pandemicflu.gov/the_pandemic /index.htm, accessed on June 1, 2008. American deaths in World War II are estimated at 418,000; see http://en.wikipedia.org/wiki/World_War_II_casualties#Casualties_by _country, accessed on June 1, 2008.

workers are simply staying at home or calling in sick with "flulike" symptoms—thereby ensuring they will be told to self-isolate until their health is restored. The global economy's machinery has not quite ground to a halt, but the pandemic has, in the words of U.S. secretary of commerce Juliette Perriman, "thrown a bucket of sand in its gears."[7]

As grim as the situation is here in the United States, the hardships that many Americans are experiencing pale in comparison to what is happening in other parts of the world that have neither America's wealth nor its advanced public health system, flawed though it may be. Apparently large parts of southern China are under martial law or under no law at all. Some areas of sub-Saharan Africa have descended into chaos, with gangs looting and killing anyone who opposes them. The images of human bonfires of the dead in Nigeria, to name but one sub-Saharan state where this is occurring, cannot be described in any other way but as horrifying. Similar circumstances exist in parts of the Middle East, South Asia, and Latin America. With nearly all states hard pressed to preserve order at home, the United Nations' request for humanitarian relief supplies and peacekeeping forces has found no takers.[8] Consequently, while Americans are having a hard go of it, much of the rest of the world thinks of the United States as an oasis of peace and order.

AN IMPOSING ENEMY

THE ONGOING PANDEMIC IS SIMILAR TO THE 1918 "SPANISH" INfluenza pandemic.[9] As epidemiologists have observed, influenza is peculiar among infectious diseases, as it is transmitted so effectively that it literally exhausts the supply of effective hosts. As the reader has doubtless experienced, most victims of the flu endure several days of discomfort and then recover fully within a week or so. But in a minority of cases the virus exhibits extreme virulence, as it does in the United States

7. Stanley Friedberg, "Global Economy at Dead Stop," *International Herald Tribune,* June 22, 2011, p. 8.
8. James Singer, "UN Request Goes Unanswered," *Washington Post,* June 10, 2011, p. A1.
9. The term "Spanish influenza" is a misnomer. While stories of the pandemic were first reported in the Spanish press, the viral strain is believed, at least by some, to have originated in the United States.

today, where the flu strains currently circulating are causing pneumonia in roughly 10 percent of the population. The numbers are far higher in many parts of the developing world. Here again the symptoms are well known: the mucosal membranes of the nose and throat become inflamed. The eyes redden. Headache, body ache, congestion, coughing, chills, and fever afflict the exhausted victim, often accompanied by vomiting and nausea.[10]

The virus is producing in some cases symptoms that have rarely been seen in great numbers since the pandemic of 1918. As Dr. Evelyn Grey of New York's Mount Sinai hospital describes it:

> Patients exhibit the most intense forms of pain and suffering. They bleed through their nose, and blood is found in their saliva, along with a kind of yellowish mucus that also appears from nasal bleeding. Partial paralysis is not uncommon, with motion oftentimes severely impaired. The patient's features take on a dull, dusky leaden hue. Cyanosis is typical in these patients. Others who have suffered for weeks often turn melancholy, become hysterical and exhibit suicidal tendencies.[11]

In many parts of the country hospitals are collapsing under the strain, as ever greater numbers of Americans succumb to the virus. While doctors, nurses, and hospital administrative staff are being given priority access to antiviral drugs, these drugs are not a panacea. For hospital staffs, the combination of exhaustion from bearing such a heavy patient load and constant exposure to infected individuals compounds the danger to what is being called America's "thin white line."[12]

10. John M. Barry, *The Great Influenza* (New York: Penguin Books, 2005), pp. 231–32.
11. "Special Report: Death of a Mayor," interview of Dr. Evelyn Grey, CBS News, July 20, 2011, at http://wcbstv.com/, accessed on July 24, 2011. Cyanosis occurs when the patient's lungs cannot transfer oxygen to the blood, resulting in the patient's acquiring a bluish pallor. The case of New York mayor Joseph ("Joey") Johnson is perhaps the worst notable case in the United States. Mayor Johnson fell (or jumped) from his fourteenth-floor hospital room window on July 6. The symptoms described by Dr. Grey are highly consistent with those elaborated upon in John M. Barry's superb account of the 1918 influenza pandemic. See Barry, *Great Influenza*, pp. 230–38.
12. The "white line" is, of course, a reference to the white garb traditionally worn by doctors and nurses, even though in many hospitals they no longer wear it.

With the nation's public health system overwhelmed in some areas, many hospitals are effectively shut down, save for treating all but the most severe cases of influenza and other life-threatening diseases. Others are able, albeit barely, to care for their patients but are not admitting anyone who is not in an immediately life-threatening condition. The result is that tens of thousands, and perhaps many more, Americans are suffering and dying in their homes, bereft of all but the most basic medications, such as over-the-counter drugs.

"PLAGUE" IN THE INFORMATION AGE

TODAY IF AMERICANS REQUIRE ANY INCENTIVE TO AVOID THE WORK-place, or one another, they need only look at some of the graphic visuals and descriptions of those who have succumbed to the pandemic influenza virus right here at home. In 1918 there were no television broadcasts or Internet sites showing vivid images of the suffering to spread fear throughout the country. The advent of modern communications has almost certainly helped to produce a climate of fear and foreboding among Americans. Until recently these images have been available on a continuous basis, from twenty-four-hour televised news services like CNN and Fox News, from major media websites, and from websites such as YouTube that provide unvarnished, uncensored, and not necessarily objective video accounts of events. Videos of poor inner-city alleyways populated with human corpses convey a message of fear and hopelessness to the viewer, as do clips of hospitals, looking increasingly like fortified zones, turning away the sick and infirm.

Only recently, following a swift eight-to-one ruling by the U.S. Supreme Court in early May, has the government imposed a tight censorship on what can be broadcast by the media and posted on websites. Enforcement on the Web, however, has been difficult to achieve. Indeed, one cannot underestimate the impact of the government's loss of its once near-monopoly over information. Where only a generation ago a few major television networks and press services dominated the news, today Americans and much of the rest of the world get their "news" from a wide range of sources, many of them more intent on sensationalism than on providing information.

CHAOS ON AMERICA'S DOORSTEP

THE COMBINATION OF THE PANDEMIC, THE LACK OF GOVERNMENT preparedness, and sensationalist media is diminishing the American people's confidence and trust in their government. While minor breakdowns in order have occurred in parts of the United States and Canada, the situation is far worse in Mexico and in many Caribbean states. The consequences of Mexico's agony for the United States are both real and immediate.

As news of the lack of vaccines and shortage of antiviral medications spread throughout Mexico, and as the descriptions and images of Mexicans succumbing in ever-greater numbers to the virus flooded the various media, desperation took hold among the people. The influenza hit Mexico City especially hard. Many of the city's poor were denied medical care. As the death toll in the poor communities mounted, so did fear and a sense of helplessness. These feelings soon turned to anger when rumors spread that wealthy Mexicans were hoarding antiviral drugs and vaccines for themselves.[13] In mid-May many public and private hospitals where vaccines and antiviral drugs were reputed to be stored were ransacked, accelerating the collapse of the country's public health system. A video of Mexican troops at several hospitals firing on rioters, and apparently killing scores of them, was quickly censored in the United States.[14]

Compounding the problem, Mexico's rogue drug industry and its distributors have been peddling "generic vaccines" and "antiviral drugs" at steep prices to desperate citizens. As these "cures" have failed to produce results, the dying—and the desperation—are increasing.

13. The rumor that antiviral drugs were being hoarded is likely true. However, the second rumor, that vaccines were being hoarded, is certainly false, as neither Mexico nor any other country has been able to produce or acquire vaccines in any significant quantity. Michael Joseph, "Mexico City Nears Collapse," *Los Angeles Times,* May 30, 2011, p. 1.
14. The author can attest that as of late July 2011 the video remains on certain websites and can still be found by those with good Web-surfing skills and some persistence.

In Mexico, the collapse in public order, when it comes, is quick and devastating. Within the span of a week in late May 2011, civil order in many parts of that country simply ceases to exist. The pandemic's effects, which also include economic disintegration brought on by the workforce's evisceration from disease and self-isolation, triggers a growing crime problem, as people now seek to gain access, by whatever means, to vaccines and drugs as well as food. The Mexican police and military, themselves without immunization or access to antiviral drugs, have seen their ranks depleted by the disease and are simply unable to arrest the rapidly growing mass disorder. Large parts of Mexico City have become the equivalent of a Wild West frontier town on a massive scale, with looting in some sections and eerily deserted streets in others.

Then there are the bodies. Many of the dead can be seen lying near the curb, much as one would put out the trash for pickup, waiting vainly for the arrival of the city's public ambulances to collect them. The images call to mind the inhabitants of Europe during the Black Plague, who were told to "bring out your dead." Upon seeing images of the devastation, Mexico's ambassador to the United States tearfully remarked, "My country no longer exists."[15]

GO NORTH, YOUNG MAN . . .

WELL OVER A CENTURY AGO HORACE GREELEY ADVISED THOSE Americans seeking opportunity to "go west." The American West has long since been settled, but it now finds itself host to a new wave of settlers, who come not from the east but from the south, at as rapid a pace as they can. For decades many Latin Americans, principally Mexicans, have sought a better life for themselves and their families by immigrating to the southwestern United States, most of them illegally. Despite periodic efforts by Washington and state governments to address the problem, it has not only persisted over time but grown.

The problem is, in part, self-induced. The decline in the native U.S.

15. Jasper Burgess, "Mexico Descending into Chaos," *Washington Post*, May 29, 2011, p. A1.

birthrate has accentuated the need for workers to support an expanding American economy. As one wag put it, "We didn't know that when European-Americans decided to stop having children, we had also decided to have mass immigration."[16]

Efforts to construct a barrier along the U.S.-Mexico border encountered resistance on the part of an odd coalition: liberal pro-immigration groups, and conservative business leaders that benefit from the low wages paid to illegal immigrant labor. Protection was provided them by unscrupulous politicians who hoped to win votes by supporting the "rights" of illegals to become U.S. citizens, while failing to meet their responsibilities to enforce U.S. laws against illegal entry. The United States' inability to control its own borders is only part of its growing immigration problem. Periodic amnesties for illegal aliens increase the incentives for Latinos, especially those from Mexico and Central America, to enter the United States illegally. American laws that grant citizenship to children born in the United States, even if their parents are there illegally, further reward illegal entry. Then there is the U.S. social welfare system. Although these aliens have broken the nation's laws by entering the United States illegally, they are generally provided with access to the nation's public schools, health care system, and certain social welfare benefits. Those who defend this practice—typically the same people who would benefit from a more liberal policy on immigration—do so on the grounds of humanitarianism and the fact that many illegal workers do pay taxes. (Indeed, some even file tax returns!)

Simply stated, the U.S. government's inability—or unwillingness—to fulfill its responsibility to secure the nation's borders has created a problem that it compounds by providing incentives for foreigners to enter the country, legally or illegally. This has created a de facto open-door policy, helping to lay the groundwork for the humanitarian crisis America confronts today.

16. Jefferson Daniels, "U.S. and Mexican Demographic Trends and the Reconquest of the Great Southwest," *Political Science Quarterly* 125, no. 2 (Summer 2010), p. 25.

THE SHADOW OF DEATH

OVER THE PAST SEVERAL DECADES THE WORLD HAS EXPERIENCED A wave of globalization, far surpassing the great surge that swept over the globe in the years leading up to World War I. The growth of the world economy—facilitated by lower trade barriers, global supply chains, international financial networks, and global communication—has yielded many benefits, including increased wealth and greater economic efficiencies. It has also yielded an unprecedented level of mobility—in the movement of capital, goods, and services, in people (including migration), and last but not least, in disease.

For nearly a century the world has been spared the specter of mass deaths induced by a killer disease. The last great global pandemic occurred at the end of World War I, when the misnamed Spanish influenza killed an estimated 20 million people—including nearly 700,000 Americans—before it ran its course.[17] To a significant degree, the spread of influenza was aided and abetted by the world war, which saw the armed forces of many nations on the move from their home countries to other parts of the world. Even then, however, human mobility and trade were far more constrained than they are today, when every year millions of passengers pass through U.S. airports alone.

There have been several canaries in humanity's mine shaft, warning of impending disaster.[18] According to the scientific community, the world has been overdue for some form of pandemic. On occasions too numerous to count, members of the medical profession have stated that "it is not a matter of if such an event will occur, but when." As the World Health Organization met in Geneva in the summer of 2009, health officials were citing the "near-misses" the world had recently experienced with the AIDS virus, tuberculosis, and avian flu (commonly referred to as bird flu), and warning that, absent a major effort to improve the globe's public health system, humanity's good fortune could not—and

17. The term *pandemic* refers to a disease that strikes on a global scale, as opposed to an *epidemic*, which is limited to a specific region. More recent estimates have put the global death toll of the 1918 pandemic at between 50 million and 100 million.
18. Miners would put canaries in their mine shafts to provide early warning of dangerous gas leaks. If a canary were to die suddenly, it signaled to the miners that poisonous gas had seeped into the shaft and that evacuation was imperative.

would not—last. But the issue had to struggle to get on the global agenda. Here in America the 2008 presidential campaign (which began in early 2007) was dominated by the wars in Afghanistan and Iraq, the broader problem of militant Islam, rising energy prices, a falling economy, and growing concerns about global warming. Neither public health concerns over a pandemic nor the country's illegal alien problem appeared prominently on the political radar screen. Call them the "stealth" issues—the ones that we failed to detect.[19]

HOW DID IT HAPPEN?

HOW DID THE AVIAN INFLUENZA, OR "BIRD FLU," ABOUT WHICH WE have heard for over a decade, become a pandemic? The process, familiar to most readers who have been following recent events, requires only a brief summary here.

There are three main types of influenza viruses—A, B, and C. Of these, Type A can produce an influenza pandemic. This occurs when a Type A virus undergoes a genetic modification involving genes for two surface proteins: humagglutinin (H) and neuraminidase (N). If a virus acquires genes for a new H or H+N, a "novel" virus is created. But this is only the first step in creating a pandemic. Two additional conditions must be satisfied. The new virus must have the capability to spread easily from one person to another, and it must be highly lethal. Fortunately, this is not easily accomplished, and most novel viruses have not caused pandemics.

But some do.

The reservoir for Type A influenza is wild birds, although it may infect pigs, horses, and humans. Prior to the current outbreak, the previous two pandemic viruses were combinations of bird and human viruses. Scientists believe that wild aquatic birds are the primordial reservoir of all influenza viruses for both avian and mammalian species. The best chance of averting a pandemic rests in stopping the further spread of the disease in poultry populations.[20] One method that has proved effective,

19. To be sure, President George W. Bush and Congress made several attempts in his second term to arrive at a solution for the country's illegal immigration problem. However, their efforts failed to produce results.
20. Knobler et al., *Threat of Pandemic Influenza,* pp. 30–31.

and that was tried in many areas where the virus spread, involves culling flocks of birds, either wild or, especially, domesticated.

Vaccinating birds to prevent their succumbing to the disease has also been tried. However, vaccination of poultry must be accompanied by effective surveillance to prevent the spread of asymptomatic infection among vaccinated birds—a "silent epidemic." Such an infection occurred on at least one occasion in the past. In 1995 thousands of chickens in Mexico were vaccinated against the highly pathogenic H5N2 influenza, which led to the spread of antigen-distinct genetic variants of the vaccine strain among the country's poultry flocks.[21] Fortunately, that episode did not produce a pandemic.

There were other influenza pandemics between the 1918 Spanish influenza and the current bird flu. In 1957 the Asian flu killed nearly 70,000 Americans, while the 1968 Hong Kong flu, though milder, accounted for over 30,000 American deaths. More recently there have been several "scares": the Swine Flu of 1976, the Russian Flu of 1977, and the Avian Flu of 1997. The failure of these outbreaks to expand into pandemics may have been at least partly responsible for the sense of security that led to the lack of preparedness throughout the world to address the current situation.

The Avian influenza that is very severe in birds involves H5 and H7 subtypes. Once the H5N1 flu strain is passed from wild birds to domesticated livestock birds (e.g., chickens and turkeys), it spreads rapidly. Hundreds of millions of birds have been destroyed in attempts to stop the flu's progression. Nevertheless, these efforts have not prevented the flu from spreading to humans, beginning with those who work or live in close contact with domesticated birds. The species "jump" from animals to humans probably occurs through a process known as "reassortment." If a person (e.g., a poultry worker) becomes exposed to both animal and human viral infections, the "genetic mixing" that occurs between them can produce a strain that is transmissible from human to human, one that is highly resistant to vaccination or antiviral treatment.[22] Between 2003 and 2008 nearly 300 cases of human

21. Ibid., p. 28.
22. Lawrence O. Gostin, "Public Health Preparedness and Ethical Values in Pandemic Influenza," ibid., p. 358.

infection with H5N1 were identified, and over half of these individuals died. This mortality rate of over 50 percent vastly exceeds the rate of roughly 2.5 percent estimated for the Great Pandemic of 1918, which in any case killed more people than died in combat in all of World War I.[23]

THE WORLD'S WEAK DEFENSES

THE WORLD HEALTH ORGANIZATION (WHO) HAS SPEARHEADED global influenza surveillance efforts since 1948 and coordinates a network of over 110 national influenza laboratories in over eighty countries. The network, while strong in the West, has major gaps in Africa, parts of Asia—and, as it turns out, in Latin America as well.[24] Consequently, the WHO has not been able to respond effectively to halt the disease's progression.

While the first line of defense against avian influenza, to prevent the disease from spreading to humans, is to kill off flocks of infected birds, especially domesticated birds such as chickens and turkeys, in many parts of the less-developed world small farmers have sought to evade directives to cull their flocks, as the birds are their source of livelihood. Some governments, particularly those in the undeveloped world, fearing that early reporting of the disease and widespread culling will have potentially harsh economic consequences on tourism and the agriculture sector, have been a barrier to effective early warning and action.[25]

By 2006 the disease, which originated in Asia, had spread to Europe and Africa. At that point the disease had not yet been detected in North or South America and was still limited almost exclusively to birds. While some humans had contracted bird flu, there was no indication that the conditions for a potential pandemic—the easy spread of the flu from one human to another—had been met. Late that year, however, the journal *Nature* reported that H5N1, which had difficulty infecting the cells

23. Aubrey Noelle Stimola and Gilbert L. Ross, eds., *Avian Influenza, or "Bird Flu": What You Need to Know* (New York: American Council on Science and Health, 2006), p. 2.
24. Knobler et al., *Threat of Pandemic Influenza*, p. 32.
25. Ibid., p. 27.

lining the nose and upper parts of the lungs, had mutated to become more infectious in humans.[26]

GLOBALIZATION: THE GREAT ENABLER?

AS THE PERIODIC DEMONSTRATIONS OUTSIDE WORLD BANK MEET-ings declare, globalization's effects, while positive as a whole, have, like every other great economic shift, produced both winners and losers. Capital and labor—jobs—have migrated to places where they can add the greatest value. Thus areas with poor infrastructure and poorly edu-cated populations have found themselves falling farther and farther be-hind the rest of the world. In the 1990s the Clinton administration's so-called "Mother Teresa" policies targeted these areas, such as Haiti and Rwanda, deploying U.S. military forces to impose some form of order and provide humanitarian relief where the political system had simply broken down. But these efforts failed to produce lasting results. The world still remains divided between the "rich millions" and the "poor billions."

At the same time the United States' reputation for being at the fore-front in helping people recover from natural disasters—such as the tsunami that devastated Indonesia in 2004, the Pakistan earthquake in 2005, and Colombia's earthquake last year—has, in this age of global communications, led many to expect that Americans will "be there for them" under all such circumstances.[27]

In March 2010 the first signals of impending disaster came when scientists discovered that the Avian Flu had mutated into a form that could be transmitted relatively easily from humans to humans. The first cases were traced to a small village in southern China.[28] From there the

26. "One Step Closer," *Economist*, November 18, 2006, p. 85.
27. The reader will doubtless recall the famous "Be There for Them" slogan as the unoffi-cial theme of the relief operations undertaken by the U.S. government (as well as the title for the popular song produced by over a dozen popular singers) in the wake of the Colombian earthquake in June 2010.
28. The migration of influenza from birds to humans is best accomplished in areas where people, pigs, and poultry live in close proximity. These conditions are predominantly found in Asia in general and in China and Southeast Asia in particular. Most pandemics have their origins in China. Robert G. Webster and Elizabeth Jane Walker, "Influenza,"

disease spread quickly. Initially it was hoped that the flu's progression could be confined to southern China, but soon cases were discovered in North Africa, in the Persian Gulf region, and in Latin America. In Latin America, the spread has been traced to a Mexican woman, Maria Gonzalez, who returned to Mexico City by plane following a stay in South Africa, where the disease had supposedly not yet spread. Others assert that the pandemic has been spread by transcontinental wind currents.[29] Still others, fueled primarily by accusations of political leaders seeking to place the blame for their country's lack of preparation elsewhere, are accusing the United States of employing biological warfare against them.[30]

For those old enough to remember, the pandemic's spread recalled the 1950s, when fallout was tracked from atmospheric nuclear tests. Day by day Americans and others around the globe watched the flu's slow, seemingly inexorable series of outbreaks, like an unstoppable army ravaging and pillaging one town, one city, one nation after another, despite the restrictions placed on travel and attempts to identify and isolate those with the disease. Yet the disease has not progressed uniformly, either geographically or in its virulence. Rather, it has popped up in hot spots, here and there, like a guerrilla army showing up unexpectedly to wreak havoc. The best example of its spread may be that given by John M. Barry in his description of the 1918 pandemic, which mirrors our own in many ways.

American Scientist, March–April 2003, at www.americanscientist.org/template/AssetDetailNoFrame?assetId=18570, accessed on May 30, 2008.

29. There is some debate in the scientific community over whether the virus may have been spread by dust clouds. Epidemiologists note that dust clouds can travel over the Pacific Ocean from the Gobi and Taklimakan deserts in Asia to the northwestern United States, carrying hundreds of tons of dirt with them. Scientists originally thought no viruses or bacteria would survive such a trip, given their exposure to ultraviolet radiation and extreme temperatures. Yet on a dusty day over a decade ago in the Virgin Islands, microbiologists collecting air samples found thirty colonies of microorganisms, each with billions of cells. Doug Struck, "Dust Storms Overseas Carry Contaminants to U.S.," Washington Post, February 6, 2008, p. A2.

30. The leaders of Iran, Myanmar, and North Korea have accused the Dickson administration of developing and employing biological weapons against them. James Singer, "Tehran Accuses U.S. of Germ Warfare," Washington Post, May 28, 2011, p. A1. Such charges are not new. In 2008 Indonesia's health minister, Siti Fadilah Supari, stated that the United States was developing biological weapons using bird flu strains found in Indonesia. "Bird Flu as Biological Weapon 'Nutty' Idea, Says Gates," Jarkarta Post, February 26, 2008.

When water comes to a boil in a pot, first an isolated bubble releases from the bottom and rises to the surface. Then another. Then two or three simultaneously. Then half a dozen. But unless the heat is turned down, soon enough all the water within the pot is in motion, the surface a roiling violent chaos.[31]

In early 2010 as in 1918, the initial bursts took place in southern China, then spread to other areas. Now, however, the pot is rising to a full boil. Hardly a country has not been hit hard by the influenza pandemic. Today the heat of this "violent chaos" is being felt in many parts of the world, including the United States and Mexico.

WAGING WAR ON PANDEMIC INFLUENZA

VACCINES CAN PREVENT INFLUENZA, BUT THE UNITED STATES' CApacity to produce vaccines is limited and production is time consuming. The developing world's production capacity is meager in comparison to America's. Simply put, access to vaccines is beyond the reach of the vast majority of the global population.[32] Even here in America, the world's richest and most technically advanced country, supply of the vaccine has proved wholly insufficient to meet demand. The reasons are simple and in some cases disturbing.

Five years ago the federal government established the goal of creating and maintaining stockpiles of pre-pandemic vaccine adequate to immunize 20 million persons against influenza strains that present a pandemic threat. It also declared it would expand domestic influenza-vaccine-manufacturing surge capacity, so that pandemic vaccines could be produced for the entire domestic population within six months of a pandemic's appearance. Moreover, the government stated its intention to stockpile existing antiviral medications sufficient to treat 75 million persons, or roughly a quarter of the total U.S. population.[33] Unfortunately, these stockpiles had not yet been fully established at the time the

31. Barry, *Great Influenza*, pp. 231–32.
32. Knobler et al., *Threat of Pandemic Influenza*, p. 6.
33. Homeland Security Council, *National Strategy for Pandemic Influenza* (Washington, D.C.: n.p., May 2006), p. 9.

pandemic struck the United States. Nor is there surge capacity sufficient to produce large quantities of vaccine along the government's six-month timeline.

As the Centers for Disease Control and Prevention (CDC) noted repeatedly in the face of mounting public criticism, developing a vaccine to deal with a novel strain of influenza can take nearly a year. The CDC's judgment is proving to be on the mark. Just identifying the new strain—an effort that began here and in Europe in September 2010—and producing initial supplies has taken eight months, with the initial vaccines available only in late April. As President Dickson noted in his address to the nation, the U.S. production capacity will be unable to meet the demand for months to come.[34] Many have asked: Why wasn't the vaccine stockpiled? The answer is simple: due to antigenic shift and drift, influenza vaccines cannot be stockpiled.[35] The vaccine must be developed to deal with the specific strain producing the pandemic. Consequently, while a flood of the vaccine is needed, a lag of months passes before even a trickle can be produced.

America—indeed, the world—is now paying a fearful price for its lack of vaccine production capacity. This shortfall can be traced to the law of supply and demand, and to a mix of government inaction when action was needed, and intervention when it would have been better to leave well enough alone. Despite warnings from the medical community, global annual immunization rates were less than 500 million persons per year prior to the pandemic's outbreak. Only about a third of the U.S. population, fewer than 100 million, received vaccinations in 2009, the last year before the pandemic began to manifest itself. Remarkably, less than half of all U.S. health care workers were immunized.[36] This is a major factor in the near collapse of parts of the nation's public health system.

Absent a strong demand for vaccinations, the pharmaceutical industry has had little incentive to expand its production capacity. Compounding the problem, those in the business of vaccination production

34. President Norville Dickson, "The Pandemic Challenge," Address to the Nation, May 17, 2011, at www.whitehouse.gov, accessed on July 9, 2011.
35. Knobler et al., *Threat of Pandemic Influenza*, pp. 33–34.
36. Ibid., p. 34.

have, on occasion, failed to perform to standard. Twice in the past decade authorities have suspended the licenses of major vaccine producers due to contamination problems during the manufacturing process. One case, in 2004, saw British authorities suspend Chiron Corporation's license.[37] In February 2010 a U.S. producer had its license suspended for the same reason.[38]

But the problem does not end here. Currently the vast majority of the influenza vaccine in the United States—over 80 percent—is sold, distributed, and administered by private health care providers.[39] The first major public disorders in the United States, including the riots at hospitals and clinics in several major metropolitan areas, are the result of the Dickson administration's decision to nationalize the country's vaccine and antiviral drug stocks. As President Dickson stated in his address to Congress:

> My fellow Americans, we must fight this silent killer with every weapon at our disposal—and we must fight it together, as one nation, indivisible. All must share in the effort—and in the risk. Those in the front lines of this war—our doctors, nurses, police, and military—must be given the weapons they need to succeed. This means vaccinations and antiviral drugs. That is why I have directed that all stocks of these drugs be brought under federal control.[40]

The president's actions (or inaction, depending upon your point of view) have been the source of great controversy. At the time of his speech

---

37. At the time Chiron was one of only two suppliers of influenza vaccine to the United States, providing roughly half of the country's vaccines. Some assert that the unnamed U.S. firm has been recertified for vaccine production sooner than warranted in order to address the pressing demand for vaccines. Other firms have been pressed into service for producing the vaccine. This has led to a two-tier market for the vaccine: The vaccines produced by the new firms are typed as the "inferior" brand. Still, with supplies scarce, even these vaccines are highly sought after. David L. Kalbaugh, " 'Generic' Flu Vaccine Also in Short Supply," *New York Times*, April 13, 2011, p. A1. See also Knobler et al., *Threat of Pandemic Influenza*.

38. The Department of Health and Human Services has not released the name of the company involved.

39. Knobler et al., *Threat of Pandemic Influenza*, p. 34.

40. President Norville Dickson, "The Pandemic Challenge," Address to the Nation, May 17, 2011, www.whitehouse.gov, accessed on August 4, 2011.

many accused him of acting too slowly. But many of his critics, particularly individual rights groups like the American Civil Liberties Union (ACLU) and so-called survivalist groups, vigorously opposed taking strong measures during the pandemic's initial stages. They argued, with some justification, that serological tests might prove unreliable, that vaccines and treatments are not always safe and effective, that the economic losses from declaring national "snow days" to isolate the population as a means of addressing the "pandemic blizzard" are unacceptable violations of an individual's freedom of movement and association, and that coercive interventions to preserve the public's health are violations of civil liberties. But to be effective, agencies need to intervene at the earliest stages, before the threat level is clear.[41]

The president's decision to nationalize the nation's stocks of antiviral drugs and vaccines appears to have been motivated in large part by the need to enable the government and public health community to confront the pandemic, from the federal level all the way down to the local level. As the events of recent months have shown, the primary battles against pandemic influenza are being waged at the state and local level. Yet even with the federal government giving priority to local health and law enforcement authorities, many communities are left to combat the influenza pandemic with minimal external resources and support.[42] The nation's hospitals are being overwhelmed by the massive "casualties" inflicted by the virus. Making matters worse, hospital workers themselves are becoming agents for the spread of infection, as sick workers continue reporting to work due to staff shortages, spreading their illness to patients whose immune systems have been compromised.[43]

The growing number of Americans succumbing to the virus, combined with the declining economy, is eroding public confidence in the administration's ability to cope with the pandemic. Rumors circulating on the Internet are adding to the administration's woes. One of many

41. John M. Barry, "1918 Revisited: Lessons and Suggestions for Future Inquiry," in Knobler et al., *Threat of Pandemic Influenza*, p. 366.
42. Knobler et al., *Threat of Pandemic Influenza*, p. 24.
43. In a number of hospitals, the staff is now required to stay on-site, even when not on shift, to isolate them from the surrounding community. This requirement also stems from growing fears that hospital workers might be attacked by angry citizens or subjected to extortion by those who want access to antiviral drugs or vaccines. Ibid., p. 25.

rumors making the rounds alleges that the president's wife and three children have received inoculations and antiviral drugs, even though they are not "key and essential personnel" in the fight against the disease.[44] Other rumors assert that the families of congressmen and other senior government officials have received the same preferential treatment. While there is as yet no evidence to support these allegations, their effect on public morale and confidence in the government is corrosive.

Unsubstantiated reports are also circulating on various blogger sites that wealthy Americans are securing vaccines and antiviral drugs through a black market that has developed, purportedly linked to organized crime. Still another rumor has it that vaccines and antiviral drugs are plentiful in Canada—clearly not the case. Yet traffic still trickles northward across the country's border, for those seeking to improve their perceived odds of surviving the pandemic.[45]

Despite efforts to develop quick and effective vaccine production methods to address the avian influenza scourge, egg-based production remains the only proven and rigorously tested method of producing vaccines on a large scale.[46] While shortages have created desperate

44. See, for example, www.PanAlert.com, accessed on June 29, 2011.
45. Oddly enough, several online *Mexican* drug manufacturing firms are providing a "vaccine" for sale.
46. In an effort to accelerate influenza vaccine production, four years ago the government awarded five contracts totaling more than $1 billion to develop cell-based technologies. The objective was to create an alternative to growing flu vaccines in eggs, thereby boosting U.S. production capacity. The funds were part of a $3.3 billion fund that Congress appropriated in 2005 for pandemic preparations. The firms involved are GlaxoSmithKline; MedImmune; Novartis Vaccines & Diagnostics; DynPort Vaccine; and Solvay Pharmaceuticals. At the time the Bush administration's goal was to develop the capacity for domestic production of sufficient vaccines for every American within six months. Egg-based production takes about six months, and the eggs must be ordered well in advance. Growing vaccines in laboratory cell cultures has the potential to produce larger amounts of a vaccine in a given time period. The method is used for a number of other vaccines, such as polio, hepatitis A, and chicken pox. Cell-based production enables the producer to skip the step of adapting the virus strains to grow in eggs. Unlike eggs, cells can be frozen in advance and large volumes can be grown quickly. Cell-based methods also sidestep the risk of a shortage of egg supplies owing to poultry disease, and they eliminate the problem of helping those who are allergic to eggs and thus cannot receive vaccines grown in eggs. Unfortunately, the cell-based approach is not yet sufficiently mature to enable large-scale production. See www.cidrap.umn.edu/cidrap/content/influenza/panflu/news/may0406vac cines.html, accessed on May 20, 2007.

conditions in many parts of the United States, as noted earlier, the situation in the underdeveloped world is much more precarious. The basic reason is simple: 95 percent of the world's vaccine is produced by countries comprising only about 10 percent of the world's population. Simply—and devastatingly—stated: nearly 90 percent of the world's people *have little or no hope* of gaining timely access to the vaccine.[47] Mexico is among those countries. In China, where the pandemic is believed to have started, estimates are that 2 percent of the population has succumbed to the disease and another 30 percent or so are infected. If true, this means that China alone has already lost over 20 million people to the disease.

Modern medicine has another weapon in its antiviral arsenal, one in which Americans have developed an intense interest in recent weeks. The gap between the onset of pandemic influenza and the production of vaccines can be covered, albeit imperfectly, through the use of antiviral drugs, some of which have a long record of demonstrated effectiveness in influenza treatment and as a prophylaxis. Once again, however, the United States lacks production capacity. Only two U.S. manufacturers produce these drugs, and their surge capacity is inadequate to meet the demand being generated by the pandemic. In the past, it was possible to tap into Europe's production when a surge in demand occurred. Not now. Like the Americans, the European Union producer states have all nationalized their existing stocks.[48]

The good news is that antiviral drugs can be stockpiled. Thanks to efforts by the past two administrations, and several members of Congress working with the CDC and the Department of Health and Human Services, there is a significant stockpile of antiviral drugs. The bad news is that once the stockpile is exhausted, there is no surge capacity to reconstitute it quickly. And according to reports, the existing stockpile is far from adequate to meet the nation's needs.[49] Furthermore, resistance

47. Knobler et al., *Threat of Pandemic Influenza*, p. 37.
48. James Singer, "EU Cuts U.S. Off: Cites Emergency," *Washington Post*, January 17, 2011, p. A1.
49. One key issue is how to measure out the supply of antiviral drugs. If the disease hits in waves, as seems to be the case, government health officials run the risk of depleting their stock in the first wave of a pandemic, leaving little or no reserve remaining for a

to the drugs can build fairly rapidly with their widespread and indiscriminate use.

The U.S. government has kept the stockpile's precise size and location a closely guarded secret. The reason given is to avoid panic and disorder. The government fears that were this information available, and the stockpile close to being exhausted, some citizens might be tempted to take desperate measures to obtain the drugs.

MEXICAN EXODUS

IN EARLY FEBRUARY, AFTER SOME RELATIVELY MINOR OUTBREAKS in the fall of 2010, the pandemic hit Mexico in full force, with Mexico City suffering perhaps the worst outbreak. Fortunately, at that time the United States had still suffered only small flare-ups of the disease. Given the gift of time, Americans took steps to limit the flu's damage by stockpiling foodstuffs in their homes (to enable self-quarantine) and to exploit the potential, wherever possible, of telecommuting.[50] Still, Americans would not long remain unaffected by the tribulations of their southern neighbor. Beginning in March, just as the pandemic was becoming more widespread in America, senior decision-makers in Washington began receiving reports of an increase in illegal immigration across the U.S.-Mexican border—a surge that by all accounts risks becoming a flood this summer. Despite past proclamations of politicians that they have "secured" the border, it remains easy to penetrate, both for illegal aliens and for drug-runners.[51] Among the relatively few illegals detained and questioned at the time, a growing number cited their fear of the pandemic as their principal reason for entering the

---

successive pandemic wave that might arrive. This concern has led the president to rule out providing any antiviral medicines to foreign governments, despite their petitioning the United States to remember its pledge to "Be There for Them." Janice Morrow, "Foreign Pleas Fall on Deaf Ears," *Los Angeles Times,* June 3, 2011, p. 1.

50. Dry runs of telecommuting plans have been conducted in recent years, with mixed results. As one leading member of the financial community observed, "99 percent of the business interruption plans [of the financial sector] are based on telecommuting." "The Drawbacks of Homework," *Economist,* December 2, 2006, p. 78.

51. Washington's assertion that it has closed the border with Mexico has been mocked by a number of television news outlets, whose correspondents have run segments showing Mexicans crossing the border at some of its many weak points.

United States. Their logic was both simple and compelling: they believe their chances of surviving the pandemic are much better in the United States than in Mexico.

The Congress, reflecting the American people's fears that massive numbers of illegal aliens—many of them likely carrying the disease— will spread influenza in the United States, and collapse the increasingly fragile U.S. health care system, is demanding the administration take whatever steps are necessary to stem the advance of this human wave. As we move into August, Washington faces an internal public health crisis of the first order and an immigration crisis as well. The political leadership knows that there is insufficient medical support for the U.S. population, let alone for large numbers of illegal aliens. The consensus is that America must secure its borders or become an irresistible magnet for massive numbers of desperate foreigners who are seeking medical services and are willing to do practically anything to secure them.

The dozens of illegal aliens who were intercepted daily along the country's southern border in March grew to hundreds by May. By late July the numbers were approaching a thousand a day, even though the full force of Mexico's mass migration north has yet to be felt. Last week, within hours of one another, the governors of the border states—Texas, New Mexico, Arizona, and California—declared a state of emergency and began calling up their Army National Guard units to support the U.S. Border Patrol, whose numbers are wholly inadequate either to seal the border or to intercept large numbers of illegals.[52] As one U.S. government official who requested anonymity put it, "The Border Patrol is full of little Dutch boys trying to plug holes in the dike. Well, the dike has burst."[53] Both Washington and the border state governors are also concerned by the appearance of self-described armed "militia" units, small groups of Americans who are determined to protect their communities by preventing illegal aliens from crossing the border. Literally

52. The Border Patrol has fewer than 10,000 agents to cover a U.S.-Mexican border spanning roughly 2,000 miles. Interestingly, one of the reasons cited in the Delaration of Independence for America's separation from Britain was the king's refusal to provide the people of America with a secure border. See www.usborderpatrol.com/Border_Patrol87 .htm, accessed on June 1, 2008.
53. Harry Williamson, "Border Patrol Being Reinforced," *Dallas Morning News*, August 8, 2011, p. 1.

dozens of these groups, some numbering in the hundreds, are patrolling the border, despite the efforts of both the federal and state governments to discourage them.

These militia groups have appeared in surprisingly large numbers and are, in the view of many, disturbingly well armed. The National Guard and local law enforcement forces, stretched thin as they are, their numbers depleted by the influenza, are hard-pressed to confront these groups and require them to disband. Indeed, in some areas, especially in Texas, the militias—which include a surprising number of Latinos—appear to be operating with the tacit approval of the National Guard and law enforcement organizations.[54]

The U.S. Latino population is torn between desire for self-preservation and protection for their families and community, and memories of their own entry into the United States in search of a better life. While the ban on public gatherings has eliminated the opportunity for public demonstrations in support of admitting what would amount to millions of Mexicans into the country on humanitarian grounds, Latino websites have kept up a spirited discussion on the issue and how it might be accomplished—or prevented.[55]

The president is no doubt aware that failing to stem the tide of illegals entering the country risks producing a breakdown in public order along the U.S.-Mexican border that could extend from San Diego and El Paso to Los Angeles, Dallas, Houston, Albuquerque, and Phoenix. The collapse of the public health system in these areas could lead to thousands of American deaths. And any decision by Washington to send resources from other parts of the country to assist areas attempting to absorb the wave of Mexicans would, according to one wag, "be robbing Peter to pay Paul, when Peter has nothing to

54. William McCauley, "A Militia-Guard Alliance?" *San Antonio Express-News*, July 5, 2011, p. 1. There are unconfirmed reports of militia units firing on Mexicans attempting to cross the border illegally.
55. Many of the "solutions" to this emerging crisis that are found on the websites are fanciful. One, for example, argues that the problem could be solved by simply arresting those involved in the alleged vaccine and antiviral drug black market, which would "provide more than enough medicines to save us all." Another would have the U.S. public health system come to the rescue, when it is already overburdened with the (relatively) small number of Americans who have contracted the disease.

spare."[56] Put bluntly, attempts to "rob" the rest of the United States to provide support for illegals is a political third rail that no politician dares touch.

There is now overwhelming agreement that the United States must secure its borders, but how? One way may be to provide at least some level of assistance to the Mexican people, if only to keep them from attempting to cross into the United States. Again, the question arises: Given circumstances in the United States and in Mexico, how can this be accomplished?

President Dickson has established an executive committee, somewhat reminiscent of the group of senior advisers brought together by President Kennedy during the Cuban Missile Crisis in 1962. The "ExCom," as it is known, comprises a dozen or so senior government officials, including Secretary of Homeland Security Jonathan Wales, Joint Chiefs of Staff chairman General Harry Wilson, Army Chief of Staff General James Stanton, Secretary of State Brian Durantz, Secretary of Health and Human Services Denise Cordoba, and FEMA director Duhayne Johnson. The ExCom has been meeting almost daily since July 8, as the administration attempts to navigate its way through the crisis. Based on various reports, it is possible to piece together the major elements of President Dickson's strategy, of which there are three.

First, the military is being directed to secure the country's border with Mexico, including the maritime approaches, and to provide humanitarian relief in the form of food, shelter, and "basic medical treatment" to those persons who are trying to enter the United States illegally.[57]

Second, the National Guard is being federalized—that is, placed under the control of the federal government. In announcing the decision, strongly opposed by many state governors, the president declared that this step is necessary to provide him with the ability to shift these forces to areas where the need for pandemic relief is greatest. This

56. Congresswoman Nancy Jamison, quoted in Todd Lowery, "U.S. Fleet Confronts Human Wave," *Time*, July 23, 2011, p. 33.
57. It is not clear what the administration means by "basic medical treatment," save that it includes neither vaccines nor antiviral drugs.

decision is proving unpopular in many states, where governors suffer from a lack of public safety personnel. The governors are either using, or have plans to use, their Guard units to maintain order and provide relief services to communities hit particularly hard by the influenza.[58] Several governors, including those of California, New Mexico, and Oklahoma, have already declared they will defy the president's order unless all U.S. National Guard units serving overseas are brought home first.[59]

Third, FEMA is coordinating with the Defense Department to establish a pandemic relief strategic reserve known as Task Force Blue Eagle, comprising six active Army brigade combat teams and seventeen National Guard brigade combat teams and support brigades to be deployed within the United States if order breaks down as a consequence of the surge of Mexicans across the border. There are concerns that, as a consequence of repeated deployments overseas, these units are suffering from excessive wear and tear on both their soldiers and their equipment. Lieutenant General Cy Brannigan, the commander of this force, could only declare that his soldiers were at "adequate" levels of readiness in "most" critical categories.[60] This reserve can be deployed quickly, using the Air Force's cargo aircraft fleet, to reinforce local law enforcement units that are either decimated by the influenza, confronting widespread disorder, or both. This move has received strong congressional

58. A significant number of men and women serving in the National Guard also work in public safety jobs—as policemen, firemen, etc.—in their civilian capacity. Consequently, National Guard units serving overseas are weakening an already fragile U.S. public safety sector.

59. Over 40,000 American National Guard units are serving overseas, most of them in Afghanistan, the Horn of Africa, Iraq, and Kenya. Those in Africa have been directed to remain in their bases in "isolation" until the pandemic has passed. There are reports that U.S. troops have been forced to fire on local inhabitants seeking to force their way onto American bases, either to gain access to medical materials or simply to loot. Peter Browning, "U.S. Troops Fight to Survive in Africa," *Chicago Tribune,* August 3, 2011, p. 1. There are growing public demands to bring these troops back to America, both to protect them from an increasingly chaotic environment and to help enforce order.

60. John Stamos, "Pandemic Reserve Force Lacks Troops, Equipment," *Dallas Morning News,* August 2, 2011, p. 1. Over eight years of war in Afghanistan and Iraq have left many units returning from service short on people and equipment. It typically takes a year or more for these units to become fully manned and equipped in time for their next rotation overseas. Making matters worse, these units have not been immune from the pandemic—some have lost up to 10 percent of their authorized strength due to the virus alone.

support, but only after the president agreed to authorize use of this reserve force to *any* U.S. community threatened by a loss of civic order. However, the president will clearly need to dispatch this force to the border quickly if his plan is to have any chance of succeeding.

"MOONSHINE"

ACCORDING TO SEVERAL EXPERTS, INCLUDING RETIRED SENIOR military officers, the administration's plan for dealing with the growing threat to the nation's borders and its domestic tranquillity represents wishful thinking more than a course of action that can be effectively implemented. Even at full strength and operating in conjunction with the Border Patrol and local public safety personnel, the U.S. military's active and reserve forces are clearly insufficient to secure the 2,000-mile-long U.S.-Mexican border while meeting their overseas commitments as well. Yet the influenza's progression has left many of these units at far less than full strength, despite most having received antiviral drugs.

Highly credible sources report that if and when the strategic reserve is in position along the border, the U.S. armed forces plan to establish forty-mile-deep buffer areas inside Mexico opposite key crossing points and near major U.S. border cities like El Paso and San Diego. The hope is to avoid a surge of humanity on the U.S.-Mexican border itself and to intercept would-be illegal aliens well before they reach the United States. In military parlance, U.S. forces will provide "area security in depth." Of course, large numbers of Mexicans are already residing in this area, especially in so-called border cities like Juárez, near El Paso; and Tijuana, near San Diego. How would these cities be secured? Or would their residents be fairly displaced? If so, to where? This matter has apparently yet to be determined.[61] According to retired General Peter Dawson, who commanded the massive U.S. relief operations in Nigeria in 2009–10:

61. One option apparently is to quarantine the cities in place—prohibiting all human movement into or out of these cities. The quarantine would be enforced by U.S. (and perhaps Mexican) forces manning roadblocks and inspecting cargo entering and departing the sealed area.

The plan is someone's fantasy. Even under ideal conditions we cannot adequately man our border with Mexico. The idea that we can do it with a plague-depleted military against what may be millions of desperate people is moonshine.[62]

Within this buffer zone (to be named the Humanitarian Relief Zone, or HUMARZ), the plan calls for the military to establish displaced person camps where Mexicans can receive the basic necessities—food, clothing, and shelter—and perhaps some primary medical care. According to retired Army General Harry Pitrelli, Task Force Blue Eagle, comprising barely 100,000 soldiers and a few thousand Border Patrol agents, represents "a series of islands dealing with a tidal wave of humanity."[63]

Accompanying the American troops will be U.S. Border Patrol agents and customs officials, who will (again, according to the plan) support the overall effort while also attempting to certify commercial traffic—primarily eighteen-wheelers—bound for the United States. The goal is to maintain a sufficient "velocity of trade" to enable U.S. businesses that are critically dependent upon parts and other supplies from Mexico to continue functioning, thereby propping up the increasingly wobbly U.S. economy. Of course, given the chaotic situation in Mexico, it is not clear just how much commercial traffic will be forthcoming. It may not matter. As one Border Patrol official put it, "Even before the current crisis we could only inspect a small fraction of the traffic crossing our borders."[64] Furthermore, neither state and local governments nor the federal government, including the armed forces, is capable of disinfecting large numbers of vehicles crossing the border, or their contents.[65]

---

62. General Peter L. Dawson, "Dickson's 'Fantasyland,'" *New York Times,* July 22, 2011, p. A25.
63. Michael Milzuski, "U.S. Border Force Activated," *Washington Post,* July 31, 2011, p. A1.
64. Harry Williamson, "U.S.-Mexican Trade Slows to Crawl," *Dallas Morning News,* August 5, 2011, p. 1.
65. Beginning in 1982, Mexican commercial vehicles were required to stop at a buffer zone area along Mexico's border with the United States and transfer their cargo onto U.S. trucks. A pilot effort in 2007 to allow up to one hundred Mexican carriers access to the United States proved controversial and was abandoned by the Dickson administration in 2009. "Free Trade and Fireballs," *Economist,* September 15, 2007, p. 40; and Tom Curtis, "Administration Drops Cross-Border Cargo Plan," *Dallas Morning News,* March 28, 2009, p. 3.

The administration's plan has come under withering criticism on the political front as well. Senate majority leader Mary Logan, considered the principal spokesperson for the "loyal opposition," has stated that "the idea that we are going to have our troops mingling with these people, who are coming from an area of high influenza concentration, and providing them with assistance that should be going to needy American citizens is simply absurd."[66] Even members of the president's own party, such as House Speaker Tim Kulchak, are questioning the plan's workability. In a recent hearing Kulchak observed:

> Much as I and many other members would like to believe that the president's plan is the right plan, our military leaders are telling us in these hearings that it simply will not work, while at the same time it risks the lives of hundreds of thousands of our finest young men and women serving our country in our armed forces. It is simply not possible for us to stop the danger that is approaching our borders in a traditional humanitarian fashion. Attempting to do so will almost certainly forfeit the lives of many American soldiers and civilians while providing little in the way of actual relief to the unfortunate citizens of Mexico. And the idea of stopping these people without threatening the use of deadly force is simply wishful thinking. We must face facts. There is no alternative but to declare that we intend to protect our citizens' health and well-being by whatever means necessary, to include the use of deadly force against those who seek to enter our country unlawfully and illegally.[67]

In attempting to avoid the use of lethal force against civilians, President Dickson has authorized the military to employ a range of "nonlethal agents," as they are called, to stop the movement of Mexicans across the U.S. border. These agents include, among other things, rubber

66. Senator Mary Logan, *Face the Nation*, July 25, 2011, transcript at www.cbsnews.com/sections/ftn/main3460.shtml, accessed on July 28, 2011.
67. Representative Tim Kulchak, "Hearings on the Current Crisis," House Armed Services Committee, July 24, 2011, transcript at www.house.gov/hasc/hearing_information.shtml, accessed on July 28, 2011.

bullets, "sticky foam" (an immobilizing liquid), directed energy weapons, sound generators that induce nausea and disorientation, and tear gas. However, as these nonlethal agents are evidently in short supply, many units will likely have far less than they need. Others will have none at all. The general feeling among many senior military officers is that stemming the flow of illegals will likely mean resorting to the use of deadly force.[68]

In the face of mounting skepticism about the plan's efficacy, rumors have been circulating that the administration is already working on a "Plan B" alternative. Plan B involves helping the Mexican government reconstitute itself so it can begin to reestablish order inside the country, thereby taking the heat off U.S. forces trying to control the southwest border. This plan also has major problems, which have led one anonymous NSC staffer to observe:

> While I give those involved in developing the plan an A for effort, the fact is that while it may have had a chance of succeeding four or five months ago, it is unworkable now. There is no Mexican government to speak of that can be reconstituted quickly enough to impose order in the country on anything approaching a national level. To pretend otherwise is to set ourselves up for failure and the loss of precious antiviral medications and, at some point, vaccinations.[69]

THE COMING WAVE

DATA FROM RECONNAISSANCE FLIGHTS BY UNMANNED AIR FORCE aerial systems (pilotless drone aircraft) as well as U.S. satellites in space indicate that the leading edge of the large-scale Mexican exodus will likely reach the border within a few days. Reports are that the Air Force is prepared to drop nonlethal crowd control agents on a large scale to arrest the Mexicans' movement, at least long enough to allow U.S.

68. James Singer, "Deadly Force Needed, JCS Say," *Washington Post*, July 27, 2011, p. A1.
69. James Singer, "Plan B Being Debated," *Washington Post*, July 27, 2011, p. A1. The plan purportedly involves providing key Mexican political and military leaders, along with essential forces, with antiviral medication and some vaccine as well.

ground forces to deploy to the border area. But that seems to be all the nonlethals will accomplish. As JCS chairman General Harry Wilson notes:

> People who believe that getting into the United States spells the difference between life and death are not going to be deterred by nonlethal weapons. Parents who believe their childrens' lives depend on getting across that border are not going to go home just because they are subjected to a nonlethal attack. They are going to keep coming. And we are going to have to stop them.[70]

A large-scale mobilization of an additional forty-three Army combat and support brigades—nearly 200,000 troops in all—along with elements of a Marine Corps division, is under way to provide the president with the option to reinforce the undermanned forces along the U.S.-Mexican border, or to deal with a crisis that may emerge overseas. Unlike Task Force Blue Eagle, whose troops are to be concentrated at main border crossing points, these additional forces (named Task Force White Eagle) apparently will be deployed along the entire length of the border, covering gaps as they are identified. However, if the task force is deployed, as now seems likely, this would leave Washington with very little in the way of military capability to address outbreaks of civil disturbance in the United States.[71]

At sea, the Avian Armada's few lead elements of Mexicans have already been encountered along the coasts of California and Texas. The Navy and Coast Guard have succeeded in turning dozens of watercraft back, or incarcerating those who refuse to obey the command to leave

70. General Harry Wilson, *Face the Nation*, August 1, 2011, transcript at www.cbsnews .com/sections/ftn/main3460.shtml, accessed on August 7, 2011.
71. Michael Milzuski, "Pentagon Cupboard Bare," *Washington Post*, August 4, 2011, p. A1. It will also leave the Pentagon with few troops to deal with two rapidly growing crises, the accelerating breakdown in order in Pakistan, a country possessing dozens of nuclear weapons, and the rise in attacks on Saudi Arabia's oil-production facilities. In the case of the former, U.S. troops might be needed to help secure Pakistan's nuclear arsenal and protect it against forces seeking to overthrow the government, including militant Muslim elements. In the case of the latter, U.S. forces might be needed to help defend Saudi Arabia's vast oil facilities, which produce over ten million barrels per day.

American waters. In a few instances nonlethal weapons have been used to defend the nation's coastal borders. While the effort has been successful to this point, U.S. maritime reconnaissance aircraft reveal that the number of ships approaching the United States is projected to increase dramatically within the next four to six days, testing the U.S. fleet's ability to protect the country's coastal waters, and Americans, from this surge of humanity.

But with nonlethal munitions in short supply and unlikely to be broadly effective in any event, the question that is being increasingly asked in Washington is: Will the president sanction the use of lethal force against Mexican men, women, and children? Or has he already done so?

4

ARMAGEDDON:

THE ASSAULT ON ISRAEL

You should know that the criminal and terrorist Zionist
regime, which has sixty years of plundering, aggression, and
crimes in its file, has reached the end of its work and will
soon disappear off the geographical scene.

President Mahmoud Ahmadinejad,
Islamic Republic of Iran (quoted by Reuters)

AN ECHO FROM THE PAST

PRECISELY ONE HUNDRED YEARS AGO, ON JUNE 28, 1914, IN THE
town of Sarajevo in the province of Bosnia-Herzegovina, then part of the
Austro-Hungarian Empire, a Serbian nationalist, Gavrilo Princip, a
member of the terrorist group Black Hand, assassinated Archduke Francis Ferdinand, heir to the throne. The murder occurred while the archduke and his devoted wife, Sophie, rode in an open car through the city
streets. This despicable act set in motion a series of events that, within
a few months, found all of Europe's great nations engaged in a war that
would destroy four empires and permanently cripple the surviving two.

Yet in the days immediately following the assassination war did not seem inevitable or even imminent. Historians would later pore over the documents and memoirs of the time, trying to apportion blame for the conflagration that followed, without ever coming to anything approaching a consensus. It might truly be said that none of the great powers actively sought war, yet none proved able—or perhaps willing—to avoid the calamity that followed.

The war disproved many of the assumptions that military planners of the time had come to accept as gospel or "conventional wisdom." Noting that European conflicts of the previous hundred years, since the Napoleonic Wars, had been relatively brief affairs, many "experts" believed that the armies that marched off to war in that summer of 1914 would be "home before the leaves fall."[1] They recalled how short the conflicts surrounding German unification had been, when Prussia went to war with Austria in 1866 and France in 1870. Few bothered to recall the four years of grinding warfare that the Americans had waged against one another across the Atlantic in their civil war, but then the Americans were viewed as not being of the caliber of European armies. Only a few could envision a far darker outcome. One was Great Britain's foreign secretary, Sir Edward Grey, who remarked at the onset of the war, "The lamps are going out all over Europe. We will not see them lit again in our lifetime."[2]

The war found military experts wanting in other ways as well. The conventional wisdom of the time foresaw victory as emerging from aggressive, offensive action: fighting spirit would overcome the new

1. Barbara Tuchman notes, "The Germans took that chance [of going to war] because they expected a short war . . . Clausewitz, a dead Prussian, and Norman Angell, a living if misunderstood professor, had combined to fasten the short-war concept upon the European mind. Quick, decisive victory was the German orthodoxy; the economic impossibility of a long war was everybody's orthodoxy. 'You will be home before the leaves have fallen from the trees,' the Kaiser told departing troops in the first week of August. A diarist of the German court society recorded on August 9 that Count Oppersdorf came in that afternoon and said things could not last ten weeks; Count Hochberg thought eight weeks, and after that, 'You and I will be meeting again in England.'" Barbara Tuchman, *The Guns of August* (New York: Dell, 1962), pp. 141–42.
2. Quoted in Robert K. Massie, *Dreadnought: Britain, Germany and the Coming of the Great War* (New York: Random House, 1991), p. 907.

machinery of war. This belief persisted despite evidence to the contrary in the recent war in 1904–05 between Russia and Japan and, of course, in the American Civil War. Four years of butchery (there is no other suitable way to describe it) followed the archduke's assassination, as massed formations of soldiers on both sides were mowed down by modern firepower, leaving an indelible stain on the military profession and a lasting scar on European societies.

The military plans themselves embodied the accepted beliefs. The most famous (or perhaps infamous) was the Schlieffen Plan, formulated by the German General Staff. The plan held that if Germany found itself in a two-front war with France and Russia, it would adopt a defensive posture in the east while the main German armies executed a quick, decisive campaign against the French Army in the west. Thereafter the full weight of German military might would be pitted against Russia. But France was not defeated quickly, and the German high command, which had staked everything on a rapid victory in the west, found itself without a plan—as the Americans would do nearly a century later once they toppled Saddam Hussein in the Second Gulf War. The result of the German planning was a war that few had anticipated and that fewer still wanted—one whose horrific costs are felt to this day.

Recent events in the Middle East have put the region—indeed, the world—on a path that promises, if not guarantees, an outcome similar to the cataclysmic events that were triggered a century ago this summer. As in that fateful summer of 1914, a series of small events, many of which seemed rather unimportant at the time to many expert observers, have combined to propel us along the path of yet another war between Muslims and Jews, a conflict between Arabs, Persians, and Israelis. It is a war in which the principals seem to be dragged along by events, only some of which are of their own making. This time, however, the war, if we fail to avoid it, may be the first in nearly seventy years in which nuclear weapons are used.

Have we been along this path before? Yes, but the situation then was nowhere near as serious as the one we now confront. Toward the end of the last decade there was considerable discussion in American and Israeli policy circles regarding the need to arrest Iran's moves to develop a nuclear-weapons-manufacturing capability. As the Iranians dispersed their program and placed many key facilities deep underground, the feeling was that only the use of relatively low-yield nuclear weapons would be able to knock out Iran's nuclear-production facilities. The Americans, absorbed at the time with the wars against radical Islamists in Afghanistan and Iraq, and with the U.S. economy suffering from a variety of ills, had no stomach for this sort of thing. Instead, they supported efforts by the leading European powers—France, Germany, and Great Britain, often referred to as the EU-3[3]— to seek a diplomatic solution.

The Israelis, we now know, concluded at the time that a strike against Iranian nuclear-production facilities on their part would require at least some cooperation from the Americans.[4] Israeli aircraft carrying low-yield or tactical nuclear weapons (the military now uses the term "mini-nuke" or "precision nuke" to describe them) would have had to fly over Iraq to reach their targets in Iran. That would have required an okay from the U.S. military, which controlled the airspace over Iraq at that time. Not only might Israel encounter political difficulties in negotiating for U.S. approval, but sharing Israel's plans with the "city of leaks" (i.e., Washington) would make secrecy difficult to maintain.[5] The logistics surrounding the attack, including the long distance from Israel to Iran, and the large numbers of strike aircraft, tanker aircraft, and helicopters required, made such an operation a high-risk enterprise.[6] However, the prospect that Israel would have to use nuclear weapons to achieve success led Tel Aviv to rule out the operation.

---

3. The term *EU-3* is an abbreviation for "European Union 3."

4. Duane Williams, "Israelis Planned Attack on Iran in '09," *Washington Times*, June 7, 2014, p. 1.

5. William Davies, "Israel's Plan to Attack Iran," *New York Times*, January 29, 2010, p. A3.

6. The Israeli Defense Forces (IDF) conducted a series of maneuvers to determine how they might execute an attack on the Iranian nuclear facilities. One representative exercise, conducted in June 2008, involved more than 100 strike aircraft, which flew roughly 900 miles, the distance between Israel and Iran's nuclear facilities at Natanz. Jay Solomon and Yochi J. Dreazen, "Israel Manuevers Demonstrate Unease Over Iran," *Wall Street Journal*, June 21, 2008, p. A5.

THE SECOND LEBANON WAR

WHILE TENSIONS BETWEEN ISRAEL AND THE MUSLIM STATES HAVE existed since Israel came into existence in 1948, conflict between the two has traditionally been moderated by the influence wielded by the Great Powers. For much of the 1960s and 1970s the United States stood as Israel's benefactor and main arms supplier. The frontline Arab states (Egypt, Jordan, and Syria) and key nonstate groups like the Palestine Liberation Organization were often backed by the Soviet Union. When the two sides clashed in conventional conflict, as they did in 1956, 1967, and 1973, the results were clear Israeli victories.

Toward the end of the Cold War, radical Arab Islamist groups like Hamas in Palestine and Hezbollah in Lebanon, with the growing support of the militant Islamic mullahs ruling Iran, were willing to challenge the Israelis, using a sustained campaign of terrorism and guerrilla warfare. The First Intifada[7] (1987–93) and the Second Intifada (2000–11) pitted Palestinian nationals against Israel. Palestinian tactics ranged from mass protests and general strikes, which dominated the First Intifada, to armed attacks on security forces, suicide bombings, and firing Qassam rockets[8] into Israeli residential areas.

By 2006 Hezbollah had acquired a sizable arsenal of fairly sophisticated weapons, with thousands of rockets in its inventory, and had become a state-within-a-state in Lebanon. The Second Lebanon War, waged between Israel and Hezbollah in July and August 2006, marked a significant watershed in the long struggle between Jews and Muslims in the Middle East. During the span of little more than a month Hezbollah fired some 4,000 rockets of various types into Israel. Of them, over 900 rockets hit near or on buildings, civilian infrastructure, and industrial plants. The ferocity of the attack, which averaged some 130 rockets per day, far exceeded any attack suffered by Israel up to that time, including the Iraqi Scud missile attacks during the First Gulf War in

7. *Intifadah* is an Arabic word that literally means "shaking off," as in "shake off an oppressor." Most Israelis see the intifadas as simply terrorist campaigns.
8. The Qassam rocket is a crude short-range (less than ten miles) unguided weapon used by Hamas.

1991. Some 2,000 homes were destroyed, and more than fifty Israelis died, with several thousand being injured. Haifa, Israel's major seaport, had to be shut down, and its oil refinery as well.[9] Hezbollah also launched four unmanned aerial vehicles (UAVs) against targets in Israel and hit an Israeli corvette with a C-802 Silkworm, a Chinese-built, Iranian-supplied antiship cruise missile (ASCM).

As enemy rockets rained down on northern Israel, the Israeli Defense Forces (IDF) initially sought to defeat Hezbollah using air power and precision firepower-based operations. When this failed, the IDF employed its ground forces in limited raids and probes into southern Lebanon, Hezbollah's center of power. Yet Hezbollah managed to sustain the rocket campaign during the entire thirty-four days of conflict. Hezbollah's use of antitank guided munitions and rocket-propelled grenades against Israeli tanks proved both clever and effective. Over 25 percent of the 114 IDF personnel killed during the war were tank crewmen; out of the 400 tanks involved in the fighting in southern Lebanon, 48 were hit and 40 damaged.[10]

Hezbollah proved to be a highly dedicated and professional fighting force that had transformed itself from "a predominantly guerrilla force into a formidable quasi-conventional fighting force."[11] As one Israeli expert concluded, "Stealth, cunning, and simple technology clashed against massive firepower and the best and latest of high technology, and to the surprise of many experts, the [Hezbollah] militia prevailed."[12]

Hezbollah had won, and won big. Unlike the armies of Egypt, Syria, and Jordan, which had fought wars with Israel and been defeated very one-sidedly, Hezbollah had more than held its own. For Arabs, Hezbollah had restored their pride and dignity. Hassan Nasrallah, Hezbollah's leader, became a hero in the Arab world, while the stock of Egypt's Mubarak and Syria's Assad declined.

9. Uzi Rubin, *The Rocket Campaign Against Israel During the 2006 Lebanon War* (Ramat Gan, Israel: Began-Sadat Center for Strategic Studies, 2007), pp. 10–11, 14. Additionally, some 100,000 to 250,000 Israeli civilians fled their homes.
10. Matt M. Matthews, *We Were Caught Unprepared: The 2006 Hezbollah-Israeli War* (Fort Leavenworth, Kan.: U.S. Army Combined Arms Center Combat Studies Institute Press, 2008), p. 64.
11. Ibid., p. 63.
12. Rubin, *Rocket Campaign Against Israel,* p. 22.

IRAQ AND THE SUNNI ARAB STATES

TWO YEARS AFTER THE WAR, IN 2008, THE UNITED STATES—THE only remaining Great Power with a substantial military presence in the region—began gradually drawing down its forces in Iraq, while it remained fully engaged in its protracted conflict in Afghanistan against militant Muslim insurgents. To many, the disengagement from Iraq, gradual though it was, signaled that the United States would be reluctant to assume anything more than a light burden to preserve order in the region. This view was best expressed by President William Redding in his inaugural address in 2013, when he declared, "America cannot—and should not—and *will not,* under this administration—try to maintain stability everywhere. To do so would make us secure nowhere."[13] The drawdown of U.S. forces from Iraq was accomplished, to the surprise of many, with minimal casualties. The measured U.S. withdrawal also produced another surprise: despite the predictions of some, Iraq did not descend into widespread and bloody civil war. The country's Shi'a Arab leaders proved willing to work with the Kurds to their mutual advantage and with their Sunni Arab brethren as well.

The Iraqi government is dominated by the Shi'a, who comprise some 60 percent of the country's total population. But they share power with both the Kurds and the Sunnis. The Kurds, concentrated in the northern part of Iraq, enjoy a great deal of autonomy and a sizable share of the oil riches around Kirkuk. The Sunnis, who dominated Iraq under Saddam Hussein and ruled the country for most of the twentieth century, comprise less than 20 percent of Iraq's population. Some radical elements associated with al Qaeda continue waging a low-level insurgency against the regime in Baghdad, employing the same means as they did against the Americans and their coalition partners: suicide bombers, roadside improvised explosive devices ("IEDs"), car bombs, kidnappings and assassinations, and sabotage against the country's economic infrastructure. But they are now more a violent nuisance than an existential threat. The government, with the backing of the United States, has

---

13. President William M. Redding, Second Inaugural Address, January 20, 2013, at www.whitehouse.gov, accessed on July 18, 2013.

fielded security forces that are capable of providing for Iraq's internal security but that have little capability to defend the country from overt foreign aggression from neighbors like Iran, a strong supporter of Hezbollah, Hamas, and several Iraqi Shi'a political factions.

The Arab world, which is dominated by Sunni Muslims, began establishing diplomatic relations with its only Shi'a-led state toward the end of the last decade. This came to pass primarily due to the Shi'a Iraqis' willingness to work with their Sunni countrymen in a spirit of shared power and shared wealth, and out of concern that the fragile new regime was vulnerable to ongoing Iranian efforts to destabilize or subvert it. The Sunni Arabs, wanting Iraq not to emerge as an Arab state governed by puppets of the radical Persian Shi'a regime in Tehran, proved willing to engage seriously with the government in Baghdad. As one Arab diplomat remarked,

> If Iraq sees itself as an Arab state, we are happy to cooperate with it. If it sees itself as an ally of the Persians [i.e., Iranians], we can only view it as a threat. We will resist any attempt to recreate the Persian Empire, or a Shi'a Empire.[14]

To address what was seen as a rising Iranian challenge to the power balance in the region, Saudi Arabia invested heavily in expanding its oil- and natural-gas-production facilities following the spike in oil prices during the late 2000s. Its reasons for "helping to meet the needs of our friends," as Saudi ambassador Sheikh Abul al-Saud has repeatedly stated to the Washington press corps, owed more to strategic factors than to any sense of goodwill. Saudi Arabia has managed to increase the supply of oil available on the market by nearly 2 million barrels per day. Expanded Saudi production (which has been partially matched by increased production elsewhere), combined with global efforts to move toward alternatives (e.g., coal- and nuclear-fired power plants), heightened conservation efforts, a sluggish global economy, and the bursting

---

14. Paul Dimsdale, "Arabs See Iraq as Potential Ally Against Iran," *Wall Street Journal*, October 28, 2011, p. A1. At its height around the year 500 BC the Persian (or Achaemenid) Empire stretched from present-day India in the east to Greece and Libya in the west.

of a speculation bubble in oil and gas, has helped to keep oil prices at a "reasonable" range of $80 to $115 a barrel since 2012.

This price has served two key Saudi strategic objectives. First, it has prevented oil prices from rising to the point where the industrialized world aggressively pursues energy alternatives. Should it do so, oil, which has had a stranglehold on advanced industrial societies for a century, would decline in importance, and significant Saudi leverage would be lost. Second, by keeping the price of oil relatively low, the Saudi royal family hopes to exert pressure on Iran, which needs high oil prices to cope with popular discontent at home and the demands of its clients— Hamas, Hezbollah, the Shi'a regime in Baghdad, and Syria—for financial support.

IRAN ASCENDANT

THE FIRST DECADE OF THE NEW CENTURY SAW IRANIAN POWER ON the rise in the region. The mullahs of Tehran quickly adapted to the post-9/11 world, initially adopting a more accommodating position toward an enraged United States, then adeptly exploiting Washington's poorly executed attempts to stabilize Iraq following the invasion of that country in 2003 by a U.S.-led coalition. Not only did Iran position itself as the principal supporter of the Shi'a-dominated government that emerged from U.S.-sponsored elections in Iraq, but a combination of Iranian military assistance and economic support enabled Hamas to displace the inefficient and corrupt Palestinian Authority in Gaza and eventually the West Bank, and for Hezbollah to become a state-within-a-state in Lebanon. When Syria's despot, Hafez al-Assad, looked to be "going wobbly" in the early stages of the American invasion of Iraq, it was the Iranian leaders who offered support and convinced Assad that the Bush administration was an aberration that would eventually be replaced by a more pliable regime in Washington.

Iranian influence likely reached its apogee in 2011. Hezbollah's success against Israel in the Second Lebanon War in 2006, combined with the U.S. inability to cope effectively with Shi'a militias in Iraq, convinced many that, after decades of Western military domination, the

Muslim nations had at last found the key to defeating the "infidel armies." As one Israeli general ruefully noted, "These people believe they have broken the code on how to defeat us. If we don't find a way to disabuse them of that idea, we are destined to see more and more of the same."[15] Israel's director of its Defense Ministry's Political-Military Bureau, Major General Amos Gilad, warned that "the Iranians could create a belief that they can beat us, and under their [nuclear] umbrella create an axis that will destabilize the Middle East."[16] Iran's outspoken president, Mahmoud Ahmadinejad, declared his country was on the verge of becoming a "superpower,"[17] while Iran's "Supreme Leader of the Islamic Revolution," Ayatollah Seyyed Ali Khamenei, bluntly stated that "Israel's weakness . . . was well proved in the thirty-four-day war in Lebanon."[18]

The last oil spike—the one in 2011—found Iran at the center of what some observers have called a "New Persian Empire" or "Persian Crescent" stretching from Tehran through Baghdad and Damascus, on to Beirut, and down the Mediterranean coast to Gaza. When oil reached $135 a barrel that year, Tehran was generously subsidizing its clients while also containing growing internal unrest at home through expanded public assistance programs and appeals to national pride. Iranian Quds Force[19] members apparently are still embedded with several Iraqi Shi'a militias. Syria continues to serve as a conduit for Iranian influence, funneling support from Iran to Hezbollah in Lebanon while serving as a

15. William Davies, "Israeli General Cites Lessons of War with Hezbollah," *New York Times,* August 13, 2009, p. A11.
16. Richard Boudreaux, "Israel Sounds Alarm on Iran's Nuclear Efforts," *Los Angeles Times,* February 7, 2007, p. 3.
17. Nazila Fathi, "Iran Leader Calls Nuclear Sanctions Ineffective," *New York Times,* February 2, 2007, p. A10.
18. IRNA.com, "Khamenei Urges Stronger Iran-Pakistan Relations," February 5, 2007.
19. The Quds Force ("Jerusalem Force") is a special unit of the Iranian Revolutionary Guard Corps (IRGC). Its principal mission involves training Islamic fundamentalist terrorist groups, including those in Lebanon, Palestine, and Iraq. The Quds Force also gathers intelligence and is responsible for gathering information required for targeting and attack planning, while building and maintaining relationships with Islamic militant organizations throughout the Islamic world. See "Qods (Jerusalem) Force Iranian Revolutionary Guard Corps (IRGC—Pasdaran-e Inqilab)," at http://www.globalsecurity.org/intell/world/iran/qods.htm, accessed on February 21, 2007.

base for Iranian Quds units aiding Hezbollah and Hamas. This enabled both organizations, the latter of which continues to dominate in its relationship with the rump Palestinian Authority, to maintain their low-level war against Israel.

But for the United States, which saw its position in the region decline dramatically in less than a decade, the worst was yet to come. On the night of September 14–15, 2011, seismic recorders detected a sharp uptick in the eastern desert of Iran. The Iranians, who according to U.S. and European intelligence services were "at least five years" away from being able to fabricate a nuclear device, had detonated an implosion fission weapon with a plutonium core whose yield approached that of the Nagasaki blast sixty-six years before.[20]

While Iran's actions quickly brought the world's opprobrium down upon it, neither the United Nations nor the European Union proved willing to do anything more than posture and authorize minor sanctions. Former International Atomic Energy Agency director general Mohamed ElBaradei repeated his now-famous statement, "We must abandon the unworkable notion that it is morally reprehensible for some countries to pursue weapons of mass destruction, yet morally acceptable for others to rely on them for security."[21] Thanks to Chinese and Russian support for Iran, even these modest sanctions proved unenforceable. The West continued to line up for the privilege of buying Iranian oil—even at $135 a barrel. The United States, having roughly halved its forces in a still-fragile Iraq, was unwilling to act alone, without UN or EU support. In Israel, an atmosphere of grim resolve took hold as Tel Aviv prepared for the storm to come. Former head of the IDF General (Ret.) Yitzak Naveh declared bluntly (and prophetically), "This clears the way for the Iranians to ratchet up the efforts of their proxies in Lebanon, the West Bank and Gaza."[22]

20. The "Fat Man" weapon dropped on Nagasaki is estimated to have had a yield of between 19 and 23 kilotons. See www.warbirdforum.com/hiroshim.htm, accessed on June 12, 2008.
21. The earliest quotation of this declaration may be found in a 2004 *New York Times* editorial by ElBaradei. See Danielle Pletka and Michael Rubin, "ElBaradei's Real Agenda," *Wall Street Journal,* February 25, 2008, p. A14.
22. Simon Ghazak, "Iranian Storm Clouds Approaching," *Jerusalem Post,* September 28, 2011, p. 3.

How had Iran managed to acquire nuclear weapons so far in advance of the West's intelligence estimates? On October 24, in a speech before the UN General Assembly, President Redding revealed:

> Airborne samples taken by U.S. reconnaissance aircraft following the Iranian nuclear detonation that took place in the predawn hours of September 15 reveal that the plutonium used in these weapons—and perhaps the weapons themselves—may have come from the Democratic People's Republic of North Korea. The government of Iran likely is continuing to purchase plutonium from North Korea, and may be importing entire weapons, to include the designs and triggers. These transfers have occurred despite the efforts of the United States and its partners in the Proliferation Security Initiative. I call upon the Security Council to take this matter up in an emergency session as a clear and immediate threat to international peace and security.[23]

The Security Council did meet, but the international community greeted U.S. intelligence reports with great skepticism. The Iranian media declared the U.S. reports to be another attempt to suppress the accomplishments of the Muslim peoples through lies and deceptions. In any event, both Russia and China refused to support harsh sanctions against Tehran.[24] The United States had proposed a strict trade embargo against

23. The Proliferation Security Initiative (PSI) "is a global initiative aimed at stopping shipments of weapons of mass destruction (WMD), their delivery systems, and related materials worldwide." The Bush administration announced the PSI in May 2003. Department of State, "The Proliferation Security Initiative," at http://usinfo.state.gov/products/pubs/ proliferation/, accessed on September 16, 2008. By 2008, ninety countries had become participants in the PSI. Department of State, "Morocco Endorses the Proliferation Security Initiative," at http://www.state.gov/r/pa/prs/ps/2008/may/105143.htm, accessed on September 16, 2008.
24. The matter of sanctions against North Korea was also taken up at that time. Again, the Chinese and Russian representatives refused to support strong measures. The Chinese called for "renewed negotiations" with Pyongyang, which denied providing any nuclear materials, designs, or weapons to the Iranians. The North Koreans did express a willingness to permit some limited inspection of their nuclear facilities in exchange for technical and financial aid. Only South Korea took the bait. See William Davies, "Beijing, Moscow Block Sanctions," *New York Times*, September 30, 2011, p. A1.

the Iranians but found no backers in either London or Paris. Even at home, the American people were unenthusiastic about the oil price spike that would occur if Iran's oil were taken off the market. Analysts estimated it would cause prices to jump to $170 or $200 a barrel.[25] Once again the international community had failed to act. As U.S. secretary of state John Kirkland observed following his speech before the Security Council, "This is what it must have been like at the League of Nations in the 1930s. I hope to God our lack of resolution does not produce the same result."[26]

As for China, its extensive deals with Tehran for access to oil and its desire to assist Iran in developing a capacity to ship liquid natural gas to satisfy growing Chinese energy needs has made Beijing a strong backer of the mullahs. Russia, which along with Iran controls nearly half the world's proven reserves of natural gas, hopes to form an OPEC-like cartel with Tehran to control the world market[27] and is in no mood to oppose the Iranians. Moreover, both China and Russia see little benefit in helping the United States stem nuclear proliferation in the Middle East. From their perspective, proliferation will curb American "adventurism" by making it riskier to deploy U.S. forces into the region, a capability that neither Moscow nor Beijing possesses.

THE MULLAHS' DESCENT

ASTONISHINGLY, IRAN'S DESCENT FROM ITS SELF-PROCLAIMED PERCH of regional superpower has been even more rapid than its rise. In the

25. Dudley Farrington, "Over a Barrel," *Financial Times*, October 13, 2011, p. 1.
26. During the 1930s the League of Nations failed to take forceful action against the actions of Nazi Germany, Fascist Italy, Imperial Japan, and Soviet Russia to overthrow the international system. Ultimately the actions of the first three led to World War II. Joseph Breyer, "UN Deadlocked over Iran," *Christian Science Monitor,* November 22, 2011, p. 1.
27. The discussions between Moscow and Tehran over establishing a natural gas cartel have been ongoing for nearly a decade. There are long-standing fears throughout the West that Russia and Iran would use such a cartel to Westerners' detriment, both economically and politically. See Russell Gold and Gregory L. White, "Russia and Iran Discuss a Cartel for Natural Gas," *Wall Street Journal*, February 2, 2007, p. A1. China is now investing heavily in supporting Iran's belated effort to develop its natural-gas-export infrastructure.

span of only three years a combination of factors and events have transformed the regime in Tehran from a confident quasi-regional hegemon to one that is very much on the defensive and contemplating dramatic action to right its declining fortunes. The advantage gained by Iran's nuclear capability is proving short-lived. Other states in the region, the Egyptians and Turks in particular, are now aggressively pursuing their own nuclear programs with support from France and Russia, creating worries of a "Sunni/Arab Bomb" (take your pick) and a "Turkish Bomb."[28] The Saudis reportedly have an option to buy up to twenty nuclear bombs from the Pakistanis.[29] Iran now finds itself in a Middle East where a number of other Muslim states—all of whom are generally hostile to Tehran—may soon possess the bomb. The window of opportunity that Iran possessed as the only Muslim state able to oppose a nuclear-armed Israel on roughly equal terms is likely to close soon. Some estimates are that Egypt and Turkey will be capable of having the bomb by 2018, at the latest, and the Saudis much sooner if they exercise the Pakistan Option. These states—Saudi Arabia and Turkey in particular—are generally hostile to Tehran, thanks to its expansionist behavior.

As Arab states and the Turks push to develop their bombs, many Iranians are beginning to ask why billions of dollars were spent on developing a nuclear weapons capability that has not made Iran more secure. The questions are even more pointed when one considers the increasing hardships the Iranian people have had to endure with the recent decline in oil prices. While the mullahs pursued their nuclear option, they failed to maintain and upgrade their oil- and gas-production infrastructure. While oil prices were over $130 per barrel, the country enjoyed a financial windfall even as its oil production remained stagnant. Now as

28. The Middle Eastern nuclear arms race began late in the last decade, driven by the "Persian Bomb" and high oil prices. See Henry Sokolski, "Atomic Non-Allies," *Asian Wall Street Journal,* January 18, 2008, p. 13; Hassan M. Fattah, "Arab Nations Plan to Start Joint Nuclear Energy Program," *New York Times,* December 11, 2006, p. A10; and "Nuclear Succession," *Economist,* September 30, 2006, p. 57.

29. As one wag recently put it, "The Saudis, being the Saudis, are not going to go to the trouble of developing their own nuclear weapons. That's hard work. Their approach is to use the Pakistanis like a Domino's Pizza: ring 'em up and order a bunch." See William Davies, "Nuclear 'Take-Out': The Saudi Option?" *New York Times,* February 21, 2012, p. A1.

more mature fields become less productive, as Saudi production increases, and as global energy conservation and the maturation of the search for oil substitutes is beginning to bear fruit, Iran's sluggish efforts to develop its energy resources—its enormous natural gas fields in particular—and its neglect of its infrastructure are exacting a toll. Oil and gas revenues have declined significantly from where they were only a few years ago, dropping by over a third, according to some estimates.[30]

All this could not have come at a more inauspicious time, given the "demographic bulge" of young Iranians entering the job market, trying to begin careers and start families. Over a quarter of Iran's population is under the age of twenty-one. This wave of young Iranians is victim to the "disease" of rising expectations. Raised during a period when the country was in the ascendant, they looked forward to an adulthood in which they enjoyed the fruits of Iran's growing stature and influence in the Middle East and its oil-induced economic boomlet. Recent events have disillusioned many Iranian youths. Their unusually large numbers have made the problem even more difficult for the mullahs, compounding the effect of the country's economic slowdown.[31] Unemployment in Iran, which hovered at around 10 percent a decade ago, nearly doubled between 2011 and late 2012. Iran's underemployment rate is quite possibly twice that figure. The percentage of Iranians living below the poverty line, nearly 20 percent a decade ago, now exceeds 25 percent, as government subsidies dry up along with oil revenues. Public disturbances in Iran directed toward the government have increased precipitously over the past three years. The mass demonstration earlier this year in Tehran drew a crowd estimated at nearly half a million. Even more important, for the first time the mullahs used large-scale force to break up the protest. Reports indicate that eleven of the protesters were killed and scores arrested.[32]

The Iranian people's dissatisfaction is mirrored by the growing

30. See Mohammed Falah, "Iran's Growing Economic Crisis," *Washington Post,* November 20, 2013, p. A1.
31. Interestingly, Iran has succeeded in reducing its population growth. By the middle of the last decade the country's fertility rate stood at 1.8 children per woman—below the 2.1 rate needed to sustain the population at its current level. But that is of little comfort to the Supreme Leader in Tehran.
32. Paul Dimsdale, "Mullahs Under Siege," *Wall Street Journal,* March 25, 2014, p. A1.

unrest in Lebanon and in the Palestinian territories. In Lebanon, Hezbollah's current dominant position came about in large part because it was able to provide order and—perhaps even more important—social services at a time when the regime in Beirut failed to do either. The Second Lebanon War, in which Hezbollah fought the IDF to a standstill, cemented the organization's role in the mind of many Lebanese as the legitimate protector of their state.[33] Hamas's rise was very much along the same path, displacing the PLO/Palestinian Authority through its ability to provide a modicum of social services where there were none (thanks to both Iranian support of Hamas and the PA's pervasive corruption).

The problem, for both Hezbollah and Hamas, is that their assumption of a de facto leadership role in their countries has raised expectations that are proving increasingly difficult to meet. Both groups are increasingly plagued by corruption, which has undermined their ability to meet their people's expectations for social services and a better quality of life. The security wall constructed by the Israelis has not only better protected them from Palestinian acts of terror, it has also slowly but surely loosened the links between the Palestinian and the Israeli economies, much to the Palestinians' disadvantage. While until recently the Israeli economy proved remarkably resilient in the face of sporadic Arab attacks, the same cannot be said for the Palestinians' economy. In Gaza and the West Bank, unemployment and underemployment hover at over a third of the workforce. Once significant numbers of Palestinians enjoyed relative prosperity working in Israel, but those days are long gone. Israeli demand for Palestinian workers dried up following the Second Intifada, as some displayed a worrisome habit of blowing themselves up. To be sure, their numbers were relatively few, but it was the many that suffered. And Iran is not the only country in the region suffering from an unhelpful demographic "youth bulge," which has yielded a harvest of undereducated, urbanized, underemployed males who have little hope for a better life. Over 40 percent of the Palestinian population is under the age of twenty-one. And what do they hear and see from

33. Lebanon has become overwhelmingly Muslim in orientation, with the Shi'a Muslims dominating.

their leaders and the media? That Israel and the United States are the principal source of their hardships.

The decline in Iranian subsidies to Hamas and Hezbollah has served only to worsen matters. The Palestinian leadership, despite its recovery of Gaza and most of the West Bank, cannot help but note the disparity between their land and that of the Israelis. While the Israelis have been able to make even parts of the Negev desert bloom, Hamas and Fatah have nothing comparable to show for their efforts.[34] Nor does Hezbollah, which is also beset by growing internal opposition from its minority Christian and Sunni Muslim communities.[35] Although it lays no claims to Israeli lands, Hezbollah has found common cause with Hamas in asserting that Israel is at the core of the region's problems. The focus on Israel also serves as a useful way to deflect the Palestinian and Lebanese peoples' attention away from their own leaders' shortcomings.

THE GROWING CRISIS

INITIALLY, HAMAS AND HEZBOLLAH LIMITED THEIR VITRIOL AGAINST Israel to verbal assaults. But there is little doubt that the campaign was well coordinated among Beirut, Damascus, Ramallah,[36] and Tehran. The region's broadcast media, principally al-Jazeera and al-Arabiya, picked up the drumbeat beginning in January 2013. The initial results were exactly what the Anti-Zionist Front (as these states are often referred to) had hoped for. Demonstrations against the regimes in Beirut, Ramallah, and Tehran were supplanted—albeit temporarily—by protests against Israel's purported depredations. Still, the level of military activity between these states and Israel remained simmering at the relatively low level it had assumed following the Second Lebanon War. There was the

---

34. The tendency of the Palestinians to foul even their own nest was perhaps best on display shortly after the 2006 war between Israel and Hezbollah, when Fatah and Hamas destroyed each other's universities. See Zev Chafets, "Israel's Home Run," *New York Post,* February 28, 2007.

35. The Saudis are reputed to be funding the Sunni opposition groups in Lebanon and perhaps the Christian opposition as well. See Vanessa Sczerbick, "Saudis Support Anti-Hezbollah Efforts," *Washington Post,* December 3, 2013, p. A1.

36. Ramallah is the location of the Palestinian Authority's governing body, which has been effectively displaced by Hamas. Its intention is to relocate eventually to Jerusalem.

sporadic firing of a rocket or two into Israeli territory, followed by the Israeli retaliatory strike on a minor target in the offending area. The occasional suicide bomber slipped through Israeli security, but there was nothing like the rash of attacks that occurred back in the early 2000s. Privately, senior Israeli officials saw the verbal attacks for what they were: a traditional attempt by weak and unpopular Arab governments to deflect criticism of their failure at home toward an external scapegoat.[37] Now the chorus included the Iranians as well.

The argument advanced by Iran's mullahs is certainly familiar to longtime observers of the Middle East: Israel is aiding and abetting U.S. efforts to depress the global energy market as a means of weakening key Muslim states in the region—especially those like Iran that have "stood up to the Great Satan's imperial interests"[38]—and expanding U.S. influence into the region through subversion following the fitful stabilization of Iraq. Yet the people's attention could not easily be deflected from their personal hardships. After several months the protests against Hamas, Hezbollah, and the Iranian mullahs resumed. But the protests against Israel and the United States continued.

As U.S. presence in the region has been very much reduced, its forces present less of a target for Muslim wrath than they once did. This makes Israel the target of choice, not only because of its proximity to Muslim-dominated states but also because of a widespread belief that "the Americans will not come back for a generation."[39]

Events took a distinct turn for the worse last summer. The seventh anniversary of Hezbollah's "victory" over Israel in August 2006 was marked by parades in Lebanon and on the West Bank. Hezbollah's

---

37. As former Israeli prime minister Benjamin Netanyahu remarked, "We Israelis have seen this all before. It is the time-honored practice of despots looking for bogeymen abroad to mask their utter failure at home. Sadly, we have also seen this kind of popular response before: the willingness of downtrodden peoples to allow themselves to be exploited for malevolent purposes." Shimon Navrone, "Tehran Backs Nasrallah Attack on Israel," *Jerusalem Post*, February 14, 2013, p. 3.

38. Paul Smith, "Iran Cites U.S. Threat to Region," *Chicago Tribune*, December 20, 2013, p. 1.

39. This quote is attributed to Muqtada al-Sadr, an Iraqi Shiite who headed one of Iraq's most powerful militias—the Mahdi Army—until his assassination, probably by Iranian Quds Force elements, on August 24, 2011.

longtime leader, Hassan Nasrallah, repeated his oft-stated position toward Israel in declaring:

> I am against any accommodation with Israel, and do not accept the presence of a state that is called "Israel." Its existence is a vile construction of the Zionists and their American patrons. It is an affront to all peoples in the region, and to all civilized people around the globe. My only interest with regard to Israel is in terminating the existence of the Israeli state.[40]

THE 28 MORDAD

ON AUGUST 19 (KNOWN AS 28 MORDAD IN IRAN), IRAN'S SUPREME Leader, Ayatollah Seyyed Ali Hossayni Khamenei, issued a statement marking the sixtieth anniversary of the Anglo-American-inspired coup that removed the Iranian nationalist Dr. Mohammed Mossadeqh from power and placed the shah at the head of Iran's government.[41] In his statement Khamenei denounced both the United States and Israel as the principal agents of instability in the Middle East and the Persian Gulf regions. The message included Khamenei's threat to block oil shipments from the Persian Gulf if the Israelis and Americans tried to "undermine" regional security. Iran's policy, he declared, has long been that "the Gulf is either safe for everyone, or it is safe for no one."[42]

40. This statement is similar to many Nasrallah has made over the past fifteen years. For example, in 2000 he declared, "I am against any reconciliation with Israel. I do not even recognize the presence of a state that is called 'Israel.' I consider its presence both unjust and unlawful. That is why if Lebanon concludes a peace agreement with Israel and brings that accord to the Parliament our deputies will reject it; Hezbollah refuses any conciliation with Israel in principle." "Sayyed Hassan Nasrallah Q&A: What Hezbollah Will Do," *Washington Post,* February 20, 2000.
41. Funded with money from the U.S. CIA and the British MI6, pro-monarchy forces gained the upper hand against Mossadeqh on August 19, 1953 (28 Mordad). Pro-Shah tank regiments stormed the capital and fired at the prime minister's residence. Mossadeqh surrendered the next day. Dr. Donald L. Wilbur, "Overthrow of Premier Mossadeq of Iran: November 1952–August 1953," Clandestine Service History, Central Intelligence Agency, March 1954, at http://web.payk.net/politics/cia-docs/published/one-main/main.html, accessed on September 17, 2008.
42. Paul Dimsdale, "Iran Threatens West Access to Gulf Oil," *Wall Street Journal,* August 20, 2013, p. A1.

But words could only go so far to salve the frustrations of the increasingly angry Palestinians and Lebanese. In September militia groups in southern Lebanon, in Gaza, and on the West Bank stepped up their attacks on Israel. While the United States asserted that this initial surge in violence was engineered by the leadership of Hezbollah and Hamas (and that its roots extended all the way back to Tehran), no compelling evidence has yet been presented to sustain this allegation. The attacks—employing suicide bombers, car bombs, and rockets—represented a significant escalation in the level of violence.

As in the past, the Israeli leadership initially fell back on tit-for-tat reprisal strikes. By early October, however, it was clear the violence had reached a new level, and that reprisal strikes were not going to cause it to abate. At that time word began circulating in the open press that Hezbollah and Hamas possessed several hundred Russian-made precision-guided rockets that had originally been sold to Iran.[43] This threatened to bring about a significant change in the military balance. Whereas the rockets used by Hezbollah in the Second Lebanon War had had significant range, they could not be effectively aimed against specific targets. Guided weapons, by definition, could be, and precision-guided weapons could be aimed at a given target with high confidence of hitting the target.

Since the Second Lebanon War, Hezbollah, with Iranian backing, has dramatically increased its inventory of rockets and can now threaten most of Israel. Iran provided Hezbollah rockets with a range of about 185 miles, enabling it to strike any major city in Israel and to hit Dimona, the location of Israel's nuclear reactor.[44] Estimates are that Hezbollah has more than 10,000 long-range rockets and in excess of 40,000 short-range rockets in southern Lebanon. Hezbollah is also reported to have a few hundred unmanned aerial vehicles and a similar number of antiship cruise missiles. These may be under control of Quds Force troops embedded with Hezbollah. It is believed that Hamas has

43. Paul Dimsdale, "Israeli Intelligence: Hezbollah Armed with 'Smart Rockets,'" *Wall Street Journal,* December 4, 2013, p. A1.
44. Matti Friedman, "Israel: Hezbollah Increases Rocket Range," March 27, 2008, at http://apnews.myway.com/article/20080327/D8VLNEFO0.html, accessed on June 29, 2008.

6,000 to 8,000 short-range rockets positioned in Gaza and on the West Bank. The rearming of Hezbollah is in violation of UN Security Council Resolution 1701 that ended the Second Lebanon War. Attempts by Israel to have the resolution enforced have been blocked at the Security Council by China and Russia.

THE SINKING OF THE MOSHE DAYAN

ON DECEMBER 11, 2013, THE ISRAELI LITTORAL COMBAT SHIP *Moshe Dayan* struck several advanced-design antiship mines off Israel's Mediterranean coast. The ship quickly sank, with twenty-seven sailors perishing. The mines were apparently emplaced by Iranian-trained Hezbollah saboteurs, although neither party has yet owned up to it.[45] The Iranian president, Mohammed Rushtani, asserted that the mines had been put in place by the United States and Israel as a pretext for increasing the latter's military pressure on Lebanon and the Palestinians.[46] This interpretation was quickly picked up by the Arab media. During this speech Rushtani went on to declare, "Two can play at this game. Let me make it plain to the Zionists and their backer, the Great Satan, that the Islamic Republic of Iran can block the Strait of Hormuz whensoever it chooses."[47]

The author, like a number of other political observers, believes Rushtani's threat was aimed principally not at protecting the Lebanese from Israeli retaliation, but at warning the Sunni Gulf oil states, the Europeans, and the Americans not to get involved in the growing conflict. Simply put, Rushtani's threat was to cut off a significant portion of the Arabian peninsula's Sunni Arab oil production outlet (and Iran's as well, it should be noted), and along with it a significant portion of the world's oil supplies. In the short term Tehran got what it wanted: fears over

45. The Hezbollah frogmen who planted the mines are rumored to have been led by Quds Force commandos. Jonathan Larrabee, "Israel Alleges Iranian Attack Connection," *Chicago Tribune*, December 29, 2013, p. 1.
46. William Davies, "Tehran Asserts U.S.-Israeli 'Conspiracy,' " *New York Times*, December 14, 2013, p. A1.
47. President Mohammed Rushtani, speech to the Conference on Greater Muslim Affairs, Tehran, December 20, 2013, at www.IslamicRepublicIran.com, accessed on April 27, 2014.

a possible disruption saw the spot market for oil prices spike, providing Iran with a much-needed financial transfusion. Moreover, unlike the Iran-Iraq War of the 1980s, when commercial vessels were reflagged as American ships and protected by the U.S. fleet, this time the Americans did not offer to take steps to ensure the safe passage of Gulf shipping.

"GREATER THAN ENTEBBE"

ON JANUARY 22, 2014, HEZBOLLAH ELEMENTS EMPLOYING A STRING of IEDs ambushed an Israeli military convoy traveling in northern Israel near the border with Lebanon. Eleven Israeli soldiers were killed and over twenty injured. Following the attack Raffi Leteim, Israel's prime minister, and his coalition came under severe pressure to do more than order a reprisal air strike. Heeding the demands from within his own party and the nation at large, Leteim authorized an undercover raid into Lebanon. On February 2 Israeli intelligence agents of the famed Mossad[48] and Israeli Special Forces elements executed their raid. Through a combination of luck, skill, and superior intelligence, the Israelis abducted and spirited away via helicopter Hezbollah's number-two man, Mohammad Rida Zahidi. In the process, the Israelis killed over two dozen members of Hezbollah and, as it turns out, several members of the Quds Force. The Israelis also captured two Quds Force officers who were present at the time.

The *Jerusalem Post*'s headlines cheered, "Senior Hezbollah Henchman Captured" and "Greater than Entebbe."[49] The broadcast media

48. The full name is Ha-Mossad le-Modiin ule-Tafkidim Meyuhadim, or "The Institute for Intelligence and Special Tasks" (סירחוים סירייקפהדו ויעיומך רסומה). *Mossad* in Hebrew means "institute" or "institution."
49. On June 27, 1976, two German nationals and two Palestinians boarded Air France Flight 139, en route from Tel Aviv to Paris, during a stopover in Athens and hijacked it first to Benghazi, Libya, then on to Entebbe Airport in Uganda. There the hijackers linked up with another group of radicals, whereupon they divided up the passengers into Jews and non-Jews and released the non-Jews. On the night of July 3, some 150 Israeli commandos aboard three C-130 cargo aircraft landed and stormed the airport terminal at Entebbe, where over a hundred hostages were kept, killing all eight hijackers and numerous Ugandan soldiers. The Israeli commander, Lieutenant Colonel Yonatan Netanyahu, and three hostages were killed during the operation, which lasted some forty-five minutes from landing to takeoff. (An elderly Jewish woman who had been hospitalized and was

trumpeted the feat as the Mossad's greatest since its capture of Adolf Eichmann[50] over half a century ago. But the Israeli action set off a wave of protests in the Arab and Muslim worlds and beyond. The bubbling crisis seemed on the cusp of boiling over as it entered a new and more dangerous phase.

Documents captured in the raid revealed that the Iranians and their clients in Syria, Lebanon, and Palestine are pursuing a strategy of persistently wearing away at Israel while sustaining the international media's support. The papers argue that victory can be achieved if the Anti-Zionist Front can keep the United States from intervening. The formula for defeating Israel, the documents assert, was discovered in the Second Lebanon War and in America's persistent inability to wage irregular warfare effectively. Now all that remains is to apply these principles under conditions where the "Great Satan" cannot "intervene decisively" as it did in 1967 and 1973.[51] The documents reveal a widespread belief that "the Americans do not have the stomach to confront the forces of Islam."[52] Indeed, given the United States' desire to avoid stirring up anti-American opposition in Iraq (which is not yet out of the political woods with regard to the tensions surrounding its principal factions), Washington is expected to assume a low posture and let Israel fend for itself.

---

not present during the rescue was later murdered.) The jets refueled at Nairobi, Kenya, and returned to a tumultuous welcome the following morning in Israel. "The Rescue: We Do the Impossible," *Time,* July 12, 1976, at
http://www.time.com/time/magazine/article/0,9171,914272,00.html, accessed on September 17, 2008; Terence Smith, "Hostages Freed as Israelis Raid Uganda Airport," *New York Times,* July 4, 1976, p. A1; and David E. Kaplan, "An Historic Hostage-Taking Revisited," Jerusalem Post Online Edition, August 3, 2006, at
http://www.jpost.com/servlet/Satellite?cid=1154525798527&pagename=JPost%2FJP Article%2FPrinter, Accessed on September 17, 2008.
50. Eichmann was head of the Nazi Germany's Gestapo Jewish section from 1939 to 1945. He was chiefly responsible for the murder of millions of Jews during World War II. After the war he fled to South America, where he was captured by the Israeli secret service in 1960. He was tried and executed in Israel.
51. To assuage their wounded pride, many Arab states maintain that U.S. and British air strikes were part of the initial attacks during the 1967 Six-Day War. Michael Oren, *Six Days of War* (New York: Ballantine Books, 2002), p. 209.
52. Speech, "The Way Forward," Mohammed Rushtani, June 19, 2013, at http://www.parstimes.com/audiovideo, accessed on May 18, 2014.

When Israel refused to release its captives without receiving major concessions from Lebanon and Iran, Hezbollah stepped up its rocket attacks. The rate of the attacks ranged from a few a week, on average, to a few a day. Revealingly, none of the strikes appear to have involved the use of the precision-guided rockets that Hezbollah is believed to possess. The conflict, which has gone from a simmer to a low boil, was finally taken up by the UN Security Council in early February. There the debate centered on accusations that the real problem is Israel's refusal to return to the pre-1967 borders and its alleged "disproportionate" response to provocations by Hezbollah and Hamas. The Israelis responded that abandoning the remainder of the West Bank while its enemies offer no security guarantees and refuse to sign a formal peace treaty is unacceptable. On February 16 the Security Council voted on a resolution to condemn Israel's "excessive" and "nonproportional" retaliatory strikes. The resolution failed to carry, being blocked by a U.S. veto with Britain abstaining.

SLIDING TOWARD ARMAGEDDON

THE FAILURE TO WIN A UN RESOLUTION CONDEMNING ISRAEL, COMbined with the Israeli refusal to return its Lebanese and Iranian captives, put the Anti-Zionist Front in a quandary.[53] In retrospect, it seems clear that while Tehran and its allies would have preferred to continue with their strategy of slowly squeezing Israel, their people were now demanding more aggressive action. This feeling stemmed in no small part from the actions of the Arab media, which trumpeted the crisis on a daily basis, repeatedly emphasizing the "shame" that had befallen the Anti-Zionist Front compared to the honor won by the "heroes of the Thirty-Four-Day War" (i.e., the Second Lebanon War).[54] The leaders of the

---

53. Israel had offered to return the captives following the cessation of rocket attacks and a commitment from Hezbollah to allow U.S. forces to occupy and monitor the southern part of Lebanon. The offer was refused. Moreover, Washington also signaled that it would not send what would have likely amounted to over 25,000 troops to monitor the border areas. Sara Goldsmith, "Israeli PM Sets Conditions for Release," New York Times, February 18, 2014, p. A1; and Paul Dimsdale, "Joint Chiefs Caution Against Lebanon Deployment," Wall Street Journal, February 28, 2014, p. A1.

54. Years of Honor: Days of Shame, al-Jazeera, broadcast on March 30, 2014.

Anti-Zionist Front now found themselves following popular passion on this issue rather than setting the agenda. In early March several large government-orchestrated demonstrations in Iran, the West Bank, and Lebanon against the "Great Satan" (the United States) and the "Little Satan" (Israel) morphed into spontaneous calls for decisive action against Israel. The demonstrations were broadcast by al-Jazeera and al-Arabiya throughout the Arab world, triggering further demonstrations. For Iran's mullahs, some of whom remember well the mass protests that led to the shah's fall nearly forty years ago, the population's growing anger and frustration, against both Israel and the regime, no doubt had a chilling effect.

All this was but a prelude to the event that has sent the world hurtling along a path toward a major war. On the night of April 2–3 a salvo of rockets fired from the West Bank into Jerusalem struck and damaged the Al-Masjid El-Aqsa mosque ("المسجد الاق " or "The Farthest Mosque," sometimes referred to as the "Dome of the Rock").[55] U.S. reconnaissance satellites clearly showed that the rocket launches occurred at locations in the West Bank, but Arabs and Iranians claim that the attack was in fact a U.S.-Israeli strike designed to further humiliate Muslim peoples. Unfortunately, the "Arab street" and the Anti-Zionist Front states generally dismissed the U.S. intelligence reports confirming a West Bank launch as a repeat of the intelligence "fabrications" that preceded the Second Gulf War in 2003. In Lebanon, Nasrallah voiced the views of most people in the Middle East when he asked:

> The Israelis have the American Patriot missiles,[56] and yet they did
> not bother to intercept these attacking missiles. Why? The answer is

55. Ten years after the Prophet Muhammad received his first revelation, he made a miraculous night journey from Mecca to Jerusalem and to the Seven Heavens on a white flying horse. While in Jerusalem, Muhammad prayed at the rock, the site of which is now covered by the golden dome. There Muhammad was commanded to pray five times a day. Muhammad instructed Muslims to worship where they lived in Mecca, but also to travel to the "Farthest Mosque" in Jerusalem. Rizwi S. Faizer, Ph.D. McGill, "Rizwi's Bibliography for Medieval Islam," at http://us.geocities.com/rfaizer/reviews/ book9.html, accessed on September 17, 2008; and http://www.answers.com/topic/ dome-of-the-rock, accessed September 17, 2008.

56. The Patriot Advanced Capability-3 (PAC-3) is the only antiballistic missile (ABM) system to have successfully engaged and destroyed a tactical ballistic missile (TBM) in combat. However, it is not designed to deal with the kind of rocket attacks employed by Hezbollah.

simple: they wanted to destroy one of the holiest places in all of Islam as a way of deflecting attention from their failures. How can one do anything with such people other than destroy them?[57]

While no one has come forward to claim responsibility for the rocket attacks that night, the evidence clearly points to a Hamas militia group (or perhaps a Hezbollah element operating on the West Bank). It is unlikely that the rockets were aimed at the Dome of the Rock; rather, it appears to have been a case of poor targeting. The rocket attack may have been planned, but given the rocket's poor guidance capabilities, it is unlikely the Dome of the Rock was the target.

Israel has been exploring defenses against Hezbollah's rocket arsenal ever since the 2006 war. These rockets are difficult to intercept owing to their small size and uncertain flight path, very low trajectory, and very short time of flight. The Israeli Arrow ballistic missile defense system and the PAC-3 system, which Israel has deployed to protect itself from Iranian Scud-D and Shahab-3 missiles, are basically useless against the smaller rockets. Furthermore, the firing of interceptors that cost tens of thousands of dollars against rockets costing a few thousands of dollars is simply impractical. Israel has fielded the Iron Cap defense system designed to fill its Ultra-Short Range Missile Defense needs. The Iron Cap comprises truck-mounted launchers and several thousand interceptor missiles, which are cued from the IDF's early-warning radar network that stretches across northern Israel.[58] With its limited range, the Iron Cap is designed to protect high-value targets, such as key military and industrial facilities. In military parlance, the Iron Cap is a point-defense system, not an area-defense system. As with other interceptors, however, the problem is cost, with each interceptor missile priced at roughly $35,000.

The Iron Cap defenses have proved marginally successful. Estimates

57. Jonathan Larrabee, "Nasrallah Assails 'Zionist Atrocity,'" *Chicago Tribune*, April 22, 2014, p. 1.
58. "Israel Embarks on a Third Ballistic Defense System," *Defense Update*, at www.defense-update.com/newscast/0207/news/010207_iron_cap.htm, accessed on June 19, 2008.

are that roughly half the rockets fired at high-value Israeli targets are successfully intercepted, with many of the "leakers" (i.e., attacking rockets that breach the defenses) missing the target owing to poor accuracy.

The Israelis have long been exploring, with the Americans, deploying the Tactical High-Energy Laser (THEL) defense system.[59] They have conducted several successful tests, but the system is still too cumbersome for mobile operations. The Israelis are especially interested in a derivative of THEL, the Skyguard, a chemical laser-based air defense system designed to provide defense against short-range ballistic missiles, short- and long-range rockets, artillery shells, mortars, unmanned aerial vehicles, and cruise missiles. Each Skyguard system is capable of establishing a protective shield roughly ten kilometers in diameter over key point targets, such as an airport, military installation, or small city.[60] Crucially important, each shot of the Skyguard laser costs only about $2,000, more than many of the short-range rockets it

59. The Tactical High Energy Laser (THEL), which includes a mobile version (M-THEL), is a high-energy laser weapon system designed to provide an active defense capability in counter air missions. The program, initiated by a memorandum of agreement between the United States and Israel in 1996, has the objective of intercepting short- and medium-range threats, including aircraft, rockets, and missiles. A particularly attractive aspect of the THEL is its low cost-per-shot, roughly $3,000. This contrasts sharply with the cost of many other interceptors, such as the Rolling Airframe Missile ($400,000-plus). The THEL, employing a chemical-based laser, can fire up to sixty shots before having to replenish its chemical supply. Despite its "mobile" designation, the system, which also goes by the name of Nautilus, suffers from a lack of mobility, and some argue it is relatively ineffective against the kind of extended-range rockets employed by Hezbollah during the Second Lebanon War. In 2000–01 the THEL successfully intercepted twenty-eight *Katyusha* artillery rockets and five artillery shells. However, the project was discontinued. It was later revived under the name of Skyguard. The U.S. military also has been working on solid-state laser missile defense systems, for both aircraft and ground systems. See Defense Update, "(Mobile) Tactical High-Energy Laser Program," at http://www.defense-update.com/directory/THEL.htm, accessed on September 17, 2008. See also MSNBC News Services, "Laser Weapon Passes Biggest Test: Nautilus System Shoots Down Long-Range Missile," May 7, 2004, at http://www.msnbc.msn.com/id/4926840, accessed on September 17, 2008; "Tactical High-Energy Laser," accessed at http://en.wikipedia.org/wiki/Tactical_High_Energy_Laser, on September 17, 2008; and "M-THEL: Mobile Tactical High-Energy Laser," at http://www.israeli-weapons.com/weapons/missile_systems/systems/THEL.html, accessed on September 17, 2008.
60. Sharon Weinberger, "Second Life for Laser Defense?" August 7, 2007, at http://blog.wired.com/defense/2007/08/second-life-for.html, accessed on June 24, 2008.

is looking to intercept but far less than other interceptor alternatives. For the Israelis the cost factor is crucial. Former Israel Air Force (IAF) chief General (Ret.) David Ivory declared years ago that "eventually, lasers will be the solution against rockets."[61] But the solution, it seems, has not appeared quickly enough for Israel.

There have been rumors about rushing U.S. Skyguard prototypes to Israel. While Israel would like access to U.S. solid-state laser (SSL) missile defense systems, none are as yet ready for deployment.[62] Meanwhile, the U.S. Air Force's Airborne Laser (ABL) and Advanced Tactical Laser (ATL) programs, which involve mounting a megawatt-class chemical oxygen iodine laser (COIL) aboard a 747 aircraft and an AC-130 gunship, respectively, have experienced continued difficulties in their development and may not yet ready for deployment.[63] Ideally, these airborne platforms would loiter over enemy forces and intercept missiles as they were launched, in their boost phase. With a magazine of only a few

61. Alon Ben-David, "Barak Seeks to Revisit Skyguard, Steel Curtain," *Jane's Defence Week,* January 2, 2008, p. 16.
62. The Defense Department began a major effort to develop SSL systems late last decade when they demonstrated 100 kilowatt (kW) power levels as a result of progress made under the Joint High-Power Solid State Laser (JHPSSL) program. The 100 kW power level is sufficient to enable an SSL system to provide a range of force-protection, battlefield, and precision-strike missions. The Pentagon is also researching fiber lasers that promise to be even more powerful and reliable than the so-called "slab" SSLs. Jim Desmond, "Finally More Than an 'Interesting Toy'?" *New York Times,* April 26, 2012, pp. B1, B4–B6. The big advantage of the SSL over the chemical laser (such as the chemical oxygen iodine laser, or COIL, used on the troubled Airborne Laser) is that using chemical fuel to generate laser power both limits the number of shots that can be fired before the laser's magazine is exhausted, and requires a considerable supply of chemicals on hand for reload purposes. An SSL, on the other hand, requires only a sufficient electric power source (e.g., electric grid, batteries) to be able to fire.
63. The Airborne Laser (ABL) weapons system, designated YAL-1A, is a megawatt-class COIL designed to shoot down tactical ballistic missiles (TBMs) similar to the Scud missiles fired by Iraq in the First Gulf War, while in their boost phase (i.e., initial ascent). The ABL is mounted on a modified Boeing 747 aircraft. The Air Force currently has one ABL prototype. The ABL's method of intercept involves heating the attacking missile's skin, thereby weakening it and causing it to fail due to the flight stresses imposed on it. As their name indicates, directed-energy weapons focus energy in a particular direction through electromagnetic radiation (e.g., laser beams—the ABL is a directed-energy weapon) or by particles possessing mass (particle beam weapons). Interview, General Harry Davidson, CNN, April 28, 2014, at http://www.cnn.com/2008/DEFENSE.Israel-Iran/index.html, accessed on May 4, 2014. See also "Airborne Laser Backgrounder," at http://www.boeing.com/defense-space/military/abl/doc_src/ABL_overview.pdf, accessed on September 17, 2008.

dozen shots at best before it would have to return to base to reload, these systems may not be worth the effort of deployment, given that Hezbollah has thousands of rockets at its disposal. As retired Air Force chief of staff General Harry Davidson noted recently:

> We can't afford to spend several hundred thousand dollars on a missile to shoot down an enemy rocket that cost only a small fraction of that amount. That's where the laser interceptors come in. The cost-per-shot on these systems runs you only a few thousand dollars. That's something we can live with.[64]

One major problem with the laser defense system is the difficulty of maintaining the laser beam's coherency as it moves through the atmosphere, which induces a distorting effect. This can greatly limit any laser's effectiveness.[65] Consequently, the Israelis are contemplating a complex combination of forces to address the so-called G-RAMM threat.[66] As one Israeli military expert described it:

> Ideally, you would have aircraft loitering over suspected rocket and missile launch sites, along with strike aircraft. The moment you detected a launch, the strike aircraft would hit the launch site, destroying the launcher and killing the crew. If you have airborne laser interceptors, they may be able to destroy the rocket as it begins to ascend, but this would likely be useful against long-range missiles that are of high value. The American Airborne Laser is an expensive

64. General Harry Davidson, interview, CNN, April 28, 2014, at http://www.cnn.com/ 2008/DEFENSE.Israel-Iran/index.html, accessed on May 4, 2014.
65. The atmosphere comprises pockets of slightly varying temperatures arrayed in random fashion. This condition causes the beam's intensity to fluctuate. Atmospheric attenuation—the interaction of the laser beam with gases and particulate matter in the air— results in a reduction in the beam's power level. Finally, atmospheric turbulence causes the beam to lose coherence, so that its power fluctuates. Work is under way on technologies, to include adaptive optics, to attenuate these problems. "Laser Zaps Communications Bottleneck," *Science and Technology Review,* at www.llnl.gov/str/December02/Ruggiero .html, accessed on June 18, 2008.
66. G-RAMM is an abbreviation for "guided rockets, artillery, missiles, and mortars."

system that has only a few shots before it must return to base and re-load. You'd want to put that up against the ballistic missiles that might be carrying a nuclear warhead or chemical [munitions]. It would be good to have small ground units—commando teams—operating to detect enemy launch sites and communicate their location back to our loitering strike aircraft or long-range artillery.

That's the front-end piece of this network.

On the back end, you need interceptors to deal with the incoming rockets, artillery missiles and mortars that cannot be destroyed before they are launched or destroyed while they are in their boost phase. Here you need a combination of what the IDF is trying to put together on the fly: cheap interceptors like Iron Dome[67] and Skyguard, but also Steel Curtain[68] to deal with the short-range rockets, and Arrow, THAAD, and Patriot to deal with the longer-range systems. The problem with the laser systems like Skyguard, of course, is that they don't function as well in poor weather, while the problem with these other systems is that the IDF only has so many interceptors. They have to be concerned that Hezbollah will strike soon, and in large numbers before the IDF can get or make additional interceptors. In a sense, Hezbollah and Hamas have been doing the IDF a favor up till now by only attacking with small numbers [of rockets].[69]

67. The Iron Cap system is also referred to as Iron Dome.
68. Steel Curtain is a rocket defense system based on a proximity-kill interceptor designed to intercept rockets with a range of between 3 and 150 miles. Along with another interceptor, "David's Sling," which is designed to intercept missiles at distances between 24 and 150 miles, it has been slowed in development as emphasis has been shifted toward laser interceptors. This has much to do with cost. A Steel Curtain interceptor runs about $100,000, while a David's Sling "Stunner" interceptor costs roughly $300,000. "Israel Bets on David's Sling," Space Daily, at http://www.spacedaily.com/reports/Israel_Bets_On_David's_Sling_999.html, accessed on September 17, 2008; and Niel Keehan, "Israeli Missile Defense and Its Role in the Israeli-Palestinian Peace Process," Power and Interest News Report, at http://www.pinr.com/report.php?ac=view_report&report_id=718&language_id=1, accessed on September 17, 2008. The Israelis have also deployed the Iron Dome interceptor system, which is not effective against short-range rockets like the Qassam, used by Hezbollah and Hamas, even though at $100,000 each, the interceptors cost far more than the Qassams. Reuven Pedatzur, "Iron Dome System Found to Be Helpless Against Qassams," Haaretz.com, at http://www.haaretz.com/hasen/spages/956859.html, accessed on September 17, 2008.
69. General (Ret.) Yigal Ritzah, Fox News, April 22, 2014, at www.foxnews.com/story/0,3933,352785,00.html, accessed on July 2, 2014.

Within a week of the rocket attack on the Dome of the Rock, both Hamas and Hezbollah began firing rocket salvos in greater numbers, increasing the rate to a dozen or so a day. The Israeli Iron Cap batteries, which did in fact intercept several rockets on the night of the infamous attack, continued to perform up to expectations. Ironically, this served only to confirm what many Arab and Iranian citizens believe regarding Israel's "complicity" in the attacks.

Israel continued selective air strikes against suspected rocket launchers and against Hezbollah and Hamas leadership targets in Lebanon, and in the West Bank and Gaza. However, this failed to slow the rate of the rocket attacks. As one expert observed, "It's hard to suppress an enemy that has thousands of rockets from firing off a tiny fraction of his arsenal each day."[70]

At the same time Israeli maritime forces were also engaged in major mine-clearing operations along the approaches to its principal Mediterranean ports. Successful IED and suicide bomber attacks, while still few in number, were on the rise.

Most important, as we now know, in early May the IDF began running low on Iron Cap interceptor missiles.[71] For the Israelis, the hard truth is that the number of Iron Cap interceptor missiles is woefully inadequate to deal with the true threat level.

On May 15 the Israelis requested that the United States provide it with three Skyguard units and four Terminal High-Altitude Area Defense (THAAD) missile batteries.[72] Unfortunately, the U.S. military does not possess a substantial surplus of missile defense batteries or missiles, and the production line for them cannot be quickly geared up to produce large quantities. Washington agreed to provide Tel Aviv with one Skyguard and two THAAD units.[73] The Israelis apparently also requested seventy-two PAC-3 interceptor missiles, which are also in short supply.

70. Admiral (Ret.) Philip Stevenson, *CBS Evening News*, May 1, 2014, at www.cbsnews.com/sections/world/main202.shtml, accessed on May 8, 2014.
71. Joseph Breyer, "Israelis Short Interceptor Missiles," *Christian Science Monitor*, May 13, 2014, p. 1.
72. The THAAD system is designed to intercept short- and medium-range ballistic missiles, similar to the Scud missiles used by Iraq in the First Gulf War, by striking them with interceptor missiles.
73. Richard Boudreaux, "Pentagon Cupboard Bare, Israelis Told," *Los Angeles Times*, May 18, 2014, p.1.

With the exception of Skyguard, these missile defense systems are generally ineffective against Hezbollah's short-range rockets. However, both THAAD and the Patriot systems could prove useful in the event of Syrian or Iranian long-range ballistic missile attacks.

The Israeli government was also feeling the pressure of domestic public opinion. The Israeli people were weary of absorbing the blows of these rocket attacks, which their government seemed powerless to stop. This placed the Leteim government in a quandary. It recalled all too well the disaster of the Second Lebanon War, from which the Olmert government never recovered. The relative ineffectiveness of ongoing reprisal air strikes only reinforced this frustration. Oddly enough, both the Hamas and Hezbollah leadership were now asserting that their continuing economic stagnation was made worse due to Israeli military strikes against them. Although this should have provided encouragement to the Israelis, it did not. They saw the claims of Hezbollah and Hamas as attempts to win the propaganda war, and the continued rocket barrage as confirmation that military "half-measures" would not end the attacks.

For a few months the Israeli Navy's countermine operations enabled the country's economy to muddle along. Following the loss of the *Moshe Dayan*, Israeli littoral combat ships conducted minesweeping operations and escort operations for commercial shipping approaching Israeli ports. Owing to the maritime security campaign's success, private shipping lines were willing to enter Israeli waters. Until early June it appeared that any hope on the Anti-Zionist Front's part that it could bring Israel to the brink of economic collapse through a drizzle of rocket attacks and mine warfare alone was misplaced.

The situation changed dramatically on June 6, when Israel's major port facilities at Haifa, Hadera, and Ashdod were subjected to barrage attacks of over sixty rockets each, all precision-guided. Several commercial transport ships were hit, but fortunately no oil tankers were struck. While over half the rockets were intercepted, Israeli rapid-response air strikes failed to destroy the rocket launchers, which are suspected to be located in southern and central Lebanon. Just as worrisome, the Israeli Air Force, working with IDF Special Forces, has been unable to interdict the resupply of these rockets coming from Iran via Syria.

Following the rocket barrage, commercial shipping firms quickly reviewed the altered situation and decided to avoid Israeli waters until the "current crisis passes."[74] The situation only worsened when, on June 12, an Israeli littoral combat ship was hit and severely damaged by a Silkworm, a Chinese-built, Iranian-supplied antiship cruise missile fired from what appeared to be a commercial transport ship.[75] The ship was quickly determined to be operated by Hezbollah, and promptly sunk by Israeli Air Force fighters. Israeli intelligence reports indicate that, as in the 2006 war, the Silkworm firing units were manned by Iranian Revolutionary Guard agents, not by Hezbollah.[76] Immediately after the attack, those few commercial vessels that were willing to brave the contested waters began demanding healthy premiums over their normal shipping rates. At last, it appeared, Israel's enemies had struck a telling blow against its economy. In response, on June 17 the Israeli Navy moved to blockade the coast of Lebanon, Syria, and Gaza. The Israeli Air Force is rumored to be making preparations to disrupt or destroy the transportation and communications infrastructure of Syria, Lebanon, Gaza, and the West Bank.[77]

On June 8, following the initial attacks, the UN Security Council was called into session at the United States' request. U.S. ambassador Mary Lowe presented a compelling case on the need to respect international waters and the home waters of all nations. But with Israel running low on interceptor missiles and its port security a growing concern, the members of the Anti-Zionist Front (now widely referred to as the AZF, or "A-ziff") clearly felt they had the upper hand in the conflict, and

74. Paul Dimsdale, "Shipping Firms Avoiding Israeli Waters," *Wall Street Journal,* June 14, 2014, p. A3.
75. The Silkworm has a maximum range of sixty miles, a relatively advanced guidance system that can incorporate inertial midcourse correction, radar homing, and GPS (global positioning system). The attack recalled the 2006 conflict, when Hezbollah hit an Israeli corvette warship with a Silkworm.
76. Shiman Navrone, "Iranians Behind Silkworm Strike," *Jerusalem Post,* June 14, 2014, p. 1.
77. Sarah Jackson, "IAF Planning Major Air Campaign," *New York Times,* June 20, 2014, p. A1.

their key Security Council supporters—China and Russia—focused principally on AZF's demands that Israel unconditionally withdraw from all territories it occupied after the 1967 Six-Day War and pay reparations for the recent damage inflicted on Lebanon, Gaza, and the West Bank. Once again the path through the United Nations produced a diplomatic dead end.

As for the UN's 4,000-troop peacekeeping force in southern Lebanon, it began to withdraw on June 10.[78] Both sides' unwillingness to respect the agreement ending the Second Lebanon War, and the increasingly dangerous situation, put the peacekeepers' safety at risk. Consequently, the constituent states whose militaries comprised the force agreed on a pullout. The withdrawal was completed on July 6.

Faced with abandonment by the international community and a United States that was clearly reluctant to become directly involved in another open-ended conflict in the region, Tel Aviv seemingly stood alone. But its very isolation seemed to increase its resolve. Former Israeli prime minister Benjamin Netanyahu, newly named to a unity Israeli war cabinet, may have expressed it best in a speech in Washington. Paraphrasing Winston Churchill during Britain's darkest hours in World War II, he declared:

> Here is this Israel which so many count down and out, which the world has consigned to the task of quivering on the brink of surrender to the multitude of enemies arrayed against her. Let them know that we fear nothing and will stop at nothing to secure our survival and our freedom.[79]

78. Following the Second Lebanon War, a force of some 15,000 peacekeepers was dispatched to southern Lebanon. Their mission, under UN Resolution 1701, called for Hezbollah to be disarmed; full control of Lebanon to be exercised by the government of Lebanon; and no paramilitary forces permitted south of the Litani River. None of these objectives were accomplished. By 2012 the force had dwindled to less than half its original number. By 2014 it could barely count 4,000 troops.
79. Sara Goldsmith, "Netanyahu Strikes Defiant Note," *New York Times*, July 4, 2014, p. A1. The paraphrase can be found in Winston S. Churchill, *Their Finest Hour* (New York: Houghton Mifflin, 1949), p. 205.

On July 1 the IDF called up the first group of reservists. The Israeli economy, already strained, cannot long withstand the additional stress of a large segment of its labor pool abandoning their jobs as they respond to the call to the colors. Simply stated, Israel appears to be on the cusp of all-out war against Hamas, Hezbollah, Syria, and perhaps Iran.

If the recent press reports are true, the Israeli war cabinet has been meeting on a daily basis to discuss options for breaking the economic stronghold being imposed by its neighbors. Several plans seem to be at the forefront of these discussions. One plan, dubbed Seize and Hold, calls for the IDF to occupy Gaza, the West Bank, and all of Lebanon up to Beirut. This operation is designed to push most Arab rocket forces back beyond their effective range. The rationale behind this plan is that it would render Israel safe from rocket attack. But it would mean putting large IDF ground forces in densely populated Arab territory for what might be a protracted period of time. The Israeli sea blockade of Lebanon would, according to this plan, also reduce the threat from antiship mines and antiship cruise missiles like the Silkworm.

An alternative plan (again, assuming press reports are correct),[80] known as the Slow Squeeze, calls for a massive aerial bombardment of the transportation and communication infrastructures of Lebanon, Gaza/West Bank, and Syria, partly to inflict comparable economic damage on Israel's enemies and also to hopefully stem the war supplies reaching Hezbollah. The economic pressure would be further heightened by a maritime blockade of Gaza, Lebanon, and Syria. Critics argue that this would only likely redouble the determination of Israel's enemies to continue their rocket campaign.

A third option—what some are calling the Armageddon Option—involves Israel taking action against the source of its travails: Iran. It calls for Israeli missile attacks on Iran's principal ports, to stress that country's already fragile economy. This would bring the war home to

---

80. These options were drawn from sessions of the Israeli cabinet whose deliberations were leaked to the press. The most detailed account can be found in Shiman Navrone, "Cabinet Weighs Options," *Jerusalem Post,* July 4, 2014, pp. 1, 4–9.

Iran by striking directly at the source of aggression.[81] The Armageddon Option is aptly named. If Israel pursues this course of action, it will be the first direct attack by one nuclear power against another.

AN IRANIAN "GUARANTEE"?

AS NEWS OF THE ISRAELI MOBILIZATION IS REPORTED IN THE PRESS, both Iran and Syria threaten retaliation should Israel cross international borders in an "act of aggression." The threats hark back to those of Nasser, Saddam, and bin Laden and speak of turning Israel into a "sea of fire" and a "vast Zionist tomb."[82] Complicating matters, in what may be the final days of a weakened and battered peace in that troubled part of the world, Iran has threatened Israel with the use of nuclear weapons. President Mohammed Rushtani recently stated that "any escalation by Israel against the peace-loving Muslim states must take into account Iran's nuclear potential," or what some are now calling the "Persian nuclear umbrella." Estimates are that the Iranians may have a half dozen to a dozen weapons. Many experts doubt, however, that these weapons can be fitted atop Iran's ballistic missiles for launch against Israel.[83]

Rushanti's statement has led to speculation that the Iranians may have already prepositioned several nuclear weapons with their forward-deployed special forces units (the Quds) in Syria or perhaps even in Lebanon. Such a move would serve two purposes. First, it would preclude the Iranian nuclear capability from being disarmed by a preemptive Israeli strike.[84] Second, the weapons can be used to attack Israel or, if threatened with interception, be detonated on Lebanese or West Bank soil, thereby enabling Iran and its allies to assert that the weapon was Israeli and the Israelis used nuclear weapons first.

81. Paul Dimsdale, "The IDF's 'Armageddon Option,'" *Wall Street Journal,* July 5, 2014, p. A1.
82. Duane Williams, "Anti-Israeli Axis Threatens All-Out War," *Washington Times,* June 24, 2014, p. 1.
83. During an interview with the BBC following his speech, Rushtani was asked whether Iran's small nuclear arsenal could seriously threaten Israel's existence. He replied, "With four such weapons we can cleanse the land of these infidels." "An Interview with President Rushtani," at www.bbc.co.uk/, accessed on July 10, 2014.
84. Most experts believe disarming Iran's small nuclear stockpile is beyond the IDF's

Perhaps most worrisome is the June 29 speech given by Rushtani in which he alludes to the coming of the twelfth Imam.[85] Some have interpreted this to mean that the Iranians are willing to light the fire of a large-scale conflagration, one that would extend from the shores of the eastern Mediterranean to the Iran and involve the possible—and perhaps even likely—use of nuclear weapons.

THE VIEW FROM WASHINGTON

AS EVIDENCED BY HIS DISPATCHING OF SECRETARY OF STATE JANET Schmidt to the Middle East for several rounds of diplomacy beginning in February, President Redding has not remained inactive in the face of the growing crisis. In particular, Secretary Schmidt's trip to Tehran in April, the first by a senior U.S. public official since the shah's days, is the most visible indication that the administration is exploring every possible diplomatic solution. Unfortunately, the United States finds itself with little leverage, since it is reluctant either to abandon Israel to the designs of the Anti-Zionist Front, or to use military force on a decisive scale to tip the balance in the Israelis' favor.

The administration has been subjected to growing criticism, however,

---

capability. However, Iran must take into account the United States' ability to execute a disarming strike. While the United States has publicly ruled out a preventive attack against Iran's nuclear forces, such an option might be considered favorably if it seemed the only way to stop a nuclear war.

85. Speech, "A Call to Sacrifice," Mohammed Rushtani, June 29, 2014, http://www.parstimes.com/audiovideo, accessed on July 6, 2014. Imam Hujat al-Mahdi (or Muhammad ibn Hasan ibn Ali) is, according to Twelver Shi'as, the twelfth Imam and the Mahdi, a figure considered by both Sunnis and Shi'as to be the ultimate savior of mankind. While the historical existence of Muhammad is questioned, Twelver Shi'as believe that Muhammad went into occultation (hiding) to escape from his enemies, and that his life has been miraculously prolonged by Allah until the time is right for him to emerge as the Imam Mahdi (the Qa'im) and fulfill his mission. Ja'far, the brother of Hasan al-'Askari, Imam Hujat's father, refuted this whole story, claiming that his brother had had no children. Others assert that the Imam Qa'im has yet been born but would be born in the Last Days and, in accordance with God's command, bring justice and peace by establishing Islam throughout the world. Importantly, given the context of Rushtani's speech, the Mahdi's return is to be presaged by a period of great hardship for Muslim peoples. It may be the prospect of—or perhaps desire for—a general Middle East war that animates Rushtani's comments. Moojan Momen, "Shi'a Islam," at http://www.northill.demon.co.uk/relstud/shiislam.htm, accessed on September 17, 2008.

for not doing enough militarily to keep the lid on the Middle East cauldron. Two congressional hearings in May involved more than member grandstanding over the administration's "failure" to anticipate the need for additional interceptor missiles.[86] The hearings also found the Joint Chiefs of Staff elaborating (as much as security would permit in open session) on military options for defusing the crisis.

Senator David Dilwood (R-Va.) posed a series of questions as to how the U.S. military might protect threatened maritime trade in the Middle East.[87] Admiral Weston Phillips, the chief of naval operations, informed the Senate Armed Services Committee that this would involve deploying U.S. naval forces—primarily squadrons of littoral combat ships—to conduct minesweeping operations and escort commercial ships in the Gulf of Aqaba to the Israeli port of Elat, as well as along Israel's Mediterranean coast. These ships would be protected by four carrier strike groups, two each in the eastern Mediterranean and the Red Sea. American naval forces would also be needed to patrol the Persian Gulf as a sign of U.S. willingness to protect shipping in the Gulf, including Iranian shipping. The U.S. fleet would also need to defend itself in these coastal waters, not only against mines but also against antiship cruise missiles, which have proliferated in recent years, and against potential attacks by explosives-laden suicide speedboats using what the Navy refers to as "swarm" tactics. When questioned on the risk of U.S. forces incurring casualties, the admiral responded, "The risk is significant even if the Iranians are not inclined to challenge us. It is unclear whether they can control the actions of their clients."[88]

86. Congress has actually *reduced* the number of interceptor missiles to be procured from the Pentagon's budget in three of the last four years and also reduced funding for the THEL program.

87. House Armed Services Committee, Hearings on the Middle East Crisis, May 19–20, 2014, www.house.gov/hasc/hearing_information.shtml, accessed on June 11, 2014; and Senate Armed Services Committee, Hearing on the Middle East Conflict, May 27, 2014, http://armed-services.senate.gov/hearings2006.cfm, accessed on June 11, 2014.

88. Apparently the admiral was asked in closed session how the fleet would fare in the Gulf if the Iranians were actively hostile. He reportedly replied, "It depends on whether we get in the first blow or he does. Deploying in the narrow waters of the Persian Gulf limits our attack warning and our freedom to maneuver our ships. If we're not careful, it could be a Pearl Harbor." Vanessa Sczerbick, "Chiefs Fear 'Pearl Harbor' in Gulf," *Washington Post,* June 20, 2014, p. A1.

Admiral Phillips also declared that fleet ballistic missile defense forces could be deployed to protect Israeli and other ports from Iranian and Syrian ballistic missile attacks. The JCS chairman, General Anthony DiSilva, informed the committee that the military also had the option of deploying U.S. Army land-based PAC-3 and its new THAAD missile units in Israel for such purposes. There is speculation that the military might also deploy the Air Force's ABL along with several of the military's new Skyguard units.[89] However, the problem of numbers remains: PAC-3 and THAAD missile defense systems are not effective against most of Hezbollah's rocket forces. The Skyguard units, which may prove effective, are untested in combat, and there are only a handful of firing units available in the entire U.S. military. In short, Hezbollah and Hamas have far greater numbers of rockets than the U.S. military has interceptor missiles (or chemical laser rounds) with which to engage and defeat a concerted salvo attack. Making matters worse still, the U.S. defense industrial base has a very limited capacity to surge its production of these interceptors, be they the traditional missile-type interceptors or the laser-based defenses.[90] As noted earlier, the more advanced U.S. defense systems, those based on solid-state laser technology, have not gone far beyond the prototype stage.

Clearly the most sensitive issue pertains to the possible use of nuclear weapons by either side or perhaps both. When asked his opinion on U.S. options in the event a war were to "go nuclear," General DiSilva responded:

> We are capable of intercepting a nuclear-armed missile with one of our missile defense systems, assuming they are deployed to the region, are in a position to affect an intercept, and are directed by the

89. Deploying the ABL, which is still in development, has some precedent. In the First Gulf War, for example, the U.S. Air Force deployed the E-8 Joint Surveillance Target Attack Radar System (Joint STARS) battle-management aircraft, which was still in development at the time. The aircraft performed well.

90. Former Air Force chief of staff General Scott Tuesday expressed this cost dilemma best when he said, "It is going to take time to ramp up production of these interceptors. Meanwhile, Israel's enemies have literally tens of thousands of these rockets in their possession." *Face the Nation*, CBS, June 28, 2014, transcript at www.cbsnews.com/stories/2014/06/28/ftn/main2491338.shtml, accessed on July 3, 2014.

national command authority [i.e., the president] to do so. The Israelis have a highly capable air defense system to protect them against nuclear attack by an aircraft carrying a nuclear weapon. Still, neither they nor we can guarantee an intercept of either a missile or an aircraft armed with a nuclear weapon. We have little capability to detect an attempt by the Iranians to employ nuclear weapons via unconventional delivery means [e.g., covert prepositioning of the weapons]. While our ability to detect radiological materials at a distance is classified, I can say that this capability is not one that extends over hundreds of miles. Nor can it be employed effectively from remote or stand-off distances. Finally, in the event of nuclear use, we are prepared to engage in humanitarian relief operations. However, the scale on which these operations would need to be conducted may greatly exceed our capability. Furthermore, it might be exceedingly difficult, and dangerous, to conduct these operations if the war were still being fought, especially if one or both belligerents remained armed with nuclear weapons.[91]

When asked about the possibility of a disarming strike against Iran's nuclear forces, the general stated:

History has demonstrated the difficulty of gathering intelligence that can permit a military operation to disarm a country of its nuclear capabilities. In hindsight, it is clear that our understanding of the Soviet nuclear forces in Cuba during the 1962 missile crisis was incomplete. In 1991 we found we had greatly underestimated the Iraqi nuclear program under Saddam Hussein. In 2003 the opposite proved out: we greatly overestimated his WMD program. The North Koreans surprised us on several occasions with respect to how far along they were in their nuclear program. The Iranians have gone to

91. House Armed Services Committee, Hearings on the Middle East Crisis, May 19–20, 2014, at www.house.gov/hasc/hearing_information.shtml, accessed on June 11, 2014; and Senate Armed Services Committee, Hearing on the Middle East Conflict, May 27, 2014, http://armed-services.senate.gov/hearings2006.cfm, accessed on June 11, 2014.

great lengths to deceive the international community on the status of their nuclear program. They have taken strong measures to preclude a preemptive strike from succeeding; for example, by dispersing their program and placing key facilities deep underground. We were clearly surprised by their nuclear test. So I would say that any operation to take out the Iranian nuclear capability would not necessarily be conducted with high confidence of success.[92]

THE LAST HOURS OF PEACE?

HAVING FAILED TO DEFUSE THE CRISIS THROUGH THE UNITED NAtions or through Secretary Schmidt's "shuttle diplomacy," including her unprecedented trips to Tehran, the Redding administration is left with very few options for preserving the peace, especially since AZF seems intent on war. Nor, as the recent congressional hearings on the crisis have revealed, is the United States in a particularly strong position militarily, should a general war engulf the region. At present, it remains unclear whether the president will request that Congress authorize the deployment of U.S. forces to the region, or in what capacity. Clearly if American ground and air forces are based in Israel, the United States risks being drawn directly into the conflict. While Iran may be reluctant to take on U.S. naval forces escorting ships in the Persian Gulf, the fact remains that these ships would be highly vulnerable to a range of attacks, including from mines, antiship cruise missiles, strike aircraft, and suicide boats. As one military expert noted, "It'd be like Millennium Challenge all over again."[93]

92. House Armed Services Committee, Hearings on the Middle East Crisis, May 19–20, 2014, at www.house.gov/hasc/hearing_information.shtml, accessed on June 11, 2014; and Senate Armed Services Committee, Hearing on the Middle East Conflict, May 27, 2014, http://armed-services.senate.gov/hearings2006.cfm, accessed on June 11, 2014.
93. Admiral (Ret.) Philip Stevenson, *CBS Evening News,* July 8, 2014, at www.cbsnews .com/sections/world/main202.shtml, accessed on July 11, 2014. Millennium Challenge was a joint U.S. military field exercise conducted in 2002. During the exercise, the Red (enemy) side employed antiship cruise missiles, strike aircraft, and suicide boats, among other forces, in a surprise attack that severely damaged most of the U.S. fleet operating in the constricted waters of the Persian Gulf.

If the president decides to deploy missile defense systems to the region to reduce the prospect of a nuclear missile attack, the Iranians will almost certainly view it as an effort to compromise their nuclear capability. Under these conditions, the Iranians have made it clear that they will, without hesitation, strike U.S. interests around the globe. Whether Iran has the capability to do this is unclear. Nevertheless, the threat is there. As one former Iranian diplomat declared,

> Iran's supporters are widespread—they're in Iraq, they're in Afghanistan, they're everywhere. And you know, the American soldiers in the Middle East are hostages of Iran, in the situation where war is imposed upon it. They're literally in the hands of the Iranians. The Iranians can target them wherever, and Patriot missiles aren't going to defend them and neither is anything else. Iran would suffer, but America would suffer more.[94]

As for the Sunni Arab Frontline States—Egypt, Jordan, Kuwait, and Saudi Arabia—they clearly have no interest in seeing Iranian (or Shi'a) influence expand in the region. The Kuwaitis, Saudis, and other Arab states along the Persian Gulf also have an interest in keeping the flow of oil coursing through the Gulf. But they also fear the Iranians, who have been building up their military forces for well over a decade. Not only are the Iranians a threat to maritime traffic in the area, but their missiles can be used to target oil- and natural-gas-production and distribution facilities all along the Arab side of the Persian Gulf. Consequently, the Sunni Frontline States have remained on the sidelines and are likely to remain there, especially given their lack of effective missile defenses. If war comes, they hope to avoid it and would be happy to see it produce a disaster for both the Israelis and the Iranian coalition, thereby strengthening their position in the region. What we do know is that Washington's efforts to bring these states

94. Najaf Ali Mirzai, quoted in Anthony Shadid, "With Iran Ascendant, U.S. Is Seen at Fault," *Washington Post,* January 30, 2007, p. A1.

to support its diplomatic initiatives to maintain the peace have gone un-requited.

President Redding has been informed by the Pentagon that even more difficult decisions may soon confront him. One involves reinforcing U.S. troops in Iraq should the Iranians move to destabilize the regime in Baghdad. Toward this end, the Iranians could activate Shi'a militias and sleeper terrorist cells supported by Quds advisers to target U.S. troops, including the possible use of chemical and biological weapons. Depending upon how well the Iraqi Army reacts to the Iranian proxy offensive, large numbers of U.S. reinforcements might have to be sent to Iraq. However, it is not likely they could be sent quickly, since routing them through the Persian Gulf might provide the perfect opportunity for an Iranian maritime ambush. Nor is it clear the Turks would allow U.S. troops to transit their country. Even if the Turks give the okay, it will likely take considerable time to deploy sizable reinforcements. In short, for at least the next three or four months, the American troops in Iraq will be on their own.

The president is also reminded that he may face the difficult choice of allocating scarce U.S. G-RAMM defense systems, like Skyguard, Patriot, and THAAD, as well as maritime defense systems like the Aegis,[95] between U.S. forces in Iraq, and requests by the Israelis and Arab Gulf states for protection.

Where does this leave the United States? Diplomatically, it is running out of time. Militarily, its options seem remarkably limited, given that its armed forces are considered to be far and away the world's finest and most technically advanced. To be sure, the U.S. military is, at this point, the only armed force capable of exerting a significant, and perhaps decisive, influence on the outcome of this crisis or the war that may follow. The problem has to do with inadequate numbers of key military capabilities and a dearth of allies who are both willing and capable of contributing.

95. The Aegis ballistic missile defense system is capable of providing defense against ballistic missiles after their post-boost phase. The system would be of use against longer-range ballistic missiles and thus of limited use against most of the Hezbollah G-RAMM inventory.

In the meantime, the Middle East slides toward a war that, in retrospect, few heads of government seem to want, none seem capable of avoiding, and all will likely come to regret. History may not repeat itself, but the echoes of 1914 can increasingly be heard, exactly one hundred years after they led the world into the abyss of war.

5

CHINA'S "ASSASSIN'S MACE"

All war is based on deception.

Sun Tzu, *The Art of War*

THE LAST DAYS OF PEACE?

AS THESE WORDS ARE BEING WRITTEN, WHAT EXPERTS ARE CALLING the greatest aggregation of naval power the world has ever seen is assembling in a long arc several hundred miles off the maritime approaches to China. The leaders of the United States and Japan, the two naval powers whose fleets fought each other in the world's last great naval battles over seventy years ago, are now allies in what many fear may be the opening gambits in a new world war. The warships now arrayed against China are preparing to conduct what Washington and Tokyo assert is a "counterquarantine" of Chinese ports, in retribution for the People's Liberation Army's blockade of Taiwan. The term *quarantine,* an artifact of the Cuban Missile Crisis, is a mere euphemism. In reality, it is simply a counterblockade. But as the diplomats will tell you, a blockade is an act of war. In a last-ditch attempt to avoid the first open conflict between great powers in over half a century, the term *blockade* is being shunned, even by the world's media.

Similarly, the Chinese government is calling its blockade of Taiwan "coastal trade enforcement" operations. Beijing's view is that the military power it has arrayed to choke off the island's maritime links to the outside world is really nothing more than a sovereign power's right—duty, really—to exercise control over the seaborne traffic entering the territorial waters of its "wayward province."

In the span of several weeks what seemed to be the latest in a series of Chinese internal crises has now put the world's two greatest military powers on the cusp of a war that neither seems to want but that neither seems capable of avoiding. Making matters worse, the situation threatens to expand into a global conflagration. The foundation of the current crisis was laid decades ago, and the signs of impending confrontation, which now seem obvious in retrospect, were also clear for those who took the time to look for them. Unfortunately, the voices of those who raised the alarm were often drowned out by a chorus of political and military leaders who found it easier to hope for the best and to avoid preparing for the worst.

THINKING ABOUT THE DAY AFTER TOMORROW

DAUNTING SECURITY CHALLENGES NEED NOT BE JUST AROUND THE corner. Some will arise farther down the road, in a decade or so. How does one prepare for them? It pays to begin early. In today's Pentagon effecting major change can easily take a decade or more. The modern fighters rolling off the production lines today were first conceived well over a decade ago. Changes in military doctrine—the way the United States' armed forces conduct their highly complex operations—can take years to develop and test. Witness the four-year lapse between the beginning of irregular warfare in Iraq and the "surge" campaign, the first coherent effort to apply a new doctrine to address the challenge. There is a saying in the Pentagon that the secretary of defense can greatly influence the character and shape of the military that his future successors will lead, but he must content himself with directing the military built by his predecessors' decisions a generation ago. Simply put, today's defense secretary, more than any other, will determine the kind of military in which today's grade-school children will serve—but he is also stuck with the equipment and doctrine decided upon by his (sometimes distant) predecessors. As former defense secretary Donald Rumsfeld famously remarked, "As you know, you have to go to war with the army you have, not the army you want."[1]

A decade ago the Pentagon's attention was almost wholly absorbed by the war with radical Islamist elements and their allies. Not surprisingly, and certainly understandably, Pentagon planners focused on winning the war confronting them, while according lower priority to other threats, especially those that seemed distant and improbable. If you had met one of these senior civilians in the Pentagon, or their military counterparts—junior generals and admirals directing their service's strategic planning efforts—and asked them if they were concerned about getting a bad case of strategic myopia, they would have likely answered that if you want to win the next war, it's a good idea first to win the one you are fighting. Then Secretary of Defense Robert Gates went so far as to caution his generals and admirals against "Next-War-itis," or focusing on preparing for future military challenges as opposed to immediate dangers.[2] While this retort has a certain logic to it, the fact is that strategic planning must balance near- and longer-term risks. Surely the nation must win the war it fights today. But if that only positions the nation to lose the war that follows, it is cold comfort in the long run. Still, many defense experts today wonder if the Pentagon played a role in encouraging China's recent aggressive moves by not paying sufficient attention to developments in the Far East during the height of U.S. military operations in Afghanistan and Iraq.

While every American is now aware of the grave situation confronting the nation, few are familiar with how the current circumstances came to be.

1. Secretary of Defense Donald Rumsfeld, remarks to Iraq-bound soldiers in Kuwait, December 8, 2004, at www.cnn.com/2004/WORLD/meast/12/08/rumsfeld.troops/, accessed on July 5, 2007.
2. Secretary Gates said, "I have noticed too much of a tendency toward what might be called 'Next-War-itis'—the propensity of much of the defense establishment to be in favor of what might be needed in a future conflict." Secretary of Defense Robert M. Gates, remarks to the Heritage Foundation, Colorado Springs, May 13, 2008, at www .defenselink.mil/speeches/speech.aspx?speechid=1240, accessed on June 22, 2008.

DRAGON OR PANDA?

IN THE LATE TWENTIETH AND EARLY TWENTY-FIRST CENTURY POL-
icy planners compared the rise of China to the rise of Germany a century earlier. China's seemingly endless ability to sustain high economic
growth rates recalled Wilhelmine Germany's rapid economic expansion
that threatened to displace Great Britain as the world's dominant power.
Some have feared that China, like Germany, might move aggressively to
change the balance of power and, in the process, trigger a war. Thus for
over a decade the conventional wisdom among one group of China experts viewed as hawkish (and sometimes referred to as the "Dragons")
is that Beijing's rising power would lead to conflict with the United
States.

The Dragons' view has been counterbalanced by a school of thought
that sees China as a country dominated principally by a desire for
economic growth. This growth, they argue, requires good relations with
the United States, which until recently for years ran an enormous trade
deficit with China, often exceeding $200 billion per year. China, they
argue, does not want war with the United States; it has too much
economic interest at stake to seek a conflict with the world's superpower. In fortifying their argument, the "Pandas" (or "Panda Lovers"
as their critics often refer to them) note that the United States
and China have a strong symbiotic relationship with each other—
China's accumulation of U.S. debt enables American consumers to
buy the Chinese goods that help sustain that country's economic
growth. Were China to dump its U.S. debt, it would drive up American
interest rates and slow consumer demand—including the demand for
Chinese goods. The result would find China's economic growth compromised.

The Dragons' counterargument, which now seems prophetic, has
been that "it's *not* the global economy, stupid." They note that in 1914,
on the eve of the war that would nearly destroy them both, Britain and
Germany were major trading partners. They have also criticized the Pandas for failing to realize that China could not continue buying up
U.S. debt in perpetuity as American consumers piled up a staggering

mountain of IOUs that their "children would owe to the children of their Chinese debtors."[3]

Despite their differences, nearly all China watchers, Dragons and Pandas alike, have long agreed on one thing: the Chinese leadership needs a rapidly growing economy to ensure its legitimacy. With communism a dead letter in China, long gone are the days when the Beijing leadership could credibly claim that they alone know the true path to a workers' paradise. Nor can the Beijing ruling group claim legitimacy as a result of free elections: democracy has not replaced the iron fist of communist rule. Rather, Chinese leaders, after witnessing the failure of democracy in Russia, have opted for an open economy and a closed political system. Mao once said that power comes from the barrel of a gun, and that remains true in China, where the government represses any signs of dissent. But the regime's legitimacy—and the Chinese people's general passivity—rests on sustaining the blistering economic growth that, until recent years, enabled most Chinese to enjoy a progressively better life, while limiting their resentment toward the government.

China is a large country marked by geographic, social, and demographic diversity. Consequently, there has traditionally been considerable anxiety over the government's ability to maintain order and to hold China together. Given the country's long history of exploitation and warlordism, especially during the "century of shame" prior to the communist revolution of 1949, Chinese leaders are anxious that China not be broken up again. In their eyes, the Taiwanese and Tibetan separatist movements risk triggering a return to a period of weakness and foreign intervention. One of the reasons Mao Zedong continues to be admired by many Chinese despite his murderous regime is that he imposed order on China.

Ironically, neither the right-wing Dragons nor the left-wing Pandas anticipated that conflict with China would emanate out of Beijing's sense of its growing weakness more than its increasing strength. Yet that is precisely what appears to be happening. Once again the conventional

3. Fred Downey, "GOP Leaders Decry US-PRC Trade Gap," *New York Times,* September 4, 2012, p. A8.

wisdom has proved wrong, while the "experts"—both Dragons and Pandas—have moved on to explain why our current situation was really "inevitable." But the experts have failed us when we needed them most—in helping us to anticipate the unexpected. Unfortunately, if war cannot be averted, the same may be said regarding our military preparedness.

But how has China's phenomenal growth engine stalled? Why has it led Beijing to look for confrontation abroad instead of solving its problems at home? And most important, why has the United States military, by far the world's most experienced and capable, proved so ill prepared to address the threat posed by China?

THE SPUTTERING ENGINE OF GROWTH

SEVERAL FACTORS HAVE CONSPIRED TO SLOW CHINESE ECONOMIC growth at a time when the country can least afford it. Principal among them are energy, demography, and the economic laws of gravity. Regarding the latter, it is only a matter of time, say most economic experts, before a developing country's high economic growth rates begin to level off. Annual growth rates of 8–10 percent or more are not unusual for countries that are in the "takeoff" phase of their economic development. These countries have a lot of catching up to do with more advanced economies, and they typically benefit from copying the production processes and incorporating the superior technologies of first-world countries. At some point, however, a developing country wrings out most of what it can from these benefits. At that point growth typically levels off. This happened with China beginning around 2015. Had that been the only factor pressing down on the country's economy, it would have been worrisome enough for the regime. But economic "gravity" was not China's only problem.

Many say that rising energy prices are the sand that gummed up the gears of China's economic juggernaut. The Persian Gulf region, with its huge oil reserves and production capacity, remains the heartbeat of the global economy. Unfortunately, lagging investment in extraction and production capacity and the ongoing instability in the region have combined to produce a situation in which production growth frequently lags behind global demand. In addition, consumers must pay a hefty risk premium due to two major disruptions in supplies over the past six years.[4] The result has been a slowdown in the global economy. Oil prices that hover around \$130/barrel and, during crisis periods, spike to over \$180/barrel have had significant effects on the world's two principal oil importers, the United States and China. While both countries are exploring alternatives to oil, progress has been fitful at best. There are no quick fixes to the hefty "oil tax" that both countries must pay to slake their enormous thirst for crude.

Aggravating matters for both countries is China's changing attitude with respect to the enormous amount of U.S. debt that it holds. To encourage U.S. consumption—and the purchase of Chinese goods—Beijing was, for the longest time, willing to allow the United States to run huge annual trade deficits, at one point exceeding \$300 billion. Low-cost Chinese goods and low interest rates (thanks to China's willingness to buy up U.S. debt) facilitated this arrangement. But of course, this could not last indefinitely. Higher energy prices and the continuing lingering effects following the bursting of the real estate bubble reduced U.S. consumer demand for Chinese products and led China to spend a significant amount of its currency reserves to offset increased oil prices. To be sure, Beijing initially tried to bring about a "soft landing" to maintain the economic health of its principal customer. However, the resulting increase in U.S. interest rates owing to Beijing's declining willingness to buy America's debt has further slowed U.S. demand, dragging the Chinese economy down along with it.

As the economic climate steadily worsened in 2016, the U.S. Congress deliberated imposing trade sanctions against China to force Beijing

---

4. The descent of Nigeria into a condition of near anarchy in 2012 deprived the world's energy market of nearly two million barrels of high-quality crude every day. It took nearly a year for a U.S.-led international force to restore sufficient order and for repairs to be completed. For an excellent account of the event, see Louis N. Donnatin, *The Oil Fields Are Burning* (New York: Random House, 2014). Three years later Russia suffered a dramatic drop in oil and natural gas production due to a combination of poor pipeline maintenance and a series of attacks on its infrastructure by Muslim separatists. See Owen Delaney, "The Fragile Energy Economy," *Foreign Affairs,* March–April 2016, pp. 37–51.

to revalue the yuan upward against the dollar. This produced a concerted campaign of economic threats against the United States—the Chinese government hinted that it might liquidate its vast holding of U.S. treasuries, an act referred to as China's "nuclear option" in the state media. Such an action would likely trigger a collapse of the dollar, leading to a spike in U.S. bond yields, weakening the U.S. economy and tipping America into a deep recession. At the time China held over $1.3 trillion in a mix of U.S. bonds. China's principal trade negotiator with the United States, Zhou Yong, declared:

> China has accumulated a large sum of U.S. dollars. Such a big sum, of which a considerable portion is in U.S. treasury bonds, contributes a great deal to maintaining the position of the dollar as a reserve currency. China is unlikely to sell off its dollars as long as the yuan's exchange rate is stable against the dollar. However, the Chinese central bank will be forced to sell dollars once the yuan appreciates dramatically, which might lead to a mass depreciation of the dollar.[5]

Congress backed off, but the underlying structural problems could not be resolved. Analysts have looked for ways to arrest this economic malaise, but barring a sustained drop in energy prices, the prospects appeared dim, at least over the near- to mid-term future.

China's energy and trade problems would, alone, be worrisome enough. But still other factors have compounded China's problems and generated additional greater economic stress and growing popular frustration with the nation's political leadership. Principal among them is the country's demographic profile.

IS DEMOGRAPHY DESTINY?

AUGUSTE COMTE ONCE REMARKED, "DEMOGRAPHY IS DESTINY." For China, this observation is proving all too true, but in a negative way.

5. Harriet Brisbane, "China Threatens to Dump the Dollar," *Wall Street Journal,* August 22, 2016, p. A1. This was not the first time Beijing threatened to exercise the "nuclear option." See Ambrose Evans-Pritchard, "China Threatens 'Nuclear Option' of Dollar Sales," *London Daily Telegraph,* August 8, 2007.

A major factor for the slowdown in Chinese economic growth is its declining demographic profile, which has become a major source of concern for Beijing. China is growing older and its demographics increasingly unstable by historical terms. The U.S. population, by comparison, which was one-quarter that of China's less than twenty years ago, is projected to rise to roughly half that of China's by a little over twenty years from now. Today the United States has, and will continue to have, a better balance between its working cohort and its elderly population.[6] And America's sex ratio—a topic of increasing interest in recent years—is much more stable than that of China. As one Columbia University demographer recently noted, "With the exception of periods when nations were recovering from war or widespread internal upheaval, no nation since the Industrial Revolution has enjoyed sustained high economic growth rates in the absence of substantial gains in its working-age population."[7] China has proved no exception; as its demographic profile has weakened, so too has its economic growth.

In the Information Age (and the emerging Biotechnologies Age), the human intellect is an increasingly important factor in generating a nation's wealth. Just as capital replaced physical labor during the Industrial Revolution, human intellectual capital—for example, in developing just-in-time production and distribution processes—has enhanced the value of capital and labor in the world's more advanced economies. Alas, China has yet to join the ranks of the world's most technically

6. See Nicholas Eberstadt, "Power and Population in Asia," *Policy Review,* February–March, 2004, p. 15.
7. John L. Keane, "Asia's Growing Sex Imbalance," *Foreign Affairs,* September–October 2013, p. 76. For example, the period of rapid British economic growth, from the onset of the Industrial Revolution to the Pax Britannica era, was matched by an impressive leap in its population. Similarly, during the great U.S. economic expansion in the half-century after the Civil War, its population tripled (from 31 million in 1860 to 99 million in 1914). Germany's population also expanded rapidly, growing from 41 million in 1871 to 49.7 million in 1891 and 65.3 million in 1911. That is, Germany's population grew by over 50 percent in forty years. This data is cited at www.workmall.com/wfb2001/germany/germany_history_the_economy_and_population_growth.html. In Japan the population increase was not quite as dramatic (34 million in 1868 to 51 million in 1913), although the urban population more than doubled between 1890 and 1913 as the country became an industrial power. Thus while history may not repeat itself, it certainly offers a cautionary tale for those Chinese leaders who are betting on sustained rapid economic growth. See www.census.gov/population/censusdata/table-4.pdf and http://www.census.gov/population/estimates/nation/popclockest.txt. All sites accessed on April 17, 2008.

sophisticated economies. Compared to the United States, the European Union, and Japan, China's economy remains far more labor-intensive. So even though the "quality" of a nation's human capital plays an increasingly important role in its economic success, human quantity still carries great weight.

The matter of health figures importantly in calculations of the value of human resources. How long can a nation's health care system enable its citizens to remain not only alive but productive? Physical longevity is linked to economic progress and a corresponding enhancement of a nation's health care system. An aging population means that health care costs will consume an increasing amount of the nation's wealth. At the same time an aging population makes increasing demands on the nation's social welfare system, and/or upon the families of the elderly, to sustain it during a period marked by declining productivity or outright departure from the workforce. Simply put, an aging population is, all other things being equal, a relatively less productive population—one that draws more out of a nation's store of wealth than it puts in. By definition, countries that are moving toward this demographic profile are almost certain to have fewer resources—human and material—available to sustain economic growth.

What has this to do with China's economic slowdown? The roots were established nearly forty years ago, in 1980, when the country's one-child policy was initiated to check population growth. The inevitable consequence of this policy has been the shift toward an aging China. Some demographers refer to this as the "4-2-1" phenomenon: a large number of Chinese children have four grandparents, two parents, and him/herself. Oftentimes, neither of the child's parents have a sibling, and even more striking, many grandparents lack a sibling. Is it any wonder then that these children are often referred to as the "Little Emperor" or "Little Empress"? The mathematics are devastating: the number of elderly Chinese relative to those in the workforce is increasing, and they are rising relative to the numbers of Chinese entering the workforce.

With the exception of Japan, China's population will age more rapidly than that of its more economically advanced Asian neighbors. This gives the Chinese less time to react. Furthermore, China has nowhere near the resources of Japan to devote to this challenge. Japan grew rich before it grew old; China is growing old before it grows rich. When Japan had the same percentage of population at retirement age (i.e., sixty-five) as China, its per-capita productivity was nearly three times as great.[8] Consequently, China faces the prospect of a relatively smaller working-age population attempting to support a growing elderly population. This portends internal unrest as the elderly struggle along in the absence of a Western-style social safety net. Of course, making matters worse, the "4-2-1" phenomenon means that there will be relatively fewer children to support their elderly parents.

Who will care for China's elderly? How might they extend their productive years beyond age sixty-five? The answers to these questions are sobering. China's national pension system is effectively nonexistent. For most Chinese, the family *is* the pension system. Yet in just a few years (by 2025) the ratio of elderly to workers is projected to be roughly 1:1.[9] Since China's economy is still relatively dominated by manual labor, the ability of elderly Chinese to remain productive is more problematic than in modern industrial societies like the United States and Japan. Simply put, the elderly can be far more productive in a service-driven economy than in an economy that relies more on physical labor. Compounding the problem is the Chinese health care system, which is not up to the standards of modern industrial societies. So not only do elderly Chinese need to work longer and harder, they lack the health care infrastructure to help them do so. Consequently, elderly Chinese experience more health problems than their American or Japanese counterparts, further compromising their ability to extend their productivity into their golden years. It scarcely requires saying that the Chinese people are increasingly dissatisfied with the ruling elites whose policies have created this situation.

8. Eberstadt, "Power and Population in Asia," p. 15.
9. Carsten A. Holz, "Why China's Rise Is Sustainable," *Far Eastern Economic Review,* April 2006, pp. 42–43.

THE LITTLE VIOLENT EMPERORS

SINCE THE 1980S, CHINA'S ONE-CHILD POLICY AND THE COUNTRY'S cultural valuing of males over females, combined with prenatal sex identification and sex-selective abortions, have produced a worrisome sex-ratio imbalance that the leadership has failed to address. Historically, the sex ratio between boys and girls has stood at roughly 103–105:100. That is, for every 100 girls that are born, one could expect between 103 and 105 boys to be born. In 1982, at around the start of the one-child policy, China's male:female birth ratio stood at 1.09:1.00. By 1995 it was 1.16:1.00. In 2000 the ratio had grown to 1.2:1.0. And by 2010 it had advanced to 1.28:1.00.[10] While data are now more difficult to come by, current (2017) estimates have the ratio still exceeding 1.2:1.0.[11] Today over 95 percent of China's unmarried population in the 28–49 age cohort is male. Privately, the Chinese leadership talks of a "demographic death spiral" and a "depopulation time bomb."[12] Their fear is driven by the structural problem that the sex-ratio imbalance has created. Even if the government were to encourage larger families, there are relatively fewer females to accommodate such a policy than in recent previous generations. As one respected demographer put it: "One male can impregnate many females; it doesn't work the other way 'round."[13] Where Chinese women appear in relatively large numbers is in the elderly cohort, beyond the years of childbearing.

As large numbers of unmarried males have entered, and are entering, adulthood, many of these "barren branches"[14] have little prospect of ever finding a mate. Experts estimate that by 2020 China will have 30 million more men of marriageable age than women.[15] How much does this matter? Some argue that, as the surplus male demographic increases, the result will be considerable internal instability. Young

10. Nicholas Eberstadt, "Four Surprises in Global Demography," *Orbis*, Fall 2004.
11. John Tobrial, "China's Sex-Ratio Crisis," *New York Times*, January 28, 2018, p. A7.
12. June Kilgore, "China's Economic Woes Linked to Population Shifts," *Wall Street Journal*, November 14, 2016, p. A1.
13. Harriet Lewis-Dawes, "China's Coming Demographic Bust," *International Security*, Summer 2017, p. 88.
14. The "barren branches" are unattached Chinese males who will never produce heirs.
15. Harriet Lewis-Dawes, "Where Are China's Women?" *New York Times*, October 22, 2017.

adult males commit the preponderance of violence within a society, and most of this group's violence is caused by unattached males. Surplus males typically come from the lowest socioeconomic class (hence their difficulty in attracting a mate), suffer from low self-esteem, and feel alienated from (and rejected by) "mainstream" society. Some scholars, studying the consequences of historical cases of profound sex-ratio imbalances, argue that this situation may set the stage for high levels of internal stability. They also ominously note that at times governments faced with this prospect have attempted to redirect that frustration against external rivals.[16]

WATER

CHINA'S ECONOMIC EXPANSION HAS ALSO SLOWED AS A CONSEquence of its leadership's poor stewardship of the environment. Although the Communist regime in the Soviet Union gave the world a lesson in the long-term human and economic consequences of environmental rape, the regime in Beijing has not absorbed it. The rapid construction of coal-fired electrical generation plants during the rapid run-up in oil and natural gas prices during the mid-2000s contibuted to China's already-poor air quality and, most likely, to the rapid rise in respiratory-related disease, as has the dramatic increase in the country's fleet of automobiles.[17] Acid rain falls on a third of the country's territory; China boasts fifteen of the world's twenty most polluted cities.[18] The smog is so bad that respiratory diseases have become a leading cause of death.

Perhaps most noteworthy, however, is China's growing water crisis, which has exerted a significant drag on the country's ability to sustain high economic growth rates.

Water has been a key factor in China's remarkable economic

16. See, for example, Valerie M. Hudson and Andrea Den Boer, "A Surplus of Men, a Deficit of Peace," *International Security,* Spring 2002, pp. 5–38.
17. Jared Remonak, "China's Growing Health Crisis," *New Yorker,* February 20, 2015, pp. 42–53; and "China Rolls," *Economist,* August 13, 2016, pp. 47–48.
18. Jonathan Watts, "100 Chinese Cities Face Water Crisis, Says Minister in Shenzhen," *Guardian,* June 8, 2005, at www.guardian.co.uk/world/2005/jun/08/china.jonathanwatts, accessed on June 26, 2008.

expansion, but water pollution is now rampant. The poster child for China's water problems is its Three Gorges Dam, the largest hydroelectric power station in the world. Although the dam offers economic benefits, increased pollution has had adverse effects upon the regional ecosystem. A decade ago water pollution was already so widespread that a major environmental incident occured nearly every other day, while municipal and industrial dumping left broad sections of many rivers "unfit for human contact."[19]

Nowhere is the problem more severe than on the North China Plain. A century or so ago a farmer digging a well could strike water in less than ten feet. Streams, creeks, swamps, natural springs, and wetlands were common. Today the region, comparable in size to New Mexico, is parched, as roughly five-sixths of the wetlands have dried up. Most of its natural streams or creeks have simply disappeared, while several rivers that once were navigable are now mostly dust and brush. China's largest natural freshwater lake in the region, Lake Baiyangdian, is drying up at an alarming rate. What water remains is highly polluted.[20]

While China scours the world for increasingly expensive commodities to sustain economic growth, it can neither import water nor easily reverse the pollution that has already occurred. The shortages have forced Beijing to make tough choices, such as ending its hopes of maintaining self-sufficiency in grain production. As grain production has been scaled back, so too has the diet of many Chinese, as the leadership has been reluctant to import large amounts of grain from the United States.

---

19. Jim Yardley, "Though Water Is Drying Up, a Chinese Metropolis Booms," *International Herald Tribune,* September 27, 2007. Most industry in China still uses two to five times more water, depending on the product, than industries in developed countries. Ten years ago the range was three to ten times more water. The Communist Party is engaged in a massive engineering project to address the country's water problems, the centerpiece of which is the South-to-North Water Transfer Project, designed to move 45 billion cubic meters, or 12 trillion gallons, northward every year along three routes from the Yangtze River basin, where water is relatively abundant. The project, if fully built, will be completed in 2050. The eastern and central lines are already well under way, while the western line, despite environmental concerns, is now in the early stages of construction. Disconcertingly, pollution problems are already arising on the eastern line. Moreover, water quality has badly deteriorated in the south. Some 50 percent of China's waste water is dumped into the Yangtze, increasing the risk that diverting clean water to the north will exacerbate pollution problems in the south.
20. Ibid.

Other countries like Yemen, India, Mexico, and the United States have aquifers that are being drained to dangerously low levels. However, when compared with the United States, China is at a severe disadvantage. It has a smaller water supply but almost four times as many people. Put another way, China has about 7 percent of the world's water resources but roughly 20 percent of the world's population. The country also suffers from a severe regional water imbalance—about four-fifths of the water supply is in the south.

Scientists say the aquifers below the North China Plain may be drained within ten years, and Chinese experts warn that by 2030 per capita water resources will drop to 1,760 cubic meters—perilously close to the 1,700-cubic-meter level, the internationally recognized benchmark for water shortages.[21]

In the last five years China has invested hundreds of billions of dollars in an attempt to reverse the decline in both the quantity and quality of its water. It has invested in desalination plants along the coast and waste-treatment plants, and in more efficient use of water and conservation. The price of water has been raised significantly in an effort to reduce consumption. Nevertheless, the bottom line is clear: water is increasingly scarce and increasingly expensive. Merely trying to limit the growth of the problem is diverting huge sums from the economy. The result is yet another brake on China's economic growth.

THE LONG PATH TO WAR

HOW DID CHINA'S ECONOMIC WOES CONTRIBUTE TO PERHAPS THE most dangerous great power confrontation since the Cuban Missile Crisis over half a century ago? One clear factor is the leadership's fears that economic stagnation is undermining its legitimacy, coupled with a determination not to allow foreign powers to exploit China's weakness.[22] Even during its period of astounding economic growth, Beijing went to considerable lengths to encourage strong feelings of nationalism among

21. The danger was forecast long ago. See, for example, Liang Chao, "Experts Warn of Water Crisis," *China Daily,* April 20, 2005, at www.chinadaily.com.cn/english/doc/2005-04/20/content_435724.htm, accessed on June 24, 2008.
22. Jonathan Kapinski, "China's 'Century of Humiliation,'" *Commentary,* April 2017, p. 30.

the Chinese people, citing the "century of humiliation" that the country had endured at the hands of European powers and Japan, and never letting the people forget the depredations inflicted on China during its long war with imperial Japan.[23] Thus nationalism and economic growth emerged as the twin pillars of regime legitimacy. As economic times have become more difficult and as popular unrest in China has increased, the government has ratcheted up its condemnation of what it perceives to be hostile intentions on the part of other countries, especially the United States and Japan, with an eye toward deflecting blame from itself.

Japan and Taiwan are beset with some of the same problems as China—especially in demographics and energy dependency—but their more advanced economies, their high-quality health care systems, their better environmental stewardship, and their democratic forms of government have enabled both to weather the economic storm far better than China. At the same time their investments in China have been curtailed, owing both to their own economic slowdowns and to concerns about China's future. In Taiwan, talk of independence, which was muted following the 2008 Beijing Olympics, has gradually retaken center stage in the country's political discourse. To many Taiwanese, the example of Japan and South Korea appears increasingly more attractive than that of Hong Kong, which, some twenty years after its absorption back into China, is experiencing difficult times. Tibetans are growing increasingly restive. Militant Muslim insurgents in China's northwestern provinces are engaging in serious acts of violence against the government.

One enduring characteristic of China's activities during this period of relative economic stagnation has been the continued growth of its military. The People's Liberation Army (PLA) enjoyed double-digit annual growth in its budgets during nearly two decades of rapid Chinese economic gains.[24] While the increase in China's military budgets has slowed somewhat in recent years, its advance remains within the very healthy 5 to 10 percent range. Despite these gains, China's defense

23. Japan occupied Manchuria in 1931 and invaded China in 1937, beginning a war that lasted until 1945.
24. Jim Yardley and David Lague, "Beijing Accelerates its Military Spending," *New York Times,* March 5, 2007, p. A8. Chinese defense outlays increased an average of 15 percent a year from 1990 to 2005.

expenditures remain only a fraction (albeit a significant fraction) of the United States' defense funding. As we are now discovering, the effectiveness of China's military is a function of how wisely the leadership invested its military funding as much as how much it invested.

CHINA'S MILITARY TRANSFORMATION: THE ASSASSIN'S MACE

THE PLA'S DRIVE TO ADAPT, AS ITS MILITARY THEORETICIANS PUT IT, to "local war under modern high-technology conditions" derives its original stimulus from the lessons drawn by the Chinese military from the two Gulf wars. During the two wars the Chinese were impressed by the Americans' ability to coordinate large, complex operations among the military services. In particular, the effectiveness of U.S. precision-strike capabilities surprised them. The Chinese were also impressed that U.S. space forces provided American forces with reliable navigation and communications, as well as near-real-time weather and missile-warning data.[25]

The U.S. precision strike on their embassy in Belgrade during the 1999 Balkan War angered and embarrassed the Chinese. While the Americans claimed the attack was the result of a targeting error, the Chinese, ascribing far greater proficiency to American precision warfare than it likely merited, were convinced the attack's purpose was to display Beijing's vulnerabilities to this kind of weaponry.

25. Roger Cliff et al., *Entering the Dragon's Lair: Chinese Anti-Access Strategies and Their Implications for the United States* (Santa Monica, Calif.: RAND, 2007), pp. 20–22. One Chinese expert noted:

> U.S. troops had at least five *shashoujian* [Assassin's Mace capabilities] on the battlefield [during Operation Desert Storm], i.e., the F-117A stealth fighter bombers, the B-1B [*sic*] stealth bombers, the B-52H bombers (specialized in launching cruise missiles outside the air defense zone), the ship-based Tomahawk cruise missiles, and the B-2A stealth bombers, which can take off or touch down from domestic airbases to carry out shock tasks. Moreover, the U.S. troops would also use various kinds of ammunition which are more powerful and more accurately guided.

Dong Wenxian, "Diplomatic Success Comes from the Sky—Analyzing U.S. Troops' Military Deterrent During the Iraqi Arms Inspection Crisis," *Jiefangjun Bao,* April 14, 1998, translated in the Foreign Broadcast Information Service; quoted in Jason E. Bruzdzinski, "Demystifying *Shashoujian*: China's 'Assassin's Mace' Concept," in *Civil–Military Change in China: Elites, Institutes, and Ideas After the 16th Party Congress,* ed. Larry Wortzel and Andrew Scobell (Carlisle, Pa.: U.S. Army War College, 2004), pp. 316–17.

This incident followed on the heels of the demonstration of Chinese impotence during the Taiwan Crisis of 1995–96. At that time the U.S. aircraft carrier *Nimitz* entered the Taiwan Strait, following a series of Chinese missile firings that landed off the coast of Taiwan. This was the first time a U.S. warship had entered the Strait since 1976. The first set of missiles fired in mid- to late 1995 were intended to signal Beijing's displeasure over the Taiwan government of Lee Teng-hui, who was believed to be moving Taiwanese foreign policy away from the One China policy. The second set of missiles, fired in early 1996, were likely intended to intimidate the Taiwanese electorate in the run-up to their 1996 presidential election.[26] The display of U.S. naval power angered the Chinese, adding to their determination to curb the United States' unfettered access to the East Asian region.

Senior Chinese political and military leaders, reflecting upon their position relative to the United States, clearly decided it would be foolhardy to challenge the U.S. military head-on for military dominance. As one senior Chinese military theorist argued, "We should not mechanically follow the U.S. theory." Rather, "We should try to create our own superiority." This was possible, since "the other side may be strong, but they are not strong in all things . . . and our side may be weak, but we are not weak in all things."[27] But how would China, with resources inferior to those of the Americans, create its advantage? The answer, in the words of one senior PLA general, was to "combine Western technology with Eastern wisdom. This is our trump card for winning a twenty-first-century war."[28] To the Chinese, this meant seizing the initiative by exploiting surprise; breaking up the U.S. military's communications networks; and launching preemptive attacks to the point where such attacks, or even the threat of such attacks, would raise the costs of U.S. action to prohibitive levels.[29]

---

26. For an assessment of the crisis, see Robert S. Ross, "The 1995–1996 Taiwan Strait Confrontation: Coercion, Credibility, and Use of Force," *International Security*, Fall 2000, pp. 87–123.
27. Bruzdzinski, "Demystifying *Shashoujian*," pp. 319, 336.
28. Ibid., p. 317.
29. For a discussion of long-standing Chinese perceptions of U.S. military vulnerabilities, see Cliff et al., *Entering the Dragon's Lair*, pp. 44–50.

The Chinese have a name for the set of military capabilities that support this strategic philosophy: Assassin's Mace, or in Chinese, *Shashoujian*. The current crisis has made painfully evident the potential of Assassin's Mace to threaten the United States' ability to defend its allies and interests in the Far East, its own well-being, and perhaps even its survival.

Among the capabilities associated with Assassin's Mace are advanced air defenses, information warfare, ballistic and cruise missiles, advanced fighter aircraft, attack submarines, and counterspace capabilities. Chinese military writers also mention the use of limited nuclear strikes (perhaps with electromagnetic pulse[30] warheads) as a means of achieving information advantage. Assassin's Mace forces are designed to enable the "inferior" (China) to defeat the "superior" (the United States).[31] However, only a small fraction of modern weaponry is seen as supporting the Assassin's Mace concept.[32] The concept is consistent with the long-standing Chinese military thinking noted above and is centered on information warfare (achieving an information advantage over the enemy) and extended-range strikes.

The PLA's embrace of these capabilities represents a "great leap forward" in that it deviates sharply from the military's strategic culture, which through the 1980s had been centered on Mao Zedong's concept of people's war. During the early development of Assassin's Mace capabilities, the Chinese took steps to deflect U.S. intelligence from identifying their emergence. Consequently, American leaders were continually surprised by Chinese military developments of a range of systems and

30. An electromagnetic pulse is a broadband, high-intensity, short-duration burst of electromagnetic energy. Such a pulse can damage and even destroy unshielded electrical equipment.
31. Mark A. Stokes, *China's Strategic Modernization: Implications for the United States* (Carlisle, Pa.: U.S. Army Strategic Studies Institute, 1999), p. 27; and Michael Pillsbury, "China's Military Strategy Toward the U.S.: A View from Open Sources," November 2, 2001, pp. 8–10, at www.uscc.gov/researchpapers/2000_2003/pdfs/strat.pdf, accessed on June 20, 2008.
32. Militaries have notably succeeded in effecting a dramatic shift in the military balance by transforming a relatively small portion of their force. Examples are Germany's mechanized *(blitzkrieg)* forces in World War II, the U.S. Navy's carrier forces in that war's Pacific theater, and the Imperial German Navy's submarine force in World War I.

capabilities, including long-range missiles, attack submarines, precision-guided munitions, and advanced surface-to-air missiles. Unfortunately, Chinese developments in information or cyberwarfare have generally remained a well-kept secret until just recently.

Yet, for those who cared to look closely, the warning signs have been there to see for at least two decades. Writings on *Shashoujian* began to appear in the Chinese military journals in the late 1990s. In August 2000 Jiang Zemin, China's president, rejected the PLA request for a greater budget increase while ordering the military to emphasize the development of *Shashoujian*. A few months later, in December 2000, the leadership called for a new generation of "strategic high-tech weapons."[33]

Again and again the themes were repeated: China must make every effort to identify and exploit the enemy's key weaknesses, rely on surprise, and use extraordinary means to attack key enemy vulnerabilities. Unfortunately, a succession of U.S. administrations, distracted by the Long War with radical Islamist states and groups, and enjoying the short-term economic benefits of trade with China, failed to take the growing Chinese military machine seriously. In a now-famous hearing in February 2012, in which the chairman of the Joint Chiefs of Staff, when asked about the Chinese threat, informed the Senate Armed Services Committee that the PLA, lacking modern, stealthy fighter aircraft, a carrier strike force, and advanced amphibious assault forces, had a long way to go before it could pose a serious challenge to Taiwan or other U.S. interests in East Asia, let alone in other parts of the world.[34] Recent events are proving otherwise.

Over time Chinese military transformation has coalesced around two pillars. One is developing and fielding what U.S. military analysts refer to as anti-access/area-denial (A2/AD) capabilities. Generally speaking, Chinese anti-access forces seek to deny U.S. forces access to—or the ability to operate from—forward bases, such as the huge U.S. air base

33. Bruzdzinski, "Demystifying *Shashoujian*," p. 328.
34. House Armed Services Committee, Hearing on the Chinese Military, February 19, 2015, at www.house.gov/hasc/hearing_information.shtml, accessed on June 4, 2015; and Senate Armed Services Committee, Hearing on the People's Liberation Army's Assassin's Mace, February 24, 2015, at http://armed-services.senate.gov/hearings2013.cfm, accessed on June 4, 2015.

at Kadena on the Japanese island of Okinawa. The Chinese have done this by fielding large numbers of ballistic missiles and low-observable (or stealthy) cruise missiles, along with strike aircraft. Although directed-energy technology may enable the United States to field highly effective missile defense systems in the next decade, at present its defenses against ballistic and cruise missile attacks, especially those that employ penetration aids and stealth, are rather limited—especially when confronted with barrages involving large numbers. The Chinese military's high command recognized this fact long ago and for several decades now has steadily (one might say relentlessly) continued to expand and improve its missile forces. The message to the United States and its East Asian allies and partners is clear: China has the means to negate the American advantage in precision strike by holding at risk of destruction the forward bases from which U.S. strike aircraft must operate.

Area-denial capabilities are generally directed at denying U.S. forces freedom of action in the seas, out to what the Chinese refer to as the second island chain—a line stretching from east of Japan through Guam and well east of the Philippine islands.[35] It is the PLA's way of ensuring, among other things, that there will be no repetition of the embarrassment of 1995–96. To accomplish this task, the PLA has invested in submarines that might use their stealth to stalk American carriers and other surface warships. Some readers may recall the surfacing of a Chinese submarine in the midst of a U.S. carrier task force early in 2006.[36] For the PLA Navy (or PLAN), this embarrassment to the American fleet only ten years after the latter's carriers had patrolled the Taiwan Strait was sweet revenge. Since then the PLAN has been launching two general types of submarines: quiet diesel subs that can form a "picket line" near the second island chain, squatting silently while waiting to ambush an approaching U.S. fleet; and, more recently, nuclear-powered attack submarines, with greater range and endurance to threaten U.S. interests in other parts of the globe, thereby diverting American attention from East

Asia. While American Virginia-class attack submarines remain far superior qualitatively to their Chinese counterparts, there are over two PLAN subs for each Virginia-class boat.

The Chinese are relying on more than submarines to keep the U.S. fleet at bay. They have constructed over-the-horizon radars, fielded unmanned aerial vehicles, and invested heavily in space reconnaissance satellites to better detect American surface warships at progressively greater distances. The PLA has also improved its ability to strike U.S. warships. Its submarines are equipped with advanced torpedoes and high-speed, sea-skimming antiship cruise missiles (ASCM), most of which were either bought from Russia or are derivatives of Russian-made weaponry.[37] The PLA Air Force has concentrated on investing in aircraft that can carry high-speed ASCMs. China has also acquired advanced antiship mines from Russia, many of which can be emplaced remotely. These further limit the maneuverability of U.S. naval forces and in so doing, increase their vulnerability. As these capabilities entered the Chinese military's arsenal, U.S. naval forces were progressively denied the ability to operate in the seas close to China, at least at an acceptable level of risk.[38]

CHINA'S THREAT TO THE GLOBAL COMMONS

BEIJING HAS BEEN DOMINATED BY MORE THAN A DESIRE TO PUSH U.S. military presence ever farther from its borders. It is also involved

---

37. The U.S. Navy's general lack of preparedness extends back a decade. One example concerns the high-speed ASCMs now aboard PLAN submarines, the Sizzler in particular. The Pentagon revealed in 2008 that PLAN Kilo-class diesel submarines were deploying the missile. Most ASCMs fly below the speed of sound and on a straight path, making them easier to track and target. The Sizzler, like other ASCMs, starts at subsonic speeds, but as it approaches ten nautical miles of its target, a rocket-propelled warhead separates and accelerates the Sizzler to three times the speed of sound, as it flies no more than ten meters (33 feet) above sea level. Making the defense's job more difficult, the missile "has the potential to perform very high defensive maneuvers," including sharp-angled maneuvers, reports the U.S. Office of Naval Intelligence. It took the Navy until 2015 to begin testing its fleet defenses against the missile. See Tony Capaccio, "Navy Can't Test Defense Against China's 'Sizzler' Until 2014," *Bloomberg News,* April 3, 2008; and Fran Darby, "Fleet Lacks Defense Against Chinese Missiles," *Bloomberg News,* April 14, 2015.
38. Bill Gertz, "China Buildup Seen Aimed at U.S. Ships," *Washington Times,* November 22, 2006, p. 5.

in a long-standing competition with the United States for access to the "global commons," a concept that has changed greatly over the past century. During the heyday of the Pax Britannica in the late nineteenth century, Great Britain's control over the high seas and key maritime choke points was the equivalent of control over the global commons. In modern times, the definition has expanded greatly. The global commons now includes the skies and space, cyberspace, and the seas and undersea. In the late twentieth century, following the Soviet Union's collapse, the United States occupied the role that Britain had had a century earlier, except that now the Americans dominated in all areas of the commons. Other powers made little of it, as the Americans, like their nineteenth-century British cousins, proved good stewards of the commons. But this would not last. China, a rapidly rising power suspicious of the Americans and increasingly able to field advanced military capabilities, had little reason to permit the United States to have unfettered access to the global commons, while it could deny China the same. China's leaders realized it would be decades before they would be in a position to challenge the United States directly for control of the commons. Consequently, they adopted the strategy typically pursued by inferior powers—a strategy of denial. In its simplest form, this strategy states that "while I may not be strong enough to wrest control of the commons from you, I am strong enough to deny you the use of the commons." Or in the vernacular of playgrounds around the world: "If I can't have it, you can't have it, either."

CHINESE CHALLENGE TO U.S. COMMAND OF THE SEA AND UNDERSEA

OVER TWO DECADES AGO CHINA EMBARKED ON A MAJOR EXPANSION in the size and capabilities of its submarine fleet.[39] Submarines represent an important element of China's Assassin's Mace capabilities. Employed in combination with other Assassin's Mace forces, submarines make it highly risky for U.S. naval forces to operate within the "first

---

39. Lyle Goldstein and William Murray, "Undersea Dragons," *International Security*, Spring 2004.

island chain" off China's coast. The first island chain comprises the Korean Peninsula, Japan, and Taiwan. The greater the risk it poses to U.S. naval forces, the easier it becomes for Beijing to deter the American fleet from coming to Taiwan's rescue—hence, the easier it becomes for China to coerce Taiwan. Forcing U.S. surface warships farther out from China's littoral region enhances the prospects for Chinese control of the Taiwan Strait in support of an Operation Sea Lion–style invasion of Taiwan.[40] Alternatively, this Chinese sea-denial capability could, along with extended-range reconnaissance and targeting (e.g., employing space-based systems, unmanned aerial vehicles, and covert operatives) and various strike means (e.g., ballistic and cruise missiles; advanced underwater mines; covertly embedded PLA Special Operations Forces) be an important part of Chinese blockade operations against Taiwan, South Korea, or even Japan. Of course, Beijing's goal is not to establish its preeminence in the region by fighting a war. Rather, the Chinese want to do so by winning a "bloodless" victory, by convincing Seoul, Taipei, and Tokyo that, given the altered military balance in East Asia, they should accommodate Chinese interests and reduce ties with the United States. In short the PLA success would lead to China's "Finlandization" of East Asia.[41]

Viewed in this manner, China's emphasis on surprise may be less focused on achieving it at the onset of war than on the world's sudden recognition that a new balance of power exists in East Asia, one dominated by Beijing. As the current crisis reveals, Chinese military leaders well remember Sun Tzu's admonition: "For to win one hundred victories in one hundred battles is not the acme of skill. To subdue the enemy without fighting is the acme of skill."

By engaging as it has in a decades-long sustained building of its submarine fleet, China also possesses a serious sea-denial capability that

40. Operation Sea Lion was the German plan for invading England during World War II. It called for a rapid movement across the English Channel to negate Great Britain's advantage in naval forces. The invasion would be enabled by the German Air Force, whose mission was to establish air superiority over the channel, thus making British naval operations to disrupt the seaborne assault impractical.
41. Finlandization is the influence that one powerful country may have on the policies of a smaller neighboring country. During the Cold War a "Finlandized" country might maintain its national sovereignty while accommodating its foreign politics to those pursued by a more powerful neighbor, as Finland did vis-à-vis the Soviet Union.

enables it to threaten both regional and (some naval analysts say) global shipping. As the current crisis makes clear, this has profound implications for the global economy and, by extension, the well-being of the United States and its key allies. China could employ its sea-denial capability to destroy or disrupt critical undersea economic infrastructure and offshore energy production, platforms, and pipelines, as well as the global fiber-optic grid. China's submarine fleet is also a threat to interdict cargo that is central to the global economy's "just in time" supply network. As the commander of U.S. forces in the Pacific, Admiral Jerry O'Hare, recently testified:

> Mr. Chairman, our submarines are qualitatively better than those of the PLAN, and by a substantial margin. But their submarines outnumber ours and our allies' by better than two to one. Now our subs can only be in one place at one time. Over time I am confident we can deal with the submarine threat. But if a conflict were to break out, especially one where the PLAN initiated action, they could do substantial damage to shipping and offshore facilities like oil platforms. It reminds me of what Admiral Yamamoto told his Japanese leaders prior to Pearl Harbor, that he could run wild in the Pacific for six months. Well, the PLAN can probably run wild for a while before we eliminate their submarine threat. And we will pay a heavy price for that.[42]

CHINESE CHALLENGE TO U.S. ACCESS TO SPACE

SINCE THE FIRST GULF WAR IN 1991 THE UNITED STATES MILITARY has come to rely increasingly on access to capabilities in space for critical information, including surveillance, reconnaissance, intelligence, targeting, and positioning. While other countries may not aspire to deploy the kind of space architecture the United States has, none have been either able or willing to devote the necessary resources and level of

---

42. Admiral Jeremiah O'Hare, Testimony, Senate Armed Services Committee, July 6, 2017, at http://armed-services.senate.gov/hearings.cfm, accessed on July 28, 2017.

expertise to realize that aspiration. However, China has developed effective space-denial capabilities, which include ground-based laser anti-satellite (ASAT) weapons, ASAT ballistic missiles, and satellite-jamming systems.[43] The first of these weapons was revealed over a decade ago in the form of an ASAT ballistic missile.

China also has been populating the heavens with satellites to enhance its military capabilities, in particular surveillance and targeting. Beijing's involvement in the European Union–led Galileo global positioning system provides China with extended-range precision-targeting capabilities that were once the exclusive preserve of the U.S. military. These capabilities are proving of great value now that China has decided to resolve some "outstanding internal security matters" in East Asia. In particular, Chinese space-based elements are likely providing important intelligence on U.S. troop movements and on naval task force locations as well.

CHINESE THREATS TO CYBERSPACE

AS THE U.S. MILITARY INCREASINGLY RELIES ON INFORMATION as a critical component of its military effectiveness, and the use of networks to gather, organize, and move that information, PLA theorists have, for years, argued that the Americans' heavy reliance on cyberspace may be their Achilles' heel. As one PLA officer put it, "By striking directly at the 'brains, heart, and nerve centers' of the enemy's systems, this method paralyzes powerful troop formations and makes them collapse without being attacked."[44] Chinese military journals for years have discussed how they might combine "decapitation actions together with precision lightning strikes" to blind enemy forces and produce a climate of disorientation and disintegration.[45]

But how might the PLA accomplish this goal? The Chinese are

43. Like China's efforts in other military areas, its military space program dates back at least a decade. See Office of the Secretary of Defense, *Military Power of the People's Republic of China, 2006*, pp. 31–35.
44. Quoted in Office of the Secretary of Defense, *Military Power of the People's Republic of China, 2013* (Washington, D.C.: Department of Defense, 2013), p. 48.
45. See Office of the Secretary of Defense, *Military Power of the People's Republic of China, 2011* (Washington, D.C.: Department of Defense, 2011), p. vii.

capable of employing precision-guided ballistic missiles and cruise missiles to attack the U.S. military's forward-based command and control "nerve centers." Some argue that the PLA might employ nuclear weapons or other means to generate a widespread or discrete electromagnetic pulse—a short-lived, overlapping series of intense radio waves that can induce a destructive surge in the electrical currents coursing through electronic equipment, including electrical power grids, telephone networks, radios, and computers. Alternatively, specially equipped PLA submarines might cut key undersea fiber-optic cables providing data links both to U.S. military forces and to the civilian economy. Then there are the PLA's ASAT weapons, which can blind or even destroy satellites upon which the U.S. military relies for such important information as position location, targeting, and communications. Finally, there are the "hackers," or "cyberwarriors." Even senior U.S. intelligence officials admit they do not know to what extent the Chinese have developed an ability to introduce a wide range of viruses, worms, Trojan horses, and other cyber "weapons" into the information grids of the United States in general or U.S. military computer networks in particular.[46]

What *is* known is that since the late twentieth century a low-level cyber "war" has been ongoing with China. Attacks on U.S. government information systems originating in China have occurred on nearly a daily basis for over two decades. Over time these attacks have grown in number and sophistication. Widespread attention was first attracted when attacks emanating from China compromised computer systems at the Pentagon, the U.S. Naval War College, and the National Defense University. Far more serious was the revelation, in 2015, that several major U.S. national laboratories and defense firms had been penetrated and substantial amounts of classified data relating to U.S.

---

46. A "Trojan horse" is a piece of malware that presents itself to the user as a program that performs one function but actually performs another. For example, a Trojan horse program claiming to be a screensaver, when run, will download other, potentially malicious programs surreptitiously or enable unauthorized access to the computer. A computer worm is a computer program that self-replicates in order to exploit a computer network by sending the copies to other computers on the network. This can degrade the network and individual computers, as worms can absorb bandwidth. Worms are different from computer viruses, which can corrupt or modify a computer's files. See http://en.wikipedia.org/wiki/Computer_worm, accessed on June 27, 2008.

weapon designs and key characteristics had been compromised.[47] While the attacks originated in China, Beijing—as it had on all other occasions when accused of cyberwarfare—strongly denied any involvement or responsibility. Recently cyberattacks originating in China have "spiked," or increased dramatically in number. Leaked closed testimony from the U.S. director of national intelligence before the House Select Committee on Intelligence last month reveals that these attacks are

> well organized and well executed. They have been probing our defenses for years. What concerns me is that we don't know whether they have already inserted software "bombs" in our key military, government, and civilian information grids that are only awaiting a command from Beijing before they are activated. We've done the usual—tried attacking our own systems, building firewalls and security protocols, etc., for our systems. But there is a lot of uncertainty involved here.[48]

Revealingly, the U.S. business sector has generally refused to cooperate with the government on these matters, preferring to develop its own means of defense.[49]

CHINA'S STRATEGIC DEPTH

DURING THE COLD WAR WITH THE SOVIET UNION, THE UNITED States military had to confront the problem of its rival's strategic depth. The enormous size of the Soviet Union meant that, unless the United States was willing to allow Moscow to enjoy de facto sanctuaries for some critical military capabilities, such as long-range missiles and

47. David Loran, "China's Cyber Windfall," *New York Times,* March 29, 2015, pp. A1, A9–13. Loran won the Pulitzer Prize for his reporting.
48. Statement of the U.S. Director of National Intelligence before the House Select Committee on Intelligence, June 22, 2017, p. 17.
49. See Jamison Commission, *A Nation Unprepared* (Washington, D.C.: Commission on the Threat to the United States Information Technology Infrastructure, October 2016), p. 2. Corporate America's reluctance to cooperate with Washington is based primarily on its lack of confidence in the government's ability (or even willingness) to keep secret how it goes about defending its information technology infrastructure.

command facilities, American forces had to be able to hold them at risk of destruction. Failing that, Washington's ability to deter Soviet attempts at coercion or even aggression might be eroded. Of course, the consequences of deterrence failing would likely have been catastrophic.

The Pentagon's need to worry about strategic depth faded after the Cold War ended. The United States' immediate post–Cold War rivals, such as Iraq, Iran, and North Korea, did not possess anything like the Soviet Union's geographic density. Even after the Afghanistan campaign of 2001–02, when U.S. forces had to project power deep into Central Asia, it was difficult for this issue to get a hearing in the Pentagon's planning and programming efforts. A few senior Pentagon leaders noted that China's development of Assassin's Mace capabilities was clearly designed to erode U.S. influence in East Asia, and the PLA's mantra "the inferior defeats the superior" could only be interpreted as directed toward the United States.[50] America must, they cautioned, strive to maintain a military balance in the region, such that China would never feel it could achieve its ambitions through the use of coercion or aggression. This means that U.S. defense planners must take into account China's great strategic depth. In the past, China has used its strategic depth to great advantage as, for example, in its war with Japan from 1937 to 1945, and in developing its nuclear capability in the 1950s and 1960s.[51]

Several Assassin's Mace assets, such as ballistic missiles, ground-based ASATs, command and control centers, and leadership facilities, are exploiting China's strategic depth to advantage. By positioning these assets deep in the country's interior, Beijing is both driving up the cost for the U.S. military to hold them at risk, and creating a semisanctuary for them against shorter-range U.S. reconnaissance and strike systems. Owing to a general lack of U.S. long-range targeting and strike forces,

50. The most widely noted argument along these lines was published by the Navy's chief of naval operations and the Air Force's chief of staff. See Admiral David Ritzak and General Walter Brock, "China's Challenge to America's Security," *Foreign Affairs*, May–June, 2013, pp. 27–42.
51. At that time the Chinese positioned much of their nuclear development assets and missile forces deep in the country's interior.

the Chinese have posed the United States with an increasingly worrisome problem.

CHINA'S CRISIS

BEGINNING IN MARCH 2017, CIVIL PROTESTS AGAINST THE BEIJING regime, which had been on the rise for the past several years as the country's economic woes worsened, increased sharply. Not only had the protests grown in number, they were also larger and more violent than those that preceded them during the past winter. They were animated by the now-familiar list of grievances: falling living standards; declining health care support; a worsening of environmental conditions (especially along the coast and in Manchuria); the "Little Emperors'" inability to support their family elders; and rumors of widespread government corruption. These demonstrations, and the work stoppages often associated with them, put a growing strain on the government's security forces and worsened an already difficult economic situation.

In a series of speeches to the nation, China's president, Li Zhong, in elliptical fashion acknowledged what many Chinese know to be true: conditions had been worsening, and significantly, for over four years. But the president argued that the country's economic slowdown was an aberration, not a new fact of life. He sacked several of his most corrupt deputies. But rather than accepting responsibility for the situation, Li blamed "foreign elements" who were not content to accept China's "peaceful development" and sought to create for China a new "century of humiliation."[52]

China's woes, the president asserted, stem primarily from the efforts of foreign powers—principally the United States and Japan—to undermine the country's economic growth and, in so doing, its security as well. To this end, he alleged, "hostile foreign powers" were engaged in the following:

---

52. The year prior, Chinese leaders attempted to placate their people by removing over a dozen high-level officials from power for incompetence and corruption. Two were executed. This might have mollified the public had conditions in China not continued to decline. But as we now know, this is not the case.

- collaborating with key oil- and other commodity-exporting nations to keep energy prices high as a means of subverting China's economy;
- imposing unfair trade practices against China, which have the effect of reducing American demand for Chinese goods;
- fomenting internal disturbances within China to undermine the economy and weaken the government; and
- encouraging Taiwan to reduce investment in China, and to move toward formal independence from the mainland.[53]

President Mary Collingwood promptly and vigorously denied the allegations in a press conference two days later, as did the leaders of Japan and Taiwan. Financial analysts gave no credence to Li's assertions, noting that the commodities markets continue operating on a supply-and-demand basis. The high prices, they noted, are a function of growing demand and concerns over supplies, especially given the relatively high level of instability in many major commodity-exporting states. As for American "unfair" trading practices, the decline in U.S. demand for China's goods had more to do with a sluggish American economy, the weak dollar, competition from other developing economies, and increasingly shoddy Chinese products, the result of corruption and lax standards.[54]

Unmoved either by the logic of the market or by the assurances of foreign leaders, in a speech given on May Day Li declared that China must respond vigorously to these attempts to undermine the well-being of the Chinese people, which threaten the very existence of the nation.[55] The president backed this up with a series of "initiatives" intended to establish conditions under which China's "peaceful development" could continue. In particular, three strongly worded "initiatives" attracted attention.

The first demanded that Taiwan cease all debate over the merits of separating from the mainland, and that it grant Beijing economic

53. Deborah Wallenhaven, "PRC President Declares U.S., Japan to Be 'Threats,'" *New York Times,* April 17, 2017, p. A1.
54. A refutation of Li's allegations is found in "Harsh Truths," *Economist,* April 29, 2017, pp. 50–56.
55. Deborah Wallenhaven, "Beijing Threatens Action Against Taiwan," *New York Times,* May 2, 2017, p. A1.

concessions and loan guarantees, and augment its investment in China as a sign of its good intentions. The second major initiative restated, in the strongest terms, China's decade-long "desire" that the United States divest itself of its bases in the region and "end its attempts to encircle China" through its expanded basing agreements with several central Asian states, as well as India and Singapore. Finally, the Chinese president urged "in the strongest possible manner" that the United States encourage its Persian Gulf "clients" to increase the production of oil as a means of moderating prices and helping the lagging global (i.e., Chinese) economy. [56]

According to well-placed sources, the leadership in Beijing had already decided in February to resolve the Taiwan issue, with force if necessary.[57] Apparently the decision was taken following a review of China's economic prospects. The island's growing sentiment to distance itself progressively from China's growing and seemingly intractable problems has apparently been seen as a threat to the Beijing regime's other pillar of legitimacy: nationalism. As one China expert put it:

> The [Chinese] leadership could be motivated by a genuine fear that Taiwan has come to represent a more attractive model than the Beijing regime. Or it could be an attempt to redirect the Chinese people's attention away from internal problems while also placing the blame for them on external forces. Or it could well be a combination of the two. If so, it may be, too, that the [Chinese] president's speech was also intended to win some measure of support from the international community for what has since transpired.[58]

56. June Kilgore, "China Lists Demands," *Wall Street Journal,* May 2, 2017, p. A1. The United States retains several major bases in the Persian Gulf region and is viewed by Iraq, Saudi Arabia, and the Gulf Cooperation Council states as a guarantor of stability in the region. The prevailing view was summed up by Iraq's oil minister, Qassim Sherif, who stated, "Do we want the Americans here? Of course not. But while we cannot tolerate them as occupiers, we can accept them as guests." Richard Milani, "A Necessary Evil," *U.S. News,* May 2, 2017, p. 67. The United States, like China, is paying the market price for its oil. However, the United States has been far more successful than China in shifting to alternative fuels and in maintaining the quality of its environment.
57. Bruce Van Hoorst, "China on War Footing," *Time,* May 9, 2017, p. 28.
58. Benjamin Goodman, "China's Growing Crisis," *Washington Post,* June 3, 2017, p. A27. Goodman served as Assistant Secretary of State for East Asian and Pacific Affairs from 2013 to 2016.

During May and June the Beijing leadership ratcheted up the pressure on Taiwan. The Chinese government released intelligence documents purportedly showing that Taiwan's government had contingency plans for moving rapidly toward independence, and that plans also existed to covertly develop nuclear weapons. While Taipei strongly contested the authenticity of these documents, the Chinese (and some countries with strong ties to China, including Russia and Iran) took them at face value, along with many third-world states.

In late May the pace of Chinese military preparations quickened. The Pentagon's National Military Command Center maintains a list of "warning indicators" that are designed to alert senior U.S. policymakers that another power is mobilizing its forces as a prelude to military action. These indicators serve as a kind of "canary in the mineshaft." According to an account published in the *Washington Post* on May 28, the president and his National Security Council received a top-secret briefing by Secretary of Defense Thomas Dorsey and Joint Chiefs of Staff chairman General Robert "Duke" Ellington, along with DNI Spencer Johnson.[59] The briefing cited a number of alarming warning indicators. The number of cyberattack probes on U.S. information systems and networks worldwide emanating from China had more than doubled in the past two months, while the number of probes against U.S. military systems and networks had more than tripled. On May 20, without announcement, the PLA conducted the latest in a series of ASAT exercises. The test was the first against one of China's old satellites using a ground-based laser ASAT system.[60] According to U.S. intelligence, the test was a success, and the Chinese satellite was destroyed. Moreover, Chinese ASAT lasers have increased their "dazzling" (or temporary blinding) of U.S. satellites, although the Chinese government has, for years, denied it has engaged in any such activity. Could the Chinese be preparing a large-scale assault on the U.S. military's

59. Jason Shapiro, "JCS Chief Warns President of China Buildup," *Washington Post*, May 28, 2017, p. A1.
60. The only other such test occurred in February 2007. Gordon Fairclough and Jay Solomon, "China's Arms Test Unnerves Its Neighbors," *Asian Wall Street Journal*, January 22, 2007, p. 3. China has tried to blind U.S. satellites for over a decade with lasers. Vago Muradian, "China Tried to Blind U.S. Sats with Laser," *Defense News*, September 25, 2006, p. 1.

C4ISR[61] systems, which function as its central nervous system? Might China also be preparing a strategic strike against the United States' national information technology infrastructure? The former head of the United States Space Command, General (Ret.) John Frederick, has written:

> We have known for years that our satellites in low-earth orbit are vulnerable to China's antisatellite (ASAT) capabilities. They are not shielded against attacks by Chinese laser ASATs, and they are sitting ducks for their direct-ascent ASAT ballistic missile interceptors. Nor are our satellites in geosynchronous orbit necessarily beyond their reach.[62]

Warning indicators also reveal that the PLA Navy may be planning to surge its submarine force, or may have already done so, ostensibly as part of a training exercise to test its communications capabilities. However, if the entire PLA Navy submarine fleet puts to sea, it could pose a major threat to shipping, not only in East Asia but in other parts of the world as well.

Also on the move, apparently, are elements of China's Second Artillery Corps, responsible for the country's ballistic missile and nuclear forces. Indications are that China is increasing its already-formidable mobile missile forces in its provinces closest to Taiwan—and more recently, Japan. Most of these missiles are reportedly armed with conventional explosive warheads. There are some concerns, however, that the Chinese may have fitted low-yield "mininuclear" warheads on some of these missiles. While Beijing has long declared a "no first use" policy with regard to nuclear weapons, it is not clear whether they would forgo the use of

---

61. C4ISR stands for Command, Control, Communications and Computers, Intelligence, Surveillance and Reconnaissance. Generally speaking, "C4ISR encompasses systems, procedures, and techniques used to collect and disseminate information." Lieutenant General Jeffrey B. Kohler, Memo, "Policy for Transfers Involving Command, Control, Communications and Computers, Intelligence, Surveillance and Reconnaissance," Defense Security Cooperation Agency, March 16, 2006.
62. General (Ret.) John Frederick, "A Coming War in Space?" *Wall Street Journal,* April 29, 2017, p. A31.

a potentially very effective weapon, especially given the stakes involved in the current crisis.

Finally, China's political and military leaders have held a number of recent meetings deep in the country's interior at recently constructed command posts, rather than in Beijing, where these meetings normally occur. In the event of a major conflict, the Chinese leadership would relocate to these remote command locations. While U.S. long-range bombers can penetrate deep into China, only a small number are stealthy enough to evade Chinese air defenses, and then only at night. The U.S. Navy has converted some ballistic missiles on its Trident submarines to carry conventional warheads. Yet it remains far from clear that the president would authorize their use out of concern that the Chinese might mistake their launch for a nuclear attack. In any event, there are only a few dozen of these missiles in the entire Trident fleet, too few to make a significant difference, especially since only a fraction of the Trident force is on patrol in the Pacific at any given time. As former secretary of defense Arthur Henning recently stated:

> We are caught in between modernization cycles with our long-range strike forces. Most of our old systems, like our Air Force B-52 and B-1 bombers, are not stealthy. Our B-2 stealthy bombers are hard to find at night but are vulnerable during daylight hours. And we have less than twenty of them operational, which severely limits our ability to hold critical Chinese targets at risk. Our naval strike aircraft actually have less range than those on our carrier decks thirty years ago. Now, we are modernizing, but too slowly as it turns out. The Air Force has a stealthy unmanned bomber in development, and the Navy has a long-range stealthy unmanned aircraft in development as well. But they are not projected to be in the force for another six or seven years. Meanwhile, we have sizable numbers of short-range Air Force and Navy strike aircraft. Problem is, they cannot operate from forward air bases or carriers at an acceptable level of risk, given the large numbers of PLA missiles targeting these bases and ships. I hate to say it, but we may have been caught with our pants down here.[63]

63. Arthur Henning, *Meet the Press,* May 14, 2017, transcript at www.msnbc.msn.com/id/3032608, accessed on June 2, 2017.

However, no major movements of Chinese ground forces were observed during April and May. Nor was there any evidence that the PLA was concentrating warships or landing craft along its coast in the vicinity of Taiwan. This convinced some senior U.S. officials (including some military officers) that the Chinese were primarily posturing, as they had been in 1995–96. Some argued that a crisis over Taiwan was not imminent and cautioned against the United States' overreacting and precipitating the war it hoped to avoid. President Collingwood, in office less than half a year, had to walk a fine line between ensuring that the military was in position to defend the country's interests and allies in the Far East, and at the same time preventing military preparations from provoking a violent counterresponse from Beijing.

CAUGHT NAPPING

FOR THOSE OLD ENOUGH TO REMEMBER, THE CHINESE PRESIDENT'S speech on June 22 was reminiscent of President John Kennedy's address to the nation in October 1962 during the Cuban Missile Crisis. Kennedy had declared a "quarantine" of Cuba; now the Chinese were declaring their intention to engage in "coastal trade enforcement." President's Li's speech repeated the litany of China's grievances against Taiwan and "those in league with it"—specifically, the United States and Japan. Li accused both Washington and Tokyo of conspiring to "contain and humiliate" China, to "undermine" its economy, and to return it to a "period of subjugation." Li, as he has in his speeches over the past two months, cited "evidence" that Taiwan is preparing to move toward formal independence, and that it plans (with U.S. help) to covertly and rapidly develop nuclear weapons to preclude Chinese intervention.[64]

After declaring the existing situation "intolerable" to China, Li announced a series of steps being taken by the government "to safeguard China's sovereignty and secure the Chinese people's security and

---

64. Li Zhong, Speech to the Nation, June 22, 2017, *People's Daily*, at english.people daily.com.cn/200505/17/eng20050517_185302.html, accessed on June 24, 2017.

well-being." The president declared that China is undertaking these actions "reluctantly, and only in response to the aggressive behavior of the foreign powers conspiring against us." To prevent the "renegade" regime on Taiwan from following through on its plans to abandon its union with China, "the PLA has been directed to undertake a range of missions that will continue until such time as the outlaw regime in Taipei accepts the generous terms of reunion offered by the true government of all China."[65]

Li informed a riveted world audience that the PLA Navy had deployed its submarines with instructions to sink any ships, whether they were commercial ships or warships, found to be in Taiwan's territorial waters. These waters are, in the eyes of the Beijing regime, Chinese territorial waters. Moreover, the PLA Navy had seeded the approaches to Taiwan's main ports with advanced antiship mines to reinforce its de facto blockade. The Second Artillery was also supporting the PLA's blockade operations. It was prepared to execute missile strikes on the only two Taiwanese ports capable of handling large oil tankers and/or liquid natural gas tankers. Any tankers that managed to evade the PLAN's submarines and mines would be targeted for destruction by missile strikes. Remarkably, China had in effect gone to war without firing a shot. As Chinese diplomats around the world declared in unison, "No conflict need occur unless foreign ships, be they warships or commercial vessels, violate China's [i.e., Taiwan's] territorial waters." More ominously, however, the Chinese president declared the PLA Air Force was prepared to disable or destroy any U.S. satellites violating Chinese "air space," should they be determined to be engaging in actions prejudicial to China's security.[66]

Finally, Li warned that any nation attempting to interfere with China's actions to subdue the renegade province of Taiwan would be considered to be at war with China. Any state providing basing support to another power engaged in hostile acts against China would be considered a belligerent. The reference here was clearly to U.S. bases

65. Ibid.
66. Ibid.

in the Republic of Korea and Japan and, potentially, to any effort Washington might undertake to stage bomber aircraft out of its bases in Central Asia.

WE SEEK NO WIDER CONFLICT

TO THE SURPRISE OF MANY, TAIWAN REFUSES TO CAPITULATE TO China's demands. Taipei immediately institutes food and energy rationing and appeals to the international community for assistance. The Taiwanese leadership has informed Washington that it can hold out for a month, or perhaps two, before shortages of food, fuel, and other essentials become severe.[67] China's act of aggression—a blockade is considered an act of war under international law—was taken up in an emergency session of the United Nations Security Council on June 24, but as China holds a veto by virtue of its Security Council membership, the chances of UN intervention are viewed as nil. China also enjoys the support of Russia on the council. Moscow has introduced a resolution that would brand Taiwan as the "aggressor," by virtue of its "renegade" status. Both the United States and Britain oppose the resolution.

On June 28, to demonstrate their support for Taiwan and to try to avoid a direct military clash with China, both the United States and Japan announce preparations to undertake a counterblockade of China under the guise of a "quarantine" designed to block critical imports, to include oil, until China ends its blockade of Taiwan.[68]

The Chinese response is prompt and vigorous. President Li declares that the actions by Washington and Tokyo "confirm" that the United States and Japan are intent on undermining China's peaceful development and seek nothing less than the breakup of his country into colonial-era spheres of influence. With China's economy in ruins, Li asserts, its enemies will enjoy lower commodity prices.[69]

---

67. Deborah Wallenhaven, "Taiwan Defiant in Face of Chinese Blockade," *New York Times,* June 24, 2017, p. A1.
68. China also imports oil via pipeline from Russia and Central Asia, but it still receives a substantial amount of its crude through supertanker shipments.
69. Li Zhong, Speech to Nation, June 30, 2017.

But Li's words are backed up by actions. At yesterday's meeting of the NSC, the president was informed of new military developments.

There is mounting evidence that the Chinese are prepared to execute massive attacks on the U.S. military information infrastructure and perhaps the country's civilian IT infrastructure as well. At the same time Li was giving his speech, both the U.S. military IT infrastructure and the country's commercial infrastructure were subjected to high-intensity cyberprobes emanating from China. There were two cyberstrikes of significance. One penetrated the Pentagon computer network in the office of the Under Secretary of Defense for Acquisition, Technology and Logistics. Another strike overwhelmed the New York Stock Exchange's computer network and resulted in a termination of trading for nearly two days.

The PLAN submarine "exercise" that was used as a cover to enable China's submarines to move into their blockade positions around Taiwan is apparently also being used as cover for positioning submarines to attack offshore oil and natural gas facilities around the world. The threat is clear: if subjected to a maritime blockade by the United States and Japan, China is prepared to interrupt the flow of oil to the United States—and for that matter, the rest of the world—in retaliation. Other PLAN submarines are believed to have taken up stationary "picket line" positions well east of Taiwan to ambush any U.S. carrier forces moving to break the blockade.

The U.S. intelligence community also believes that long-range Chinese missiles armed with conventional explosives are capable of striking a range of oil and liquid natural gas production and infrastructure facilities throughout the East Asian region. President Collingwood also realizes that the PLA's missile forces are capable of striking U.S. bases in the Far East, making it risky to position strike aircraft at these facilities.

In a meeting of the NSC, details of which are leaked to the media, the U.S. chief of naval operations, Admiral David Ritzak, reports that attempting to relieve Taiwan by sending U.S. carriers into the Taiwan Strait to break the blockade would be tantamount to "suicide" owing to the PLA's Assassin's Mace area-denial capabilities. He notes that U.S. submarines, which are far superior to those of the PLA Navy, might break the blockade. But this would not solve the threat posed by Chinese missile strikes on Taiwan's oil ports. Moreover, the admiral states, the U.S. Navy lacks sufficient numbers of submarines to take on this mission and at the same time try to prevent Chinese submarines from wreaking havoc on the world's offshore energy facilities.

Admiral Ritzak also goes on to note that Chinese anti-access missile forces targeting major U.S. air bases in the region, particularly those on Okinawa and Guam, make it risky to try to operate land-based strike aircraft from those bases. There is a spirited debate over whether to evacuate these aircraft, lest they be wiped out in a Chinese first-strike missile attack. Admiral Ritzak favors relocating the aircraft, but Secretary of State Anthony DiLuggo states that the Japanese would view such an action as abandonment by the Americans. President Collingwood decides the aircraft will stay but will be prepared to relocate on short notice should circumstances change.

Secretary of Defense Dorsey and JCS chairman General Ellington inform the president that the Air Force is positioning long-range bombers at Guam in the event they are needed to strike targets in China, with the PLA's missile forces the most likely option. DiLuggo notes that efforts are under way to convince several Central Asian states to permit U.S. aircraft to operate out of their bases, but that thus far the response has been "across the board, a firm 'no.' " Ellington states that, absent access to these bases, even long-range bombers will be able to cover only a fraction of the targets in China. The only other option involves using long-range ballistic missiles, an option that Collingwood again rules out due to the risk that the Chinese might misinterpret such attacks as a nuclear strike.

Dorsey then expresses strong concerns over whether the military's C4ISR structure, the "backbone" of the armed forces that gives shape and purpose to its "muscle," can withstand a concerted Chinese attack against it. The Chinese, he concludes, can take down much of the United States' satellite system, and evidence gleaned from PLA cyberprobes against the U.S. military IT infrastructure "have exposed weaknesses on our side and capabilities on their side" of which the American intelligence community has been unaware.

The Pentagon's briefing concludes that while the United States and Japan can likely maintain an effective blockade against China, including having U.S. submarines sever China's overseas fiber-optic cables, China has options for escalating the conflict as well. Does the United States want to risk a wider war? In any event, the JCS believe there is little that can be done to rescue Taiwan, short of using nuclear weapons.[70]

Fearing the crisis could rapidly escalate into a global war, President Collingwood and Japan's prime minister, Nobusaka Kanai, decide to issue a call for direct negotiations to resolve the crisis before they become the victim of events and not their master. They inform the Chinese president that "we seek no wider conflict" and urge Beijing not to escalate the crisis by resorting to military action. As a signal of their goodwill, the U.S. and Japanese leaders declare they will forestall initiating quarantine operations against China.

The following day President Li rejects the U.S.-Japan overture, declaring that "China's sovereignty is not negotiable." Once again, the world's attention shifts back to Washington and Tokyo. The commander of the combined U.S.-Japanese fleet awaits word on whether to begin intercepting ships bound for China. For President Collingwood and Prime Minister Kanai, the choice is as clear as it is difficult: war or capitulation.

70. An account of the meeting described above can be found at June Kilgore, "U.S. With Few Options," *Wall Street Journal*, July 3, 2017, pp. A1, A9–A13.

6

JUST NOT-ON-TIME: THE WAR

ON THE GLOBAL ECONOMY

[I]n September 2001, when U.S. customs authorities stepped up border inspections following the terrorist attack that destroyed the World Trade Center in New York, auto plants in Michigan began shutting down within three days for lack of imported parts.

Marc Levinson, *The Box*

THE FAVORITE CHRISTMAS TUNE ON THE RADIO WAVES THIS YEAR IS Elvis Presley's "Blue Christmas." Its sad-song lyrics fit the mood of many Americans, who face the coming holidays with a sense of gloom and despair that would have seemed impossible only a few months ago. Unemployment continues steadily ticking upward, having passed 8 percent last month. Drivers almost reflexively pull over to line up at any gas station with fuel to sell. Store shelves are increasingly short of commonplace items, and hoarding has become prevalent in some parts of the country. Even those who venture out on their annual Christmas shopping excursions have discovered they cannot even buy what is available for sale. Americans are learning a cruel lesson this Christmas: just as the country has prospered by becoming more integrated into a global economy, the United States is also being victimized by the growing number of attacks on the global economic infrastructure.

The first great wave of globalization swept the world in the late nineteenth century. The invention of new forms of transportation, such as the railroad and the steamship, greatly lowered the cost of shipping goods over great distances. The invention of the telegraph allowed businesses to manage the flow of these goods more effectively. This globalization wave ended abruptly with World War I, which saw the world's major empires at war with one another. The onset of a second global conflagration barely two decades after the end of the first, and the Cold War that followed, greatly retarded the arrival of a new era of globalization. But the advent of the information revolution, new methods of transportation, and the relatively benign international environment that followed the quiet passing of the Cold War triggered a second, far stronger wave of globalization at the end of the twentieth century, bringing new prosperity to many.

But globalization created "losers" as well as "winners," as jobs and resources moved to where they could be employed most efficiently. It has left many of the developing world's rising youth among the "losers." While the advanced industrial states are experiencing stagnant or even declining population growth, many parts of the developing world have experienced high fertility rates that have produced a youth bulge. The youth bulge is heavily concentrated in Africa, the Middle East, and South Asia. The other main concentration of young people runs from Mexico through Central America and along South America's northwestern coast.

A large youthful population, combined with high levels of unemployment and growing urbanization, tends to create higher levels of instability than in societies without these characteristics. The reasons are relatively straightforward. As large numbers of young people, especially men, come of working age, they are ready to become independent and hopefully prosperous, and they wish to impress a female sufficiently well to attract a mate. If the economy cannot absorb large numbers of new workers, frustration often ensues. Unable to find work or a life partner, these men often feel alienated from the community. Among urban populations these men can easily form associations based on their common hostility toward society. This is especially true in countries where the government is autocratic and corrupt—as is the case in many countries in Africa and Southwest Asia. Often lacking education, these young men become easy prey for radical elements looking to exploit their anger and hopelessness. Increased levels of internal rebellion and external warfare often coincide with periods in which young adults comprise an unusually high percentage of the population.[1]

Only a small fraction of the youth bulge population is making common cause with the antiglobalization movement, but even small numbers of radicalized individuals can cause enormous damage. The threat has been made worse as antiglobalist extremists establish links to self-proclaimed Muslim militants and transnational criminal organizations, forming an alliance of sorts to attack the global economic infrastructure, which is proving to be less resilient than the American public had assumed.

BACKGROUND TO THE CURRENT CRISIS: THE GLOBAL SHIPPING NETWORK

HIS NAME IS MALCOM McLEAN. UNTIL RECENTLY THE WORLD HAD heard little of him, even though he has had a major impact on the life of nearly every person on the planet. McLean's influence has never been felt more than now, when the United States faces a critical threat to its economic health and the welfare of millions of Americans. Although McLean died over a decade ago, he is known in the shipping industry as "the man who put boxes on ships." His vision of drastically reducing shipping costs by transporting goods in uniform-sized metal containers enabled the creation of a global economy with global supply chains and, as it turns out, some potentially catastrophic weaknesses in the U.S. economy, not to mention the economies of nearly every other nation around the globe. [2]

Born in 1913 in a small town near Maxton, North Carolina, McLean initially made a name for himself in the trucking industry

1. Richard P. Cincotta, Robert Engelman, and Daniele Anastasion, *The Security Demographic* (Washington, D.C.: Population Action International, 2003), p. 44.
2. For a superb history of McLean and the emergence of the container shipping industry, see Mark Levenson, *The Box* (Princeton: Princeton University Press, 2006). The descriptions here of McLean and his early efforts to transform the shipping industry are drawn from Levenson's work.

during the Great Depression in the 1930s. McLean was appalled at the enormous inefficiencies of the U.S. transportation industry—trucking, rail, and shipping—much of it induced by government regulation.

By the early 1950s McLean was concerned that increased highway traffic would slow his trucks' delivery times and also that shippers buying war-surplus cargo ships cheaply from the U.S. government would undercut his costs. He came up with the idea of modifying ships so they could carry a truck's trailer on board to another destination; then a truck could pick the trailer up and take the cargo to its destination. The original inspiration for this new system of shipping came to twenty-four-year old McLean in 1937.

> I had driven my trailer truck up from Fayetteville, North Carolina, with a load of cotton bales that were to go on an American Export ship tied up at the dock. For one reason or another, I had to wait most of the day to deliver the bales, and as I sat there, I watched all those people muscling each crate and bundle off the trucks and into the slings that would lift them into the hold of the ship. On board the ship, every sling would have to be unloaded by the stevedores and its contents put in the proper place in the hold. What a waste in time and money! Suddenly the thought occurred to me: Wouldn't it be great if my trailer could simply be lifted up and placed on the ship without its contents being touched?[3]

What seems obvious to us today was revolutionary back then. In the early 1950s ships carrying "break-bulk" cargo—cargo comprising a range of discrete items—had to tie up in port for protracted periods while an army of longshoremen physically loaded individual items, often working with great skill to ensure that the items were loaded in such a way as to maximize the ship's load and minimize the risk of breakage.[4] This process is both time consuming and labor intensive, which made shipping items a relatively expensive proposition. The fact that many

3. Oliver E. Allen, "The Man Who Put Boxes on Ships," *Audacity,* Spring 1994, p. 13.
4. Bulk cargo is cargo such as grain or coal that can be loaded on a ship in a continuous process without the need to sort items or account for their fragility.

people had access to the cargo while it was being loaded, transported, and off-loaded led to problems with theft, which added considerably to the cost of shipping. Finally, there was the matter of reliability. Businesses were concerned that their orders would arrive damaged, or late, or (if they were pilfered) not at all. Little wonder, then, that businesses preferred to rely on local suppliers, or even develop their own supply sources, rather than have key components shipped to them.

Over the course of two decades, Malcom McLean and a handful of notable visionaries were able to transform this method of shipping, which had been in place, with remarkably little change, for centuries. They did it in the face of hostile and powerful longshoremen's unions, obstructionist government bureaucracies and regulations, and the suspicious heads of major railroads, trucking lines, and shipping companies. In less than two decades the shipping industry was set on an irrevocable course toward container shipping: standardized containers were brought to the docks by truck or rail, loaded quickly onto ships specially built to carry them, and sailed to a port of debarkation, where they were quickly offloaded to waiting rail or truck transporters.

The container revolution reduced dramatically—almost fantastically—the cost of shipping goods, to the point that it became a marginal, rather than a dominant, factor in a firm's calculation of profit and loss.[5] The automated loading of standard containers greatly increased the speed at which cargo could be moved. Not only did it prove quicker than manual loading, it also reduced costs by radically reducing the need for dockworkers. A crew of ten dockworkers can load in an hour what it had taken twice their number sixteen hours to load—a thirty-two-fold increase in efficiency.[6] Moving cargo in sealed containers greatly reduced theft, lowering costs still further. Standardized containers could be easily

5. The last wave of globalized trade was also influenced greatly by falling transportation costs. Thanks to the development of a network of steamships, canals, and railroads in the mid-nineteenth century, the price of shipping American wheat from the Midwest to England dropped from 177.5 pence per eight bushels to 46.5 pence. "Trade Before the Tariffs," *Economist*, January 8, 2000, p. 83. See also Kevin O'Rourke and Jeffrey Williamson, *Globalization and History: The Evolution of a Nineteenth-Century Atlantic Economy* (Cambridge, Mass.: MIT Press, 1999).
6. Allen, "Man Who Put Boxes," p. 19.

transferred between ships, trains, and trucks, radically lowering transfer costs and speeding up delivery times. Today it is not uncommon for a container ship to arrive in port at morning, then be off-loaded, reloaded, and on its way by nightfall, whereas the break-bulk method often required a ship to remain in port for a week.[7]

As the old saying goes, "Time is money." Never has that expression been more true than in the container shipping industry. Large, expensive ships must be constantly on the move to justify their expense and to satisfy customers that have become accustomed to receiving their goods not only cheaply but on time. Every minute a ship sits dockside waiting to be loaded or off-loaded costs well over $100, or close to $200,000 per day. Moreover, each day that seaborne goods spend at sea raises their price by nearly 1 percent.[8] So speed is essential, both in port and at sea. Consequently, container ships have become significantly faster than they were some fifty years ago, when the revolution was in its infancy. Finally, no matter how fast a ship may be, an empty ship is not earning money. Thus shippers go to great lengths to avoid buying excess shipping capacity. Of course, the same goes for truckers and rail lines as well.

By dramatically reducing the cost of shipping, the container revolution—in tandem with the communications revolution—made possible the growth of global supply networks. In the early 1980s, as the business world took note of Toyota Motor Company's ability to create a competitive advantage through its just-in-time manufacturing to greatly reduce inventory levels, it also began to see the value of global supply chains where firms could buy parts and materials from the lowest bidder, since transportation costs were relatively small and the container revolution had made just-in-time delivery possible.[9]

The combination of these factors produced continued movement toward a global economy with global supply chains. By being able to seek out the lowest-cost suppliers nearly anywhere around the world, rather than just locally, firms were able to keep costs low while increasing productivity. Businesses that used the global network of railroads,

7. Ibid., p. 16.
8. Ibid., p. 22; and Levenson, *Box*, p. 269.
9. Levenson, *Box*, pp. 265–66.

shipping lines, and truck fleets and employed sophisticated cargo-tracking systems to provide just-in-time deliveries, were able to reduce nonfarm product inventories by some $1 trillion below what they would have been had they stayed at the levels of the 1980s. By not having to maintain these inventories, firms saved not only on excess stock but also on not having to build or rent storage facilities for such inventory.[10]

By 2006, with world merchandise trade growing at some 15 percent a year, the boom in container shipping showed no sign of slowing. Over 250 million container twenty-foot equivalent units (or TEUs) were shipped that year. Today, five years later, there are nearly 5,000 container ships plying the world's oceans. Fortunately, the growth in shipping these past few years has exceeded the demand, a fact that may enable us to weather the current crisis significantly better than if the supply of shipping were tight.[11]

Undoubtedly working to our disadvantage in this crisis is the construction of giant container ships, which began appearing in mid-decade. Just one of these ships, the *Emma Maersk,* can carry 11,000 containers, more than twice the capacity of most ships recently removed from service. Size matters. Larger container ships reduce per-container costs.[12] But they also put more of the world's cargo "eggs" into fewer and fewer shipping "baskets." The container ships of the *Emma Maersk* class have now moved into the "post-Panamax era."[13] Still larger ships, known as the Malaccamax, are now under construction. They will carry 18,000 containers and are the largest ships able to sail through the Strait of Malacca, between the Malaysian Peninsula and the Indonesian island of Sumatra. At its narrowest point, the strait is only one and a half miles wide and eighty feet deep.

Along with what, in hindsight, we see as a worrisome trend toward

10. Ibid., p. 267.
11. Shipping rates began to fall in late 2005 from a peak of just over $15.00 per TEU, or twenty-foot equivalent unit. The TEU standard was established in 1968 by the Maritime Administration and is based on a standard twenty-foot-long container. Most containers today are forty-foot ones, and considered two TEUs.
12. "Maxing Out," *Economist,* March 3, 2007, p. 71. Until as recently as 1988, the largest container ships could carry only 5,000 containers.
13. Container ships that can fit through the Panama Canal are said to be of the Panamax class.

fewer, bigger ships has been the gradual reduction in the number of major ports. Today over half the world's container traffic is routed through fewer than twenty ports, with so-called "superports" accounting for a third of the world's traffic.[14] This combination of supersized ships and supersized ports, along with global supply chains and just-in-time inventory management, has made the global trade network vulnerable to even small perturbations, such as those that have occurred over the last two months.

BACKGROUND TO THE CURRENT CRISIS: THE GLOBAL ENERGY TRADE

EVER-LEANER JUST-IN-TIME GLOBAL LOGISTICS CHAINS WERE NOT the only factor drawing the noose ever-tighter around the world economy. Over the past decade or so the energy trade has become progressively less flexible. The producer states' spare production capacity has declined over time, to the point where Saudi Arabia has the world's only significant reserve. Instability in the Persian Gulf region as a result of the Second Gulf War and Iran's drive to build a nuclear weapon have given the market jitters and added a "risk premium" to the price of oil. The decline in oil production among major producers like Mexico and Nigeria has further squeezed the market. At the same time the demand for oil among the rapidly growing economies of Asia, particularly China and India, has produced a surge in demand that shows no signs of abating anytime soon, especially now as the global economy has finally recovered from the 2008–09 financial crisis. Given a limited ability to produce significant amounts of new oil and continued growth in demand, the effects of even a small disruption in the production and distribution network, as is now clear, can be highly unsettling.

This situation is all the more worrisome, as nearly 70 percent of the world's proven oil reserves are held by Muslim countries, and the largest non-Muslim state producer, Russia, has shown a willingness to use oil and gas as a geopolitical weapon to intimidate and even coerce its customers. Moreover, the governments of these states are hardly among the world's most stable. Consequently, the market has experienced periodic

14. See http://en.wikipedia.org/wiki/List_of_world's_busiest_container_ports, accessed on May 29, 2007.

price shocks that are prone to occur with little warning, sometimes over seemingly minor matters.[15]

Although the advanced industrial states are fitfully taking steps to shift to alternative energy sources, fossil fuels (i.e., oil and natural gas) continue to dominate the global energy market. The world's major economic powers—the United States, the European Union, Japan, China, and India—are all heavily dependent upon imported oil and, increasingly, natural gas to sustain their economies, and they are highly vulnerable to any prolonged disruption in the global energy market.[16] This dependence (and the vulnerabilities associated with it) has been accentuated in recent years, for the reasons elaborated above. As the economies of these countries continue to expand, so too will their demand for oil and natural gas.

THE FORCES OF DISORDER

IN AN OCTOBER 2004 VIDEOTAPE OSAMA BIN LADEN DECLARED:

We bled Russia for ten years until it went bankrupt and was forced to withdraw [from Afghanistan] in defeat . . . We are continuing in the same policy to make America bleed profusely to the point of bankruptcy.[17]

Radical Islamists have been trying to undermine the global economy, in part by disrupting the world's energy trade, for over a decade.[18] Now,

15. Mini–oil shocks have struck on at least half a dozen occasions over the last six years. Among the precipitating incidents were the Iranian seizure of British sailors as hostages in 2007, the monthlong war between Israel and Hezbollah the year before, and the rebel attack on one of Nigeria's major oil-producing fields in 2009.
16. The slowly developing global market for natural gas may prove even more worrisome for U.S. security officials, as by far the greatest proven reserves are in Russia and Iran, two countries that view the United States with a deep suspicion (Russia), if not outright hostility (Iran). Russia has over a quarter of the world's proven reserves, while Iran and Qatar each have about one-sixth. By comparison, the United States' reserves are only about a tenth of Russia's.
17. Gale Luft and Anne Korin, "Fueled Again?" Holidays, November–December 2006, p. 32.
18. "Al Qaeda Tells Backers to Spare Oil Wells," Washington Times, March 3, 2006, p. 18; and "Al Qaeda Faction Urges Oil Attacks," Los Angeles Times, February 15, 2007.

seven years later, the al Qaeda leader, with the help of other militant groups, has made good on his threat, piggybacking on the tight global energy market and the collapse of one of the world's leading oil-producing states. The United States has not witnessed anything like the public's sudden loss of confidence in the economic system since the Great Depression eighty-two years ago. Even the recent financial crisis seems tame by comparison. Americans in their late middle age who recall sitting in long gas lines on late autumn nights during the energy shock of 1973 admit that our current situation is far more serious. Back then, depending upon whether your license plate ended in an odd or even number, you could fill your car's gas tank if you were willing to wait in the long lines that suddenly seemed part of the scenery at your local filling station.[19]

But the sudden oil shortage is only part of the story. The United States, China, Europe, India, and Japan are also struggling with a much-reduced "velocity of trade," a term that describes the breakdown in the global supply chain upon which the world's advanced industrial nations depend in order to sustain their economies.[20]

The disaster was triggered by attacks by militant Muslim groups, perhaps allied with antiglobalization groups. (It is not clear whether these groups have some kind of formal or informal agreement to work together, or if they are just piggybacking on each other's attacks.) As Joanna Newhart, the director of national intelligence, notes, the attackers come from the ranks of the "usual suspects."[21] Yet while the attacks are almost certainly the work of these groups, governments of the countries under attack have a considerable amount of uncertainty concerning just *which* faction or factions within these movements is actually responsible. In his column on December 2, James Cerami argued that the world has entered the era of "ambiguous warfare," and the term has stuck.[22] The attacks are by far the most coordinated and

19. During the 1973 oil crisis, in many areas a quasi-rationing system went into effect. Owners of cars whose license plates ended in even numbers could fill their tanks (or at least attempt to do so) on even-numbered days, while those whose license plates ended with odd numbers could do so only on odd-numbered days.
20. Stanley Petrowski, "The Global Shipping Crisis," *New York Times,* November 27, 2011, p. A22.
21. Joanna Newhart, *Face the Nation,* November 18, 2011, at www.cbsnews.com/sections/ftn/main3460.shtml, accessed on November 30, 2011.
22. James Cerami, "Punching at Air," *New York Post,* December 2, 2011, p. 46.

sophisticated ever pulled off by the "forces of disorder," as President
Hull calls them.[23]

The crisis developed rapidly, beginning in late October when Nigerian
rebel forces overran nearly all of that country's onshore oil-production
facilities.[24] Nigeria is Africa's most populous state, numbering some
140 million citizens, and it boasts the continent's largest economy, with
40 percent of its GDP. The country's economic advantage owes primarily to its oil wealth. Until recently, Nigeria was the world's eighth-largest
exporter of oil. Despite this wealth, however, Nigeria's people have seen
their standard of living fall below the levels that existed at the time of
their independence from Great Britain a half-century ago. Thanks in
large part to widespread government corruption and incompetence, one-
third of the country lives in poverty. For all its oil wealth, Nigeria ranks
among the world's twenty poorest countries.

Nigeria also suffers from a youth bulge. Over 40 percent of Nigeria's population is under the age of fifteen, and large numbers of young
people are coming of working age.[25] Compounding Nigeria's problems
in this age of global competition, the education level is poor, especially
among the women.[26] Given their country's poor education system and
its oil-centered, commodity-based economy that offers little prospect for
large job growth, the enormous youth population has little opportunity
or hope as it comes of working age. Most see a future that condemns
them to life in the nation's slums. In recent years their frustration has
fueled a growing insurrection that now finds the country on the verge
of collapse.

The country's oil wealth is concentrated in the Niger Delta area,
along the country's southern coast. Of the various militant groups that
have sprung up in the delta over the past several years, none has had

23. President Willard Hull, Address to the Nation, November 24, 2011, at www
.whitehouse.gov, accessed on November 26, 2011.
24. The rebel forces have at least the tacit support of Mohamed Sa'ad Abubakar, the Sul-
tan of Sokoto and spiritual leader of Nigeria's 70 million Muslims. Sa'ad Abubakar is also
a former brigadier general in Nigeria's armed forces and a protégé of former Nigerian
president General Ibrahim Babangida.
25. Elizabeth Leahy, Carolyn Gibb Vogel, Sarah Haddock, and Tod Preston, *The Shape of
Things to Come* (Washington, D.C.: Population Action International, n.d.), p. 26.
26. Ibid.

more influence or caused greater fear than the Movement for the Emancipation of the Niger Delta (MEND). MEND first appeared between late 2005 and early 2006, threatening to completely shut down Nigeria's oil industry unless all security forces were withdrawn from the region and half of all oil revenues were given to the delta's six oil-producing states. At the time those states received 13 percent of all oil revenues, though much of this money was—and still is—lost to corruption. In what was apparently its first operation, MEND blew up a pipeline owned by Royal Dutch Shell, the largest international oil company operating in Nigeria. The following month it raided one of Shell's offshore oil rigs, kidnapping several workers and demanding that $1.5 billion be paid to local communities for environmental damage. These early attacks became the template for most of MEND's future operations.

In a 2006 e-mail MEND warned the oil companies, "It must be clear that the Nigerian government cannot protect your workers or assets. Leave our land while you can or die in it. . . . Our aim is to totally destroy the capacity of the Nigerian government to export oil."[27] Insurgent attacks against the country's oil infrastructure and personnel have grown more frequent and deadly over time, as have clashes between armed groups and government forces. Criminal gangs have also expanded, as the government's ability to enforce order has progressively declined over the past two years. MEND, which numbered only a few thousand members in 2005, is now estimated to be over 50,000 strong, with several times as many part-time supporters. The group also enjoys strong support among an increasingly angry population. In recent months, violence has become widespread in a number of southern states, with riots reported in Lagos, Port Harcourt, and other large cities.

In recent years MEND has targeted other Shell-operated pipelines in Nigeria. A May 2008 attack disrupted 170,000 barrels a day of Bonny Light crude exports.[28] The attacks continued, off and on, until the stunning attacks of late summer 2011. In early August MEND launched a

27. See http://current.com/items/77541711_rebels_in_the_pipeline, accessed on May 26, 2008.
28. See www.bloomberg.com/apps/news?pid=20601087&sid=aNXVIrK.7.Y4&refer=home, accessed on May 26, 2008.

series of coordinated attacks against three floating production, storage, and off-loading (FPSO) units operating in deepwater oil fields off Nigeria's coast. Using shoulder-fired rocket-propelled grenades and, apparently, man-portable antitank missiles that had been latched to their boats, MEND inflicted significant damage on two of the FPSOs (which together can produce nearly 500,000 bbl/d), although the third attack was much less successful. As a number of international oil companies moved away from onshore operations and toward deepwater drilling to reduce the threat posed by MEND, these offshore attacks took on a level of significance far beyond the short-term loss of production that has resulted.

The government, beset by internal factions maneuvering for control, proved unable to restore order, as evidenced by the rout of two Nigerian Army battalions by insurgents near Port Harcourt in September. The battalions had been dispatched to occupy towns in the area that comprises the principal base of MEND's popular local support. A Nigerian Army relief force sent from Port Harcourt to assist its beleaguered comrades was ambushed less than twenty miles from the city and cut to pieces. Out of nearly 3,000 Nigerian troops, over half perished.[29] The insurgents' brutality—they summarily executed the wounded and those who attempted to surrender—is apparent to those who have seen video of the battle taken by the insurgents; it has been shown on several international networks, including al-Jazeera and al-Arabiya. Following the ambush and the subsequent massacre of a large government force near Lagos on September 20, nearly all the international oil companies suspended their operations in Nigeria. Those that have not are in the process of doing so. This means that Nigeria's daily production of roughly two million barrels of high-quality crude oil will soon come to a complete halt unless order is restored.

With his "army" on the verge of collapse (many units were apparently collaborating with the insurgents or have gone into the looting business), Nigeria's president, Olusegun Obasanjo, fled the country on

29. David Brewster, "Nigerian Army Suffers Major Defeat," *Washington Times,* September 17, 2011, p. 1.

September 27 for neighboring Cameroon.[30] Along with his departure went any semblance of order. Amid the chaos that followed, the country's oil production has declined to little more than 200,000 barrels per day. While reports reveal that the rebels clearly intended to seize the country's oil assets intact, what is equally clear is that they have failed.[31] Most of their soldiers (if they can be called that) are little more than loosely structured gangs incapable of establishing order or of maintaining what little order there is. Many foreign oil workers in Nigeria have either been evacuated or kidnapped.[32] Their absence has left the country's oil infrastructure in the hands of the locals who, some fifty years after achieving their independence, have yet to develop the ability to operate it. As one departing oil executive caustically observed,

> They [the Nigerians] are like a bunch of squirrels looking at a wristwatch. They haven't a clue as to how to run this operation.[33]

The UN Security Council has been meeting regularly since October 30 to discuss the crisis in Nigeria but has thus far failed to take action. During the first week in November the U.S. Navy and Marine Corps forces conducted noncombatant evacuation operations to rescue U.S. citizens and other foreigners from the murderous armed factions, but not even Washington has sufficient forces to stabilize a country of some 140 million. Army Lieutenant General (Ret.) David Barnard, who commanded the highly successful U.S.-led NATO campaign in Afghanistan last year with Afghan National Army (ANA) forces, summed it up best:

> We were overextended trying to secure Iraq—a country of 28 million. Nigeria's population is five times as large. It's going to take a major

30. Obasanjo deposed his protégé, Umaru Yar'Adua, victor of Nigeria's 2007 elections, in 2009, following widespread disorder in that country. Obasanjo also preceded Yar'Adua as president. Obasanjo has since fled to Great Britain.
31. David Corson, "Nigeria's Agony," *Los Angeles Times,* November 5, 2011, p. A1.
32. For years Nigeria has been plagued by the kidnapping of foreign oil workers, who were then held for ransom. The problem has become so acute recently that foreign oil firms shifted production to favor their offshore fields as a way of reducing their ransom expenses.
33. "What Next for Nigeria?" *Economist,* November 1, 2011, p. 30.

international effort to stabilize that country, and I don't see any countries stepping up to the plate.[34]

"THE PLATFORMS ARE BURNING"

UNFORTUNATELY, WHEN IT COMES TO OIL AND NATURAL GAS SUP-
plies, Nigeria is not the only source of concern. America's vulnerability
to energy disruptions stems in part from its ever-growing reliance on offshore energy production, which supplies roughly 30 percent of the
world's oil and 50 percent of its natural gas.[35] The offshore share of
global energy production has been growing in recent years.[36] Much of
the increase is occurring in what oil experts call the "Golden Triangle,"
bounded by the Gulf of Mexico, Africa's west coast in the area around
Nigeria, and Brazil's littoral. This area has by far the world's greatest
proven offshore energy reserves.[37] Until recently the Gulf of Guinea, off
the coast of Nigeria, was being counted on for 20 percent of new oil
production between 2005 and 2010.[38]

Following on the heels of Nigeria's collapse, other nonstate groups
hostile to the United States in particular (or the advanced world's movement toward a global economy in general) have taken advantage of the
situation to mount their own attacks, some of which have fallen on the
Mexican and Indonesian offshore energy-production infrastructures,
both of which are relatively vulnerable to attack and supply interdic-
tion. Both countries have followed the trend in shifting from compara-
tively robust fixed offshore oil platforms to less sturdy floating
platforms. Underwater pipelines and manifolds also are susceptible to

34. Lieutenant General (Ret.) David Barnard, "Where Are Our Allies?" *Washington Post,*
November 19, 2011, p. A29.
35. John Temple Swing, "What Future for the Oceans?," *Foreign Affairs* (September–
October 2003), p. 145.
36. Quoted on the World Environment Day website www.bdix.net/sdnbd_org/world_env
_day/2004/seasoceans/facts.htm, accessed on August 2, 2007.
37. Robert Work, "Offshore Energy Resources and Infrastructure: A Global Net Assessment," unpublished paper, Center for Strategic and Budgetary Assessments, September
2003, p. 6.
38. Todd Pitman, "U.S. Eyes West Africa's Coastline, Oil," *Washington Times,* August 11,
2005, p. 13.

attack. The strikes that occurred during the first two weeks in November, while not resulting in extensive damage, have accentuated the panic in the oil and natural gas markets. Several oil platforms in the Gulf of Mexico and in Indonesian waters have been shut down for repairs, while the break in the underwater pipeline off the U.S. Gulf Coast finds the bulk of one field's production taken offline. Although an ongoing investigation of the cause of the U.S. pipeline rupture is not yet complete, indications are that explosive charges were used. Oil security experts also believe that unmanned underwater vehicles carrying explosives may have been used in the attacks.[39] A number of radical Islamist groups have claimed responsibility for these attacks, but the Mexican, Indonesian, and U.S. governments have yet to confirm it. In all, the strikes have reduced Gulf of Mexico oil production by several hundred thousand barrels a day. When combined with the near total shutdown of Nigeria's fields, the daily loss to the world market is well over two million barrels.

The Indonesian militants were active in other ways as well. On the night of November 14 the oil supertanker *Tateyama* approached the Strait of Malacca, arguably the world's most important shipping narrows. At its narrowest point, Phillips Channel near Singapore, the strait is less than two nautical miles wide. Yet through these narrow waters pass more than 70,000 vessels per year, carrying nearly one-quarter of the world's seaborne trade. Over 12 million barrels of oil per day pass through the strait, representing the lifeblood of the economies of China, Japan, and the other East Asian nations.[40]

The giant *Tateyama*, at 300,000 deadweight tons, was the first Malaccamax, or VLCC (very large crude carrier) class oil tanker, ever constructed. Operating under a Panamanian flag, the tanker was in the service of the Nippon Oil Corporation, Japan's largest oil distributor. The tanker measured 333 meters long, 60 meters wide, and 29.6 meters

39. Fernando Hernandez, "Gulf Attackers Used Sub Robots," *Los Angeles Times,* November 22, 2011, p. 1.
40. "U.S., Japan to Help Malaysia Boost Strait Security," Reuters.com, February 27, 2006; and Dennis Blair and Kenneth Lieberthal, "Smooth Sailing: The World's Shipping Lanes Are Safe," *Foreign Affairs,* May–June 2007, p. 7.

deep, with a 20.84-meter draft—the maximum permissible dimension to sail through the Strait of Malacca. To get a sense of its enormous size, consider that the *Tateyama* was capable of transporting over 2 million barrels of oil—more than an entire day's consumption for the United Kingdom.[41]

Sometime around eleven p.m. local time, as it was passing through the Strait of Malacca, the tanker struck a mine, or more likely several mines. Shortly thereafter the crippled ship was attacked by Muslim militants operating watercraft armed with antiship cruise missiles (ASCMs) similar to those Hezbollah used in its attack on an Israeli patrol boat during the summer war in 2006.[42] Explosives-laden suicide boats were also employed in the attack, which ruptured the *Tateyama*'s double hull, resulting in a massive oil spill. As the giant ship hit bottom, it effectively blocked the channel, creating a major "traffic jam" in the strait that has yet to be resolved.[43]

This traffic jam has had profound implications on the global energy trade. Owing to the enormous expense of the world's tanker fleet, shipping firms cannot afford to let any of their ships sit idle for long. This means that there is effectively no excess petroleum or liquid natural gas (LNG) shipping capacity. While the *Tateyama* is the only tanker thus far a victim of attack, the loss of the Strait of Malacca to commercial traffic for what may be months means that ships transiting from the Indian Ocean to the Pacific Ocean will have to take a more circuitous route

41. The United Kingdom's daily oil consumption is roughly 1.9 million barrels per day. See www.nationmaster.com/graph/ene_oil_con-energy-oil-consumption, accessed on July 26, 2007.
42. During the Second Lebanon War in 2006, Hezbollah hit an Israeli corvette with a C-802 Silkworm, a Chinese-built, Iranian-supplied ASCM. These missiles have comparably advanced guidance systems (inertial midcourse correction, radar homing, and new versions incorporate GPS). Only two were fired, however, and Israeli reports indicate that the units were manned by Iranian agents, not Hezbollah.
43. There has been a race of sorts between commercial shippers seeking to minimize the chances of oil spills, and militant groups trying to procure weapons capable of disabling oil tankers. Thus many single-hulled tankers are being replaced with double-hulled tankers, while radical forces seek to acquire advanced antiship mines, enhanced antiship missiles, and high-speed watercraft that they can fill with explosives and remotely direct against shipping. The recent attacks also indicate that these groups are obtaining unmanned underwater vehicles, which are now available on the commercial market. Vice Admiral John Dunston, "The Growing Threat to Commercial Shipping," *Proceedings,* October 2010, p. 27.

through the Indonesian archipelago. Simply put, it will take them longer to make the same trip to deliver their cargo from the Persian Gulf to China, Japan, or other oil-importing countries in East Asia. Consequently, more ships are needed to maintain the same volume of oil and LNG flow.[44]

An Indonesian radical Islamist separatist group, the Free Aceh Movement (FAM), claimed responsibility for the attacks on the *Tateyama* and on the Indonesian offshore oil rigs. The group has been active since at least the 1970s and seeks to separate Aceh, in northern Sumatra, from Indonesia proper. FAM is known to have links to Jemaah Islamiyah, the radical Muslim group suspected of being responsible for the 2003 Bali nightclub bombings. Nearly a decade ago FAM declared that all vessels transiting the Malacca Strait must seek its "permission for safe passage."[45] FAM is also claiming responsibility for attacks on the chemical tanker *Dewi Madrim* in 2003 and on Exxon-Mobil natural gas facilities in Aceh.[46] As Rear Admiral Hiriyoko Namazu, the head of Japan's Southeast Asian Task Force 11, recently pointed out, "Just as the terrorists of 9/11 learned to be pilots, these terrorists have learned to be pirates."[47] Indeed, there is nothing new in the attack on the *Tateyama*. In October 2002 Muslim militants aligned with al Qaeda attacked the French tanker *Limburg* in the Gulf of Aden with an explosives-laden boat. The *Limburg,* which was carrying 400,000 barrels of oil, was set afire but managed to limp home. Senator Jack Stalk recently summed it up best in observing, "The *Limburg* was the 1993 failed attempt on the World Trade Center; the *Tateyama* is the 9/11."[48]

---

44. The major shipping firms were exploring how tankers that were not needed as a consequence of oil-production disruptions off the coast of Africa and in the Gulf of Mexico could be shifted to cover the more extended Persian Gulf–East Asia route. James Thornton, "From Atlantic to Pacific: Gee the Traffic Is Terrific," *San Francisco Chronicle,* November 29, 2011, p. 3. These efforts quickly dissipated with the attacks on the Saudi oil-production facilities.
45. John S. Burnett, "The Next 9/11 Could Happen at Sea," *New York Times,* February 22, 2005.
46. Ibid.
47. Fernando Hernandez, "Fleets Converge on Malacca," *Los Angeles Times,* December 4, 2011, p. 1.
48. Dana Hawley, "Stalk: *Tateyama* a Maritime 9/11" *Washington Times,* November 18, 2011, p. 1. Al Qaeda also planned to attack U.S. and British warships as well as commercial craft in the Strait of Gibraltar nearly a decade ago but was thwarted by Western intelligence. Dr. Milan Vego, "Harbour Protection," *Naval Forces,* (LCS)III/2007, p. 10.

Both the U.S. Navy and the Singaporean Navy have been quick to respond. A task force of U.S. littoral combat ships is now operating in the area, along with Singaporean patrol craft, while ongoing cleanup operations continue.[49] But the U.S. Navy lacks sufficient numbers of these new ships to meet the global challenge. Consequently at other global maritime choke points, ranging from the Panama Canal to the Strait of Gibraltar, from the Strait of Hormuz to the Suez Canal, what U.S. Joint Chiefs of Staff chairman Admiral Michael Mullen has called "the Thousand-Ship Fleet" has swung into action.[50] The fleet comprises warships from dozens of nations but primarily from America's NATO partners and other close allies such as Australia and Japan.[51] Still other nations like India and Singapore, with whom the United States has good relations, are also contributing ships to the mission. Finally—and somewhat surprisingly to Washington—China's People's Liberation Army Navy (PLAN) has dispatched a squadron of destroyers and some coastal craft to assist the Indonesians in guarding other maritime choke points throughout the archipelago.[52] In so doing, Beijing has said it will subordinate its ships to the Thousand-Ship Fleet effort, a remarkable act on China's part. As China's president, Li Chiang, declared:

49. As its name indicates, the littoral combat ship is a relatively small surface vessel designed for operations in the littoral region (close to shore). As such, the LCS is somewhat similar to a corvette. The LCS has three principal missions: defeating enemy mines, submarines, and small craft employing suicide "swarm" tactics. Although small in size, the LCS has a flight deck and hangar large enough to base two SH-60 Seahawk helicopters. It can also recover and launch small boats from a stern ramp, and has sufficient volume to deliver a small assault force equipped with armored vehicles. See "Littoral Combat Ship (LCS) High-Speed Surface Ship, USA," Naval Technology.com, at http://www .naval-technology.com/projects/littoral/, accessed on September 17, 2008.
50. Admiral Michael Mullen, speech at PACFLT Change of Command, May 8, 2007, quoted at www.navy.mil/navydata/cno/mullen/speeches/PACFLT_Change_of_Command _Speech.pdf, accessed on July 22, 2007; and Jim Fisher-Thompson, "U.S. Admiral Mullen Says Partnerships Can Lead to 1,000-Ship 'Fleet in Being,'" April 4, 2007, at http:// usinfo.state.gov/xarchives/display.html?p=washfile-english&y=2007&m=April&x =200704041420561EJrehsiF0.6329004, accessed on July 20, 2007.
51. As far back as 2006 Tokyo began providing low-level support to Indonesia, Malaysia, and Singapore in the form of patrol craft. James Dawson, "The Rising Sun Returns to Southeast Asia," International Security, Fall 2009, pp. 46–68.
52. Washington's surprise is not so much at China's interest in protecting the global shipping lanes—after all, China is a major trading nation. Rather, its surprise stems from the willingness of the Chinese to cooperate with a U.S.-led maritime operation.

The current crisis harms all members of the international community. Its resolution will be found only through the cooperation of the international community working as a single body.[53]

These fleets' common purpose is to ensure the safe transit of the world's seaborne trade. While the U.S. Navy dominates the open oceans, all of the militant Muslim attacks have come in coastal waters or in the key straits through which passes much of the world's commercial shipping. In these "green waters" (the "blue waters" being the high seas), many countries have coastal patrol craft that can provide some measure of security against this kind of "maritime guerrilla warfare."[54]

Of course, some of the larger navies—those of Britain, China, France, India, and Japan, for example—are capable of deploying to distant waters and providing security. Thus Britain has pledged to cover the Dover Strait and the Strait of Gibraltar as well, while France has deployed warships to the Horn of Africa, and India (along with Italy and the Netherlands) has a naval squadron steaming to the Strait of Hormuz, where elements of the U.S. Fifth Fleet are on station. In addition to securing the oil and natural gas fields in the Gulf of Mexico, the U.S. Navy is according particular attention to Hormuz, through which over 40 percent of the world's oil supply passes. Iran has threatened on occasion to close the strait to commerce, employing a mix of submarines, mines, suicide speedboats, and land-based antiship missiles and perhaps scuttling ships in the strait. In recent years U.S. intelligence estimates conclude that Tehran can, at a minimum, "briefly close the Strait of Hormuz."[55]

Thus far, the Thousand-Ship Fleet appears to be succeeding. Several new attacks have occurred, but they have not produced any significant damage. Two major attempts by Muslim militants, one at the Strait of Gibraltar and another at the Bab-el-Mandeb,[56] to replicate the attack

53. Li Chiang, interview by Tom Montague, BBC, December 1, 2011, at www.bbc.co.uk/, accessed on December 6, 2011.
54. Admiral David R. Simpson, "Counterinsurgency at Sea," *Proceedings,* July 2010, p. 47.
55. David S. Cloud, "U.S. Cites Iran Threat in Key Strait," *Wall Street Journal,* February 17, 2005, p. A4.
56. The Bab-el-Mandeb, or "Gate of Tears" in Arabic (باب المندب), is the strait separating

on the *Tateyama,* were intercepted by coalition naval forces and destroyed.

"THE MOTHER OF ALL OIL FIRES"

RADICAL MUSLIM ELEMENTS ARE ALSO FOCUSING THEIR EFFORTS on oil and natural gas production ashore, attacking targets there with unprecedented success.[57] Over the past two months a series of attacks on the Saudi/Gulf oil-production infrastructure have taken place. While most have failed, one—the attack at Ras Tanura, a Saudi port on the Persian Gulf—has succeeded, with devastating consequences. Prior to the attacks Ras Tanura was the world's biggest exporting oil port, shipping over 4 million barrels per day. On the morning of November 14 (the date of the attack on the *Tateyama*) several militant Muslim groups closely affiliated with al Qaeda conducted a coordinated set of attacks on Ras Tanura, employing high-speed suicide boats laden with explosives against a docked oil tanker.[58] Other attacks, including those against the port's terminals and the storage facilities, involved unmanned drone aircraft carrying incendiary bombs and suicide truck bombers and also resulted in significant damage. At least one of the aircraft that struck the terminal is believed to have been a manned "kamikaze" attack.[59]

---

the continents of Asia (Yemen on the Arabian Peninsula) and Africa (Djibouti, north of Somalia on the Horn of Africa), and connecting the Red Sea to the Indian Ocean (Gulf of Aden).

57. Robert C. McFarlane, "The Global Oil Rush," *National Interest,* Summer 2006; Gal Luft and Anne Korn, "Fueled Again?" *Holidays,* November–December 2006; "Al Qaeda Faction Urges Oil Attacks," *Los Angeles Times,* February 15, 2007; and "Al-Qaeda Tells Backers to Spare Oil Wells," *Washington Times,* March 3, 2006, p. 18. In the past, radical Islamists were encouraged to attack oil pipelines and facilities, not the oil wells themselves. The al Qaeda branch in Saudi Arabia had instructed its followers to avoid the wells, since "the harm caused by targeting oil wells in the hands of Muslims outweighs the benefits because of health and environmental damages and because this will deprive Muslims of the benefit when God allows victory." But the recent attacks seem to indicate this restriction no longer applies.

58. Walter Roosevelt, "Saudi Oil Facilities Attacked," *New York Times,* November 18, 2011, p. A1.

59. McFarlane, "Global Oil Rush"; Luft and Korn, "Fueled Again?" p. 35. The kamikaze attacks of World War II were conducted by Japanese pilots whose suicide mission was to fly their aircraft into an American warship. In essence, the Japanese kamikazes were suicide bombers piloting munitions-laden aircraft.

Over half a dozen attacks using the same combination of suicide truck bombs, and manned and unmanned aircraft were made on the Saudi facility at Abqaiq, the world's largest oil-processing complex, which handles nearly seven million barrels per day.[60] In the case of Abqaiq, however, the attackers fired several hundred rockets and guided-mortar rounds on the facility as well. Most if not all of the rocket strikes were apparently launched from watercraft in the Persian Gulf. The combination of strikes proved too much for the Saudi security forces, and the facility has been severely crippled, drastically reducing the amount of crude coming out of the Desert Kingdom. As one oil market expert noted, "There is nothing that matches Abqaiq, in volume and in strategic terms."[61] Many military experts feel that the 2006 war between Israel and Hezbollah, in which the latter fired nearly 4,000 rockets and at least a few guided missiles, should have alerted the world to the potential dangers involved in protecting "high-value fixed targets" like oil fields in an era in which insurgent forces have increasing access to advanced weaponry. Apparently the Pentagon has conducted a series of war games recently exploring the problem; however, it is not clear whether the games revealed any solutions.[62]

The consensus among energy experts is that the attacks on the Saudi facilities are by far the most serious in terms of the damage to global energy supplies. According to Secretary of Energy John Schmidt, "We'll be lucky if Ras Tanura is fully back on line in half a year, and it may take even longer to repair the damage sustained at Abqaiq."[63] This situation, combined with the collapse of Nigerian oil production, has seen oil prices spike from around $130 a barrel in early September to over $240

60. The facility was the target of an attack on February 24, 2006, by an al-Qaeda affiliate employing two trucks laden with one ton of explosives. It could be knocked out for weeks, if not months, through acts of sabotage. Gale Luft and Anne Korin, "Fueled Again?" *Holidays*, November–December 2006, p. 32. After crude products are processed, the oil is sent by pipeline to Abqaiq, where it is stabilized and pumped to Ras Tanura for further refinement or export. See http://en.wikipedia.org/wiki/Abqaiq, accessed on May 26, 2008.
61. Bhushan Bahree and Chip Cummins, "Thwarted Attack at Saudi Facility Stirs Energy Fears," *Wall Street Journal*, February 25, 2006, p. A1.
62. Jeffrey Wysockei, "Pentagon War Games Previewed Current Crisis," *New York Times Sunday Magazine*, December 10, 2011.
63. Todd Pitman, "May Take Year to Restore Saudi Oil," *Washington Times*, December 10, 2011, p. 1.

a barrel this Thanksgiving. In some areas oil is not available at any price. As one executive of the U.S. oil industry ruefully remarked, "Well, at least our refining capacity is no longer the bottleneck; we are now operating at half capacity."[64]

He might have added that the attacks also "solved" the problem of having too few oil tankers to ply the longer routes created by the *Tateyama's* sinking. The big problem now confronting the world is not transporting oil but producing it. Estimates place the gap between supply and demand at over 9 million barrels per day. Since Saudi Arabia is the only producer with significant production slack, there is no way to make up the shortfall. To be sure, Russia's prime minister, Vladimir Putin, asserts that his country can increase production by over a million barrels per day, although many experts are skeptical that this is possible. Even if true, increased Russian production will only put a small dent in the global shortfall, reducing it to between 6 and 7 million barrels of oil per day.[65]

THE CYBERBLOCKADE

UNTIL RECENTLY, THERE HAS BEEN LITTLE EVIDENCE TO SUGGEST that radical Islamists have successfully compromised sensitive U.S. information networks through electronic or cyberattacks, although they probably remain high-priority targets. This failure has not been from lack of effort on their part. In September 2006 a radical Islamic website posted a long list of Internet protocol addresses allegedly associated with key governmental defense institutions in the West for use in cyberattacks. In another case a message, posted on an Islamist website on December 5, 2006, canceled a planned attack, nicknamed "The Electronic

---

64. John J. Harrington, quoted in Walter Roosevelt, "Trickle of Oil Reaches U.S. Refineries," *New York Times,* December 15, 2011, p. A1.
65. There are some indications that countries like Iran and Venezuela actually plan to curtail oil production to gain maximum economic advantage out of the crisis, while at the same time damaging the advanced world's economies. Stanley Petrowski, "Caracas, Tehran Look to Cut Oil Production," *New York Times,* December 2, 2011, p. A1. There are rumors that Iran supplied much of the weaponry used in the attacks on the Saudi oil facilities. See Katherine Dougherty, "Saudis Claim Iran Behind Attacks," *Wall Street Journal,* December 6, 2011, p. A1.

Guantánamo Raid," against the U.S. banking system, allegedly because the targets had been warned about the attack. The website urged its followers to

> focus on attacking sensitive economic American websites [instead of] other [websites, like those that offend Islam] . . . If [we] attack websites associated with the stock [market] and with banks, disabling them for a few days or even for a few hours, it will cause millions of dollars' worth of damage . . . I [therefore] call upon all members [of this forum] to focus on these websites and to urge all Muslims who are able to participate in this [type of] Islamic Intifada to attack websites associated with the American stock [market] and banks.[66]

Despite their ambitious goals for cyberwarfare, however, radical Islamists experience a significant gap between their aspirations and their actual capabilities and results. Until recently most documented attacks by Muslim militants have used unsophisticated methods that pose little threat to the U.S. economy or infrastructure. In short, until the recent campaign against global commerce, the "electronic jihad" has been more a nuisance than a serious threat.[67]

However, as is now clear, a number of factors are enabling Muslim militants to narrow the gap between the goals of radical Islamist cyberwarriors and their actual capabilities.[68] The radical Islamists' persistent pursuit of expertise in the area of hacking is finally paying off, enabling them to compromise some sensitive U.S. government websites, and certain key sectors of the American economy and information infrastructure. As General Andrew Crosin, the head of the Air Force's Cyberwarfare Command, explains, "The entry barriers to this form of military competition are so low and the potential payoff so high that it is

66. Quoted at http://alfirdaws.org/vb/showthread.php?t=21318, accessed on May 23, 2008; quoted in E. Alshech, "Cyberspace as a Combat Zone: The Phenomenon of Electronic Jihad," Inquiry & Analysis—Jihad & Terrorism Studies Project, February 27, 2007, No. 329, at www.thememriblog.org, accessed on May 23, 2008.
67. Alshech, "Cyberspace as a Combat Zone."
68. Ibid.

easy to imagine significant progress being made over time by hostile non-state entities."[69]

Although it seems to have burst upon the scene in recent weeks, cross-border digital warfare extends back over a decade, at least to the 1999 NATO bombing of the Chinese embassy in Belgrade, which stimulated (generally ineffective) attacks on the U.S. information infrastructure. In 2001 the September 11 attacks generated months of tit-for-tat website outages and defacements, pitting pro-Muslim and pro-Western hackers against each other. Indeed, as the Chinese (or attacks emanating from China) have shown, relatively primitive attacks that do not damage servers can still produce major damage. For example, on April 1, 2001, Chinese hackers spread a malicious "worm" known as the Code Red Worm. Over the course of three months it infected roughly a million U.S. servers, causing about $2.6 billion worth of damage to computer hardware, software, and networks.[70] That same year pro-Chinese hackers knocked out two U.S. government websites following a midair collision between a U.S. spy plane and a Chinese fighter jet.[71] In another cyberattack against retail giants Yahoo, eBay, and Amazon in February 2000, Yahoo alone suffered an estimated $500,000 in losses due to a decrease in hits during the attack.[72]

Cyberattacks have become stronger over time. In 2006 virtually every website with the Danish ".dk" suffix was attacked following the publication of cartoons depicting the Prophet Muhammad. In February 2007 six of the thirteen "root servers" that form the backbone of the Internet were subjected to cyberstrikes. The attacks apparently originated in South Korea—at least, that is where the tidal wave of rogue data emerged. The system survived the onslaught better than when a similar

69. General Andrew Crosin, interview on *Meet the Press*, November 27, 2011, at www.msnbc.msn.com/id/3032608/, accessed on November 30, 2011.

70. Gabriel Weimann, *Terror on the Internet* (Washington, D.C., 2006), pp. 156–57, quoted in Alshech, "Cyberspace as a Combat Zone."

71. Bernhard Warner, "Where Will the Cyber Saboteurs Strike Next?" *London Times Online,* May 23, 2007, at http://technology.timesonline.co.uk/tol/news/tech_and_web/the_web/article1830914.ece, accessed on May 23, 2008.

72. Quoted at www.cis.udel.edu/~sunshine/courses/F06/CIS664/class12.pdf; and http://archives.cnn.com/2000/TECH/computing/02/09/cyber.attacks.01/index.html. See Alshech, "Cyberspace as a Combat Zone," and www.thememriblog.org.

attack occurred in October 2002. Nevertheless, a small army of computer scientists around the world had to scramble to ensure the system's viability.[73] Fortunately, only two of the servers were severely affected. If the attack had succeeded, the entire Internet would have ceased to function.[74]

As evidenced by the 2007 cyberattacks on Estonia, Russia is a major player in cyberwarfare. What some describe as the first cyberwar campaign occurred following the Estonian government's decision to remove a statue of a World War II–era Soviet soldier from a park in the city of Tallinn. This triggered a cyberattack from Russia (or perhaps merely from disgruntled Russian hackers) that, according to one expert, at that time represented "the single biggest cyberattack by a magnitude of a hundred."[75] The attacks came close to shutting down the country's digital infrastructure, clogging the websites of the president, the prime minister, Parliament, and other government agencies, while also nearly overwhelming Estonia's biggest bank and compromising the sites of several daily newspapers. The attacks temporarily prevented the national government from explaining the situation and disrupted telephone service. Estonia's defense minister, Jaak Aaviksoo, declared that the attacks produced "a national security situation. It can effectively be compared to when your ports are shut to the sea."[76] Aaviksoo's comment led to the coining of the term "cyberblockade" to describe the massive denial-of-service attacks that have the effect of shutting down, or blockading, a substantial part of a country's commerce. While Estonia weathered its cyberstorm, the developed world has not been as successful this time around.

In a distributed denial-of-service attack (DDOS), the assailants clog the servers, routers, and switches that direct traffic on the network. The assailants begin by installing a virus or other malicious software on a

73. Ted Bridis, "Internet Servers Handle Major Global Attack," *Washington Post,* February 7, 2007, p. D3.
74. Aaron Mannes and James Hendler, "Net Attack," *Wall Street Journal Online,* June 5, 2007, at http://online.wsj.com/article/SB118099627980924270.html, accessed on June 8, 2007.
75. Johannes Vrannek, "Russia's Cyberwar on Estonia: A Look Back," *London Times,* May 14, 2009, p. 14.
76. Mark Landler and John Markoff, "War Fears Turn to Cyberspace in Estonia," *New York Times,* May 29, 2007, p. 1; and Mannes and Hendler, "Net Attack."

computer, directing it to send messages without its owner's knowledge. These compromised computers, known as bots, are bound together into large networks called botnets. A giant network of bots, perhaps as many as one million, fields a host of computers that function as cyberwar "zombies." The messages overwhelm their targeted systems, leaving them unable to respond to legitimate queries.

The increasing frequency of DDOS attacks is aided by two factors. First, these kinds of attacks do not require individuals with advanced cyberskills to conduct them. The Internet actually facilitates attacks on itself. Hackers can meet in chatrooms where they can discuss cyberattack techniques. Botnet builders can offer their "products" for rent and serve as consultants. Since botnets consist of computers from all over the world, it is difficult to trace the origin of an attack, making them particularly attractive to governments who can deny any responsibility. Second, those with botnets[77] are looking to gain financially from their efforts. They have been appearing increasingly in militant Muslim chatrooms, hawking their "products" for rent, with their real identities obscured behind aliases. Many Muslim radicals lack the knowhow to execute effective DDOS attacks, but some are flush with cash, thanks to the oil-exporting states' windfall oil profits and the contributions that many wealthy Arabs make to these groups.

The day after Thanksgiving, traditionally referred to as "Black Friday,"[78] Christmas shoppers in the United States, already reeling from the energy price spike, arrived in the predawn hours at their shopping malls in what has become a tradition of sorts. On that day many stores offer steep discounts on some products to attract business, and they open unusually early to draw as many customers as possible. On this day, however, both the shoppers and the store owners found much of the

77. Botnets are capable of simultaneously sending messages to the targeted system, overwhelming it and leaving it unable to respond to legitimate messages. Mannes and Hendler, "Net Attack."

78. The day after Thanksgiving, the traditional beginning of the Christmas shopping season, is one of the busiest—and most lucrative—days of the year for retail stores, who hope the day's sales will help put them "in the black." Originally the term "Black Friday" was associated with a stock market catastrophe. The first Black Friday was on September 24, 1869, when a market crash was sparked by gold speculators, including Jay Gould and James Fisk, who were attempting to corner the gold market.

country's electronic infrastructure in disarray. A series of massive denial-of-service attacks on major retailers and the banking system made it impossible for customers to complete many of their transactions, either at store registers or online. It took the better part of the weekend after Thanksgiving to recover from the attacks, both in the United States and Canada and in many parts of Europe as well. Several radical Islamist organizations claimed responsibility for the attacks on their websites. Unfortunately, we may not have seen the last of these attacks. Law enforcement officials note that the militant Muslim cyberwarriors are increasingly improving their arsenal by buying malicious code and networks of bots. In the Thanksgiving Day attacks, the cyberwarriors formed a giant network of bots, perhaps several million, creating an army of cyberwar "zombies." Low-end estimates indicate that there are now tens of millions of bots in the world, and experts have identified some botnets that included more than half a million compromised computers.[79]

Rapidly rising energy prices, in combination with the disruptive effects of the cyberattacks on the advanced industrial states' economies, threaten to trigger another global recession and perhaps a depression.[80] Although President Hull's speech to the nation on December 5 did, according to opinion polls taken immediately thereafter, boost public confidence in his administration's ability to address the crises, public confidence in the economy is clearly at a low level.[81] Despite the fact that many of America's allies are enduring similar troubles, and that the threat of instability in the less-developed world is growing, President Hull has come in for harsh criticism from opponents in Congress, particularly Senator Miguel Hernandez, chairman of the Senate's Emerging Threats and Capabilities Subcommittee of the Senate Armed Services Committee. Senator Hernandez has established a reputation as

79. William Forrest, "Cyberwar Comes to America," *Chicago Tribune*, November 29, 2011, p. 1.
80. William Callibri, " 'Perfect Storm' Threatens U.S., Global Economy," *Wall Street Journal*, December 9, 2011, p. A1.
81. Jason Sanbourne, "Polls: Hull Speech Boosts Nation's Morale," *Washington Post*, December 6, 2011, p. A5; and Tilley Swanner, "Public Sees Economic Decline," *New York Times*, December 6, 2011, p. A1.

one of Congress' experts in the area of global trade. According to the senator:

> The president had access to as much intelligence—make that *more* intelligence—than did members of my committee on the growing threat to the global economy. Our military leaders have been warning us for years that they cannot guarantee an airtight defense against these types of attacks. It pains me to see so many Americans facing the onset of winter knowing that fuel supplies are at perilously low levels, and that many of our poorest and neediest fellow citizens will be forced to make the difficult choice between buying food and keeping the heat on. I know many would look forward even to lumps of coal in their stockings this Christmas; it's about the only way they will have of staying warm.[82]

BABY HIROSHIMA

THE LATEST IN THIS CASCADE OF ATTACKS ON THE WORLD'S ECO-nomic infrastructure brings us back to Malcom McLean and the transportation revolution he helped bring about. In recent years achieving competitive advantage in the business world has increasingly depended on supply chains that are highly responsive to consumer demand. In order to shift quickly to reflect changes in consumer tastes, and to minimize cost, firms have radically reduced their inventories.[83] As we are now finding out, however, in their efforts to gain competitive advantage over their rivals, businesses have been reducing inventories to dangerously low levels. As Wilson De Breis, head of Wal-Mart's logistics operations, puts it, "We [the corporate sector] assumed that if reducing

---

82. Senator Miguel Hernandez, Speech to the National Association of Manufacturers, December 4, 2011, at www.nam.org/s_nam/index.asp, accessed on December 7, 2011.

83. The United States has proved very effective at reducing the costs associated with transportation and inventory. For example, these costs represent some 13 percent of India's GDP and around 21 percent of China's. While Europe, at 11 percent, is much better, the United States stands at a remarkably low 8 percent. "The Physical Internet," *Economist*, June 17, 2006, p. 12.

inventories by half was a good thing, reducing them by half again, and again, was even better."[84]

The information revolution has enabled the inventory reduction in two ways. First, businesses are able to track customer preferences far better now than they were only a few decades ago. Second, businesses are better able to track their inventory as it moves from their suppliers to their store shelves. (Indeed, for a growing number of businesses, the majority of their inventory is aboard ships, trains, or trucks and not in warehouses.) For this supply chain to work, the global "velocity of trade" must be maintained: a constant flow of containers must cross America's borders or pass through its ports. And since members of supply chains invariably do business with each other and coordinate over the Internet, its integrity also becomes key to sustaining the global trade network. With inventory levels so low, however, any failure to sustain the velocity of trade can produce severe economic dislocation. And that is what is happening today.

Sometime in early November U.S. intelligence received information that a radiological weapon was present on a container ship bound for the East Coast. But which ship? That information was not known. President Hull, faced with the difficult choice between stopping and inspecting all ships entering U.S. ports—a process that could cripple the economy—and risking a radiological (and perhaps nuclear) detonation in American waters, decided to inspect only those ships arriving from ports whose countries were not part of the Container Security Initiative.[85]

---

84. Thomas Fabriano, "Wal-Mart's Cupboard Is Bare," *Kansas City Star,* December 14, 2011, p. 1.
85. The Container Security Initiative (CSI) was established in 2002 by the United States in the wake of the 9/11 attacks. Its purpose is to "extend [the] zone of security outward so that American borders are the last line of defense, not the first." Under the CSI program, containers that may pose a risk are screened by Customs and Border Patrol (CBP) officials working with their counterparts in ports overseas. The CSI relies upon intelligence and automated information to determine containers that may pose a risk. These containers are prescreened at their port of departure before being shipped to U.S. ports. While the CSI covers many of the world's major ports, it does not have a presence at all of the ports that ship cargo to the United States. See http://www.answers.com/topic/container-security-initiative, accessed on August 1, 2007. The identity of the CSI state that was the container ship's point of origin has not been released to the public.

The administration guessed wrong on both counts. There was a "dirty bomb"[86] in a container on a ship that had debarked from a port of a CSI member. When the container was opened at the port of Norfolk, Virginia, on December 3, the bomb detonated, spewing radioactivity over roughly a two-square-mile area. The contamination would have been worse, but the container helped muffle the blast.[87] At present the port of Norfolk, the nation's sixth largest, is shut down until decontamination efforts are completed.

In his speech to the nation on December 5, President Hull defended his decision:

> Our country cannot raise a drawbridge and isolate itself from the problems of the world. Today our security and economic well-being are intertwined with the rest of the world. Our homes, schools, and industry depend upon reliable supplies of oil and natural gas from abroad. Our standard of living, the world's highest, is made possible through our participation in the global trading network.
>
> About 90 percent of the world's trade is transported in cargo containers. Almost half of incoming U.S. trade arrives by ship containers, nearly seven million of which are offloaded at U.S. seaports each year. It is simply impossible to maintain the flow of trade needed, at the volume needed, and inspect every container that crosses our borders. But we can, and we will, do better.[88]

Thus far doing better involves inspecting every container crossing the border into the United States. But since these containers are being inspected at the U.S. border, if they contain dirty bombs or other destructive materials, *they have already reached their target.* When Rear

86. A dirty bomb comprises a conventional explosive, like TNT, and radioactive isotopes. The bomb is designed to spread radioactive contamination over a wide area. Dirty bombs are less devastating than nuclear devices but easier to create.
87. William Callibri, "Radioactive Weapon Hits Virginia Port," *Wall Street Journal,* December 4, 2011, p. A1.
88. Willard Hull, Address to the Nation, December 5, 2011, at www.whitehouse.gov, accessed on December 10, 2011.

Admiral Mary Scott-Warren was queried by Congress regarding the Coast Guard's role in protecting the nation's coastline from attack, she responded:

> If we have intelligence that a container ship may pose a threat to our security, your Coast Guard can intercept the ship before it reaches a port. We have boarding parties that can seize the ship and stop it. What we do not have is the ability to screen a container ship's densely packed cargo of containers. Nor is there any way to offload these containers at sea. So, in response to your question, Senator, we are not able to screen ships at sea. Nor do we have the capacity to stop and board large numbers of ships at sea.[89]

BLUE CHRISTMAS

WHAT ONCE SEEMED UNLIKELY, AND PERHAPS IMPOSSIBLE TO MANY, has happened: the global economy has been crippled by small groups of Muslim militants, aided by luck and circumstance (i.e., the collapse of Nigeria). Reports from several intelligence services, both in the United States and in Europe, indicate that militant Muslim groups had been preparing a series of spectacular attacks on the global economy for several years. The crisis in Nigeria apparently accelerated these efforts, in the hope that they would have a boosting effect. The simultaneous attacks at the Strait of Malacca and on the Saudi oil-production facilities indicate that, although loosely linked, at least some militant Muslim groups are capable of acting in conjunction with one another to great effect. Rumors of Iranian involvement in supplying at least some of the attackers raise the question of whether Muslim Shiite Khomeinists and Sunni Salafist-Jihadis have formed an alliance of convenience. Although the U.S. government has not named the group responsible for the dirty

89. Rear Admiral Mary Scott-Warren, House Armed Services Committee, Hearings on the Global Trade Crisis, December 7, 2011, at www.house.gov/hasc/hearing_information .shtml, accessed on December 11, 2011; and Senate Armed Services Committee, Hearing on U.S. Border Security, December 8, 2011, at http://armed-services.senate.gov/hearings 2011.cfm, accessed on December 11, 2011.

bomb attack, claims by Muslim militant organizations allied with al Qaeda suggest that it was part of their overall effort to strike a deadly blow at the global economy and the U.S. economy in particular. The same can be said of the cyberattacks that befell the United States in late November.

The "forces of order" (as President Hull refers to them) have responded fitfully and not entirely effectively to the coordinated attacks. On the brighter side, many of the world's major navies, and those of several notable minor powers like Singapore as well, have moved quickly to patrol key maritime choke points like the straits of Hormuz and Malacca. They are also providing security in other key littoral areas, such as alternative shipping routes through the Indonesian archipelago. But it is far from clear that they can cover all of these routes continuously. Many of the major powers' maritime forces were built to combat other large navies and execute major air and missile strikes against targets ashore. This is especially true of the U.S. Navy. In his recent testimony before Congress, Secretary of Defense Wilford Dawson admitted:

> Our Navy cannot be everywhere at once. We are working with our allies and partners—the Thousand-Ship Fleet coalition—to secure as many key trade route locations as possible. But even together we cannot cover all offshore oil- and [natural] gas-production facilities that may be liable to attacks. We must rely on the producer states to defend their own property.[90]

When pressed as to who would defend Nigeria's oil fields, now that its government had ceased to function, Dawson could promise only that the fleet would make "regular visits" to the area.

Defense experts assert that the Pentagon simply lacks the resources—with or without the cooperation of other major powers' navies—to secure offshore energy facilities from attack, especially if the "forces of disorder" possess significant numbers of unmanned underwater vehicles (UUVs). As one expert put it:

90. Secretary of Defense Wilford Dawson, testimony, Senate Armed Services Committee, Hearing on Global Commerce Protection, December 15, 2011, at http://armed-services.senate.gov/hearings2011.cfm, accessed on December 28, 2011.

UUVs are like small submarines, and you know how hard it is to track a submarine. Well, it's even more difficult with these things. Then you put them in coastal waters, with all the commercial traffic, and it's almost impossible to pick up an acoustic signal on them. If they [the UUVs] have enough cargo space to carry explosive charges, these oil platforms and their associated FPSOs [floating production, storage and off-loading vessels] and FSOs [floating storage and off-loading vessels] could be sitting ducks.[91] Especially the FSOs, since most of them are old single-hull supertankers that have been converted. So they're even more vulnerable than the newer double-hull tankers.[92]

Perhaps more to the point, after receiving a White House briefing on the administration's planned maritime operations, House Armed Services Committee chairman Michael O'Malley declared:

Look, even if the Navy can somehow accomplish the mission of protecting the choke points and the energy production locations, the militants win. After all, to do this we are going to have to spend billions—and I mean hundreds of billions—to increase the fleet to a size that is capable of maintaining constant presence to police these areas. So once again, they spend a few tens of millions, and we end up spending thousands of times more.[93]

The ability of militant Muslim groups armed with guided weapons to strike at oil- and gas-production facilities will likely only grow over

91. An FPSO vessel is a type of floating tank system that takes aboard oil or gas produced from a nearby platform or platforms, processes it, then stores it until the cargo can be transferred onto a tanker or sent through a pipeline. An FSO vessel is similar, save that it does not process the oil or gas. A number of FPSOs have routinely operated off the coasts of Nigeria and Angola, among other offshore oil and gas fields.
92. Professor Harry Sundstrom, testimony, Senate Armed Services Committee, Hearing on Global Commerce Protection, December 15, 2011, at http://armed-services.senate.gov/hearings2011.cfm, accessed on December 28, 2011.
93. Representative Michael O'Malley, interview on *Meet the Press*, December 18, 2011, at www.msnbc.msn.com/id/3032611, accessed on December 30, 2011. The 9/11 attacks are estimated to have cost roughly $1 million to plan and execute, while the United States today spends over $50 billion on homeland security, a spending ratio of 50,000 to 1.

time as these weapons continue to improve and proliferate. General David Barnard notes:

> It's not only the rapidly growing accuracy of these weapons—everything from mortars to rockets to missiles—it's their increased range. The day will come when they can launch some of these things 30 or 40 miles away, and it becomes almost impossible to create a "safe zone" that far out from your critical asset, whether it's an oil refinery, or a dock, or an embassy. You simply don't have enough troops to blanket an area that big. And that means at times we are just going to have to sit there and take it.[94]

The United States and many other countries are not willing to simply "sit there and take it" if they can avoid it. Global manhunting efforts against militant Muslim leaders, which began shortly after the attacks of 9/11 a decade ago, have been expanded, in part due to the increased efforts of other countries' special forces. Manhunting operations[95] have succeeded in killing many militant Muslim leaders. Yet even as they are killed, others have risen to take their place. This has produced the growing belief that these operations, while useful in many respects, are not a solution to the challenge posed by the recent attacks. As Senator Elena Rousseau argues, "We have been waging Global Whack-a-Mole for a decade now and are less secure than when we began."[96]

There is great uncertainty over the nation's ability to defend itself against cyberattacks. The government keeps a tight veil of secrecy over

94. Lieutenant General (Ret.) David Barnard, "An Era of Ambiguous Precision Warfare," *Wall Street Journal,* October 19, 2011, p. A28.
95. Manhunting involves operations by Special Operations Forces and Intelligence organizations to identify, track, and either kill or capture key high-value targets, especially the leaders of radical groups.
96. Whack-a-Mole is a children's game that involves moles popping up randomly from their holes; the player is supposed to force the individual moles back into their holes by whacking them on the head with a mallet. During early U.S. military operations in Iraq, units would rush around an area in an effort to keep antigovernment insurgents at bay by suppressing them whenever they appeared. Some have viewed the global manhunting operations as employing these tactics on a grand scale. Senator Elena Rousseau, interview on *Face the Nation,* December 18, 2011, at www.cbsnews.com/sections/ftn/main3460.shtml, accessed on December 30, 2011.

its cyberweapons, those used both to attack rival networks and to defend its own. While no government systems were brought down by the Black Friday attacks, they did suffer—and withstand—several apparent denial-of-service attacks. The commercial sector is apparently far more vulnerable.

Demands that the administration take forceful action against those responsible for the Black Friday cyberattacks have put President Hull in a difficult position. While the attacks are believed to have originated primarily from countries in the Arab world, proving that the governments of these states were complicit in them is difficult. State computers may be part of a botnet, but so are other computers around the world. Many computers in the botnets are located in Europe, still others in Asia. During the heaviest phase of the attacks, over two million computers were participating. One expert called the attacks the result of a cyber *levée en masse*. Some speculate that the Pentagon is engaged in cyber-counterstrikes against the Arab countries that appear to have hosted the attacks, but Secretary of State Luis Romero has strongly denied it. Most Americans feel the government was caught napping by the recent attacks, then responded in an ad hoc and ineffective manner, as it seems to have done in every major crisis since 9/11. The opposition party's front-runner for the 2012 nomination for president, Governor John Brickerhoff of Ohio, summed up the feeling of most Americans when he recently declared, "We have the world's best military, the world's most advanced technology, the world's most innovative private sector—and the world's most incompetent administration."

7

WHO LOST IRAQ?

Tell me how this ends.
General David Petraeus (quoted in the *Washington Post*)

THE "BLAME GAME"

IT HAS BEEN NEARLY A QUARTER-CENTURY SINCE AMERICAN FORCES entered Iraq in the First Gulf War, eleven years since the U.S.-led coalition invaded Iraq and overthrew the predatory regime of Saddam Hussein, and only two years since American combat forces withdrew from that country and the current "difficulties" began.[1] Arguably, the geopolitical situation in Iraq, and in the Middle East region, has changed more in the last two years than in the two decades that preceded it—and not for the better.

President John Dannemeyer's decision to begin withdrawing the remaining 80,000 U.S. troops in Iraq in September 2012 is generally viewed to have reversed his decline in the public opinion polls and enabled his come-from-behind, narrow election victory over Senator George Clayton that fall. What happened during the course of that with-

---

1. "Difficulties" is, of course, a reference to President Dannemeyer's speech announcing the phased withdrawal of U.S. forces from Iraq in July 2012. There he uttered the now-famous words, "Of course there will be difficulties [following a withdrawal]; but I believe they are outweighed by the benefits and, with America's leadership, can be minimized." See Danielle Johnson, "President Announces Troop Cut," *Los Angeles Times*, July 18, 2012, p. 1.

drawal, and the events that followed, presented the United States with perhaps its greatest national security crisis since the Cold War along with the most vicious and partisan political debate this country has seen since the 1950s, when the question "Who lost China?" (to the Communists) initiated the modern, mass-media-era "blame game."[2] The blame, depending upon your political affiliation and level of objectivity, belongs to any one of the last four administrations extending back to President George H. W. Bush, although Dannemeyer and his immediate predecessor, George W. Bush, have drawn most of the political fire.

While President Dannemeyer's decision was popular among a majority of Americans when it was announced, from the very beginning most Hawks strongly opposed the troop withdrawal as "reckless" and likely to destabilize not only Iraq but the region at large. As Senator Clayton argued in the candidates' final debate on October 28, 2012:

> The president calls for withdrawal but says nothing of the consequences. In recent years it has become fashionable to attack President [George W.] Bush for not having a plan for what would follow the overthrow of Saddam Hussein. But where is the president's plan for the day after withdrawal? All we have are unfounded predictions about how the Iraqis will be forced to work things out among themselves, and how the countries in that part of the world have too much at stake to let things get out of hand. Well, hope is not a policy or a plan. If we proceed to abandon Iraq with no clear course to follow, this president will be doing exactly the same thing he criticizes his predecessor of having done.[3]

President Dannemeyer famously replied:

> My fellow Americans, U.S. troops have been in Iraq for nearly a decade now. Over 6,000 of our finest young men and women, heroes all, have died and over 50,000 have been wounded as a consequence of the Bush administration's decision to invade Iraq on the false

2. The question was purportedly posed to Secretary of State Dean Acheson, who is reported to have responded, "I didn't know China was ours to lose."
3. "Final Debate Highlights," *New York Times,* October 29, 2012, p. A14.

assumption that it possessed weapons of mass destruction, and its incompetent leadership following the capture of Baghdad. We have paid a heavy price in our efforts to provide the Iraqi people and their leaders an opportunity to come together, to share power and to equitably allocate that country's abundant natural resources.

We have spent too much—in blood and in dollars—for too long, and have stayed too long in Iraq. The Iraqi people know it; the American people know it; the Iraqi government knows it; and this government knows it. This administration has worked too hard to enable us to recover from the mistakes made by the previous administration to be lectured by them [*sic*] as to how best to move forward. Iraq is now, thanks to our efforts, far more stable than anyone could have hoped in the dark days following our invasion. We have done much to achieve domestic tranquillity in that country and assist the Iraqi people. Now they must chart their own future, and we must tend to our own pressing problems here at home. Whatever happens in Iraq, the way ahead should not, and will not, be paved with the blood of our young men and women in uniform, too much of which has already been shed.[4]

The president's remarks—particularly the last passage, which he had made a part of his standard stump speech, and which was viewed by millions on TV campaign spots and on websites like YouTube—have become grist for the opposition. The same is true of Senator Clayton's remarks, which are constantly referred to as clearly warning of the dangers inherent in pursuing a U.S. troop drawdown.

NOT SO FAST

DANNEMEYER REACHED HIS DECISION SOMEWHAT RELUCTANTLY and only after months of deliberation and debate within the administration's senior policy circles.[5] The president came into office in 2009

4. Ibid., pp. A14–15.
5. This debate is captured in Bob Woodbury's recent book, *Never Call Retreat* (New York: Random House, 2014), pp. 27–56. Many of the administration's internal deliberations recounted are drawn from Woodbury's book. He obtained direct access to many of the key

promising to withdraw all U.S. troops from Iraq by the end of his first administration and to leave Iraq on a "solid and secure footing, with Iraqis in charge of their own destiny and the region more stable than it is today."[6] Over the next three years the president did reduce U.S. force levels, which once stood at nearly 200,000, to 80,000 in the summer of 2012.

During that time the administration worked to bring about a "Grand Bargain" among Iraq's three main factions: the Kurds, concentrated in the country's north; the Shi'a Arabs, who reside mainly in the south and comprise over half the country's population; and the Sunni Arabs, who represent barely 20 percent of Iraqis but had ruled the country for generations prior to the Second Gulf War. The Sunni Arabs are found primarily in western Iraq, an area bereft of the oil that generates most of the country's wealth.[7]

The president's policies seemed to please no one. Hawks argued that the troop reductions represented "defeat on the installment plan," while many Doves were angered by what they saw as the drawdown's unacceptably slow pace. For their part many Iraqis feared that the Americans' departure would remove a source of security that had enabled some level of accommodation—if not reconciliation—to occur among the country's factions. But Iraqis also found the American presence an affront to their pride and honor, recalling as it did the period of colonial rule. Simply put, like many Americans, many Iraqis had mixed feelings regarding the U.S. military presence in their country.

---

players involved, including National Security Advisor Sean O'Callaghan, Secretary of State William Peterman, and Defense Secretary James Burke. While the picture Woodbury presents is incomplete—a number of key principals, including senior military commanders, did not consent to discuss their role with him—the account is the best we have at present.

6. Donald Benson, "Dannemeyer Announces Iraq Plan," *Washington Post,* September 11, 2008, p. A1.

7. Iraq's Shi'a population predominates in the oil field areas that extend up from Saudi Arabia and through Kuwait into southern Iraq. These fields produce over a million barrels of crude per day. The Kurdish population dominates the area around the country's northern oil fields, which are concentrated around Kirkuk. The city, long dominated by Kurds, was repopulated by Sunni Arabs under the orders of Saddam Hussein. Following his fall, the Kurds have worked diligently, successfully—and often violently—to repossess what they believe is rightfully theirs and to "cleanse" the Sunni Arab population from the area through a process that has become known as "Kurdification." Currently the country's oil wealth, including that pumped from Kurdish dominated areas, is shared under an agreement reached by Iraq's three main factions.

The Grand Bargain sought by President Dannemeyer was essentially the same objective as that pursued by the Bush administration, which called it by other names: national compact, national reconciliation, and national accommodation. Dannemeyer's objective was to achieve stability by convincing Iraq's three main factions to come to a power-sharing agreement and to agree as well on a method to share the country's oil wealth. However, fundamental problems have been associated with this approach. First, after centuries of mutual antagonism and, in many cases, outright repression, the Kurds, Sunni Arabs, and Shi'a Arabs simply do not trust one another. Some experts believe that to have a chance of holding up, any Grand Bargain would have to be enforced by an external power, and for an extended period of time. The only external power that could possibly muster sufficient will and force is the United States. As noted columnist Edward Akins wrote at the time:

> During the Cold War it was said that NATO existed to keep the *Americans in* Europe so we could keep the *Soviets out* of Europe and the *Germans down*—that is, from starting another war. Well, today the Americans are needed in Iraq to keep the predators—Iran, al Qaeda, the Turks—out, and the country's radical factions down—from rising up and subverting the agreement. And we will be needed in Iraq for a long time. Republicans and Democrats alike seem to believe that although the Iraqi constitution is less than a decade old, a "Grand Bargain" agreement will disperse generations of acrimony into the ether. And yet in 1861, over seventy years after we crafted our own constitution, a time characterized by far more benign conditions than the Iraqis have enjoyed, an American as revered as Robert E. Lee still saw himself more Virginian than American. How long will it take for a Sunni Arab, or a Shi'a Arab, or a Kurd to see himself as an Iraqi first? I suspect it will take decades. And if that is the case, then it will take decades—not months—of U.S. troop presence in Iraq to achieve our goals.
>
> But let's not be too harsh on the political leaders. In our democracy, dear reader, the people get the government they deserve. Our inattention, our intellectual laziness, our unwillingness to demand

more of our leaders than platitudes paved the way to our current difficulties. If you want to know "Who is losing Iraq?" just look in your mirror.[8]

Indeed, if the Americans wanted out, there was little incentive for Iraq's factions to do more than position themselves for the inevitable power struggle that would follow. In fact, this is what has been happening, albeit gradually, for several years now. Today's crisis is the result of several factors that together produced a major shift in the geopolitical environment, apparently to the United States' detriment.

These factors did not immediately make themselves felt. Some called for a rapid withdrawal of U.S. forces following the end of the Bush administration, but the Dannemeyer administration that came into office in January 2009 opted for a gradual drawdown of U.S. forces, in line with recommendations from senior commanders in the field.[9] After a symbolic withdrawal of one U.S. Army brigade combat team (BCT) shortly after taking office, President Dannemeyer withdrew only three more BCTs over the next twelve months, bringing the total in Iraq down to ten Army brigades and Marine regiments. Despite its reluctance to admit it, the Dannemeyer administration was pursuing its predecessor's approach of gradually standing down the U.S. military commitment as the Iraqi Security Forces, who were being trained and equipped primarily by Americans, gradually assumed greater responsibility for the country's security.

STAGFLATION AND DECLINING U.S. SUPPORT

THE ADMINISTRATION MIGHT HAVE DOWNPLAYED ITS CAMPAIGN withdrawal rhetoric, but it could not ignore the United States' weakened economy and increasingly worrisome financial condition. The

8. Edward Akins, "The Long, Hard Slog," *Wall Street Journal,* October 4, 2012, p. A22.
9. For a summary of the military's assessment and recommendations, see General Robert Hunter, Commander, U.S. Central Command, testimony before the Senate Armed Services Committee, February 13, 2009, at http://armed-services.senate.gov/hearings.cfm, accessed on June 18, 2011.

bursting of the housing bubble and the financial crisis on Wall Street and beyond, combined with the spike in energy prices, produced a whip-saw effect on American consumers, the principal drivers of the nation's economy. As housing prices declined, homeowners were no longer able to pull equity from their homes to finance consumption. Their purchasing power declined even further as billions of dollars flowed from American wallets into the coffers of the Organization of the Petroleum Exporting Countries, better known simply as OPEC.

The U.S. economy was further compromised by inflation, which was stimulated not only by rising energy prices (and broad advances in many commodity prices) but also by the continued growth of the U.S. federal budget deficits and trade imbalance. Finally, as the country's baby-boomer generation, born between 1946 and 1964, began to retire in large numbers, the country's Social Security Trust Fund, from which the federal government borrowed to help reduce the effects of its large deficits, eroded at an accelerated rate.[10] By 2010 the country was, for the first time since the 1970s, experiencing "stagflation," in which unemployment, economic stagnation, and inflation all increase at the same time.

The recession, the most severe in nearly forty years, brought ever-growing attention to the federal government's spending, including defense spending, and in particular spending on military operations in Afghanistan and Iraq. As operations in Iraq absorbed roughly 70 percent of the war's costs, and as the Iraqi government was enjoying a huge windfall from its oil exports, many Americans questioned why the country was spending nearly $100 billion each year to help a country whose oil reserves were among the world's largest,[11] when Washington was cutting spending on so many domestic programs.

10. The Social Security Trust Fund's monies are invested in nonmarketable U.S. *government bonds*. Thus the trust fund indirectly helps to finance the federal government's budget deficits. As the trust fund is reduced, the U.S. government has, all other things being equal, less demand for its bonds. To attract sufficient demand, the U.S. Treasury has to raise the interest rate it is willing to pay on its bonds, creating greater debt for the government.

11. While there is some debate about the size of Iraq's proven oil reserves in relation to those of other countries, Iraq is clearly in the top tier and likely in the top five. Energy Information Administration, "Iraq," at www.eia.doe.gov/emeu/cabs/Iraq/Oil.html, accessed on July 7, 2008.

President Dannemeyer was forced to balance putting the country's financial house in order with protecting the country's security interests in the Persian Gulf region. After the 2010 midterm congressional elections resulted in unexpected losses for Dannemeyer's party in both the House of Representatives and the Senate, the pressure increased to cut America's presence in Iraq. Negotiations with the Baghdad government had produced an agreement for a continued U.S. military presence in Iraq, along with a number of bases (referred to as "support facilities," to take account of Iraqi sensibilities owing to the country's colonial past). But the government of Iraq steadfastly refused to provide any financial support to offset the expense of the American security forces.[12]

This became an issue during the fall 2010 elections, as members of both parties thumped the administration on the issue. One campaign ad, run by a private interest group, was widely embraced by Republicans and Democrats alike. It featured an out-of-work autoworker, wearing a plaid shirt and jeans, standing by his old family car at a gas pump. Looking into the camera, he asks why his government is spending money to protect a government that charges its people pennies for a gallon of gas and over three dollars a gallon to the country whose young men and women are shedding their blood on its behalf. The ad ends with the man looking into the camera and asking "How much is a gallon of American blood worth? Someone needs to ask our 'friends' in Baghdad."[13]

As the 2012 presidential campaign heated up during the autumn of 2011, so did the rhetoric on how best to right the U.S. economy, and Iraq was inevitably part of that debate. Shouldering much of the blame for

12. The Iraqi government's refusal to provide "host nation support" is rooted in its experience as part of the Ottoman and British empires. The idea that American "occupation" forces would actually be funded by the Iraqi people struck many Iraqis as a return to its time as an imperial outpost. The Baghdad government would find it difficult to weather the storm of criticism that would follow such an accommodation, seen as an affront to the country's pride and honor. See John Ellsworth, "Iraq at the Crossroads," *Foreign Affairs*, November–December 2012.

13. The ad, which rocketed to number one on YouTube, can still be seen at www.youtube.com/results?search_query=iraq+videos&search_type=&aq=4&oq=Iraq, accessed on February 18, 2014. A similar ad ran with an Afghanistan theme, in which a woman surrounded by her three young children wonders why Washington is building roads in Afghanistan and providing food to Afghan schools while the infrastructure in her community is in disrepair and the government has cut back on the local school lunch program.

the country's economic woes, President Dannemeyer faced a challenge in his own party for the nomination. During the 2012 primary season Dannemeyer made several modest cuts in U.S. force levels in Iraq, bringing them down to slightly less than 80,000. While Dannemeyer won renomination, he was running behind his rival in the polls up until the last debate in late October, when he made his pledge to bring the troops home. Dannemeyer's performance in the debate and his unequivocal declaration are generally credited with securing his exceedingly narrow victory over Senator Clayton.

IRAQ'S FACTIONS REEMERGE

THE PRESIDENT HAD REASONS FOR BOTH OPTIMISM AND CONCERN regarding how Iraq would fare following the withdrawal of all American combat units and most support units. On the positive side of the ledger, the Shi'a-led government of Prime Minister Nouri al-Maliki, once derided by many as the "Government of the Green Zone,"[14] proved remarkably resilient. Maliki was able to reach out to both the Kurdish and the Sunni factions, inducing them to participate in the political process in exchange for significant local autonomy and a guaranteed share of the country's oil revenues. Kurds and Sunnis were also appointed as heads of several government ministries. The Kurds, who fear both the Turks and Iranians, were willing to participate rather than try to fend for themselves. The Sunnis, horrified by the depredations of al Qaeda in Iraq and disappointed in the lack of support from Sunni Arab states, were willing to give the arrangement a try.

Both Kurd and Sunni confidence in the Maliki government grew when the prime minister began extending the government's writ to the Shi'a-dominated areas of southern Iraq. Several key areas, including the southern oil hub of Basra, had fallen under the control of radical Shi'a militia elements, in particular the Mahdi Army led by the young firebrand cleric Muqtada al-Sadr. The Mahdi Army, along with criminal gangs, had undermined the government's efforts to establish order in the

---

14. The Green Zone is a four-square-mile area in central Baghdad that is the center of the international presence in the city, as well as the Iraqi government. Its official name, beginning under the Iraqi Interim Government, is the International Zone.

region. These groups, and the Mahdi Army in particular, were heavily infiltrated by Iranian intellgence and members of the Quds Force.[15]

By 2008, however, Maliki was confident enough in his young American-trained army to dispatch it to Basra, where it succeeded in asserting control over the city. Rather than contest Maliki openly, Sadr ordered his militia to lie low for the time being and bide its time. As later events were to prove, the Mahdi Army was not the only nongovernment force in hibernation. Both the Kurds and the Sunni Arabs retained sizable armed groups in the form of local security forces, tribal organizations, and territorial militias as a hedge against the possibility of Baghdad's duplicity or America's fecklessness. The Kurds were particularly well organized. Two principal Kurdish armed groups, the Kurdish Democratic Party (KDP) and the Patriotic Union of Kurdistan (PUK), who exercised control over northern Iraq since the First Gulf War in 1991, solidified their hold, prohibiting the central government from establishing a major presence there.

The announcement by President Dannemeyer that the United States would begin the phased withdrawal of its remaining combat forces (leaving behind a residual force of training units, advisers embedded in Iraqi Army units, and some logistics support units, roughly 12,000 soldiers in all) refocused the attention of Iraq's factions increasingly away from working within the agreed (but fragile) political framework and toward positioning themselves to fill, as best they could, the power vaccuum that would follow the departure of the only credible force for stability in the country. As one Sunni political leader expressed it, "The Americans spent ten years establishing trust here, only to throw it away."[16]

The first indicators that the Baghdad government might be losing its grip over the country came in southern Iraq, where the dormant intra-Shi'a power struggle reemerged as U.S. troops began preparing for

---

15. The Quds (Jerusalem) Force is an elite unit of the Iranian Revolutionary Guard Corps (IRGC). It is responsible for extraterritorial operations, with emphasis on training and advising Islamic fundamentalist groups and on gathering information for targeting and attack planning. Federation of American Scientists, "Qods (Jerusalem) Force Iranian Revolutionary Guard Corps (IRGC—Pasdaran-e Inqilab)," at http://www.fas.org/irp/world/iran/qods/, accessed on July 11, 2008. The Quds have long supported Shi'a groups like Hezbollah, the Mahdi Army, and the Badr Organization.
16. William Denton, "Pullout Fever," *Newsweek*, November 19, 2012, p. 34.

their withdrawal. Iranian intelligence agents and Quds Force elements, which had gone underground and remained there for several years, provided substantial support in particular to Sadr's Mahdi Army, even while Tehran continued providing assistance to the Baghdad government and to Sadr's principal rival, the Badr Organization. However, the Iranians clearly felt that Sadr, who had spent nearly half of his time in Iran in recent years, and who still retained a popular following with the Shi'a masses, was their best opportunity to exert increased influence once the Americans had departed. The Iranians had so infiltrated Sadr's organization that it was now unclear who controlled the Mahdi Army: Sadr, or the Iranian Quds (Revolutionary Guard) members.

Tehran also likely had a hand in the assassination of the Grand Ayatollah Ali al-Sistani, widely revered by Iraq's Shi'a population and considered by many in the period immediately following the overthrow of Saddam Hussein to be the most influential man in Iraq. Like Sadr's, Sistani's influence waxed and waned over time. Thus in September 2006 Sistani declared his intention to forgo making political observations, declaring that "I will not be a political leader anymore; I am only happy to receive questions about religious matters." Sistani's decision to assume a lower profile reflected his declining influence and the growth of Muqtada al-Sadr's power among the Shi'a. This was made clear when fighting broke out in Diwaniya between Iraqi soldiers and Sadr's Mahdi Army. When Sistani's appeals for calm were ignored, Sadr ended the fighting with one telephone call.[17]

Still, Sadr and his Iranian patrons were leaving nothing to chance. In 2007 several of Sistani's closest advisers were assassinated. As Sadr's stature diminished following the government's assertion of its control over Basra, Sistani's influence grew once again. Plans to assassinate Sistani himself were foiled on January 29, 2007, when three gunmen were captured at a hotel near Sistani's office. The aging grand ayatollah was

17. Gethin Chamberlain and Aqeel Hussein, "I No Longer Have Power to Save Iraq from Civil War, Warns Shi'a Leader," Telegraph.UK.Co, September 9, 2006, at www.telegraph .co.uk/news/main.jhtml?xml=/news/2006/09/03/wirq03.xml, accessed on September 8, 2007. See also Sami Moubayed, "Iraq Loses Its Voice of Reason," *Asia Times Online,* September 6, 2006, at www.atimes.com/atimes/Middle_East/HI06Ak01.html, accessed on September 8, 2007.

not as fortunate six years later, on May 11, 2013, when masked gunmen broke in to his office in Najaf and gunned him down along with over a dozen of his followers. While it is generally accepted that the assassination was the handiwork of Quds elements embedded in Sadr's Mahdi Army (or Jaish al Mahdi), many Shi'a are convinced he was killed by Sunni Arabs. The grand ayatollah's death once again frayed relations between Iraq's Sunni and Shi'a Arabs, and the level of sectarian violence rose again, at the very time when the newly elected President Dannemeyer was promoting his Middle East peace initiative.[18]

The principal source of concern, however, was intra-Shi'a conflict. Southern Iraq witnessed a struggle for power that ended with the destruction of the Badr Organization[19] and the death of Muhsin Abdul Aziz al-Hakim, the leader of the Supreme Islamic Iraqi Council (SIIC), at one time the largest political party in the Iraqi Council of Representatives.[20] With Hakim out of the way, and with the Iranians' help, Sadr's goal of undermining government control in the south no longer seemed quixotic.

And what of the Sunnis? Both the Bush and the Dannemeyer administrations were seeking a durable partnership with Iraq's factions. To some extent they had such a partnership with the Kurds, prior to the U.S. troop withdrawal. But such connections were always "alliances of convenience," based on short-term interests, and never "alliances of conviction," based on enduring values, as America had formed with countries like Australia, Great Britain, and Japan. Following Saddam Hussein's fall, the Sunni Arabs were the U.S.-led coalition's principal enemy, going so far as to join forces with the al Qaeda elements

---

18. Some argue that the assassination was specifically intended to ensure that America's new leaders would be disabused of any thoughts that they could marginalize the Shi'a radicals—Sadr, specifically—or his Iranian sponsors. See Tamil Khariri, "Sadr's Master Plan," *Los Angeles Times,* May 28, 2013, p. 26.

19. The Badr Organization (previously known as Badr Brigade) was the armed wing of the Supreme Council for the Islamic Revolution in Iraq (SCIRI), which now goes by the name Supreme Islamic Iraqi Council (SIIC).

20. Muhsin Abdul Aziz al-Hakim, a son of Sayyed Abdul Aziz al-Hakim, was the leader of the SIIC before his death in 2009. He was killed by an improvised explosive device, or IED, on August 17, while riding to a meeting in Najaf. The bomb that killed Muhsin was so powerful, it obliterated the car and killed eight bodyguards who were riding in that car and in two others.

that had infiltrated to join the insurgency. But as the power of the Shi'a Arabs grew, and as it became clear the Sunni Arab states were not coming to their aid and that al Qaeda in Iraq (AQI) was more interested in dominating the Sunni tribes than in supporting them, the Sunni Arabs found themselves increasingly weak and isolated. In 2007 a growing number of Sunni tribes did the seemingly unthinkable: they joined with the Americans to suppress AQI. While this "alliance of convenience" succeeded in reducing the AQI threat to the Sunnis and the Americans, both allies eventually realized that their interests in other matters were at odds. The Sunnis distrusted the Shi'a-led Baghdad regime, which they saw as both hostile to their interests and incapable of protecting them. As for the Kurds, the Sunnis saw them consolidating their hold over Iraq's northern oil fields as the Shi'a were doing in the south, leaving the Sunnis, literally, to "pound sand" should the fragile agreement calling for shared power and wealth ever lose its irreplaceable guarantor: the American military presence. As one key Sunni tribal leader expressed it, "We hated the Americans as occupiers, but have grown fond of them as guests."[21]

The U.S.-Sunni alliance, however, faltered even before the 2012 election. In 2009, following the effective defeat of AQI, the Sunnis went about the business of securing their part of Iraq, primarily the west and northwest. They accomplished this in no small measure thanks to the American funding provided during the time when both were working to eliminate the common threat posed by AQI. This enabled the Sunnis to buy arms and munitions and to declare that Iraqi Army units would be welcome to remain in the area only as long as they did not challenge tribal prerogatives.

The lid on this slowly bubbling pot of sectarian stew was kept on tight by U.S. soldiers and marines. But their numbers continued to dwindle. From a peak of some 170,000 in 2007 during the surge, U.S. troop strength in Iraq declined significantly following the Bush administration's end in January 2009. Over the next three years President Dannemeyer, true to his campaign pledges, did gradually reduce troop

21. Jasmine Heradith, "What Next for Iraq's Sunnis?" *Wall Street Journal,* January 18, 2013, p. A1.

numbers, but to 80,000, not zero. By then, all of America's coalition partners had pulled out of Iraq.

During the first Dannemeyer administration, U.S. casualties declined substantially. Prior to the 2007 Anbar Awakening[22] U.S. casualties had been sustained principally at the hands of the Sunni insurgents; they were now inflicted primarily by the Shi'a militias closely affiliated with the Iranians. It became increasingly clear that Iran wanted the United States out of Iraq and intended to keep the pressure on by ensuring a steady stream of U.S. casualties to remind the American public that it was paying a human, as well as a financial, cost for staying in that country.

If that was Tehran's strategy, it seemed to produce results. For three years the Dannemeyer administration confronted a seemingly unending trickle of U.S. casualties. Despite its repeated attempts to work with Iraqi political leaders to fashion a Grand Bargain, it was never able to concentrate within the Baghdad government a monopoly on the use of force. In a dramatic speech on the eve of the 2010 midterm elections, the president proposed a regional peace conference, but it was scuppered when the Arab states and Iran refused to attend if the Israelis were present, and the Turks refused to participate lest they legitimize the Kurds' relatively high level of autonomy in northern Iraq.[23] The administration then defaulted to a series of bilateral diplomatic initiatives with the frontline Sunni Arab states (Egypt, Jordan, and Saudi Arabia), Turkey, and the "Persian Axis" (Iran and Syria). These efforts achieved little. The Saudis proved unwilling to embrace a Baghdad government they saw as little more than a front for Shi'a Arabs or, worse still, Shi'a Persians. Iran has long believed that time is on its side and has been content to let the situation fester.

22. The Anbar Awakening was the coalition of Sunni tribal sheikhs that was formed in 2007 in Anbar province to ensure security. This coalition was facilitated by American support and oriented toward defeating AQI. While the government in Baghdad planned to absorb a quarter of these forces into its security forces and disband the rest, the Sunni tribes generally successfully resisted both efforts.
23. What the Kurds refer to as Kurdistan has long been divided among several states, including Iran, Iraq, Syria, and Turkey. In each of these countries the Kurds are a minority. At the end of the First Gulf War, the Allies established a safe haven in northern Iraq, much to the consternation of Turkey, a U.S.-NATO ally with a sizable Kurdish population, some of which is engaged in a separatist campaign to join its Iraqi brethren to the south. Iraqi Kurdistan has enjoyed a high level of autonomy, with its own local government and

THE SHORT RECESSIONAL

PRESIDENT DANNEMEYER'S WITHDRAWAL PLAN CALLED FOR A SMALL residual force of advisers to remain with the Iraqi Army, which would be tasked with providing for Iraq's internal security. American advisers would mentor their Iraqi officer counterparts as well as monitor the agreement that called for the Iraqi Army to ensure that militia forces stayed in their own regions and did not engage in sectarian violence. Some American training units would also remain to assist the Iraqis in fielding, over time, a military capable of defending Iraq from an attack by its neighbors. In the interim Washington would provide Baghdad with a guarantee of support should Iraq be a victim of aggression. In a move viewed as a diplomatic coup, President Dannemeyer secured UN Security Council approval for dispatching an international peacekeeping force of 8,000 troops to Baghdad to secure the city and keep ethnic tensions down.[24]

The administration argued this plan would prove successful, based on several considerations. First, the residual U.S. adviser contingent, numbering nearly 2,000 officers and sergeants (noncommissioned officers), would function as a tripwire. If any Iraqi factions challenged the government, Americans would be on the scene to identify the culprit. Second, the United States would maintain a strong military presence in the region in the form of air units based in Kuwait and an aircraft carrier in the Persian Gulf, to send a strong signal that it would react strongly if order began to break down. Third, Washington offered to continue training the Iraqi Army to give it the capability to repel an attack by an external power. This was seen as a key "carrot" in the plan, since all of Iraq's factions would be vulnerable to external predators until the country had built its military arm up far beyond its current capability levels. Fourth, the presence of a UN-sanctioned peacekeeping force

---

parliament, since 1992. As a portion of Iraq's oil revenues began flowing to the Kurds, the Turkish government became increasingly concerned that the Kurds would eventually declare their full independence from Iraq—and demand that the parts of Turkey that are predominantly Kurdish be ceded to the new state.

24. The force would comprise a mix of Latin American and Southeast Asian troops, including significant contributions from Argentina, Brazil, the Philippines, and Thailand. Josh Kravitz, "UN Force for Iraq," *New York Times,* January 12, 2013, p. A5.

in Baghdad was seen as a key expression of the international community's desire for Iraq's stability (and, no doubt, its continued oil production). Finally, the administration had worked out an agreement among the factions whereby the Sunni Arabs would continue to receive 18.5 percent of the country's oil revenues. Oversight on the country's oil production would be provided by the United States and UN representatives. Violations would lead to sanctions against the offender.

Predictably, the president's plan drew opposition, especially as many regarded it as an "October Surprise" designed to assist the president's uncertain political fortunes at the time. The administration, realizing the importance of winning broad political support for its plan, took pains to consult with like-minded members of the opposition and to explain the plan to the American people. As President Dannemeyer stated in his address to the nation following his reelection:

> For those who argue this plan has its flaws, my response is: What plan is devoid of flaws? This plan is not perfect. It is far from perfect. But it is the best plan that we have. Had others advanced a better plan, this administration would have gladly embraced it. Our plan is clearly an improvement over the current situation, which finds young American men and women risking their lives, and American taxpayers footing the bill, doing for Iraqis what it is high time Iraqis start doing for themselves. The Iraqis say they are ready to sustain the process of reconciliation, and we are ready to help them. And the international community is ready to assist. As our forces are withdrawn from Baghdad, they will be replaced by an 8,000-strong force of United Nations peacekeepers. They will be supplemented by nearly 2,000 American advisers embedded in Iraqi Army units,[25] which will ensure that those various factions that might engage in sectarian violence are identified and defeated. And we have worked out an agreement in which Iraq's energy wealth will be available to all the Iraqi people, and provided in an environment that will enable continued reconstruction of the country's infrastructure and its economy. These initiatives

25. The president did not mention the nearly 10,000 U.S. trainers and support troops that would remain in addition to the advisers.

will be backed by a strong residual U.S. force that will remain in the region after we complete the withdrawal of our combat forces.

It is time to move beyond partisan politics and turn the page to what can be a better future for the Iraqi people, the peoples of the Middle East, and the American people as well. But our chances of success are enhanced if we pull together on this effort, lest our hopes, and those of the Iraqi people, be pulled apart.[26]

By Inauguration Day 2013 U.S. troop levels in Iraq were under 70,000. Initially, things proceeded according to plan. Iraqi Army units with their American advisers stood ready to take on any renegade militia organization that might challenge the government's authority. American advisers had the ability to requisition supplies for their Iraqi units, along with fire support from American strike aircraft located in the region.[27] A UN force comprising some 8,000 Argentinians, Brazilians, Filipinos, and Thais, along with a smattering of Indonesians, Malaysians, and Ukrainians, took up positions in and around Baghdad, primarily along the lines dividing the city's ethnic populations. After years of the Army and Marines shouldering the burden in Iraq, the administration was now turning to American air power and sea power to back the Iraqi Army in its mission to maintain internal stabilty and keep potential neighboring predator states at bay.

While the plan looked good on paper, the military will be the first to tell you that "no plan survives contact with the enemy" and that "the enemy gets a vote." In fact, the American plan provided opportunities to several of Washington's enemies, beginning with the Iraqi factions themselves, who viewed the U.S. pullout as signaling a return to bareknuckle, survival-of-the-fittest politics. The Sunni Arabs had no doubt that corruption would prevail in the distribution of Iraq's oil revenues,

26. President John Dannemeyer, Address to the Nation, November 20, 2009, cited at www.whitehouse.gov, accessed on July 24, 2014.
27. They could also request support from U.S. Special Forces units operating in Iraq against residual AQI elements. The special forces operated from a few remote bases in Iraq and, it appears, in Jordan as well. With their own helicopters and AC-130 gunships, they also represented a rapid-reaction force that could come to the assistance of the advisers themselves, should their own units turn on them. This possibility was clearly understood at the time, given the progressive infiltration of radical militia elements into the Iraqi Army. See Woodbury, *Never Call Retreat*, pp. 32–34.

and every confidence that the U.S. plan to oversee production figures was a farce (which it proved to be). Hence they felt compelled to settle scores with the Kurds and perhaps, down the road, the Shi'a as well. What they needed was strong support from the Arab world, which is dominated by Sunni regimes with one exception: Iraq. With Saudi and Kuwaiti financial support, and Arab "volunteers" from Egypt and other Sunni Arab states (and Turkey's approval), the Sunnis could, they believed, retake the oil fields around Kirkuk. Once the north was consolidated, the Sunnis might be able to challenge the Shi'a for control over the southern part of Iraq. The risk of American disapprobation was seen as small, given Washington's concerns over Iran's strong influence in southern Iraq, which sits on the doorstep of both Saudi Arabia and Kuwait.

The challenge was to create a level of Sunni unity, which had been absent since Saddam Hussein's Tikriti clan had emerged as dominant following his seizure of power in 1979. The leadership problem was solved, however, by the Shi'a-led government's actions, which soon put the Sunnis in desperate straits, and the Saudis' insistence that the Sunnis rally around Sheikh Ahmed Abu Reesha, the brother of Sheikh Abu Reesha, the founder of the Anbar Awakening Conference, a coalition of over forty Sunni tribes that, along with U.S. troops, fought al Qaeda between 2007 and the American troop withdrawal.[28]

The Shi'a militias are perhaps most responsible for the rapid breakdown in the administration's efforts to preserve a stability underwritten by fewer than 2,000 American advisers. What is now widely known as the Stand at Najaf, viewed by the Shi'a as a great victory, arguably has laid the foundation for the calamity that confronts us today.[29]

THE STAND AT NAJAF

THE WITHDRAWAL OF LARGE NUMBERS OF AMERICAN TROOPS WITHIN a fairly short time span—less than ten months, beginning in January 2013—created a logistical nightmare. Not only did U.S. soldiers and

28. Sheikh Abu Reesha and three of his bodyguards were assassinated by AQI in September 2007.
29. While the Stand at Najaf actually occurred roughly ten miles to the city's south, initial press reports coined the phrase, and it has stuck.

marines have to be moved to Kuwait before boarding aircraft or ships to return to the States, but large amounts of equipment had to be moved as well. This meant hundreds of convoys moving along roads in southern Iraq on their way to staging areas in Kuwait. During the summer of 2013 these convoys moved generally without incident. To be sure, there was the occasional IED, but casualties were generally low. Both the Mahdi Army militia and its Iranian sponsors were happy to have the U.S. military depart and saw no reason to do anything that might delay the withdrawal. By October, U.S. troop strength was under 20,000 in Iraq, on its way down to the 12,000 stipulated by President Dannemeyer, the majority being support troops. In the late afternoon of October 16 a large U.S. convoy of nearly 200 vehicles approached the bridge spanning the Euphrates near the town of Abu Sukhayr, around eleven miles southeast of Najaf. Roughly half the convoy had crossed the bridge, at which point Shi'a militia forces opened fire with small arms and anti-tank guided munitions (ATGMs)[30] on the convoy from both sides of the river. Simultaneously, a dozen or more IEDs with explosively formed penetrators (EFPs)[31] were detonated. A firefight ensued between U.S. troops caught on both sides of the bridge and elements of the Mahdi Army. The fighting raged into the evening and throughout the night, as U.S. Army attack helicopters and Air Force strike aircraft rushed to assist in the convoy's defense.[32] Around eleven o'clock that night, as the convoy's soldiers manned a "thin green line" defensive perimeter at both ends of the bridge, a heliborne rapid-reaction force arrived, landing some 500 soldiers two miles from the battle scene. Shortly after two o'clock that night the relief force broke through to the besieged force and enabled it to hold its position against repeated militia assaults until morning, when a column of tanks arrived—the lead elements of a brigade combat team, one of only two such units remaining in Iraq.

---

30. The Iranians have been supplying the Shi'a militias with ATGMs since 2009 to defeat all but the heaviest U.S. armored vehicles in Iraq.

31. An EFP is a special type of shaped charge designed to penetrate armor.

32. An Iraqi Army brigade was stationed less than ten miles from the battle scene. Although the U.S. command in Iraq called upon the Baghdad government to order the brigade into action, it did not arrive on the scene until nearly six hours after the battle ended. Jason Seybourne, *The Stand at Najaf* (New York: Random House, 2014), pp. 235–37.

Fifty-seven Americans died in the Stand at Najaf, and over 300 were wounded. While it is not known how many Shi'a militia casualties were suffered, independent estimates put the figure at over 600 killed and perhaps twice that many wounded. Two American soldiers won the Congressional Medal of Honor for their heroism in the battle, which at several points witnessed mass charges by the Shi'a militiamen and scenes of hand-to-hand fighting. Much of the battle was videotaped by the Mahdi Army. While the quality was poor owing to the fact that most of the battle took place at night, both the initial stages and the aftermath—a long line of burning, wrecked vehicles—were widely available on the Internet and shown repeatedly on Arab television. The Arab media, in particular, picked up on the Mahdi Army's line: "America's Highway of Death." This, of course, is a reference to the road between Kuwait and Basra on which the retreating Iraqi Army was attacked by American aircraft during February 26–27 during the First Gulf War.[33]

While many Arabs greeted news of the battle with general elation, Arab leaders, seeing the hand of Tehran at work, were deeply concerned. Americans hotly debated the battle's significance. Opponents of withdrawal argued that the battle indicated that the president's plan was already falling apart, while defenders asserted it showed the need to get U.S. troops out of harm's way even more quickly. Perhaps the best assessment of the battle is that of the Saudi ambassador to the United States, Adel A. al-Jubeir:

> The Shi'a, they have sent a powerful message to Iraqis and the [Muslim] world: "We have defeated the Americans. Just as they cast Saddam's army from Kuwait, we are driving them from Iraq. We deserve both the credit and the reward for this victory. And our reward is to rule over Iraq." The fact that you Americans had the power to crush Sadr and his Madhi Army and repeatedly failed to do so when he

---

33. The battle has captured the imagination of Americans, Arabs, and Iranians. Hollywood is producing a movie titled *Stand at Najaf*, and there have been several documentaries on the battle. There are video games, Arab ("Highway of Death"), American ("Stand at Najaf"), and Iranian ("Shining Sword") depicting the battle from their respective sides. The Arab version has become one of the top-selling games in the Arab world. See Paul Davies, " 'Stand at Najaf' or 'Highway of Death?' " *Wall Street Journal*, December 11, 2013, p. B1.

attacked you made this battle inevitable. All this talk now of "over-watch" and "guarantees" means nothing now. You have opened the door for Iran.[34]

THE LONG ROAD HOME

PRESIDENT DANNEMEYER WORKED TO MAKE THE BEST OF A DIFFI-cult situation. He accepted at face value Sadr's assurance that the attack was conducted by rogue elements of the Mahdi Army, and that those re-sponsible would be dealt with harshly.[35] Yet at the same time Sadr's Shi'a followers were trumpeting the American defeat. Privately the president acknowledged to his advisers that the administration was on an irre-versible path. After the Iraqi Army failed to come to the assistance of the embattled U.S. troops, the American people would not hear of revers-ing the withdrawal. As General William Swanson, chairman of the Joint Chiefs of Staff, reportedly declared at the White House war council fol-lowing the battle:

> I feel like a hitchhiker walking along a highway in west Texas with
> a storm on the horizon. I can't run, and there's no place to hide. I just
> got to keep on walking and take it.[36]

Having made his point, Sadr (and presumably his Iranian benefac-tors) allowed the U.S. withdrawal to proceed without any further major incidents. Sadr did, however, continue to prosecute his propaganda campaign—what a succession of U.S. administrations have awkwardly called "strategic communications," the "war of ideas," or most recently,

34. Adel A. al-Jubeir, "Interview with the Saudi Ambassador," *60 Minutes,* CBS News, November 10, 2013, at www.cbsnews.com/sections/60minutes/main3415.shtml, accessed on May 8, 2014. The ambassador's reference to "overwatch" pertains to the part of the president's plan that stations American air strike forces in the region as a means of enforc-ing the Grand Bargain among Iraq's factions.
35. Eight senior members of the Mahdi Army were tried in a Shi'a Islamic Revolutionary Court and publicly executed. There is strong suspicion this act was, in fact, orchestrated by Quds Force elements, not so much to mollify the Americans as to further strengthen Iran's influence over Sadr and his supporters. Mary Symanski, "Tehran's Hidden Hand," *Washington Post,* November 2, 2013, p. A1.
36. Woodbury, *Never Call Retreat,* pp. 212–13.

"multicultural exchange." American convoys moving through southern Iraq after the Stand at Najaf frequently encountered throngs of Iraqis along the roadside, particularly near towns and especially near the bridge where the battle took place. Armed with nothing more than their voices, the Iraqis jeered at the passing (retreating?) Americans. The global media, and especially the Iranian and Arab media, gave considerable play to what some U.S. conservative media dubbed the "Highway of Shame." In any language, the message the Shi'a were attempting to convey was clear: *The Americans are defeated, we have defeated them, and they are retreating in shame.*

On March 14, 2014, just a few days shy of the eleventh anniversary of the U.S. invasion of Iraq, the final American convoy crossed into Kuwait, followed by the last American infantry battalion, a unit of the Army's First Infantry Division. The ides of March found no U.S. combat troops in Iraq.

THE SHI'A SURGE

AS THE LAST AMERICAN SOLDIERS WERE PASSING INTO KUWAIT, things were already beginning to unravel in Iraq. The Shi'a militias in the south, dominated by the Mahdi Army, began harrassing Iraqi Army units in their area. In Baghdad, still home to people from each of Iraq's three major factions, representatives of Sadr's militia began informing leaders of the Sunni and Kurdish communities that they had best relocate their people in the city. The methods employed are familiar to any aficionado of American mafia movies, or to students of Stalin's forced collectivization of Soviet agriculture.[37] Residents were informed that it would be in their best interest to depart their homes immediately—typically within forty-eight hours—and to take only what they could carry with them on foot. Those who refused were typically beaten, arrested, or killed. Women and children were not spared. As a neighborhood was vacated, Shi'a families moved in. Sometimes they inherited the former occupants' possessions, including furnishings, clothing, and

---

37. It is said that Saddam Hussein's favorite movie was *The Godfather* and that he was an avid reader of biographies of the Soviet tyrant Joseph Stalin. The Shi'a seem to have learned well from their former oppressors.

an automobile. Sometimes these assets were seized by Shi'a militiamen and kept for their own use, or sold.

The Shi'a revival of ethnic cleansing in Baghdad was generally underreported in the media. Arab networks like al-Jazeera and al-Arabiya were denied access to the city, as were the Western media. Film smuggled out by a Singaporean news team, along with interviews of Sunni Arab displaced persons who had left Baghdad, received little interest in the United States and effectively none in Europe. The general attitude of the Western powers was expressed well by the president's national security advisor, Sean O'Callaghan, who stated in December 2013:

> Is there ethnic cleansing going on in Baghdad? There may be some, but the Iraqi government informs us they have not sanctioned it and are working with the UN peacekeeping forces to ensure that the city's Sunni minority is protected. I can tell you that General Swanson, who visited Baghdad, informs me that the UN commander, General Enzo Lopez, reports no unusual activity in the city's Sunni areas.[38]

We now know that President Dannemeyer was receiving intelligence reports at the time confirming that what the Singaporean video crew had filmed was indeed occurring in Baghdad and in other ethnically mixed towns and cities nearby. The president, however, viewed this as the "natural evolution" of Iraq into a partitioned state, which he now viewed as inevitable and, under the circumstances, desirable. The White House viewed the situation as one that could be reversed only over a long period of time, perhaps several decades, and then only with persistent diplomacy. According to Bob Woodbury, the president remarked during a December meeting of his National Security Council:

> The UN peacekeeping force is not going to go against the Shi'a-led government, and expose themselves [sic] to attack. The prime minister has informed me that he has had to accommodate Sadr to avoid an all-out civil war that would be in no one's interest. All we can

---

38. Sean O'Callaghan, *Meet the Press,* December 22, 2013, at www.msnbc.msn.com/id/3032608/, accessed on February 12, 2014.

hope for is that the Shi'a refrain from a blatant ethnic cleansing campaign. I have private assurances from the Iraqi ambassador that they desire to keep a significant Sunni and Kurdish population in the city to demonstrate their commitment to an eventual reconciliation. This, in my mind, is acceptable, given that the alternative is open civil war, or the return of a large U.S. military force. The former is undesirable; the latter unthinkable.[39]

The Baghdad regime, increasingly viewed as a surrogate for Muqtada al-Sadr, also clashed with the Sunni tribes and other Sunni Arabs in western Iraq, even as they were engaged in a rapidly growing series of incidents with the Kurds in the country's north. Sadr has long declared his desire for Iraq to remain united, but it was unclear whether Sadr's united Iraq would have a place for Sunni Arabs. In any event, if the Shi'a were to control Baghdad, and with it eventually all of Iraq, they would need to control the two Sunni cities near the capital, Ramadi and Fallujah. Ramadi, about fifty miles to the west of the capital, is the largest of the Sunni cities and the capital of Anbar province, the largest in the Sunni sector of Iraq. Even prior to the completion of the U.S. withdrawal, there were increasingly frequent clashes near Fallujah, which sits roughly halfway between Baghdad and Ramadi, between Iraqi Army elements dominated by Shi'a, and Sunni tribesmen and local Sunni police.

The Shi'a apparently were looking to create a buffer zone between Baghdad and Ramadi by occupying Fallujah and encouraging its Sunni residents to leave. The city once again became a center of resistance to the Shi'a government, providing a stream of suicide bombers and car bombs for targets in Shi'a sections of Baghdad. The periodic clashes between the Shi'a and Sunnis erupted into a full-scale battle on January 16, 2014, when Baghdad ordered two Iraqi Army brigades to impose order in Fallujah, ostensibly to stop the flow of bombers into the capital.

Realizing that the loss of Fallujah would place Shi'a forces on the doorstep of Ramadi, the Sunni Arabs fought back ferociously. Hundreds of Sunni Arab volunteers from throughout the Arab world flocked to

39. Woodbury, *Never Call Retreat*, p. 228.

Fallujah to take on Shi'a-dominated Iraqi Army units,[40] which were closely supported by the Shi'a militia. Funds from Sunni Arab states—particularly the oil producers like Saudi Arabia and Kuwait—ensured the Sunni volunteers would be well armed. As the Iraqi Army has little in the way of heavy equipment, like artillery or armor, the Third Battle of Fallujah[41] quickly became a grinding affair, stretching on into the spring.

This major clash of Sunni and Shi'a in Fallujah was a clear violation of the agreements negotiated by the Dannemeyer administration and Iraq's principal factions. Despite their misgivings, the U.S. advisers who accompanied the two Iraqi Army brigades initially dispatched to Fallujah accepted the Iraqi commanders' argument that the operation was designed to stop the flow of attackers into Baghdad.[42] As the Iraqi defense minister declared:

> We are doing nothing different than the Americans did when the capital was threatened during their occupation. We are sending army forces to provide security in Fallujah, where the Sunni authorities have refused to suppress these terrorists.[43]

As the Sunni tribes fed more of their troops into the cauldron, along with several hundred foreign "volunteers" that likely included some "reformed" AQI elements,[44] the Iraqi government responded by reinforcing its forces with two more brigades in late February, along with a few hundred members of Sadr's Madhi Army, which were being advised by Quds Force troops. As the fighting increased in intensity, the UN Security Council met to determine how the international community might best respond to defuse the crisis. The Chinese and Russians, reflecting

---

40. By this time many Iraqi Army units in the southern part of the country and around Baghdad had seen their Sunni and Kurd troops desert.

41. The First Battle of Fallujah occurred in April 2004, during the uprising that followed the U.S. occupation of Iraq. The Second Battle of Fallujah, fought in November 2004, saw the U.S. Marine Corps retake the city from radical Islamist and insurgent elements.

42. The advisers were withdrawn shortly after the battle began, lest they be viewed as taking the side of one Iraqi faction against another.

43. Josh Kravitz, "Fighting Intense in Fallujah," *New York Times,* March 12, 2015, p. A1.

44. Following al Qaeda's defeat in Iraq, its leaders encouraged their members and associated groups to present a more humane face to the local populations where they operated, until they were able to secure power.

their close relations with Iraq's Shi'a government and Iran, called for all foreign troops to leave Iraq and for the United Nations to support the Baghdad government's legitimate right to restore order within its borders. Efforts by Britain and France to organize a cease-fire policed by an international force similar to the one deployed to Baghdad were ruled out by both Beijing and Moscow, which countered by proposing that the UN peacekeeping forces in Baghdad be withdrawn. As for the United States, it quickly became clear that Washington had neither the popular support of the American people to reintroduce troops into Iraq, nor the political will to do so. The inability of the UN to act and the United States' determination not to be drawn into the Iraq quagmire set the stage for the escalation in the conflict that followed.

THE TURKS MAKE THEIR MOVE

AS THE FIGHTING RAGED IN FALLUJAH AND SPREAD TO OTHER areas along the Sunni-Shi'a fault line in Iraq, and as an unusually early spring thaw began melting the mountain snows in northern Iraq, the Turks made their move. On May 4, 2014, major elements of the Turkish armed forces invaded Iraq's Kurdistan region. The Kurdish minority population in Turkey had been waging a low-level insurgency against Ankara for decades, often with the assistance of their Iraqi cousins. As it became clear that UN or U.S. intervention was now a remote possibility, the Turkish government in Ankara felt increasingly threatened by what appeared to be an emerging independent Kurdistan in northern Iraq. Such a state, with access to considerable oil wealth to support its ambition to reunite all Kurds under one state, posed a clear danger in the eyes of the Turks. With the Shi'a Iraqis and their Iranian sponsors embroiled in their own conflict with the Sunnis, the Turks were presented with a golden opportunity to deal with the Kurdish rebel sanctuary in Iraq that had been a thorn in their side. The possibility of seizing a sizable portion of Iraq's enormous oil reserves only fortified the Turks' decision to act, and to act decisively.

Claiming (with considerable justification, it must be admitted) that the Iraqi Kurds had long harbored separatist insurgents, while providing them with material support in the form of weapons and supplies,

the Turkish government declared it could no longer stand by while inno-
cent Turks were killed by Kurdish "terrorists." Over 90,000 Turkish
troops streamed across the border to "restore order" in a country that,
Ankara argued, was moving beyond partition and into disintegration.
Baghdad formally protested the Turkish incursion, but given its current
dependence on Iran and Tehran's agreement with Turkey (see below), there
was little the Shi'a could do to deflect Ankara from its chosen course.

Washington ensured the enmity of both the Turks and the Kurds by
condemning the intervention but refusing to take action either to prevent
it or to arrest it. Surprisingly, the White House was caught off guard by the
Turkish action, even though U.S. reconnaissance satellites provided clear
evidence of the Turks' buildup along their border with Iraq. Insiders assert
that the buildup seemed no different than several others that had occurred
in recent years as the Turkish government sought to coerce the Kurds into
terminating their support for the Kurdish separatists inside Turkey.[45]

The lightly armed Kurds were ill prepared to defend against such an
assault, and the Turks made quick progress toward Mosul and the oil-
rich region around Kirkuk. To the east of Kurdistan, Iran, which boasts
a significant Kurdish population of its own, sealed its border to prevent
Kurds from avoiding the approaching Turkish forces. To the west, Syria,
an Iranian ally, did the same.[46] After an emergency meeting of the UN Security Council and appeals to the United States and the European Union
failed to produce action, the Iraqi Kurds realized their fate was sealed.[47]

---

45. "Washington Caught Napping," *Economist,* May 17, 2014, p. 43.

46. There is considerable speculation that Turkey and Iran reached an understanding on Kurdistan prior to the Turkish invasion, in which Iran would support the Turkish action in return for
Turkish acquiescence to Iran's consolidating its influence in southern Iraq. Both countries, of
course, saw themselves benefiting from the end of a quasi-independent Kurdish state. Michael
Herzog, "Strange Bedfellows: The Tehran-Ankara Axis," *New Yorker,* August 12, 2014.

47. Both the Americans and the Europeans remonstrated against their NATO ally, Turkey.
The Europeans warned the Turks that their actions would harm Ankara's efforts to win
European Union membership. The Turks dismissed both warnings. As one American ex-
pert on Turkey put it:

> The Turks argued their security had been threatened for years by Kurdish
> terrorists and yet NATO did nothing, either to help defend Turkey or to
> threaten the Kurds with sanctions. And the EU threat to Turkey is laugh-
> able; everyone knows the Europeans, with their internal Muslim problems,
> will never allow the Turks into their club.

Josh Kravitz, "Turks Reject West Overtures," *New York Times,* July 4, 2014, p. A1.

But as the Kurds looked to return to the mountains and the guerrilla warfare they had waged in the past, they sent one final message to the world that they felt had abandoned them. On the night of June 3, U.S. early warning satellites reported what might have been interpreted as the bright plumes representing a series of missile launches from Kurdistan. But it was nothing of the sort; rather, these were the flames of northern Iraq's oil-production infrastructure being wrecked by the retreating Kurds. In a stroke, well over a million barrels of oil a day were taken off a global energy market that has recently, once again, become a seller's market.

Prices, which had held at around $145 per barrel prior to the U.S. withdrawal and had bumped up to over $150 per barrel following the onset of fighting in Fallujah, quickly spiked to over $230 per barrel. The Iranians and their Iraqi Shi'a allies, oil producers themselves, could not have been happier. The Turks, with the assistance of Western oil firms, are now in the process of repairing the oil fields around Kirkuk. But estimates indicate it will take many months, perhaps even a year or two, before even limited production can be resumed.

EXIT THE ADVISERS

THE PACE OF EVENTS ACCELERATED DURING THE SUMMER OF 2014. In an attempt to win active U.S. support for the "Sunni Arab front" against the "Shi'a Persian threat," the Saudis bumped up their oil production to full capacity, offsetting the loss of northern Iraq's production. The move had its intended effect. Prices declined to just over $150 per barrel, and the Iranians were denied another windfall profit. Ironically, however, the U.S. Congress used the Saudi move as an excuse to vote down the Dannemeyer administration's legislation that would have imposed strict energy conservation standards.

As the situation in Iraq unraveled, U.S. advisers still serving with Iraqi Army units found themselves increasingly at risk.[48] These advisers refused to accompany Iraqi units fighting the Sunnis in Fallujah, and

48. The U.S. military training units and their associated support elements had been withdrawn in early 2014, with over 10,000 soldiers departing Iraq in a span of less than three months.

after eleven were killed in one Kurdish-dominated Iraqi Army unit following the Turkish invasion, there was a public outcry in the United States to bring all the advisers home.[49] Their departure made headlines. The advisers departed their units unannounced, gathered at several staging points in Iraq, and were extracted by helicopters from U.S. Special Forces units operating in the region. The choppers ferried the advisers, over 1,500 of them, to an air base in Jordan, where all were transported via cargo aircraft to an American air base in Italy.[50] In a matter of hours, the long American military presence in Iraq had ended.[51]

The American media portrayed the operation as one of remarkable coordination and daring and emphasized the fact that no casualties—either U.S. or Iraqi—were sustained. The Iranian and Arab media, however, cast the operation as an American retreat in the dead of night. Domestic critics of the administration's policies declared the president's plan a shambles and angrily reminded the public that the country's security and economic well-being had been compromised less than a year after U.S. combat troops had departed Iraq.

THE WAR SPREADS

BUT THE RECRIMINATIONS OVER AMERICA'S FAILED POLICIES IN IRAQ were soon overtaken by rapidly moving events. Iran offered to replace the American advisers with its own, pledging they would not "flee in the face of danger."[52] The offer was refused by the Shi'a regime, even though it was now heavily dependent on Iran for military supplies. Nevertheless, Tehran proclaimed that Iraq was now under the protection of

---

49. The bodies of these soldiers have never been recovered, despite repeated diplomatic interventions by Washington to the Kurds, the Shi'a government in Baghdad, and more recently the Turks. Stanley Howell, "Hopes of Recovery Dim," *Chicago Tribune*, September 23, 2015, p. A1.

50. Mary Symanski, "Advisers Depart in Daring Airlift," *Washington Post*, September 30, 2014, p. A1.

51. The American supply units that had been supporting the Iraqi Army were relocated to Kuwait as part of the withdrawal of U.S. forces from Iraq. As the conflict between Shi'a and Sunni heated up, American logistical support for the Iraqis was terminated, to be replaced by support from Iran and Pakistan.

52. "Iran Extends Its Reach," *Economist*, October 15, 2014, p. 40.

its nuclear deterrent (the "Shi'a Bomb") and warned other nations not to intervene in Iraq's internal affairs.[53]

With the tide turning against the Sunnis in Iraq, they sought to focus on what many of them believed was the true source of their problems, Iran. Just before dawn on November 15 the three Persian Gulf islands of Kharg, Lavan, and Siri, which handle Iran's oil exports, were attacked by radical Sunni Islamist forces aligned with al Qaeda. Firing several dozen ASCMs from a transport ship they had leased for just such a purpose, the terrorists struck two oil supertankers. Shortly thereafter twenty-six pilotless aircraft (unmanned aerial vehicles), each armed with an estimated 1,000 pounds of explosives, attacked the islands' storage tanks. While twenty-two were shot down or malfunctioned, the remaining four hit two storage tanks on Kharg Island and one on Lavan Island. It is believed the drones were launched either from the transport ship that fired the ASCMs or from sites in Saudi Arabia. Finally, the terrorists mounted suicide fast-boat attacks on Kharg Island's port facilities. All but one of the eight boats succeeded in avoiding the Iranian defenses.[54] The al Qaeda transport ship was destroyed by Iranian aircraft and naval patrol craft late that morning, killing all aboard. But the damage had been done. Kharg and Lavan islands suffered substantial damage, and Iranian oil exports have fallen to half their pre-attack level of 3.4 million barrels a day. This time, however, there is no excess Saudi capacity to take up the slack. No other producers have any significant production capacity, although Russian president Yuri Volkogonov has hinted that his

---

53. Mary Symanski, "Iraq Protected by Iranian Nukes," *Washington Post*, November 8, 2014, p. A1.

54. The boats were laden with explosives. Perhaps only the first boats to strike the dock facilities inflicted damage, as the boats arriving behind them may have been destroyed in the blast. There are unsubstantiated claims by al Qaeda affiliates that several unmanned underwater vehicles were used to attack undersea pipelines, but this has not been confirmed. For an excellent account of the attack, see Jeffrey Schmidt, "Iran's Pearl Harbor," *New York Times Sunday Magazine*, February 1, 2015. Under the shah, Kharg Island was the world's largest offshore crude oil terminal. This is not the first time Kharg Island has been attacked. Its facilities were knocked out during the Iran-Iraq War in the 1980s, and in recent years it has experienced problems owing primarily to Tehran's lack of investment in modernizing its facilities.

country could make up for some of the shortfall in exchange for certain EU concessions.[55]

Oil industry experts from France and China have been on the scene since December attempting to repair the damage. Repair efforts are expected to take between one and two years. In the meantime, oil prices once again surged, this time exceeding $260 a barrel.

The Iranian leadership was furious over the attacks, which not only caught them napping but also removed the government's principal source of income. The Iranians publicly accused the Saudis of aiding and abetting the attack, noting that the majority of the attackers that had been identified were Saudi nationals and asserting that the drone air attacks were launched from Saudi soil. Riyadh responded that it had long cooperated with the United States and others in the war against Sunni extremists, while Iran had, for years, harbored some senior al Qaeda members. The attackers on 9/11 were mostly Saudis, as were many of the suicide bombers that bedeviled U.S. forces during the American military involvement in Iraq. Yet, the Saudis noted, Washington could tell the difference between the Saudi government and individual Saudi citizens. The Saudis also declared that several al Qaeda members believed to have had a role in planning the attack were in custody and would be aggressively prosecuted. The Iranians responded evenly that, no matter what Riyadh might say, the fact remains that Saudi oil production was at an all-time high while Iran's facilities had been devastated. On November 28, the Iranian government formally demanded the Saudis and the other Sunni oil-producing Gulf states provide it with compensation to cover the loss in production caused by the recent attacks, threatening military action if its demands were not met.

With that, Iran put its military on a war footing. In early December

---

55. Moscow argues that increased production over current rates is inefficient and will reduce the lifetime yield from several of its fields. Nevertheless, it is willing to do so in exchange for commitments on the EU's part to grant it a greater share of its market, access to certain pipelines, and approval to construct natural gas pipelines through a number of EU countries. While many energy experts doubt the Russians can make good on their claim to make up for the loss of nearly two million barrels per day of Iranian production, national security experts are expressing concern over the prospects of Europe's growing energy dependence on the heavy-handed, authoritarian regime in Moscow. See Brenda Dubois, "The Road to Perdition: Europe's Growing Addiction to Russian Energy," *Atlantic Monthly*, March 19, 2014.

2014 Iranian forces were invited into southern Iraq by Sadr, ostensibly to protect the Iraqi oil fields from attack. However, these Iranian forces now also posed a threat to Kuwait and perhaps to Saudi Arabia's oil fields, most of which are located just south of Kuwait along the Persian Gulf. The Iranians are also reported to have large numbers of sophisticated antiship mines, courtesy of Russia, that can be quickly emplaced at the Strait of Hormuz leading from the Persian Gulf out into the open sea. The strait, of course, is the principal choke point for the steady stream of maritime traffic carrying the region's oil to the world's advanced industrial economies. Press reports also say that Iranian mobile ballistic missile forces, which number nearly a thousand, have been dispatched to their launch points. Their likely targets: Saudi oil fields and main U.S. air bases and naval facilities in the region.[56] While Iran is suspected of possessing no more than a handful of atomic bombs—perhaps five or six—intelligence reports indicate that the bombs are likely too large to be delivered by missile.[57] Reportedly a handful of specially modified Iranian combat aircraft are capable of delivering the weapon to targets within a few hundred miles of Iran's borders. This, of course, puts the main Saudi oil-production facilities and several key U.S. air and naval bases at great risk. Finally, the Iranian Quds Force is reportedly attempting to infiltrate into Kuwait and Saudi Arabia for the purpose of conducting sabotage operations if war breaks out.[58]

On December 9 the European Union sent its general secretary, Lord Philip Wainwright, to Tehran in an attempt to defuse the crisis. Lord Wainwright presented a proposal to the Iranian government that includes a package of economic and financial aid to offset over half of the income the Iranians are anticipated to lose while their oil infrastructure is being repaired. By some estimates, this amounts to over $100 billion. The EU proposal has been rejected by the Iranians, in part because the

56. Paul Davies, "Iran Flexes Muscles: Gulf Oil at Risk," *Wall Street Journal,* December 11, 2014, p. A1.

57. Josh Kravitz, "Iran Threatens Nuclear Use," *New York Times,* December 17, 2014, p. A1.

58. This account of Iranian activity is derived from a variety of press reports, most of which are in turn drawn from leaked accounts of President Dannemeyer's National Security Council meetings on November 22 and 23, 2014. See Josh Kravitz, "President Weighs Options amid Iranian Buildup," *New York Times,* November 29, 2014, p. A1.

funds would be spread over ten years, and much of the amount would be in the form of credits to buy EU goods.

ON THE OUTSIDE LOOKING IN

IN CONTRAST, THE DANNEMEYER ADMINISTRATION HAS BEEN SLOW to take action, having rejected the EU's invitation to join in its economic initiative. In part, the rejection stems from the administration's very poor showing in the midterm elections in November; its approval ratings have sunk to a new low following the attacks of November 15 and the oil price spike. When the administration again put forward new energy conservation legislation last week that contained standby authority for the White House to impose gas rationing for the first time since World War II, it received a frigid reception on Capitol Hill. As the Senate minority leader, John Gavlin, put it, "The administration's policies have produced a near doubling in the price of oil, and now the president wants the American people to sacrifice to atone for his poor leadership."[59]

The Saudi government approached the White House for assurances that the United States will come to its aid in the event of war. The Saudi ambassador reportedly offered to provide the U.S. military with immediate access to Saudi bases to deflect what may be an imminent Iranian attack on the Saudi oil fields. According to well-placed senior administration sources, the Joint Chiefs of Staff have outlined the following possible missions for American forces, should the president decide that military action is necessary:

- warships patrolling the Persian Gulf to protect oil facilities and ensure the safety of maritime traffic;
- land-based missile defense units based in Saudi Arabia, coupled with missile defense radars and interceptors on warships in the Gulf to defend against Iranian (and possibly al Qaeda) missile attack;

59. Senator John Gavlin, interview, *Face the Nation*, December 7, 2015, at www.cbsnews .com/sections/ftn/main3460.shtml, accessed on January 3, 2016.

- six Army brigade combat teams and associated support units to provide security for U.S. missile defense units and, if needed, Saudi oil fields against sabotage and other forms of attack;
- Special Forces units conducting operations to identify and defeat Quds Force elements or supporters of al Qaeda should they attempt to operate covertly in Saudi Arabia; and
- strike aircraft aboard carriers, and from air bases in Kuwait, Qatar, the United Arab Emirates, and Diego Garcia, providing defense against any attempt by Iran to conduct a nuclear air strike against a Gulf state, while also conducting strikes against the full range of Iranian military assets, if necessary.

In all, the force would comprise over 100,000 American troops. Should a regime change in Iran be required, the president is informed, the force's size would need to be greatly expanded, especially the ground force. General Swanson has reportedly indicated that even the minimal force could not be fully in place for three to four months.[60]

Both General Swanson and Defense Secretary James Burke outlined the challenges associated with these actions.[61] They emphasized the risks associated with undertaking a third major military buildup in the Persian Gulf in the last quarter century. Director of National Intelligence Raymond Pfister reportedly observed:

> The last two buildups of this type preceded a U.S.-led coalition attack on Iraq. There is reason to believe that Tehran would see a third buildup, not as a measure taken to defend the Arab Gulf states, but as the prelude to an invasion of Iran.

Chief of naval operations Admiral Daniel DeMotta is said to have informed the president that, because of the narrow, crowded shipping

---

60. Mary Symanski, "JCS Present Options to President," *Washington Post*, December 18, 2015, p. A1.

61. This summary is drawn from various sources, principally ibid., pp. A1, A8–A11; and Josh Kravitz, "White House Explores Military Response," *New York Times*, December 19, 2014, pp. A1, A4–A6.

lanes in the Persian Gulf, any U.S. Navy warships in those waters would need authority to fire first at Iranian naval forces and unidentified commercial craft. Even then the Navy's ships would be highly vulnerable to high-speed Iranian antiship cruise missiles, which could be based along the Iranian coastline as well as on its warships, or even on ships masquerading as commercial transports. The admiral also pointed out that the Iranians could bring traffic in the Gulf to a halt by emplacing sophisticated antiship mines, which would be difficult to prevent as they could simply be rolled off the stern of "commercial" ships under cover of darkness. Making matters worse, former CIA director Michael Petroski noted that given the recent al Qaeda attacks in the Persian Gulf, it may be difficult to pin the blame on the Iranians even if they are responsible for the mines. In short, the Persian Gulf had become a very dangerous place in which to conduct operations. As one retired general put it:

> It's like those old Westerns where they tell the cavalry not to go into the canyon because the Indians are waiting there to ambush them. And the cavalry does it anyway. And they get ambushed. Well, this time our navy is the cavalry, and the Iranians are the Indians, and the Persian Gulf is the canyon. Only we don't have John Wayne to come to our rescue.[62]

General Thomas Davis, the Army's chief of staff, present at the meeting, is said to have also cautioned the president that the six brigades would be the "minimum" needed to provide security for the oil fields along the southern rim of the Gulf. According to the leaked transcript of the meeting, Davis described how in recent years even nonstate groups like Hezbollah have acquired substantial numbers of extended-range rockets, guided missiles, and unmanned aerial vehicles, with some capable of strikes ranging out to seventy miles. The general also noted that the Iranians have been one of the principal proliferators of these weapons, and that it would be easy for them to arm the Shi'a militias in

62. General (Ret.) John Piccarelli, *Issues and Answers,* December 21, 2015, at www.msnbc.msn.com/id/3032608/, accessed on December 30, 2014.

southern Iraq with thousands of them. In that case, Davis concluded, the Army's air and missile defenses would likely be overwhelmed by sheer numbers. Moreover, those weapons that evaded U.S. defenses were more likely to strike their targets than not, thanks to the rapid diffusion of missile guidance technology. The general went on to say that if the Iranians wanted to forgo this more ambiguous form of aggression, they could salvo-launch dozens of ballistic missiles against the oil fields and the associated infrastructure. A significant portion of these missiles would likely hit their targets.[63]

General Dana Fitzgerald, the Air Force chief of staff, informed the president that, just as the oil fields were vulnerable to damage and destruction from missile attack, so too were the region's air bases, which could be quickly eviscerated by Iranian barrage missile attacks.[64]

The newly confirmed secretary of state, Carole Hansen, soberly informed the president that the Israelis had placed their military on heightened alert. After deliberating well into the night, the cabinet supported Prime Minister Elahud Eitan's decision to respond to any Iranian use of nuclear weapons, anywhere in the region, with an Israeli nuclear attack on Iran's nuclear forces. Eitan is reported to have informed Hansen via secure telephone link, "We are a tiny country. We cannot wait for the mullahs to turn their hate on us."[65]

Secretary of the Treasury Robert Johnson concluded that, based on the information provided by the military and his assessment of the oil market, a conflict in the Persian Gulf of the type described could see oil prices exceed $500 a barrel. While Johnson conceded that was only a "rough estimate," he did feel confident that should prices reach that level, the world economy would be plunged into another severe recession and perhaps worse. He recommended that the president be prepared to put into effect standby plans for the rationing of petroleum.

63. Symanski, "JCS Present Options," pp. A1, A8–A11; and Kravitz, "White House Explores Military Response," pp. A1, A4–A6.
64. This risk was also made clear in an editorial by retired members of the Joint Chiefs of Staff. See General (Ret.) John Bucholtz, Admiral (Ret.) Kelly McDougal, General (Ret.) William Peterson, and General (Ret.) Abraham Simpson, "Gulf Ambush?" *Wall Street Journal,* December 22, 2014, p. A25.
65. This information comes from a confidential interview between the author and a senior State Department official.

Faced with this sobering military assessment, the administration temporized for twelve long days.

When the administration informed the Saudis of its concerns regarding the deployment of U.S. forces, and the extended time lines involved in putting all of them into position, it clearly deflated them.[66] But at the time they seemed to have little recourse but to continue pressing Washington for a commitment to act.

But then, in the words of National Security Advisor Sean O'Callaghan, "a most unexpected development" occurred. The Russians requested an emergency session of the UN Security Council to discuss the Persian Gulf crisis. The meeting, which took place on January 6, 2015, will go down as one of the most memorable in UN history. At the session the Chinese ambassador, Zhai Jun, announced that his government had reached an agreement with Iran and Iraq to deploy Chinese peacekeeping forces to Iraq to secure that country's borders with Kuwait and Saudi Arabia, and to assist the Iranians and Iraqis in securing their oil infrastructures in and around Basra and in the Persian Gulf. Beijing is willing to commit 70,000 People's Liberation Army (PLA) troops to the effort, along with a PLA Navy coastal patrol force to safeguard passage in the Persian Gulf. Zhai Jun also reported that Islamabad has pledged 22,000 Pakistani troops to provide a Muslim presence in defense of Saudi Arabia's oil production facilities, should Riyadh desire.[67] Given these security assurances, Tehran is willing to stand down its military forces and continue negotiating with the EU and Saudi Arabia on a package of economic assistance (or "compensation") for Iran. Beijing has agreed to participate in the negotiations and contribute a "fair share" to compensate Iran for its losses.

At the same time the Shi'a government in Baghdad announced that Russia has agreed to dispatch 6,000 advisers and trainers to assist the Iraqi Army in its efforts to defeat the Sunni insurrection in western Iraq. Moscow also declared that it has signed a $4 billion arms agreement to

66. Stanley Howell, "Saudis May Seek Other Options," *Wall Street Journal,* December 23, 2014, p. A1.
67. With the U.S. economy in the doldrums, China replaced America as Pakistan's principal backer and source of economic assistance in 2011. The PLA Navy was granted access to the Pakistani naval base of Gwadar in 2012.

provide the Shi'a regime with heavy equipment, such as tanks and artillery, along with attack helicopters and several squadrons of advanced Russian fighter aircraft. Both Beijing and Moscow pledged to work with countries in the region and the international community to ensure the integrity of the world's energy core.

The reasons behind Beijing's initiative are transparent. At relatively small cost, it offers China the prospect of displacing the United States as the key external power in the Persian Gulf. Russian, Iranian, and Chinese forces will help the Shi'a secure control over the better part of Iraq, gaining influence in the process. With the Chinese providing economic and military assistance to an increasingly embattled Iran, Beijing's influence will grow there as well. If China's initiative deflects a war between Iran and Saudi Arabia, the Chinese stand to earn the gratitude of Riyadh, and of the Europeans.[68]

The Chinese ambassador also announced that both the EU and Saudi Arabia have accepted Beijing's proposal and requested that the Security Council sanction the peacekeeping forces outlined by him. With the EU lined up to support the proposal, which offers to bring the Persian Gulf back from the brink of war, the United States has little choice but to vote along with the Security Council's other permanent members—Britain, China, France, and Russia—to support the resolution. The U.S. ambassador to the United Nations, William Curry, upon departing the session, was heard to remark to an aide, "For the first time in my lifetime, the United States is on the outside looking in."[69]

---

68. Robert Gustavson, "Beijing Bids to Shift Gulf Power Balance," *New York Times,* January 20, 2015, p. A23.
69. Jim Phillips, "Beijing Takes Lead in Gulf," *Washington Post,* January 7, 2014, p. A1.

Conclusion

LIGHTING THE PATH AHEAD

Predicting is difficult—especially about the future.

Niels Bohr

SO WHAT?

THE SEVEN PRECEDING SCENARIOS OFFER A SOBERING PICTURE OF the difficult challenges the United States, and its military in particular, may confront in the not-too-distant future. In addition to the shock of the 9/11 attacks and the ongoing wars in Afghanistan and Iraq, more dangers may be lurking ahead, dark clouds along the nation's strategic horizon.

Like Ebenezer Scrooge in Charles Dickens' *A Christmas Carol*, we are moved to ask: *Are these the shadows of the things that Will be, or are they shadows of things that May be, only? . . . . [I]f the courses be departed from, the ends will change. Say it is thus with what you show me!*[1] Fortunately, a country as powerful as the United States can often take action to deflect emerging challenges or to mitigate significantly their potential consequences. Remember, the crafting of scenarios is not an attempt to predict the future. Far too many interacting factors are at work to shape the future. It is impossible to know in advance how

---

1. Charles Dickens, *A Christmas Carol*. The entire novella is at http://www.gutenberg.org/files/46/46-8.txt, accessed on July 22, 2008.

things will turn out. Eliminating uncertainty and surprise is simply not possible.

None of the scenarios presented above will come to pass exactly as described. Scenarios have a more modest goal: to describe how the future *might* turn out. That being the case, why do these scenarios matter? Their usefulness lies in their ability to help military planners reduce the risks inherent in their work. The planners' job is to minimize the overall threat to the national security. Their ability to do this is limited, among other things, by risk and uncertainty. *Risk* is randomness with knowable probabilities; that is, we have some sense of what the probabilities might be (e.g., low, medium, high). *Uncertainty* is randomness with unknowable probabilities. These "wild card" or "Black Swan" events are essentially unanticipated.[2] Hence it is not possible to put a value on "uncertainty." However, by identifying and assessing the factors that will likely exert the greatest influence on the future security environment, and by examining the trends associated with these factors, military planners can identify significant emerging threats to the national security for which they must prepare.

These risks must be plausible or credible to be taken seriously by senior decision-makers. Toward this end the narrative path between the world of today and the world of tomorrow's security challenges must be believable. A credible scenario can help broaden senior leaders' attention beyond the immediate problems confronting them and enable them to overcome the natural mindset that sees tomorrow as simply a linear extrapolation of the world as it exists today.

Like the scenarios crafted by Pentagon planners, the scenarios presented here are the product of an examination of key geopolitical, military-technical, demographic, social, economic, and environmental trends. The path to the future will almost certainly unfold along a different route, but the kinds of challenges encountered may be roughly the same as those depicted in the preceding scenarios. Recall the

2. A "Black Swan" event is an outlier: "Nothing in the past can convincingly point to its possibility." Black Swans have profound consequences and appear to have been predictable after the fact. Nassim Nicholas Taleb, *The Black Swan* (New York: Random House, 2007), pp. xvii, xviii.

"Streetfighter State" scenario presented in the introduction. Written in 1996, the narrative saw Iran presenting a range of security problems for the United States. Some of these problems, like the threat posed to U.S. power-projection operations, were confronted in the Pentagon's Millennium Challenge field exercise six years later. Others, like modern irregular Iranian forces employing rockets and missiles against U.S.-led coalition forces, emerged a decade later in the Second Lebanon War between Israel and Hezbollah. And the challenges associated with combating a modern insurgent movement presented in the "Streetfighter State" scenario came to pass eight years later in Iraq.

"WASTING ASSETS"

ON SEPTEMBER 3, 1949, AN AIR FORCE B-29 RECONNAISSANCE AIRcraft engaged in long-range aerial detection of potential Soviet atomic activity, took an air sample on its way from Japan to Alaska. Its instruments revealed a surprising jump in radioactivity. Two days later another aircraft, flying from Guam to Tokyo, also recorded a spike in radioactivity. Other planes were quickly dispatched to take more samples. By mid-September top American scientists had concluded that the radioactivity could not have come from a nuclear reactor accident. It could only have come from the detonation of a plutonium-based atomic bomb.[3]

The Soviet Union's act meant that the U.S. nuclear weapons monopoly was a "wasting asset."[4] Once the Soviets had accumulated a sufficient arsenal of atomic weapons, the world would be a very different place. The United States could no longer rely on its nuclear monopoly to trump the Soviet Union's advantage in standing conventional military forces. Scientists on the General Advisory Committee had alerted American political leaders that the Soviets would likely detonate an atomic

3. The Soviet Union had detonated an atomic bomb on August 29, 1949, somewhere in northern Siberia. Walter Isaacson and Evan Thomas, *The Wise Men* (New York: Simon & Schuster, 1986), p. 480; and John Newhouse, *War and Peace in the Nuclear Age* (New York: Vintage Books, 1990), pp. 72–73.
4. See Marc Trachtenburg, "A Wasting Asset: American Strategy and the Shifting Nuclear Balance, 1949–54," *International Security*, Winter 1988–89.

weapon between 1948 and 1950, but for a number of reasons official Washington chose to ignore this scenario, out of either ignorance or willful disbelief. On one occasion President Truman asked Robert Oppenheimer, the "father" of the atomic bomb, "When will the Russians be able to build the bomb?"

"I don't know," replied Oppenheimer.

"I know," Truman replied.

"When?" asked Oppenheimer.

"Never," declared Truman.[5]

Confronted with this "wasting asset," the Truman and, later, Eisenhower administrations engaged in a series of national security reviews to develop a strategy to cope with the new reality.[6]

Like the "Streetfighter State" scenario, the seven scenarios presented here highlight major challenges to U.S. national security that defense planners ignore at our peril. They pose major strategic choices for the United States and for many of its allies and partners as well. The scenarios can be viewed as identifying some of the U.S. military's "wasting assets." For example, as an insular power with global interests and commitments, the United States must be prepared to project military power where it is needed and in a timely manner. The U.S. military must be prepared to defend critical assets—bases, ports, airfields, infrastructure—wherever it operates overseas, as well as here at home. Projecting power overseas requires the military to have access to the "global commons"—space, cyberspace, the skies, the seas, and undersea. Commercial access to the global commons is also essential for America's economic well-being, which is increasingly dependent upon supplies of overseas commodities and products, upon their associated supply and communications chains, and upon access to foreign markets for U.S. goods. As the seven scenarios suggest, the U.S. military's ability to project power abroad, to defend forward, and to maintain the lines of communication from those locations through the global commons to the Ameri-

5. Peter Pringle and James Spigelman, *The Nuclear Barons* (New York: Holt, Rinehart & Winston, 1981), p. 43.

6. These reviews produced some of the most well-known strategy documents of the Cold War, including NSC-68 and NSC 162/2.

can homeland is being progressively eroded and may decline precipitously in the coming years unless, like Scrooge, having "seen" what the future holds in store, the United States takes steps to create new paths to less dangerous futures.

The U.S. military's growing inability to project power in defense of the country's vital interests abroad, and to defend key assets overseas, is highlighted in several scenarios, including "China's 'Assassin's Mace,'" "Armageddon: The Assault on Israel," "Who Lost Iraq?," and "The Collapse of Pakistan." The growing risk to its ability to maintain access to the global commons is described in "China's 'Assassin's Mace,'" "Just Not-on-Time: The War on the Global Economy," and "Pandemic." The challenges associated with defending the U.S. homeland itself are presented in "Pandemic" and "War Comes to America."

Now that we have diagnosed the emerging challenges to the national security, and the associated military "wasting assets," what can be done to address them? First, defense planners need a strategic concept to identify the goals they are trying to achieve and how they might go about achieving them. Second, they need a process by which they can validate their approach.

Accomplishing this will not be easy. A number of prominent American strategists have reached the general conclusion that the U.S. government's capacity to craft national security strategy at anything approaching an acceptable level of competence is highly suspect.[7] Why is the U.S. government's capability to develop strategy so deficient? What are the principal barriers to success in this area? What might be done to overcome them?

WHAT IS STRATEGY?

ALTHOUGH MANY DEFINITIONS OF THE WORD *STRATEGY* HAVE BEEN offered, it generally involves the application of limited resources to

---

7. See, for example, Aaron L. Friedberg, "Strengthening Strategic Planning," *Washington Quarterly,* Winter 2007–08; and Barry D. Watts, "Why Strategy? The Case for Taking It Seriously and Doing It Well," unpublished paper, Center for Strategic and Budgetary Assessments, 2007.

achieve a desired goal.[8] Strategy also involves "identifying or creating asymmetric advantages in competitive situations that can then be exploited to help achieve one's ultimate objectives despite the active, opposing efforts of one's adversaries or competitors to achieve theirs."[9] A sound strategy is one that leverages our asymmetric advantages to impose disproportionate costs upon the competition, making it unfeasible for our rivals to compete effectively.[10] These differences, or asymmetries, are sources of competitive advantage; successful strategists must exploit them in order to develop the best possible approach for achieving their desired objective.[11] Thus the real value of strategic planning is not in producing a final authoritative strategy, or set of scenarios, but rather in continuously developing insights as to where asymmetric advantages lie.

Given the importance of a good strategy, why is the U.S. defense establishment so lacking in its ability to craft one?

8. Carl von Clausewitz, *On War*, ed. and trans. Michael Howard and Peter Paret (Princeton, N.J.: Princeton University Press, 1976), p. 181; B. H. Liddell Hart, *Strategy* (New York: Meridian, 1991), p. 321; Bernard Brodie, "Why Were We So (Strategically) Wrong?" *Foreign Policy*, Winter 1971–72, p. 151. Cited in Marc Trachtenberg, *History and Strategy* (Princeton, N.J.: Princeton University Press, 1991); Richard K. Betts, "Is Strategy an Illusion?" *International Security*, Fall 2000, p. 6; and Colin S. Gray, *Modern Strategy* (Oxford: Oxford University Press, 1999), p. 17. Cited in Watts, "Why Strategy?" p. 2.
9. Watts, "Why Strategy?" p. 2.
10. Richard Rumelt, one of the leading thinkers in the field of business strategy, notes that a strategist's job is "to identify, create, or exploit some kind of an edge." Barry D. Watts, Memorandum for the Record, "Strategy Seminar," Center for Strategy & Budgetary Assessments, September 25, 2007, p. 7. Business strategist Kees Van der Heijden concurs: "Success can only be based on being different from (existing or potential) competitors." Kees Van der Heijden, *Scenarios: The Art of Strategic Conversation* (Hoboken, N.J.: John Wiley & Sons, 2005), p. xv. Their views are seconded by General Rupert Smith, who states that "the essence of the practice of war is to achieve asymmetric advantage over one's opponent; an advantage in any terms, not just technological." Rupert Smith, *The Utility of Force: The Art of War in the Modern World* (New York: Alfred A. Knopf, 2007), p. 377.
11. Van der Heijden, *Scenarios*, p. 55.

BARRIERS TO GOOD STRATEGY

THERE ARE NUMEROUS BARRIERS TO CRAFTING GOOD DEFENSE strategy, and only a few of them will be presented here. One is the government's tendency to equate strategy with a list of desirable outcomes. Such lists involve little or no discussion of what obstacles stand in the way of achieving these goals or how they might be overcome. Rather than working out how best to employ scarce resources to achieve a challenging security objective, the *mere statement of a desire* to meet the objective is deemed sufficient.

For example, the Clinton administration's 2000 National Security Strategy concludes almost purely in terms of desired outcomes.

> Our strategy . . . is comprised of many different policies, the key elements of which include . . . encouraging the reorientation of other states, including foreign adversaries . . . democratization, open markets, free trade, and sustainable development . . . [and] preventing conflict.[12]

"Reorienting" adversary states' views and "preventing conflict" are not strategies, they are U.S. security objectives, which may or may not be achievable depending upon the resources at hand and the strategy employed.

The problem of mistaking objectives for strategy is not limited to the Clinton administration or to the civilian leadership. Take, for example, the Joint Chiefs of Staff document *Joint Vision 2010,* published in the late 1990s. Its intent was to show how the U.S. armed forces would operate to achieve the nation's security objectives in the 2010 timeframe. According to the document, the means would be "information superiority" that enabled "dominant maneuver," "precision engagement," "focused logistics," and "full-dimensional protection." In other words, the U.S. military had the goals of complete awareness of what is happening

---

12. William J. Clinton, *A National Security Strategy for a Global Age* (Washington, D.C.: n.p., December 2000), p. 67.

in a theater of war ("information superiority"), an ability to move its forces, which are to be completely protected ("full-dimensional protection") wherever it desires ("dominant maneuver"), and an ability to engage with unprecedented effectiveness ("precision engagement") while always being fully supplied ("focused logistics").[13] Conspicuously absent is a discussion of *how* these subgoals are to be realized. Nor is any mention made of potential enemy actions or resource limitations that could frustrate these efforts. Again, reducing "strategy" to assertions that the conditions desired will be achieved eliminates the need to consider resource limits or enemy action. The need for real strategy is assumed away.

A nation's failure to understand the enemy also severely limits its ability to identify its advantages and how best to exploit them. Consider an example from the Truman administration. After the Soviet Union detonated its atomic bomb, a revised U.S. strategic assessment—the famous NSC-68—moved away from the previous emphasis on Soviet subversion and political warfare and instead stressed the role of military capabilities in countering the Soviet threat.[14] This change generated significant debate. Chip Bohlen, one of the so-called "Wise Men,"[15] argued that the Soviet leadership's top priority was to preserve their regime and that American leaders were discounting this fact.[16] Bohlen's point was that differing assessments of Soviet motives—whether the Soviet leadership prioritized its expansionist objectives over its survival—had very different implications for strategy. Ultimately, Bohlen's argument prevailed, and U.S. strategy retained a major focus on Soviet political warfare and subversion, while accepting a deterrent posture against the coming Soviet nuclear threat in the belief that Moscow would not start a war that could cause the regime to lose internal control.[17]

Unfortunately, the United States does not currently enjoy the kind

13. General John M. Shalikashvili, *Joint Vision 2010* (Washington, D.C.: Department of Defense, n.d.), p. 19.
14. Robert R. Bowie and Richard H. Immerman, *Waging Peace* (Oxford, U.K.: Oxford University Press, 1998), p. 12.
15. Walter Isaacson and Evan Thomas, *The Wise Men* (New York: Simon & Schuster, 1986), pp. 19–20.
16. Bowie and Immerman, *Waging Peace*, p. 28.
17. *Foreign Relations of the United States, 1951*, vol. 1, pp. 177–78, cited ibid., p. 31.

of expertise regarding its rivals' thinking and operations that it did during the early stages of the Cold War. Developing a cadre of experts on militant Islamic groups, China, and other key states of concern (e.g., Iran) is an essential element of any serious effort at strategy formulation.

The varying competence of senior national security decision-makers constitutes yet another barrier to good strategy. Perhaps because the government does not do strategy well, some senior national security decision-makers seem to have lost confidence in the value of strategy or at least in recent efforts. Either way, it is bad news for those defense planners who do seek useful strategic guidance to inform their efforts.

Skepticism over the value of strategy and the possibility of doing it well is present at the highest levels of America's national security establishment. For example, President Clinton's national security advisor, Sandy Berger, put little stock in the government's strategic planning efforts, declaring that "most 'grand strategies' were after-the-fact rationales developed to explain successful *ad hoc* decisions." Berger went on to say that he preferred to "worry about today today and tomorrow tomorrow."[18] This kind of skepticism is not limited to a particular individual, administration, or political party.

Another barrier to effective strategic planning involves scarce resources. Were resources unlimited, there would be no need for strategy, since one could pursue all possible courses of action to the maximum extent possible.

Unfortunately, the Defense Department's approach to planning and budgeting actually *encourages* the services to ignore budgetary constraints through "cut drills," which are intended to reconcile the gap between a defense program that cannot be sustained given projected defense resources. In a cut drill, the service that has thought through how to work with limited means to achieve its assigned mission is likely to be penalized, while a service whose program is substantially short of the resources needed for its execution is rewarded with additional funds. The department's senior leaders tend to assist those services that are

18. R. W. Apple, "A Domestic Sort with Global Worries," *New York Times*, August 25, 1999, p. A10.

most in need. The lesson for the services is clear: put in for as large a program and force structure as you can, and hope to sustain as much as you can in the cut drill. While this may make sense from a narrow bureaucratic perspective, it hardly makes for sound national strategy.

Again, the problem is not limited to the military. The Bush administration had a goal of creating a stable, democratic Iraq but gave little consideration to the enormous resources—in time, treasure, and blood—that would be required to achieve that goal. Compounding the problem, President Bush declared, "Our strategy can be summed up this way: As the Iraqis stand up, we will stand down."[19] Here the president conflated resources—the means to be employed within a strategy—with strategy itself. Put another way, substituting Iraqi troops for U.S. troops tells us what means will be employed to achieve America's objectives in Iraq, not *how* these means will be utilized.

Finally, even senior national security decision-makers who believe in the value of strategic planning and who understand the factor of limited resources confront yet another, quite formidable barrier: the bureaucracy. Bureaucracies tend to have their own agendas, which typically offer stiff resistance to leaders' attempts to enact change.

WHAT IS TO BE DONE?

TO BEGIN, THE PRESIDENT AND THE SENIOR DEFENSE DEPARTMENT civilian and military leadership must be convinced of the value of strategic planning. Unless the national security leadership takes an active role, the strategic planning process could fall prey to narrow bureaucratic or organizational interests, leading to a suboptimal strategy or no strategy at all.

Senior national security decision-makers today could benefit from examining the success of Eisenhower's National Security Council (NSC) structure, which provided strong incentives to engage in serious discussions of strategy. Under this structure, the president chaired regular NSC

19. John D. Banusiewicz, " 'As Iraqis Stand Up, We Will Stand Down,' Bush Tells Nation," American Forces Press Service, June 28, 2005, at http://www.defenselink.mil/news/newsarticle.aspx?id=16277, accessed on August 5, 2008.

meetings and led discussions. To ensure a rich exchange of ideas, Eisenhower strictly limited the number of individuals who could participate, typically to eight.

To support the president and his senior national security lieutenants, Eisenhower also created a Planning Board, which developed policy papers to be considered by the NSC. The reason for the board, he explained to the NSC members, was:

> You Council members . . . simply do not have the time to do all that needs to be done in thinking out the best decisions regarding the national security. Someone must therefore do much of this thinking for you.[20]

A revived Planning Board's purpose should be similar to that of the State Department's Policy Planning Staff, which Secretary of State George C. Marshall intended

> to look ahead, not into the distant future, but beyond the vision of the operating officers caught in the smoke and crises of current battle; far enough ahead to see the emerging form of things to come and outline what should be done to meet or anticipate them. In doing this the staff should also do something else—constantly reappraise what was being done . . . [given that] policies acquired their own momentum and went on after the reasons that inspired them had ceased.[21]

Eisenhower adopted a similar perspective, noting that "situations of actual or probable conflict change so rapidly and the weaponry of modern military establishments increase their destructiveness at such a bewildering speed [that the president] will always need the vital studies, advice, and counsel that only a capable and well-developed staff organization can give him."[22] Dean Acheson, who succeeded Marshall as secretary of state, observed that, designed in this manner and populated with chiefs like George Kennan and Paul Nitze, the Policy Planning Staff

20. Bowie and Immerman, *Waging Peace*, p. 91.
21. Dean Acheson, *Present at the Creation* (New York: W. W. Norton, 1969), p. 214.
22. Bowie and Immerman, *Waging Peace*, p. 83.

"was of inestimable value as the stimulator, and often deviser, of the most basic policies."[23]

To ensure that the Planning Board members were not beholden to their departments or agencies, Eisenhower made it clear that their mission was not "to reach solutions which represent merely a compromise of departmental positions."[24] Former national security advisor Zbigniew Brzezinski believes that reestablishing a Planning Board could, along with persistent presidential involvement in the formulation of strategy, go a long way toward improving the quality of U.S. strategy:

> The Planning Board was a very important instrument, the elimination of which has handicapped the U.S. government ever since then. Because the consequence is that we don't have overall national security planning.[25]

There is also the matter of executing the NSC's decisions. If the bureaucracy is unable to advance its own agenda during strategy formulation, it will work to enforce its will in strategy execution. Eisenhower realized this problem and, to deal with it, established the Operations Coordinating Board (OCB), which would, at regular intervals (three to six months), prepare progress reports on how well the NSC's decisions were being implemented.[26]

The barriers to developing sound strategy are many, and they are formidable. Not only has the U.S. government seemingly lost the ability to do strategy well, but many senior officials arguably do not understand what strategy is. Nonetheless, the benefits of crafting good strategies are so great that they merit a strong push by senior U.S. national security decision-makers, the president above all, to overcome the barriers. Revitalizing strategic planning at the highest levels of government with a contemporary version of Marshall's Policy Planning Staff and

23. Acheson, *Present at Creation*, pp. 214–15.
24. Bowie and Immerman, *Waging Peace*, p. 91.
25. "The NSC at 50: Past, Present, and Future," October 31, 1997, www.cfr.org/publication/64/nsc_at_50. html (transcript), cited in Aaron L. Friedberg, "Strengthening Strategic Planning," *Washington Quarterly*, Winter 2007–08, p. 52.
26. Bowie and Immerman, *Waging Peace*, p. 93.

Eisenhower's NSC model, to include the Planning and Operations Co-ordination Boards, could be an important first step toward achieving this end.

CREATING NEW PATHS TO THE FUTURE

SCENARIOS ARE MORE ABOUT IDENTIFYING PROBLEMS (OR OPPOR-tunities) than about coming up with solutions. As in the Truman and Eisenhower administrations, today's national security leadership must contend with "wasting assets" in several key areas of the military competition. The success of their efforts to cope with emerging dangers will depend, in large part, on the kinds of military capabilities that are available or might become available over the planning horizon.[27] What follows are some indicators that can be used to assess how well the military is meeting this challenge.[28]

Once confronted with a "wasting asset," the first step is to develop a compelling vision of how the character of future military competitions will be different from those that dominate today. This provides U.S. military leaders with the basis for addressing the question "Why should the world's best military reorient itself?" The seven scenarios herein provide a vision of how America's rivals might choose to compete differently. Although the scenarios suggest areas of possible shortfalls in U.S. military capabilities, they are only a first step toward determining how the armed forces might best be adapted.

Military organizations that have in the past successfully adapted to major shifts in the security environment have benefited greatly from clear statements of how the new environment would differ from the existing

27. The range of capabilities is not limited to military capabilities but includes all forms of national power, both "hard" power like military force and "soft" power such as diplomatic and economic. However, this book focuses on the military dimension of power. For an excellent discussion of soft power, see Joseph S. Nye, Jr., *Soft Power* (New York: Public Affairs, 2004). Nye coined the phrase "soft power."
28. Among the many studies of military innovation, the author found two most useful. See Barry Watts and Williamson Murray, "Military Innovation in Peacetime," in Williamson Murray and Allan R. Millett, *Military Innovation in the Interwar Period* (Cambridge, U.K.: Cambridge University Press, 1996), pp. 369–415; and Stephen Peter Rosen, *Winning the Next War* (Ithaca, N.Y.: Cornell University Press, 1991).

one. For instance, in laying down his vision of future warfare following World War I, General Hans von Seeckt, head of the German Army's shadow general staff, rejected the army's World War I static trench-warfare experience when he declared that mass armies had become "cannon fodder for a small number of technicians on the other side." Consequently, he argued, "the goal of modern strategy will be to achieve a decision with highly mobile, highly capable forces, before the masses have begun to move."[29] Thus were the roots of the blitzkrieg established.

Similarly, the U.S. Navy's Admiral William S. Sims revealed how the character of warfare at sea would undergo a transformation when he predicted in 1925 that a "high-speed carrier alone can destroy or disable a battleship . . . the fast carrier is the capital ship of the future."[30] And the British Admiral John ("Jackie") Fisher, in the process of arguing for a fundamental restructuring of the Royal Navy at the beginning of the twentieth century, declared: "In all seriousness I don't think it is even *faintly* realised—*the immense impending revolution which the submarines will effect as offensive weapons of war.*" Fisher concluded that "when you calmly sit down and work out what will happen in the narrow waters of the [English] Channel and the Mediterranean, how totally the submarines will alter the effects of Gibraltar, Port Said, Lemnos and Malta, it makes one's hair stand on end!"[31]

Whether or not these men found agreement among their colleagues—and many strenuously opposed them—they presented a clear vision of the changes they saw coming in warfare and detailed the implications for their service. Importantly, their visions clearly implied "winners" and "losers" among the different parts of their service. Admiral Sims, for example, all but sounded the death knell of the battleship by predicting its replacement by the carrier. Needless, to say, his views stirred strong opposition in the "Gun Club," the American Navy's battleship admirals.

The Pentagon needs a compelling vision of the emerging conflict en-

29. Robert M. Citino, *The Evolution of Blitzkrieg Tactics: Germany Defends Itself Against Poland, 1918–1933* (New York: Greenwood Press, 1987), p. 71.
30. Clark G. Reynolds, *The Fast Carriers* (Annapolis, Md.: Naval Institute Press, 1968), p. 1.
31. Nicholas A. Lambert, *Sir John Fisher's Naval Revolution* (Columbia, S.C.: University of South Carolina Press, 1999), p. 83, emphasis in the original.

vironment's key characteristics. The vision must provide a clear, persuasive justification for change and some general guidance as to how the U.S. military needs to adapt in order to sustain its competitive position. Absent such a vision, civilian and military leaders are likely to focus on meeting enhanced variations of existing threats—especially when there is a war on—even though the threats are actually changing in substantial, and perhaps fundamental, ways.

As the wars in Afghanistan and Iraq understandably demand persistent, priority attention, preparations for emerging challenges have lacked the support from senior military and civilian leaders that has characterized successful efforts in the past. Secretary of Defense Robert Gates went so far as to publicly caution the military against "Next-War-itis," declaring that he had

> noticed too much of a tendency towards what might be called "Next-War-itis"—the propensity of much of the defense establishment to be in favor of what might be needed in a future conflict . . . . [I]n a world of finite knowledge and limited resources, where we have to make choices and set priorities, it makes sense to lean toward the most likely and lethal scenarios for our military . . . *Overall, the kinds of capabilities we will most likely need in the years ahead will often resemble the kinds of capabilities we need today.*[32] (emphasis added)

Secretary Gates may be correct that the challenges of tomorrow will look very much like those of today, but the seven scenarios herein argue strongly that this is not the case. Our best course of action is to find a balance between meeting the demands of today and the challenges of tomorrow.

Thankfully, the Defense Department is a large organization, and some are indeed working to develop scenarios that present emerging security threats in clearer, more detailed terms, much like the scenarios presented here. But in the process of crafting these scenarios, the military services and other "stakeholders" typically try to shape the scenarios

32. Robert Gates, speech to the Heritage Foundation, Colorado Springs, Colo., May 13, 2008, at www.defenselink.mil/speeches/speech.aspx?speechid=1240, accessed on June 28, 2008.

to support their narrow interests, rather than reflect the evidence provided by careful research and trend analysis. Here is where the direct involvement of informed senior leaders—those with vision—can make a difference.

CONCEPTS OF OPERATIONS

Once military leaders develop their vision of the underlying "drivers" of key future military competitions, they must determine whether existing and emerging military capabilities can be applied to realize that vision and decide how these capabilities will operate together. In military parlance, this is known as the "concept of operations."[33] New challenges typically require new concepts of operation. Since the challenges are new, however, it is not always clear how they might best be addressed. Hence an initial concept of operation is often a point of departure or a good "first guess." Over time concepts of operations that are deemed most effective in meeting principal military challenges are formally adopted by the armed forces and become doctrine.

For example, China's Assassin's Mace forces will likely require the U.S. military to develop new ways of conducting operations, perhaps incorporating new capabilities, in order to convince the Chinese leadership that the United States will protect its allies and partners in East Asia from coercion or acts of aggression. An initial concept of operations ideally represents educated judgments about what new mix of force elements and capabilities will be required to operate effectively in the new threat environment.

The Defense Department has been working at developing concepts of operations for two of the most demanding problems presented in the scenarios: projecting power in the face of emerging anti-access/area-denial (A2/AD) capabilities, and defeating modern irregular forces. The Mil-

---

33. The Defense Department defines a *concept of operations* as "a verbal or graphic statement that clearly and concisely expresses what the joint force commander intends to accomplish and how it will be done using available resources." Joint Publication 1-02, "DoD Dictionary of Military Terms," May 30, 2008, at www.js.mil/doctrine/jel/doddict, accessed on July 20, 2008. A "joint" force is one that includes elements from two or more services. For example, an Army brigade operating in conjunction with Air Force strike aircraft is a joint force.

lennium Challenge 02 field exercise indicated that the U.S. military could have difficulty projecting power against even a relatively minor power like Iran, if armed with rather modest A2/AD capabilities, let alone against the forces of a major power like China.

As for the challenge posed by modern irregular forces, a concept of operations developed by U.S. Joint Forces Command (JFCOM) received its baptism of fire during the summer of 2006, in the Second Lebanon War. In that conflict the Israeli Armed Forces (IAF) attempted to apply what to date had been JFCOM's centerpiece operational concept—Rapid Decisive Operations (RDO), which is closely associated with Effects-Based Operations (EBO). The RDO concept of operations is designed to "achieve rapid victory by attacking the coherence of an enemy's ability to fight."[34] This is accomplished by identifying and either neutralizing or destroying the set of targets comprising the enemy's "center of gravity."[35] As one JFCOM analyst put it, the concept of "effects-based" warfare would allow the armed forces to achieve "Desert Storm effec-

34. Colonel Chris Shepherd, "Joint Concept Development and Experimentation Program Overview," Briefing, JFCOM, Virginia Beach, Va., December 13, 2000.
35. Not long after its formation, JFCOM declared RDO to be "the major integrating concept for Joint Experimentation." Captain David W. Prothero and Major General Dean W. Cash, *Rapid Decisive Operations: Initial Concept Report, FY 2000,* (JFCOM, n.d.,) p. iii. JFCOM's official definition of RDO is "a concept to achieve rapid victory by attacking the coherence of the enemy's ability to fight. It is the synchronous application of the full range of our national capabilities in timely and direct-effects based operations. It employs our asymmetric advantages in the knowledge, precision, and mobility of the joint force against his critical functions to create maximum shock, defeating his ability and will to fight." Otto Kreisher, "The Quest for Jointness," *Air Force Magazine,* September 2001, p. 74. The strong links between RDO and strategic bombardment of the enemy center of gravity can be seen in Major General David A. Deptula, *Effects-Based Operations: Change in the Nature of Warfare* (Arlington, Va.: Aerospace Education Foundation, 2001). The paper, authored by one of the Air Force's preeminent strategists, notes that "actions to induce specific effects rather than simply destruction of the subsystems making up each of these strategic systems or 'centers of gravity' is the foundation of the concepts of parallel war, rapid decisive operations, or any other concept that seeks to achieve rapid dominance over an adversary." Deptula, *Effects-Based Operations,* p. 6. In brief, EBO is premised on the belief that it is possible to reduce dramatically the time it takes to disable an adversary's strategic center of gravity. This can be accomplished through two means. First, a greatly enhanced understanding of the cause-and-effect relationship between targets destroyed and the effect this has on "vital enemy systems" that "are relied on by an adversary for power and influence—leadership, population, essential industries transportation and distribution, and forces." Ibid. Second, the ability of precision weapons to disable many types of targets much more rapidly at much lower cost than is possible through the employment of nonprecision weapons (or "dumb bombs").

tiveness with fewer combat systems."[36] Alas, in the Second Lebanon War Hezbollah did not choose to confront the Israelis, proponents of effects-based operations, as Saddam Hussein confronted the U.S.-led coalition in the First Gulf War. Instead Hezbollah pursued a form of modern irregular warfare discussed earlier in this book. The result was an Israeli defeat, and a dramatic drop in the RDO/EBO stock as a viable concept of operations. In August 2008 General James Mattis, the JFCOM commander, declared that "USJFCOM will no longer use or export the terms and concepts EBO, EBA [Effects-Based Approch], ONA [Operational Net Assessment], and SoSA [System-of-Systems Analysis] in our training, doctrine development, and support to JPME [Joint Professional Military Education]."[37] Simply put, Joint Forces Command must now explore new concepts of operation.

WILLINGNESS TO DESIGNATE "WINNERS" AND "LOSERS"

IF THE PENTAGON HAS THUS FAR PROVIDED SO FEW SPECIFICS WHEN it comes to concepts of operation focused on emerging challenges, there is a reason. Since these challenges (especially as outlined in the seven scenarios) are substantially different from those for which the U.S. military has traditionally prepared, crafting different concepts of operations would almost certainly lead to a significantly different force structure and systems requirement mix than that of the current force. New ways of conducting operations would produce a revaluation of forces and capabilities—they would create some big "winners" and "losers"—just as the shifts in miltary competition foreseen by Fisher, Sims, and von Seeckt brought about a reshuffling of military priorities. Some capabilities would increase in value, perhaps dramatically. Others would decline in value, perhaps to the point of obsolescence.

However, by identifying "losers" within its own force, a service runs

36. Lieutenant Colonel (Ret.) Thomas M. Cooke, USA, "Reassessing Joint Experimentation," *Joint Forces Quarterly,* Spring/Summer 2001, p. 103.
37. General James Mattis, "Commander's Perspective on Effects-Based Operation and Related Concepts," Memorandum for U.S. Joint Forces Command, "USJFCOM Commander's Guidance for Effects-Based Operations," August 14, 2008, emphasis in the original.

the risk of having these programs attacked by other services competing for scarce defense resources during the Pentagon's annual "cut drills," described above. The service also will likely encounter opposition from its own subcultures that stand to see their stature decline. The dearth of specificity in current service concepts of operation is motivated, in no small measure, by a desire to avoid threatening the comfortable existing way of "doing things," or conducting operations. This leads to the absence of healthy competition among the services to determine the best kinds of military capabilities needed to meet the emerging challenges to the national security.

A SENSE OF URGENCY

IT IS TIME FOR SENIOR NATIONAL SECURITY DECISION-MAKERS TO exhibit a sense of urgency in addressing the problem of the U.S. military's "wasting assets." Not only is the national security of the United States at stake, but so are enormous human and material resources. The Pentagon spends well over $100 billion each year developing and purchasing new equipment. The sooner it identifies how best to invest this impressive sum, the better.

Moreover, bringing about substantial changes in the armed forces takes time, typically years but sometimes a decade or more. Point-of-departure operational concepts—"first guesses" of how the armed forces might successfully address the challenges posed in the scenarios—will have to be developed. This is a job for a small number of the military's best thinkers. It is not a job for large staffs whose members have been told to arrive at a solution that is acceptable to all the Pentagon's "stakeholders." But the latter approach often prevails while senior officers are all too often absorbed by the demands of their in-boxes and the issues of the moment.

If useful operational concepts are generated, then they will need to be tested, first in war games and simulations, and then through field exercises. Funding must be made available to support these exercises, to enable experimentation with new kinds of forces and equipment, including prototypes and surrogates for equipment identified as promising but which has not yet been put into the field. Unfortunately, the command most responsible for this effort, JFCOM, has found such resources hard to come by.

The clock is ticking. As several of the seven scenarios suggest, some novel threats to U.S. security may manifest themselves at any moment, while others may appear in the coming decade. Time may be as precious an asset as troops, equipment, or money. Secretary Gates' assertion that what will work against today's enemies will deter or, if necessary, defeat tomorrow's enemies as well must be either confirmed or refuted.

Consider, for example, that during the interwar period of the 1920s and 1930s the U.S. Navy conducted twenty-one fleet exercises involving large elements of the fleet, precisely for the purpose of determining whether once-successful capabilities would continue to succeed in the future. Some fleet exercises were so extensive that they comprised several major phases, each of which could have been viewed as an independent exercise. Or consider the German Army, which, having lost in World War I, was determined to identify new capabilities to avoid a repeat of that experience. The Germans continually found ways to conduct substantial field exercises even during Germany's period of disarmament from 1919 to 1935. Following the onset of rearmament, the German military moved quickly to conduct the largest field exercises of the interwar period, while concurrently conducting major operations in the Spanish Civil War.

Both of these militaries were animated by a sense of urgency among their military leaders that rapid (and perhaps profound) changes in the threat environment or character of the conflict were possible, even imminent. The U.S. Navy was acutely aware of the growing challenge posed by the Imperial Japanese Navy, both in its growing strength and in its efforts to exploit the potential of naval aviation, among other emerging capabilities. The German Army was driven by the need to avoid a protracted war of attrition on multiple fronts, the type that led to its defeat in World War I. This led to the *Wehrmacht*'s[38] vigorous efforts to exploit rapidly advancing technologies (i.e., automotive, avia-

---

38. The term *Wehrmacht* is roughly translated as "defense force" or simply "armed forces." It was the name of the German armed forces from 1935 to 1945.

tion, radio) to restore mobility to the battlefield. The need to keep pace with the competition, to determine as best as possible the direction in which warfare was headed, and to reduce uncertainty about what new (and legacy) capabilities would prove effective (and which would not) led these innovative militaries to exploit the potential of field/fleet exercises with a keen sense of urgency.

Recent surprises, such as the attacks of 9/11, the advent of modern insurgency warfare in Iraq, and the dawn of irregular forces armed with G-RAMM,[39] underscore the rapid changes in the character of conflict, stimulated in no small way by the accelerating tempo of advancing technologies. Unfortunately, JFCOM, established to identify emerging threats and support the U.S. military's transformation to address them, has progressively moved away from this mission since the Millennium Challenge 02 exercise. The command's major follow-on exercise, Olympic Challenge, scheduled to occur in 2004, was canceled following the U.S. invasion of Iraq.[40] Today the command devotes most of its time, energy, and resources to supporting the war effort, helping to identify forces to meet the needs of commanders in Afghanistan and Iraq, training joint staffs and forces, and coordinating with America's NATO allies.[41]

To be sure, focusing on the "war we've got" must take top priority. A defeat in Afghanistan or Iraq might seriously compromise the national security. However, the Defense Department does not have to make an "all or nothing" choice about addressing present threats or emerging

39. The reference is to Guided Rockets, Artillery, Missiles and Mortars—G-RAMM. Hezbollah modestly used the same (i.e., unmanned aerial vehicles, antiship missiles) during the Second Lebanon War in 2006.
40. Olympic Challenge '04 was renamed Pinnacle Vision '04 prior to its cancellation. Exhibit R-2 RDT&E Project Justification (Fiscal Year 2005 Budget Estimates), February 2004, at www.defenselink.mil/comptroller/defbudget/fy2005/budget_justification/pdfs/03_RDT_and_E/OSD_BA3/P-30603727D8Z_JWP__R-2(co)_R-2a__Feb_2004.pdf, accessed on July 14, 2008.
41. The command sees current field commanders—combatant commanders, or COCOMs in military parlance—as its principal "customer." Joint forces or staffs are those that comprise members from more than one of the military services—Army, Navy, Air Force, and Marine Corps. Establishing JFCOM for the purpose of undertaking joint exercises and experimentation was not a Defense Department initiative. Rather, it was the consequence of congressional leadership and the recommendations of an independent panel of experts. See National Defense Panel, *Transforming Defense* (Washington, D.C.: Department of Defense, December 1997), pp. 68–72.

dangers. The Pentagon is spending some $70 billion this year alone on researching and developing future military capabilities—tomorrow's planes, armored vehicles, ships, satellites, and so on. Many of these new capabilities will not be in the field for years. Prudence dictates they be viewed in terms of how they would fare not in *today's* contingencies but in *tomorrow's*.

Moreover, even in times when the danger to the United States was far greater than it appears to be today, the Pentagon's leaders were willing to balance preparing for the future with meeting immediate dangers. During the dark months following the Japanese attack on Pearl Harbor, the U.S. Navy sent some of its best carrier pilots back to the United States to train new pilots, effectively depleting the fighting force in order to build up a large cadre of well-trained aviators.[42] Around the time of the Cuban Missile Crisis, the U.S. Army, greatly outnumbered in Europe against the Soviet tank armies, took an entire division out of the line to begin experiments on the concept of air mobile operations that eventually led to the formation of today's Air Assault Division.

SUSTAINED EFFORT

AS THE SEVEN SCENARIOS SUGGEST, TIME IS GROWING SHORT, AND a sense of urgency is needed. It is also important to sustain the effort despite the never-ceasing pull of the crisis *du jour* on attention and resources.

By its nature, dramatic change in large military organizations almost inevitably involves a long-term process that spans a decade or more. Yet the U.S. military typically rotates senior leaders out of their assignments every two to four years. This personnel change may work well for leaders whose responsibilities are near-term oriented (for example, the regional commander who is responsible for the immediate war-fighting mission in his area of operation), but the mission of identifying the key emerging challenges to the national security and adapting the military to meet them can be accomplished only over a relatively long period of time.

---

42. Clark G. Reynolds, The Fast Carriers (Annapolis, Md.: Naval Institute Press, 1968), p. 27.

Not surprisingly, military organizations that have successfully addressed changing threats (or exploited opportunities to create major new advantages) have almost always had some key senior military leaders serve an extended tour of duty, often double or even triple the length of a typical tour in today's U.S. military. During the German Army's transformation to blitzkrieg, for example, General Hans von Seeckt served seven years as head of its shadow general staff. The American Navy's exploitation of naval aviation was shepherded by Vice Admiral William Moffett, who remained head of the Navy's Bureau of Aeronautics for an astounding twelve consecutive years. Admiral Hyman Rickover, widely known as the "father" of the Navy's nuclear submarine force, remained director of the Naval Reactors Branch for over thirty years. But the tour of duty for the JFCOM commander remains the same as those for senior commanders responsible for day-to-day operations. A strong case can be made for transforming JFCOM's "paper" mission of preparing the U.S. military for emerging challenges into a real mission, and for extending its commander's tenure to enable him to see the job through to its completion.

EMPHASIS ON THE OPERATIONAL LEVEL OF WAR

IN ADDRESSING THE CHALLENGES POSED BY THE SEVEN SCENARIOS, primary emphasis should be placed at the operational level of war—the level at which military campaigns are conducted. But analysis, war games, simulations, and field exercises should take place at *all levels* (tactical, operational, and strategic) of warfare and also among *all principal organizations involved,* including all the services and, where appropriate, other governmental and nongovernmental elements.[43] To

---

43. One growing challenge confronting the U.S. military concerns its role in defending the American homeland from the covert introduction and deployment of chemical, biological, or radiological agents, and from cyberattack on the national information infrastructure. Efforts to address this threat should logically involve those nonmilitary institutions and organizations that would play a significant role in dealing with an actual contingency (the FBI, Coast Guard, state and municipal governments, private industry, etc.). Similarly, those challenges that confront the armed forces with irregular warfare challenges, especially security, stability, transition, and reconstruction (SSTR) operations, would logi-

date, however, field exercises and experimentation have been heavily weighted toward the tactical level of warfare. While these efforts are desirable, they must be informed by how military organizations believe they will have to fight at the strategic and operational levels.

Consider JFCOM's first simulated experiment. It involved attacking critical mobile targets, such as mobile ballistic and cruise missile launchers, that could well destroy U.S. forward bases. Considerations at the operational level could influence the ways in which the military might accomplish this task. For example, the experiment's conduct—and outcome—could change dramatically if it was assumed either that forward bases were unavailable to U.S. forces or that U.S. forces operating from these bases prior to defeating the threat posed by enemy G-RAMM capabilities would place them at unacceptable risk. How the military goes about solving the critical mobile targeting and engagement problem at the tactical level is thus influenced enormously by operational-level factors. Consider the operations in Afghanistan to destroy both fixed and critical mobile Taliban and al Qaeda targets by combining Special Operations Forces on the ground with air strikes. Owing to a lack of forward base access early in the conflict, the workhorse arm of U.S. air power—short-range, land-based tactical fighter-bombers—had to sit on the sidelines while long-range bomber and naval strike aircraft predominated. In sum, experimentation and field exercises that focus on the tactical level of warfare in the absence of considering the operational level risk arriving at irrelevant, or impractical, solutions to accomplishing the mission.

The U.S. military plans to fight as a joint force, drawing upon all the services' capabilities. This makes sense, as modern technology has enabled each of the services to operate far outside its traditional battle space and into the battle space of its sister services. Consequently, the development and analytic assessment of operational concepts for addressing the challenges posed by the seven scenarios, as well as war games, simulations, and field exercises, should encourage a friendly but

---

cally include other relevant departments and agencies of the executive branch, such as the State Department, CIA, U.S. Agency for International Development (USAID), and perhaps similar organizations from allied and host nation organizations as well.

spirited competition among the services to determine the proper mix of capabilities required to meet the challenge. Sadly, this approach has often been the exception rather than the rule.

THE CUSTOMER

IF HISTORY IS ANY GUIDE, THOSE GENERALS AND ADMIRALS WHO will command the U.S. armed forces—commonly referred to as component commanders, or COCOMs—seven or eight years into the future should be JFCOM's principal customers. However, given that several challenges described in the seven scenarios could arise in the near-term future, current commanders should also benefit from JFCOM's efforts. As Millennium Challenge 02 showed, A2/AD threats already exist in nascent form. Today a conflict with China would almost certainly find the United States Pacific Command (PACOM) confronting a base-access challenge with respect to the major air bases and port facilities in Japan and South Korea, which can be struck by some of the hundreds of missiles currently in Beijing's arsenal. Similarly, in any near-term contingency involving conflict with Iran where U.S. sea control of the Persian Gulf is required, the U.S. Commander of Central Command (CENTCOM) would likely confront an area-denial threat along the littoral, especially at the region's key choke point, the Strait of Hormuz.

History shows that field exercises should not be viewed as some abstract effort to address challenges in the far distant future. It is preferable to focus on challenges that could emerge suddenly, over the near-to-mid-term—up to six or eight years in the future, as in the seven scenarios. For example, the training undertaken by PACOM at the operational level of warfare *today* should emphasize anti-access/area-denial contingencies (e.g., Korean Peninsula; China-Taiwan), as should those conducted by CENTCOM (e.g., defense of Persian Gulf oil facilities and protection of seaborne commerce in the Gulf). Simply put, today's senior commanders can benefit from JFCOM's efforts to develop promising new operational concepts, test system prototypes, and evaluate various force elements and capabilities employed in war games, simulations, and field exercises. To this end the U.S. military should conduct at least one major joint field exercise a year. Moreover, America's regional commands should rotate their forces through a Joint National Training Center (JNTC) for regular exercises and evaluations.

TRAINING FACILITIES

DURING THE LATTER STAGES OF THE COLD WAR, THE U.S. MILITARY invested in a number of high-fidelity training facilities that greatly enhanced the value of its field training.[44] For example, the Army's National Training Center (NTC) at Fort Irwin, California, prepared brigade-sized units for combined-arms mechanized warfare against a Soviet-style adversary. Similarly, the Air Force and Navy put their pilots through Red Flag and Top Gun training, respectively. That training is now conducted at Nellis Air Force Base and Fallon Naval Air Station in Nevada.

Comparable facilities do not yet exist to support high-fidelity field exercises at the operational level of war focused on emerging challenges, such the anti-access/area-denial threat or the G-RAMM problem. A JNTC is needed to enable both service and joint transformation field exercises. In 1997 the National Defense Panel recommended that such a facility be established.[45] While the Pentagon's 2001 Quadrennial Defense Review promised to "explore the need" for such a center, it has yet to be created.[46] Both the Army's NTC and the Air Force and Navy training centers have recently undertaken major efforts to make their training exercises more relevant for contemporary operations in Afghanistan and Iraq. This is both necessary and desirable, but it does not address the matter of helping the services determine how best to prepare to meet tomorrow's threats.

Several potential concerns arise from the absence of training facilities capable of supporting field exercises focused on preparing U.S. forces for emerging challenges at the operational level of warfare. One is that

44. For an excellent overview of the creation of the U.S. military's high-fidelity training centers, see Barry D. Watts, *U.S. Combat Training, Operational Art, and Strategic Competence: Problems and Opportunities* (Washington, D.C.: Center for Strategic and Budgetary Assessments, 2008).
45. National Defense Panel, *Transforming Defense: National Security in the 21st Century* (Washington, D.C.: December 1997), pp. 68–70. The author was one of nine members of the panel.
46. Department of Defense, *Quadrennial Defense Review Report* (Washington, D.C.: Department of Defense, September 30, 2001), p. 36.

it focuses on training at the tactical level of warfare. As noted above, however, absent significant training at the operational level—especially in a turbulent period in the character of conflict—tactical-level training may well produce flawed insights.

A second concern rests with the U.S. military's ability to determine the feasibility of operational concepts in which information architectures play a major role, sometimes referred to as networked operations or "netcentric warfare." If the military is precluded from exercising its command, control, communications, computers, intelligence, surveillance, and reconnaissance (C4ISR) architectures at the operational level of warfare, it may prove difficult to determine, with any great degree of confidence, the progress being made (or not being made) in campaigns against enemies attempting to degrade the military's communications links. For example, as the "China's 'Assassin's Mace' " scenario makes clear, U.S. space systems are becoming progressively vulnerable to Chinese antisatellite capabilities. Chinese cyberattacks on U.S. military systems are a daily occurrence. One prospective U.S. concept of operations for dealing with the Chinese A2/AD challenge involves highly mobile, highly distributed American sea and air forces that are also highly networked.[47] But can this network be sustained in the face of Chinese effort to disrupt it? A JNTC, where U.S. forces testing the concept could confront a "Red" opposing force (OPFOR) employing surrogates of Chinese military capabilities designed to defeat it, would provide as close to a true test of the concept of operations as is possible, short of war.

Recently demographers calculated that, for the first time in human history, over half the world's population lives in urban areas. Since many of the seven scenarios occur in the developing world, and as the

---

47. For a superb overview of the emerging Chinese military A2/AD challenge, see Thomas Ehrhard and Robert Work, *Range, Persistence, Stealth, and Networking: The Case for a Carrier-Based Unmanned Combat Air System* (Washington, D.C.: Center for Strategic and Budgetary Assessments, 2008). It would be desirable to conduct field exercises that address the growing challenge of maintaining space control or defending against an attack at the strategic level on the U.S. national information infrastructure. For example, the war game or exercise might be conducted under the assumption that access to space-based systems has been lost.

developing world's population is growing at a far more rapid rate than the developed world, U.S. forces confronting emerging challenges will likely often find themselves operating in an urban environment. But current training centers, such as the Joint Readiness Training Center (JRTC) at Fort Polk, Louisiana, offer facilities more characteristic of the terrain found in small towns.[48] They replicate neither the scale of an urban environment nor many of its unique terrain features (high-rise buildings, sewer and subway systems, etc.). A Joint Urban Warfare Training Center (JUWTC) should be created along the lines called for by the National Defense Panel.[49] Such a center could also be employed to conduct high-fidelity exercises to prepare a wide range of government and non-government organizations to deal effectively with terrorist attacks on U.S. urban centers, especially those involving the covert use of chemical, biological, or radiological weapons, as described in the scenario "War Comes to America."[50]

48. The JRTC is "the Army's premier combat training center." Currently training focuses on "the Contemporary Operational Environment (COE) and Counterinsurgency (COIN) operations." Soldiers at the JRTC train against opposing forces in urban terrain. See www.jrtc-polk.army.mil/OPS/INDEX.HTM, accessed on July 25, 2008. The military defines the Contemporary Operational Environment as "the overall operational environment that exists today and in the near future (out to the year 2020)." U.S. Army Training and Doctrine Command, "OPERATION ENDURING FREEDOM TACTICS, TECHNIQUES AND PROCEDURES," HANDBOOK NO. 02-8, at www.strategypage.com/articles/operationenduringfreedom/default.asp, accessed on July 18, 2008.
49. National Defense Panel, *Transforming Defense*, pp. 68–70.
50. Prior to the September 2001 terrorist attacks on the World Trade Center and the Pentagon, field exercises oriented on homeland defense were rather sporadic. One exercise, mandated by Congress, was conducted in May 2000. Named "Topoff" (short for Top Officials), the exercise was conducted by the Federal Emergency Management Agency (FEMA) and the Department of Justice. The exercise involved a chemical attack in Portsmouth, New Hampshire, and a biological attack involving the simulated release of "anthrax spores" outside Denver, Colorado. The exercise was criticized by some, who argued that it overstated the threat facing America, since multiple terrorist attacks would be unlikely to occur within such a short time span. David A. Vise, "Drill Shows Cincinnati Unready for Terror," *Washington Post*, April 28, 2000, p. 2; Lisa Hoffman, "Drill Tests U.S. Readiness Against Terror Attack," *Detroit News*, April 26, 2000; and Patrick Connole, "Catastrophic Drills Test U.S. Readiness for Terror Attack," *Philadelphia Inquirer*, May 21, 2000.

RESOURCES

JOINT AND SERVICE ANALYTIC EFFORTS, WAR GAMES, SIMULATIONS, and—especially—field exercises oriented on preparing for emerging challenges to U.S. security currently suffer from a shortage of both human and material resources. To some extent, the U.S. military writ large also suffers a significant mismatch between the size of the defense program and the resources available to support it. The deployment of large forces overseas in Afghanistan and Iraq further accentuates the problem. But if the American military is to meet future challenges, it will have to make preparing for them a higher priority. In addition to a JNTC and a JUWTC, some additional steps might prove highly useful in refining concepts of operation that address emerging challenges.

First, each of the joint training centers will require a standing joint opposing force, or JOPFOR. As its name indicates, a JOPFOR should be drawn from all the services. It should be given access to capabilities comparable to those currently in the inventories of likely or prospective rival militaries, to include irregular forces. The JOPFOR should also employ capabilities (using surrogates, if necessary) that these militaries could plausibly deploy over the next decade. One key JOPFOR mission should be to present the "Blue" (American) forces training against it with an anti-access/area-denial capability at the operational level of warfare. Another JOPFOR priority should involve fielding force elements capable of performing both as regular and as irregular forces in an urban environment. Yet another JOPFOR priority should involve presenting U.S. forces being trained with the irregular force G-RAMM problem. The JOPFOR should be manned with highly capable troops to present the stiffest possible test for those being trained and for those Blue forces attempting to validate new concepts of operation.

Second, JFCOM will need a substantial increase in funding to expand its joint field exercises and experiments at the operational level of war. As with the issue of creating a JNTC, the Bush administration's first Quadrennial Defense Review pledged to "consider the establishment of a Joint Opposing Force and increasing the Joint Forces

Command exercise budget."[51] A JOPFOR has yet to be formed, and JFCOM's exercise budget has not increased substantially since the Millennium Challenge exercise in 2002. Since any JOPFOR would be supported by JFCOM, significant additional funding will be required. In addition, the command should be given major force program (MFP) budget authority and a substantial budget to ensure that promising capabilities that lie between the mission areas of the services, or that fall victim to service parochial interests, get fair evaluations.[52] This funding could be employed, in part, to support rapid prototyping of particularly promising capabilities, whether they are weapons, munitions, or information systems.

Funding for the infrastructure initiatives and for fielding a JOPFOR might run roughly $10 billion over the next six years (i.e., over the next Future Years Defense Program, or FYDP). Funding to support vigorous field exercises supported by the use of prototype and surrogate systems and capabilities would likely add another $5–6 billion to the FYDP. Thus the average annual expenditure would be roughly $2.5 billion a year, or less than one-half of one percent of the current defense budget. The payoff in terms of improved military effectiveness and efficiency promises to more than justify the investment.

INPUT IN DEVELOPING FUTURE REQUIREMENTS

IF INNOVATION AND TRANSFORMATION ARE TO SUCCEED, THE INsights and lessons derived from field exercises must be harvested. Focusing on emerging challenges and opportunities helps to ensure that the military is addressing the right questions with respect to future warfare and thus can get the right answers with respect to new requirements. These answers mean little, however, unless they influence the way the Pentagon's requirements are determined, budgets are

51. Department of Defense, *Quadrennial Defense Review Report*, p. 37.
52. The Defense Department's budget is broken down into MFPs, or major categories. Among the MFPs are those for strategic forces (program one), general-purpose forces (program two), airlift and sealift forces (program four), and special operations forces (program eleven).

shaped, resources are allocated, institutions are adapted, and forces are developed.

At present, however, even assuming robust experimentation focused on emerging challenges, it is not clear how the insights derived from these efforts will be translated into new requirements. In recent years the Defense Department's Planning, Programming and Budgeting System (PPBS), as well as the Joint Chiefs' Joint Requirements Oversight Council (JROC), has generally proved incapable of effecting significant changes in service budget shares or program focus, despite the department leadership's declared determination to do so. Promising new capabilities and force elements have been terminated or delayed, or find themselves in jeopardy. The existing process appears heavily weighted toward evolutionary incremental improvements in existing military capabilities, as opposed to exploring aggressively opportunities that might produce a major boost in military effectiveness.

To help remedy this problem, the commander, JFCOM, should have a seat on the JROC and membership on the Defense Acquisition Board (DAB). The JROC is a key organization in the Defense Department's acquisition review process, reviewing and validating programs designated as high-interest, and making recommendations to the DAB.[53] The DAB is the Pentagon's senior advisory board, with responsibility for approving the Major Defense Acquisition Programs (MDAPs)—equipment such as warships, aircraft, and ground combat vehicles. In exercising its responsibilities, the DAB exerts enormous influence over the capabilities that the U.S. military will have available to execute any new concepts of operation.[54] As a member of the DAB, the commander, JFCOM, could present the insights gained from his command's efforts in devising new operational concepts to address the emerging challenges to the national security. He could also guard against improper influence being exerted on the DAB by the military services, who are often tempted to

53. The JROC is chaired by the vice chairman of the Joint Chiefs of Staff. Its membership also includes the vice chiefs of the four military services.
54. Among the DAB's members are the undersecretary of defense (acquisition, technology, and logistics), vice chairman of the Joint Chiefs of Staff, and the service secretaries. Department of Defense, DIRECTIVE AD-A272 410, Subject: Defense Acquisition Board, Number 5000.49, September 11, 1989.

act more out of narrow institutional interest than from a broader joint perspective.

Assuming that the commander, JFCOM, receives the extended tenure necessary to develop new concepts of operation, a logical follow-on assignment would be as vice chairman of the Joint Chiefs of Staff, the individual who chairs the JROC and cochairs the DAB. This would facilitate the Pentagon's efforts to ensure that the equipment and forces needed to execute new concepts of operations are fielded in a timely manner.

CONCLUSION

NOW, MORE THAN AT ANY TIME IN RECENT MEMORY, AMERICANS look to senior Defense officials and military leaders for reassurance that they are not only countering today's enemies but anticipating tomorrow's dangers as well. Today the Defense Department confronts major challenges regarding how the armed forces should be organized, trained, equipped, and employed to meet the emerging threats to the nation's security. Time and again throughout history, the failure of countries to anticipate new dangers has cost them a terrible price in blood and treasure. Unfortunately, the United States is no stranger to this experience, as evidenced by the surprise attack on Pearl Harbor in 1941, the 9/11 attacks on New York and Washington sixty years later, and the chaos in Iraq that ensued following the overthrow of Saddam Hussein's odious regime in 2003. If the United States wants to avoid being the victim of a new Pearl Harbor or 9/11 in the coming years—or at least be able to respond quickly and effectively when it is surprised—it must begin looking and planning ahead now. It must also understand the importance of acting sooner rather than later. More than that, the Pentagon must know where to focus scarce energies and resources in a world whose dangers threaten to challenge even the strongest militaries.

The potential gains from successful military adaptation to a changing environment are clear. One only has to look at how the German blitzkrieg overturned the military balance in Europe and how the U.S. Navy's fast carrier task forces turned the tide in the Pacific during World War II to see the payoff. The cost of preparing is relatively modest, yet the prospective price associated with failing to act is dear, including sub-optimal equipment, forces poorly organized for the tasks ahead, and the "right" solutions to the wrong threats. Ultimately, a failure to act could see the United States paying a price in compromised security, wasted resources, and lost lives of young service men and women. The choice is ours. Time is growing short. The best chance of addressing these dangers—or, better yet, deflecting them—is to start preparing for them now. For as Sir Francis Bacon warned, "He who will not apply new remedies must expect new evils."

ACKNOWLEDGMENTS

My writings rely heavily upon the advice, comments, and constructive criticism of colleagues and friends, especially my associates at the Center for Strategic and Budgetary Assessments (CSBA), where I have spent the past fifteen years of my professional life. I owe a great intellectual debt in particular to Steve Kosiak, Robert Martinage, Michael Vickers, Barry Watts, and Robert Work, longtime colleagues and dear friends.

This book benefited greatly from the efforts of Rita Colwell, Fred Downey, Richard Dunn, Michael Krepinevich, Andrew Marshall, Robert Martinage, and Matthew McGinnis, who were kind enough to review earlier versions and provide thoughtful, constructive criticism along with much-needed encouragement.

I am especially indebted to Andrew Marshall, who is the inspiration for all that the reader finds of value in this book. His rare combination of intellectual brilliance, sterling character, and selfless public service has served as a model for generations of practitioners and scholars in the field of security studies, myself included.

I want to thank the foundations that have sponsored my work, and that of my colleagues, over the years. The Bradley Foundation, the Carnegie Corporation, the Ford Foundation, the John D. and Katherine T. MacArthur Foundation, the Merrill Foundation, the Rose Foundation, the Smith Richardson Foundation, and Stuart Foundation provided financial support, along with insightful advice and sustained encouragement for the research that formed the foundation for this book. Philip Merrill and Elihu Rose, in particular, have generously shared both their time and wisdom. I also owe a special debt to Dr. Marin Strmecki, senior vice president and director of programs of the Smith Richardson Foundation, who over the years has proven to be an inexhaustible source of sage advice, thoughtful criticism, and enduring support.

My appreciation extends to my literary agent, Eric Lupfer, who was instrumental in helping me develop the idea behind this book, and who shepherded me through the commercial publication process. My editor, John Flicker, provided just the right mix of encouragement and prodding, in addition to his superb editorial skills, to ensure that the manuscript arrived at his desk on time and represented the best I had to offer. In this effort he was most ably assisted by Loren Noveck, who, in her copyediting and fact-checking role, identified a number of errors in the manuscript and greatly improved upon its presentation. Any remaining shortcomings are my responsibility and mine alone.

The greatest price paid in writing this book was not borne primarily by the author, for whom it has been a labor of love, but by his family, whom he loves deeply. Time devoted to this endeavor has been time away from my wife, Julia, my children and their spouses—Jennifer and Mark, Andrew and Nikki, Michael and Jessica—and my grandchildren, Katherine, Sean, and Alexandra. They have shown remarkable tolerance with my long-term fascination with the rather disagreeable subject of anticipating problems; specifically, of trying to identify emerging threats to our security before they arise in the hope of preventing their realization. I dedicate this book to them.

INDEX